In Search of
La Grande Illusion

March 2014   791.43

In Search of *La Grande Illusion*

A Critical Appreciation of Jean Renoir's Elusive Masterpiece

NICHOLAS MACDONALD

McFarland & Company, Inc., Publishers
Jefferson, North Carolina, and London

Excerpts from the article "Directors Go to Their
Movies: Jean Renoir" from *Action*, volume 7,
number 3 (1972), are reprinted by permission and
courtesy of the Directors Guild of America, Inc.

LIBRARY OF CONGRESS CATALOGUING-IN-PUBLICATION DATA

Macdonald, Nicholas, 1944–
In search of La grande illusion : a critical appreciation of
Jean Renoir's elusive masterpiece / Nicholas Macdonald.
    p.   cm.
Includes bibliographical references and index.

ISBN 978-0-7864-6270-4
softcover : acid free paper ∞

1. Grande illusion (Motion picture)   2. Renoir, Jean,
1894–1979—Criticism and interpretation.   I. Title.
PN1997.G68M33   2014   791.43'72—dc23   2013039864

BRITISH LIBRARY CATALOGUING DATA ARE AVAILABLE

© 2014 Nicholas Macdonald. All rights reserved

*No part of this book may be reproduced or transmitted in any form
or by any means, electronic or mechanical, including photocopying
or recording, or by any information storage and retrieval system,
without permission in writing from the publisher.*

On the cover: *La Grande Illusion*
French poster art, 1937 (Photofest)

Manufactured in the United States of America

*McFarland & Company, Inc., Publishers
Box 611, Jefferson, North Carolina 28640
www.mcfarlandpub.com*

To Elspeth, Ethan and Zack
Thanks for everything
(my life, mostly, as I've come to know it).

Table of Contents

Acknowledgments — ix
Preface: Beware the Trojan Horse — 1

Part I: The Film

1. The Blowup in the Mountains — 8
2. *La Grande Illusion*: A Misplaced Classic — 13
3. French Air Base/German Canteen — 18
4. The Film's Structure — 25
5. Aspects of Style — 27
6. Hallbach — 34
7. Wintersborn (the Opening) — 49
8. Themes and Relationships — 53
9. Maréchal and Boeldieu — 59
10. Boeldieu and Rauffenstein — 66
11. Elsa's Farm — 80
12. FIN: The Swiss Border — 102

Part II: Around the Film

13. *La Grande Illusion*: A History — 110
14. The Road Not Taken... — 121
15. ...and the End of the Journey — 125
16. An "Anti" Anti-War Film — 128
17. The Art of Collaboration — 131
18. Other Takes, Different Angles — 136

Part III: The Director

19. Jean Renoir: A Biographical Sketch — 146
20. Peaks, Valleys and Slippery Slopes (1936–1939) — 172
21. Revenge of the Treatment: *Le Caporal épinglé* (1962) — 190

Part IV: Coda

22. Film as Film — and the Music Within	198
23. The Director Among Directors	213
24. 24 Frames Per Second, Forever	216
Appendix A. Title Credits	225
Appendix B. The Story	229
Appendix C. Breakdown of Shots	233
Filmography of Jean Renoir	243
Chapter Notes	247
Bibliography	251
Index	253

Acknowledgments

When Jean Renoir released an English-subtitled version of *La Grande Illusion* in 1959, he filmed an introductory monologue. At one point, he explained that "*The Grand Illusion* is a story about people like you, or like me, caught in this horrible tragedy named a war. But it is also a story about human relationship, and I'm convinced that such a question is so important today that if we don't solve it we will just have to say goodbye to our beautiful world."

This acknowledgment of his audience, including himself also in the crossfire of war, reflected his generous nature. And he closed his introduction: "I believe that *The Grand Illusion* is timely and I decided to show it again."[1]

That timelessness has proven true, to this day.

For inviting me to see *La Grande Illusion* with him during that same year, I am beholden to my father. But, most germanely, I remain in debt to Jean Renoir and his collaborators.

More recently, in terms of this book, my debt extends particularly to Elspeth Woodcock Macdonald for reading my rudimentary second draft, as well as several later drafts, including the last major one; she gave encouragement and intelligent criticism to the very end. Her contributions, helping to keep me grounded and supporting me at every roadblock or crisis of confidence, cannot be underestimated. Not to mention putting up with my escalating bouts of hermit-like retreat from the world.

And many thanks to John Bowers, Philip Fried, Ethan Macdonald, Zack Macdonald and Sandy Miller for their valuable feedback on my fifth draft (not yet at midpoint). I am grateful for these readers. Though they made overlapping points, each contributed unique suggestions, some weighted toward grammar (a humbling experience), others toward approach or geared to the gestalt. All were supportive in this early stage and I felt that, together, they became one grand and comprehensive reader — and that was perhaps not an illusion.

Thanks are also due to staff members at the School of Continuing Studies at Long Island University's Brooklyn Campus from 2001 through 2008, for the support of the school's administration and the fellowship of my colleagues. And to the late Ernest Callenbach, for his interest in a similar project in 1979, and Mark Woodcock, for his encouragement about this one. And thanks to Steve Morris and Brian Cooke for vetting my music references in Chapter 22 to reassure me that I wasn't laughably off key, without necessarily endorsing my attempts to capture the elusive nature of an art I love but only minimally understand.

In the area of photographs and archival letters, my research during two visits to the Jean Renoir Collection at UCLA's Charles E. Young Research Library was fruitful and enjoyable, due partly to the patient guidance of Julie Graham, Special Collections Librarian. She warned me about the Byzantine process in trying to determine who owns what kind of rights to which sort of photograph — and then set me in the right direction. I'm also grateful to the staff and students at UCLA for a system that was beautifully organized; it made those visits thoroughly un-Byzantine experiences.

Ronald and Howard Mandelbaum at Photofest in New York City similarly gave me their time and expertise as I enjoyed several sessions at this treasure trove of photographs and film posters. It was a pleasure to be in an office settled comfortably in an earlier hands-on period while, at the same time, updated to be accessible. And Derek Davidson helped me secure the specific frames of *La Grande Illusion* I wanted.

Over the internet, Liz Kurtulik (Art Resource), with the aid of Katia Cordova and Noëlle Pourret (Réunion des Musées Nationaux), guided me through a thicket of rights and contract parameters for permission to publish the beautiful photographs of Sam Lévin (and of Eli Lotar and Roger Corbeau). Lévin's production stills of *La Grande Illusion* and *La Règle du jeu* especially move me, for allowing a glimpse of history-in-the-making, as if falling down a rabbit hole and finding Jean Renoir on familiar sets and locations in the 1930s, perhaps on the verge of creating movie magic or else celebrating a moment safely captured — and ready to print.

In other internet contacts, though not able to resolve certain issues with representatives of the heirs, I appreciate the efforts of Patricia Power in connecting me with Rachel McGhee at William Morris Endeavor Entertainment, who in turn helped me clarify related issues involving Renoir's works. And Martin Holz at Taschen graciously provided other clarifications in my search for photographs.

I am also appreciative of the many e-mails, back and forth, leading to permissions for photographs and quoted excerpts, from Carol Nishijima, Amy Wong and Brandon E. Barton (UCLA), Dave McCall and Sarah Wilde (British Film Institute), Peter Huestis (National Gallery of Art, Washington), Jamie Vuignier (The Kobal Collection), Jackie Lam (Directors Guild of America), and Rob Winter (*Sight & Sound*).

And, at the bewitching hour, Ethan Macdonald generously applied his creative computer knowledge to assemble the manuscript and photographs into the required format.

So many people, named and unamed, made it possible to share my labor of love with others in the world outside, beyond the confines of a cluttered desk.

To everyone who helped me, in the spirit of *La Grande Illusion*....
Спасибо (Spasibo).
Thank you.
Danke.
Merci.

Preface: Beware the Trojan Horse

> *"When I was working on the story, I discovered that the idea was very rich. But the title, to me, had another advantage, because it was so open to interpretation. We must also allow the audience to create, to be an author. To be able to say, 'Grand Illusion? That means this and this and this.' The public must have the feeling that it made the picture."*
> —Jean Renoir in "Directors Go to Their Movies: Jean Renoir"; interview with Digby Diehl (*Action*, volume 7, number 3; May–June 1972; p. 8)

Renoir's hyperbole aside, my relationship to *La Grande Illusion* has become almost a personal one. Perhaps some disclaimer is in order.

I have (alternately or concurrently): loved this film with little reservation; been obsessed, if not nearly addicted; fallen out of touch and felt guilty, as if somehow disloyal; been surprised by its freshness, on getting reacquainted and finding new reasons to champion it again; lost faith, having seen films like *La Règle du jeu* and *Citizen Kane* (back when I was keeping score as to the greatest film ever); and turned fiercely protective, upset at any slight or what seemed a lack of proper respect.

That last feeling is dangerous. The defense of a movie scorned can get out of hand. But I'm not so intoxicated now that I don't also want to be true to *La Grande Illusion* in trying to understand it clearly, faults and all.

Above everything, I feel in debt to *La Grande Illusion*— and to Jean Renoir. One possible attempt at repayment is to be honest and clear-headed about his film. And so I promised myself, starting this book, to recognize my bias. In that spirit, every sentence of my analysis has hovering over it, as guardian angels, qualifying phrases like "it seems to me" or "I think" or "in my opinion." They are implicit, as in any work of criticism. Periodically I make them visible to represent all the suppressed qualifiers that haunt these pages.

Reader be warned. I hope my prejudice is fully enough acknowledged and rendered benign — if not, even more hopefully, overcome.

An intriguing sidebar to the film is that Orson Welles has been quoted as saying: "If I had only one film in the world to save, it would be *Grand Illusion*."[1] At first blush it appears odd that Welles, a director who flaunted his style and personality in his films, offered such an accolade about a film made by a director, Jean Renoir, who seemed reluctant, at least on a superficial level, to allow much open display of himself at all.

Are there two more dissimilar masterpieces than, for instance, *La Grande Illusion* (1937) and *Citizen Kane* (1941)? The greatness of Renoir's film appears to lie in a vein far from the one mined by Welles. *Citizen Kane* grabs you by the throat immediately and (thankfully) never lets go. *La Grande Illusion* requires patience; it draws you in, quietly and deceptively. A stylized and large gesticulation as opposed to a natural, simple gesture.

But the quote attributed to Welles is not so surprising once you get by that first blush. The two directors were working the same mother lode. There's room for all — and, somewhere, a lesson to be learned.

It's easy to take *La Grande Illusion* for granted and simply dub it a "classic of the cinema." Stolid workhorse, a bit foursquare, even awkward at times. The film seems transparent and uncomplicated, in execution and in the development of familiar humanist themes — the brotherhood of man, the barriers imposed by nation and class, a striving to be free. Here is a great movie, and we can nod in agreement and move on, as though everybody knows, of course, why it's great without having to actually spend time going into it. Many critics exhibit a bored condescension toward the film. Its virtues seem too obvious to go much beyond homage duly rendered.

In addition, *La Grande Illusion*, unlike most of Renoir's films, was a success. This can be embarrassing and arouse suspicion, as in the discomfort caused sometimes by a best seller or box-office hit. The assumption is that anything popular must have something wrong with it. And some critics would rather come to the rescue of unappreciated prophets than jump on a bandwagon.

La Grande Illusion has also been overshadowed by Renoir's other masterpiece, *La Règle du jeu* (*The Rules of the Game*), made two years later in 1939 and, fitting the stereotype of great works of art, a crushing failure. *La Règle du jeu* is sophisticated, and it dazzles; *La Grande Illusion*, in contrast, comes off as eminently reliable and old-fashioned. With the modernness of its irony and cynicism, Renoir's later film inspires passion while his World War I film receives due respect, despite a myriad of qualities that may not be immediately apparent.

There exists, I believe, a general misconception that *La Grande Illusion* is not particularly cinematic and, instead, that its strengths are largely due to elements appropriated from other arts and disciplines. This makes it seemingly easy to discuss: the fully realized characters and relationships (literature and psychology); outstanding performances (theater); classic cinematography (painting or photography); the themes of brotherhood, class division and pacifism (sociology and philosophy). But getting hung up at that level of understanding misses its true genius. This film is deeply, and abundantly, cinematic. It takes time, and a certain amount of probing, to appreciate it.

La Grande Illusion proves to be more Trojan horse than plodding Percheron. You take it in only at peril to your equanimity. On the surface, the film flows easily and naturally, but it is not pedantically realistic or especially simple. A decisive hand has been at work and many scenes are charged with poetry, transformed beyond the essential realism. There is far more to the film than appearances suggest.

Similarly, the emotions stirred up seem initially to be a result of the well-developed characters (as portrayed by the actors) and the way their relationships illustrate the film's themes. This certainly accounts for a measure of its power, but the strongest feelings generated come primarily from an elusive source — Renoir's original, cinematic expression that suffuses the film's images, with little fanfare.

The deceptive simplicity of the film is belied by these complex undertones, and this play of opposites helps make Jean Renoir's *La Grande Illusion* a profound — and profoundly dynamic — movie. It deserves more than to be dismissively canonized as a "classic." It warrants a long, hard look.

My connection to *La Grande Illusion* became especially intense in the summer of 1975. Staying overnight with me and my family at our apartment on New York City's Lower East Side, my father, Dwight, a well-known writer who had been the movie critic at *Esquire* in the early 1960s, asked me, somewhat out of the blue, if I remembered whether Maréchal refers to Rosenthal's being Jewish during their confrontation in *Grand Illusion* (as we called it then). Ten years had passed since I'd last seen the film, for the tenth time, and I thought not, but was unsure. My father felt it would seem false, and be far less moving, if Maréchal didn't have such feelings at that point.

We had been talking late into the night about movies—*Citizen Kane, Children of Paradise*, Ozu, *Last Year at Marienbad*—the way enthusiasts still did in that golden age for film buffs, which was already vanishing.

I got out the published script of *Grand Illusion* that Dwight had given me on my 24th birthday almost seven years earlier. My father started reading the scene aloud. His voice began to quaver as he blew his nose and wiped his eyes, the words watery and garbled. Yet he continued to the end, forcing himself to honor the scene. I couldn't remember ever seeing him cry before. Not one to show, or even acknowledge, deep feelings, he took pride in his journalistic *sang-froid* and was famous for slashing attacks, in print and in person, on works or writers he deemed in need of deflation, if not outright savaging.

Perhaps his defenses were down, considering the late hour. But it was a measure of his intellectual commitment that, nearing 70, he opened himself to such emotions, surging up in merely reading the script. And it was a welcomed aberration as well in our relationship, which had been based largely on aesthetic or political (if often friendly) debate.

I learned more about my father's inner life after his death. Inheriting his film books, I found a comment about *Grand Illusion* in the margins of Gerald Mast's *A Short History of the Movies*, written in the thick pencil sprawl Dwight favored: "But *why* no wicked or even mean people? Maybe because Renoir sees people as essentially human (OK) as do I, and the Hitlers and Stalins are the odd monsters?" I'm not sure I would have been able to say that my father had felt that way, even knowing his sympathy for anarchism as a philosophy, and this revelation from beyond the grave was comforting. Once again the film had served as a touchstone.

It was my father who first introduced me to *La Grande Illusion* in the summer of 1959. I was 14 years old; the film had just turned 22. Dwight telephoned me from his *New Yorker* office and asked if I would like to see an old movie, playing in revival, called *Grand Illusion*, which starred someone named Erich von Stroheim. A film classic, he told me, as if that might be the clincher. But what had I to do with classics, or classics with me? And who was this von Stroheim actor anyway?

After some dithering, I agreed to join him and we met at the Baronet Theater on Third Avenue near 59th Street. I vaguely remember sitting in a dimly lit balcony. The experience marked a change—for the first time in my life, I responded deeply to a film. The scenes on the farm especially struck me, though I don't remember now what in particular did the trick. Until then, my favorite movies were *The Ladykillers, Around the World in 80 Days,* and a B-film called *The Steel Trap* that starred Joseph Cotten as an embezzling bank manager who finally becomes guilt-ridden and succeeds in returning the stolen money to his bank's vault.

Grand Illusion was also probably one of the first foreign movies I had ever seen. In any case, it was clearly a new kind of film for me. I felt grown up.

About a week later we went back to see it again. Also a first. And over the next six years I saw it eight more times. One afternoon I saw it twice at the New Yorker Theater on the Upper West Side, slipping out before the other feature on the double bill, Akira Kurosawa's *The Seven Samurai*, and returning later for my second dose of *Grand Illusion*. That was another first.

It became my favorite film, spoken about in different terms than other movies. And if music was Duke Ellington's mistress, I was married, somewhat stodgily, to *Grand Illusion*.

After making 16mm shorts in college and becoming even more of a movie fan, I began to see its cinematic side. The initial effect remained, but the film was richer now. And it intrigued me, rather than made me upset, that some people felt differently. My zealotry had waned.

Soon after that evening with my father in 1975, I wrote a long essay on the film. I got Dwight to read it, which led to one of our low points. Handing my piece back to me later, he said he hadn't read the whole thing since it was so long, but at least had gotten a sense of it and written a few comments in the margin, pro and con. I said nothing, not feeling confident enough to challenge him on his cursory reading.

Dwight may have been sparing me the full blast of his criticism since he seemed congenitally unable to tone down his critical judgment, whether directed at a grandson's drawing or the latest work of a famous author. Maybe he realized it would have been hard for me to deal with his honest take. And there was much to be criticized. Perhaps father knew best.

Renoir himself proved more encouraging in his memoir, *My Life and My Films*:

> I believe that any spectacle, film or stage play can only reach a certain level if the author collaborates with the public. Every spectator must be able in his own fashion to interpret both the situations and the general sense of the piece.... It is enough to leave a door open for him and to send him home with his personal interpretation of the situation and the feelings of the protagonists.[2]

In this book, I have certainly done a lot more than keep that door ajar; at times I've practically taken up residence. And I hope this has not been an abuse of Renoir's generous invitation.

In fact, when I started to write again about *La Grande Illusion*, early in 2001, my plan was a modest one — to adapt the earlier essay and come up with a short article, concentrating on the blowup between Maréchal and Rosenthal. But the project steadily grew. For some reason, I didn't worry about getting tired of the film, though in retrospect that was a possibility.

I spent twelve years on this book, though with substantial breaks, reviewing the film countless times on tape and DVD, sometimes going back, over and over, to count off seconds in shots (or to measure the screen-time for major characters), and at other times watching it straight through with an eye (or ear) for a specific aspect, like the background away from the action, or the dialogue. I also read as many books and articles on it as I could find and saw again a wide range of Renoir's films.

Despite this intense exposure, I never lost my enthusiasm and rarely failed to discover something new each time I saw the film or even just went over it in my head, shot by shot, walking down the street or riding the subway. This helped confirm to me both the brilliance of *La Grande Illusion* itself and the validity of what might have seemed like a quixotic journey. My obsession was paying off. And, in the last year before completing my final draft, I was still adding paragraphs analyzing some shots more closely, things I had only recently noticed. Without, I think, forcing the issue. It was simply that there were subtleties I had missed, even after all those years.

Since first seeing *La Grande Illusion* in 1959, I saw the film many times in theaters during the next thirty years. But with the fading of any resemblance to a movie culture, as classics were rarely shown theatrically, and with my own diminished moviegoing, I soon experienced my longest gap (12 years) before seeing *La Grande Illusion* twice in one week (numbers 17 and 18) during its revival in 1999. Struck from the newly found camera negative and looking crisper, the film remained, nevertheless, an old friend.

And it had lost none of its power, even on my seventeenth viewing. I was close to tears as Elsa struggled to coax out, near the end, those simple words: "Le ... café ... est prêt." Was love (hers or mine) ever more perfectly captured than at that luminous moment, shimmering ever so briefly on the screen?

This spurred me to engage Renoir's film again, but more fully this time.

Part I
THE FILM

1

The Blowup in the Mountains

> *"Well, I had written two pages of beautiful literature to explain the situation. Gabin was, you know, like a poet; explaining about what's good, what's bad in nature. It was fantastic. I was so proud of myself.... Finally Gabin told me, 'Jean, we'd better tell you: your two pages of beautiful poetry are just trash and we cannot say it.' Which was true.... Finally I had an idea—oh, perhaps Dalio had the idea, perhaps Gabin. He was humming a tune I already used in the beginning of the picture, 'The Little Sailor.' I took those very innocent words, and they became the center of the scene. The scene is good, I think. But, without the reluctance of Dalio, without my belief in the help the actors can bring you, I would have nothing. Nothing. Oh, I would have a perfectly drawn and conceived scene, but dull."*
> —Jean Renoir in *An Interview: Jean Renoir*, at the American Film Institute, April 15, 1970 (Green Integer Books; 1998; pp. 33–4)

Near the end of *La Grande Illusion*, in the midst of World War I, two escaping French prisoners of war, Maréchal (Jean Gabin) and Rosenthal (Marcel Dalio), find themselves tired, cold, hungry and on the run in enemy territory. After the claustrophobic prison camps that have dominated the movie until this point, confining French and Germans alike, the countryside offers at least temporary relief. Equally critical, after these two men had most often been part of an ensemble, they are now featured in an intimate duet.

Maréchal and Rosenthal have become progressively closer, until this moment. But tension grows. It is a gray and wintry landscape, and they are struggling.

In this context, Renoir expresses an intense crisis in a scene composed of only six shots. And one of the recurring wonders of his film is that he can briefly sketch a moment in time and yet, also, manage to evoke the depth of a novel or perhaps an Old Masters painting.

Preceding this scene, there is a mildly disorienting shot in which the camera pans down the side of a hill, with mountains beyond and music filling the soundtrack. It's difficult to figure out the perspective because of those mountains in the distance; this could be the sweeping vista of a large hill stretching far into the background. But the scale instantly becomes clear when the camera reaches Maréchal and Rosenthal sleeping on the ground, up close and momentarily seeming like giants huddled together against the cold. They rouse themselves, blearily, and get on their way.

Renoir then dissolves to the crucial scene, starting with a long shot of them on a muddy country road. It is a modest and quiet opening; the music ends with this dissolve, and the cut to natural sound, after the full strains of an orchestra, clears space for the drama to follow. Leaning on a stick to rest his twisted ankle, Rosenthal has lagged behind Maréchal, who asks grumpily if he's coming. Rosenthal starts hobbling awkwardly and when he catches up to Maréchal the camera tracks with them, heading on, and they begin to squabble.

In the next shot, the longest of the sequence (48 seconds), they lash out at each other.

Renoir again presents a somewhat disorienting composition, angled slightly from above, with the dramatic landscape of a deep valley behind them. Because of the camera angle, it's hard to tell if they are standing near a steep hillside or, more precariously, on the edge of a precipice. A sense of unease runs throughout the shot as their anger mounts. And the slight angle downward makes them appear vulnerable.

The camera tracks in, tightening the tension, and settles into a medium shot. Eye to eye, unflinching, the breaking point comes when Rosenthal blurts out that he detests Maréchal, who then spits back: "j'ai jamais pu blairer les juifs, t'entends?" ("I never could stand Jews, you hear?"). Rosenthal delivers a sarcastic barb, to regain some dignity: "Un peu tard pour t'en apercevoir" ("A little late for you to realize that"). But then, in turn, he screams for Maréchal to shove off and leave him.[1]

After many instances of fraternity in the movie, breaching class and national divisions, all seems at risk. The film has also been marked by a series of forced separations, which makes it especially painful when Maréchal accepts Rosenthal's challenge; the camera starts pulling back and he exits the frame, leaving Rosenthal behind to shout after him.

The camera continues pulling away and sets Rosenthal even more dramatically against the expansive landscape below as he staggers backward. Slumping onto a nearby boulder, he angrily begins to sing a children's song, "Il était un petit navire" ("There was a little ship"). The camera remains angled downward and makes him appear smaller, and reduced. But he is beyond caring, his face distorted as he sings.

On the run: Maréchal (Jean Gabin) screams at Rosenthal (Marcel Dalio) that he never could stand "les juifs" (*Photofest*).

The third shot in the sequence is very short (two seconds), the only brief shot in the scene — a closer glimpse of Rosenthal as he spews out the song. It had been sung earlier by prisoners to create a diversion and then was played on a pennywhistle by their compatriot, Captain de Boeldieu, who leads German guards on a wild goose chase, allowing Maréchal and Rosenthal to escape in the confusion. Thus the song of solidarity comes back as one of antagonism and separation. This kind of ironic reversal typifies the film as Renoir often reprises images, words and bits of music in changed circumstances, making tangible life's relativity and mutable nature. Nothing is fixed or certain, and Renoir makes no judgments.

The fourth shot builds the confrontation further. Maréchal, in a medium shot, walks slowly toward the camera; the landscape behind him is clearly different from the previous shot, indicating that he has already covered some distance. He starts to sing another verse of the song, turning his head back to toss it out defiantly. The camera begins to backtrack in front of him.

These successive shots of Rosenthal and Maréchal, each alone, are significant since, throughout the movie, they had always been placed together in two-shots whenever on their own and apart from others. Renoir's technical restraint pays off here. The uniqueness of their separation into adjoining shots underlines their emotional estrangement.

Maréchal soon lowers his voice and slows down the words, losing heart, perhaps remembering how this song had been used to spring their escape. He continues to walk toward the backtracking camera, with this camera movement reinforcing his movement away from Rosenthal. It is the first (and only) time that the camera tracks backward in sync with a character walking toward it. Until then, Renoir's choreography of characters within tracking shots usually indicated a communal togetherness and connection. This shot expresses isolation and stasis instead, despite the tracking movement, since Maréchal, as he walks, remains roughly the same distance from the camera.

As his anger falters and he looks over his shoulder guiltily, Maréchal's weakened resolve is also communicated visually by this image of him walking away from Rosenthal and yet, relative to the camera, making little progress. It's as if the camera captures his inner conflict by holding him fast in place within the frame and not allowing him much forward movement.

When Maréchal gets to the last words of the verse ("Ohé! Ohé!"), he barely manages to bring them out halfheartedly, having just sung about provisions that run out during the little ship's voyage — words that are a bit too obviously correlated to the scene at hand. But now he finally overcomes the camera movement and almost exits the frame left; at the cut, his blurred shoulder alone remains in the shot.

Renoir cuts back to a medium shot of Rosenthal, still sitting on the boulder. In this fifth shot in the sequence, the sound of wind at the end of the previous shot drops out on the cut, and the nearly silent soundtrack establishes a sense of anticipation. Crying to himself now, Rosenthal slightly lowers his head.

And then comes one of the most electrifying moments in *La Grande Illusion*, a moment in which content and form are inseparably meshed: the lower half of Maréchal, in his black coat, suddenly moves into view at the right-hand side of the frame, easing in gently next to Rosenthal.

Here Renoir creates an effect as powerful as signature moments in more flamboyantly "cinematic" films. An inspired bit of pure cinema. He achieves it naturally, slipped quietly into the storytelling, and it is moving not just because this signals an end to their confrontation (the narrative side of the shot) but because Maréchal has appeared all at once from the previous shot (only seven seconds earlier in movie-time) in which he was far removed from this current location and walking toward the camera, drawing him farther away from Rosenthal.

In calling on this magical, even surreal, ability of movies to distort time and space beyond real time and real space, Renoir expresses return and reconciliation mainly in cinematic terms. This abrupt elimination of the physical distance that separates the two men makes their reunion a turning point in the movie that it might not have been had Renoir followed the usual, plot-driven convention of crosscutting between them, with full disclosure of territory retraced, ending in the customary hug. Perhaps with tears in their eyes — and a string orchestra to boot.

Renoir instead uses the sort of quantum leap that is a strength of film language in undermining reality and avoiding the pitfall often inherent in an explicit and direct exposition. As when an electron instantaneously moves to a different orbit within an atom and the sudden change seems discontinuous, Maréchal's return is poetic and expressive rather than prosaically literal. In applying the illogic of film time, Renoir creates a more searing impression.

This shot also demonstrates the way that Renoir gains greater power from his effects by not squandering them. Most of the critical moments in *La Grande Illusion* are expressed by tracking shots and the choreography within a shot. But in this instance the effect is primarily achieved through editing. And, aesthetically, it makes sense. The confrontation between Maréchal and Rosenthal marks a rare breakdown in the feeling of community that permeates the film, and its restitution is convincingly indicated by such a resource. They are firmly brought back together by the editing cut.

After having built up to this moment, Renoir cashes in his chips with the shocking abruptness of Maréchal's reappearance, his hands folded at the waist over his dark coat like some penitent priest; the sound of the wind begins to pick up again, the coat flapping. And the gentleness with which he has slipped into the frame, combined with the indirection in not seeing his face, gives the scene a visceral sensation of calm in stark relief to the histrionics of the preceding shots.

The shot continues and, not looking at him, Rosenthal asks why he has returned as the camera pans up to fully reveal Maréchal, who helps Rosenthal to his feet and simply encourages him to continue. Maréchal here assumes the tact and distaste for emotional scenes of his commanding officer, the aristocratic Boeldieu (his opposite in most ways). And this reflects another motif in Renoir's film: the reversal of traits in characters, implicitly reinforcing once again the relative nature of existence as well as the ties of brotherhood.

The escaping prisoners are again eye to eye, but now also arm in arm, Maréchal supporting Rosenthal. They head off. It is the first time during their escape that these two men walk side by side, instead of Maréchal leading the way. They exit the frame as the camera pulls focus on the landscape beyond.

There are no words of reconciliation to close the shot. It has already been expressed more eloquently. That is, it has been expressed cinematically — and in a single shot lasting only 28 seconds.

Renoir dissolves to the sixth, and final, shot of the sequence as Maréchal and Rosenthal walk slowly up a hill toward the camera, which, this time, does not backtrack; they gradually make progress, unlike Maréchal two shots earlier. They pause, consider the dangers of staying in a shack ahead, joke about their lack of choice in the matter, and then continue

A quantum leap in film time — Maréchal (right) returns to Rosenthal (*Photofest*).

forward, exiting left, with Maréchal's shoulder still visible in the frame at the dissolve to the next shot (a similar composition to the one ending the earlier track).

And, with that, this last shot defuses the scene.

At this point in the film, the air has been cleared for the final sequences on a farm, scenes that hold the key to *La Grande Illusion* and provide at least tentative resolution. Now those scenes are possible.

The blowup in the mountains lasts a bit under three minutes. But one can see in microcosm some of the qualities and strategies that distinguish Renoir's film: concision and economy of means; understatement; extended takes contrasted to shorter ones; repetition and inversion; the use of a leitmotif; an effectively modulated soundtrack; the theme of brotherhood, established indirectly; and a calming grace note at the end.

This subtle cinematic expression is embedded seamlessly within the narrative, reflecting Renoir's command of technique and his apparently modest style, applied with decisive ease.

2

La Grande Illusion
A Misplaced Classic

"In the cinema the finest setting, the most beautiful photography, the greatest acting, the most inspired directing, cannot exist separately. Everything is bound up with everything else."

— Jean Renoir in his memoir, *My Life and My Films*
(William Collins Sons & Co. Ltd.; 1974; p. 138)

Why another analysis of *La Grande Illusion*? It seems to have been written into the ground—what more could possibly be said about it, for anyone's sake? But this film is in the unusual position of being famous and much acclaimed, yet only appreciated in part.

From a perspective early in the 21st century, I think that *La Grande Illusion* has been misplaced in film history. It is, to a degree, even misunderstood at some level. Saw it, got it, great movie, up there high on the list. Flattering, perhaps, but this kind of accepted wisdom relegates the film to an inappropriately comfortable niche: moving anti-war document, exceptional acting, those French and German upper-crust career officers, the class divisions. Not exactly exciting, and a bit humorless, but a standard-bearer nonetheless for the "cinema."

It has rarely been taken from that confining corner to be aired out and seen freshly. A few critics, like Alexander Sesonske and Olivier Curchod, have done the film greater justice. Others have respected it with original, if briefer, takes. But for a movie of this depth and complexity, the literature, though extensive, is constricted. The same ground has been beaten to a sodden pulp. And a common approach is to assume there's something stodgily admirable about it, and that we live in a different world now. Gone are the gentlemen at war and all that goes with it. Better to let well enough alone and send this classic film on its way with some appreciative pats.

La Grande Illusion, however, will not so easily go away. In spite of being set in World War I, it is neither dated nor moth-eaten. The clothes and manners may be antiquated, but the characters, the themes, the emotions it evokes are timelier than many fashionably up-to-date films that are weighted down by formulas and clichéd technique, even while showing off the trappings of modern technology. The Emperor's New Clothes, indeed.

But, then, why at such length?

La Grande Illusion deserves, and even needs, this amount of attention. The film is so complex that, to properly understand and honor it, there are few shortcuts. I may be obsessive in my approach, and my undertaking clearly seems outrageous on the face of it, but there is a method to this obsession. If Renoir's film stands up to such an in-depth study, as I believe it does, then my analysis at least serves to demonstrate once more that film is (or can be) an art form of the highest order. Perhaps one should not be concerned with providing another proof of what ought to be obvious. On the other hand, it might be helpful and probably can't hurt.

But why this particular analysis?

A great film not only survives exploration from distinct viewpoints, but thrives on them; new takes can clarify familiar assumptions. Renoir himself often pointed out that everything is relative.

Certainly some things covered here have been noted in other places, especially in terms of shots and dialogue that illustrate thematic elements. But my emphasis and focus is very different. And there are many ways of "looking at a blackbird," as Wallace Stevens once put it.[1]

Most notably, three major areas have not been adequately explored in the critical literature. Or even, at times, deemed important.

First, *La Grande Illusion* is largely about Maréchal and resembles, in certain ways, a coming-of-age movie, a sort of *Bildungsroman*. He opens and closes the movie, and has (by far) the most screen-time. Of more relevance, Renoir tells the story of his growth in overcoming barriers and discovering love with Elsa. Also, of everyone, Maréchal changes the most. He may be a man's man at the start of the movie but surely he has grown up by the end. And he alone pursues meaningful relationships with nearly all the other main characters.

Yet Renoir's extraordinary development of Maréchal as a fully formed character can get lost in the shuffle and is often given short shrift by critics. The role has a restrained, at times passive, feeling to it. And Maréchal's primacy in the film is sometimes reduced to discussing his half of the equation dealing with class division (opposite Boeldieu) rather than following him as he becomes a person of some maturity. Further, the relationship of Boeldieu and Captain von Rauffenstein, and the themes of class and national allegiance that it reveals, has been the usual focus. Its grand theatricality, and then its unraveling, briefly seizes control midway through the movie.

But unlike the other characters, Maréchal (and his influence) is rarely absent from the film. And he is the last one standing, with Rosenthal, in the snows of Switzerland.

Secondly, and related to the importance of Maréchal, it is during the relatively condensed final part (on the run, the farm, the border) that Renoir releases his film's affective impact, engaging various themes and conflicts in the process. This is the climax of *La Grande Illusion*. What comes before prepares for these episodes and, because of them, everything gains more significance in retrospect.

This final part is a small gem. Its startling concision and cinematic invention make it a great accomplishment. Coming after the novelistic breadth and gradual development of characters in the rest of the film, it is, by contrast, a beautifully crafted poem — the keystone without which all else would seem incomplete. Yet this dynamic is not often discussed, and some critics barely even acknowledge the last part.

The sequences on the farm, in particular, transform the movie from a prison-camp drama into a love story. Only then does *La Grande Illusion* become deeply moving — and profound. The human dimension of the film, which had been grounded in the prison camps, is enriched at the farm, as though sparked by the explosion of emotions during the blowup in the mountains. Elsa and her visitors go about their daily lives, connecting easily with each other far from the competing restrictions of camp life. And these scenes are complemented by the final one at the border.

Jean Renoir, flanked by crew, on location at the farm. Photograph: Sam Lévin (©*Ministère de la Culture/Médiathèque du Patrimoine/Sam Levin/dist. RMN-Grand Palais/Art Resource, New York*).

One reason why both Maréchal and the closing part of the film are not sufficiently appreciated may be that the ironic tone and sophistication of Boeldieu and Rauffenstein, as also with the characters in *La Règle du jeu*, appeal more to a modern temperament. There's not a lot of cachet in apparently simple values in a post-everything age.

And lastly, but crucially, I think that *La Grande Illusion* is a stunningly cinematic achievement. Renoir makes striking use of the medium, from start to finish. Of course, on a more superficial level, he masterfully develops themes and characters, and this has spurred many discussions in literary, psychological and philosophical terms. But *La Grande Illusion* is not simply a visualized play or novel. Nor is it a case study that explicates Renoir's philosophy of life, with pictures. There may be lessons in the movie but Renoir does not set about to teach them. No blackboard, no flash cards, no outline to be cribbed.

It is a film, first and foremost. And often what becomes deeply felt in seeing *La Grande Illusion* comes implicitly from the way in which composition of shots, editing choices and sound effects communicate the story and flesh out characters. Surprisingly, not a great deal has been written about these filmic qualities. But it bears stressing that a director's application of technique makes or breaks a movie and can produce a major work. Or, more often, not.

My discussion largely shifts the emphasis to Renoir's creative use of the medium. A shift from sociology and philosophy to aesthetics. Specifically, I offer a good number of detailed shot or sequence analyses and pay close attention to what is innately cinematic in them. Film as art on a basic level.

There is obviously a danger in such technical analysis, and no claim can be made that Jean Renoir necessarily made decisions with certain effects consciously in mind. Maybe some times he did, other times not at all. Nor am I implying that the viewer, as well, consciously registers effects in one way or another.

More relevantly, my interpretation is of course an attempt to communicate how I feel Renoir's decisions affect me. But, beyond that, a mystery to *La Grande Illusion* remains, especially in how it all holds together, the gestalt, with my individual points, along the way, maybe of some validity.

Surviving analysis, that mystery remains intact. What is it that goes on in this film (as in any film), particularly on the micro level of shot to shot, but also part to part and all the stages in between — sequences, scenes, episodes? What is the feel, what the visceral effect? Such a feeling is impervious to the limited scope of criticism. Something registers somewhere, for each in his or her own way. And perhaps at times, from person to person, an overlap exists.

Despite the shortcomings of criticism, to understand a movie one needs at least to look at it cinematically, rather than relying on more easily applied measures of appreciation. Renoir's film works on many levels, but it is only a masterpiece because he fully engages the medium on the cinematic level.

Renoir skillfully orchestrates the delicate combination of elements that make up a great movie — cinematic expression, emotional depth, important themes, well-developed characters and relationships, remarkable performances (for starters). But those qualifying adjectives, though perhaps applicable after the fact in looking back at the film, are only appropriate because of the verbs that produced them and do most of the work at a deeper level: "shoot" and "edit" (especially).

Yet little is schematic about the film. Its subtle and multilayered qualities reflect the genius of Renoir, a gracefulness that reaches far beyond the mere presentation of big themes and believable characters.

There is possibly one more reason for a fuller exploration. Although *La Grande Illusion* deals with war and the solidarity inherent in community, and therefore has an added impact, I would also argue that it is a moral and political movie in a far deeper sense, even more than many "political" movies that specifically advocate an impassioned point of view and trumpet their causes loud and clear. After all, politics and art are rarely compatible.

But, in any artistic achievement, the most lovingly expressed truth and realized beauty provides an implied challenge to the inequities and violence of the real world. Oscar Wilde once quipped that he spent the morning putting in a comma, and the afternoon taking it out — a quip more nuanced than its clever turn of phrase might indicate. A writer concentrating on a comma, or a particular sentence, takes the work at hand so seriously that, as an artist, the fullest possibilities of being human are, at the least, attempted.

I remember listening to a Bach organ piece, waiting for the memorial of my wife's stepfather to begin, shortly after the 9/11 attacks. Watching leaves outside flickering in the sunlight, I thought to myself: if somehow those terrorists could have fully understood and felt the beauty of this music, and enjoyed that bit of nature framed by the chapel's windows, truly felt it deep within themselves, might they have not committed that horror? A painful thought, remanded quickly to the custody of an idealized and theoretical world. And a naive flight of fancy, like the conceit in Beethoven's *Ninth Symphony* when he calls for joyful music to bring together mankind in brotherhood (in his own words).

Still, Leonard Bernstein, the conductor and composer, in talking about the shocked reaction to the assassination of John F. Kennedy, once said:

> This sorrow and rage will not inflame us to seek retribution; rather they will inflame our art. Our music will never again be quite the same. This will be our reply to violence: to make music more intensely, more beautifully, more devotedly than ever before.[2]

In the long run, even after 9/11, art has the potential to heal and bring people together.

Back in a more recognizable world, beyond unfathomable psychosis, if one reaches an appreciation for Bach, Vermeer, Proust, Egyptian art (or *La Grande Illusion*), it might be natural to feel some revulsion for evils, large and small. Great art uplifts and makes one want the best for everyone — anything less seems inconceivable. This can make it relevant politically and morally, in a way that doesn't need quotes placed around those loaded words. And that process is also like the change experienced by Maréchal, since love can stimulate a similar generosity of spirit.

La Grande Illusion is transcendent, as a film and as a humanist work of art. It has often been reduced by critics to that last category. But it's difficult to discuss these aspects separately, one apart from the other. Renoir's humanism emerges, by osmosis, from the subtlety of his cinematic expression.

And, with an added incentive provided by the curious fact that the man who made *Citizen Kane* was transfixed by *La Grande Illusion*, this film warrants fuller understanding and an investment of the highest seriousness. In any case, it is never the wrong time to celebrate such a work. Its time came. Its time remains. We need only look to Renoir's film, again and again.

3

French Air Base/ German Canteen

> After being asked about *"some thirty shots of airplanes, air fields, aerial combat"* detailed in *La Grande Illusion*'s script....
> "'No, none of that was ever shot. We couldn't get the planes for it. One day the producer told me that he just couldn't get them; he was happy because they would have been very expensive — but I was furious. Only I thought it over a little and by the next day I saw that the film would be better without them. I often have fortunate accidents like that. If I had shot those scenes and spent all that money, I probably would have used them.'"
> —Jean Renoir in *Jean Renoir: The French Films, 1924–1939* by Alexander Sesonske (Harvard University Press; 1980; p. 285)

The opening frames of *La Grande Illusion* are blank as muted music, dominated by a military drumbeat, plays on the soundtrack. An appropriately understated beginning. Continuing for six seconds, this blank screen provides space, getting ready for a complicated and large film.

After the production company's logo, the first name to appear in the credits is "JEAN GABIN," followed by "DITA PARLO"—an interesting progression, given Parlo's limited screen-time. Gallic or, more generally, male gallantry of the time? Her name is dissolved into the credit for "PIERRE FRESNAY." Then a new title card, "ERIC VON STROHEIM," pops onto the screen; his name dissolves into the film's title, which is spread out in big letters. Linking him to the title may have been as much a nod to Stroheim's stature in the film world as to his role in *La Grande Illusion*.

The next credit, "Réalisation de JEAN RENOIR" ("Direction of JEAN RENOIR"), dissolves into "avec CARETTE" ("with CARETTE"). Although film credits of that period traditionally did not end with the director, this placement of Renoir's name is still worthy of note. A certain modesty seems implicit as his name not only appears early in the title sequence but is obliterated by a credit announcing the actor who plays Cartier, the lead supporting character, after the five principals, and a role far down on the totem pole.[1]

The music gathers momentum during the credits, developing themes that will cover key scenes.

And the stage is set.

French Air Base

The first shot of *La Grande Illusion* is both classically composed and elegantly choreographed, and it features a song on the soundtrack that will become significant later. It is

3. French Air Base/German Canteen

Opening shot: Maréchal sings along with "Frou-Frou" at the French air base (*Photofest*).

efficient, wasting nothing while establishing much, but takes its time — an apt and reassuring way to set in motion this complex movie, as with the blank frames at the start. It also provides a foretaste of some things to come thematically and, of more importance, cinematically.

The shot opens with a record playing on a gramophone and a pair of hands braced on either side; a singer of indeterminate gender, but sounding perhaps like a man, croons a popular song, "Frou-Frou," in sharp, even dissonant, contrast to the orchestral music at the end of the credits. The setting is a bar at a French air squadron's base. The camera pans up to a young officer, Lieutenant Maréchal, beginning to sing along with the record; a few soldiers, out of focus in the background, place drinks on a table and someone else passes behind Maréchal, who interrupts himself to call after the passing soldier, Halphen. Renoir then pans with the lieutenant as he goes to ask Halphen for a ride to visit a woman named Josephine.

After a brief exchange, Maréchal exits the frame as the camera stays still and Halphen, about to leave the bar, salutes Captain Ringis (Claude Sainval), who is entering; the camera pans back with Ringis to Maréchal at the gramophone as the captain breaks the news to him that he must report for a mission. Renoir cuts off the music at this bit of dialogue. Such a pattern of interruption (Maréchal's reverie, the music) and separation (from Josephine) runs throughout the film and is lodged within its first shot.

A classical balance that also characterizes the film is established when the music starts up again at the end of the shot as Maréchal heads off with Ringis to report for assignment, providing a musical frame for their dialogue. The music revs up awkwardly, distorted, until it gets up to speed, and it's now clearly a woman's voice singing "Frou-Frou." Near the end of the movie, at the farm, a graphophone (a wind-up cylinder phonograph) will lose power and be distorted in the opposite direction, winding down slowly until coming to a stop. In both scenes, the snatches of music bracket important exchanges. The highlighted dialogue in this opening shot concerns a routine mission that, nevertheless, will lead directly to everything that follows.

And it is not Maréchal who starts up the gramophone when the music returns; in effect, Renoir, as the director, intervenes to make the music magically return on the soundtrack. But this poetic license is applied so casually that it doesn't disturb the naturalism of the shot. Renoir often heightens scenes this way, using the medium to transform, without sabotaging, the film's realism.

In addition, incidental music arising naturally out of the action, from within the film, plays a critical role in *La Grande Illusion*. In this first shot, "Frou-Frou" is full of ersatz emotion, a music hall song about the seductive rustling of a woman's skirt, and it comes to us via the mechanical device of a gramophone. But the journey has just begun; the song will be reprised in a scene filled with genuine feeling, as Renoir uses repetition and reprise both for structural reasons and for cinematic effect.

The fact that this opening shot pans back and forth, and is held so long (56 seconds), sets a consistent tone for the film. Often long-held panning or tracking shots of characters capture key moments, allowing Renoir to retain the integrity of the setting. And the repeated panning motions give a cohesive balance to the shot — first to the right with Maréchal, then back left with Ringis, and then back again to the right with them as they head off. This intricate camera movement recording the choreography of the action is typical of the film — an effortless movement of characters, linking one to the next in a natural and logical progression that disguises the dance taking place.

Beyond these elements, which are echoed later, the opening shot has other overtones that resonate throughout the film. Maréchal is the focus from the start; he remains the dominant presence to the end. The gathering of soldiers, drinking wine and sharing Camembert at the end of the shot (the first of many such consumptions to come), introduces the bonding of men, sometimes dining together, as another ongoing motif. And the soldiers in the background, glimpsed in passing, play a game of cards. This communal activity will yield to many games of solitaire played by a French officer who, initially, is singularly detached and remote from the group.

It also proves relevant that a woman, Josephine, is mentioned twice in the opening shot. Halphen ribs Maréchal by saying he's not the only one to go out with her; Maréchal, with bravado, says he doesn't care. Later in the shot, Ringis asks where this relationship will lead him. Maréchal ignores the question and says she'll wait. Though women are largely absent from the film until Elsa finally appears on the farm, their existence is not forgotten, with Josephine at one end of a spectrum that will be counterbalanced by Elsa near the other extreme.

At the end of the shot, the two men approach the doorway through which Maréchal will pass and leave behind the air base for a mission that changes his life. A threshold serving as a means of transition, which happens often in the film.

The opening sequence is completed with a second shot. The music continues on the soundtrack as Maréchal exits with Ringis and the camera floats past photographs of women on the wall and a bartender at his bar. These demure pinups further include women in this world of men, if only tangentially.

The camera then comes to rest on a poster, ending the sequence as it began, on a close-up of an inanimate object. The poster proclaims: "L'ALCOOL TUE! L'ALCOOL REND FOU! LE CHEF d'ESCADRILLE EN BOIT!!" ("ALCOHOL KILLS! ALCOHOL MAKES ONE MAD! THE SQUADRON CHIEF DRINKS IT!!"). A comic touch, and a frantic conjunction of capital letters and exclamation points to end these quiet and undeclarative shots.

The next sequence in the opening scene also has two shots weighted with significance. The first one is a medium shot of a haughty French officer, Captain de Boeldieu (Pierre Fresnay), adjusting a monocle in his eye, with two maps on the wall behind him in his office.

The shot is as severe as Boeldieu himself and a number of disjunctions are established. First, after the casual tracking shots that open the movie, Renoir holds this medium shot still and keeps it constrained. Second, this short shot (five seconds) is contrasted in length to those first shots (56 and 14 seconds). Third, the incongruity between the attitude of this aristocratic officer and the jaunty lieutenant in the previous shot quickly becomes clear. And there is also a contrast between the lighthearted gibe in the poster at the bar and this pinched officer about whom one could not imagine even a fellow officer daring to make such a joke. Boeldieu is a career officer, devoted to military matters; there are no pinups here, only the maps behind him. Lastly, the song from the first sequence, muffled in the distance, infects this war-minded setting.

Much has been established, but by the end of *La Grande Illusion* Boeldieu will have changed greatly, affected by his exposure to the contrasting world of Maréchal.

The differences continue in the second (and last) shot of the sequence. It is a wider three-shot, again held still, as Maréchal and Ringis enter and join Boeldieu. The faint music continues and Maréchal's cigarette sends up wisps of smoke as he discusses an aerial photograph with the two other men. After being introduced to the junior officer, Boeldieu, with his air of superiority, never bothers looking at him again, beyond a passing glance, and denies the lieutenant even his rank in addressing him as "Monsieur Maréchal." But Maréchal looks over to Boeldieu several times, visually expressing their relative positions and class-driven manners.

Nothing is spoken of much importance, beyond Boeldieu's fastidious attention to the smudge on a reconnaissance photograph that he wants to investigate by air. The image itself and the incidental music create a mood, more than the dialogue.

And this photograph, taken to yield specific information, is ambiguous. Boeldieu calls the splotch an enigma, the first of many in a film steeped in ambiguity, as no one can make sense of the bothersome smudge.

Maréchal exits and the shot ends on Boeldieu and Ringis, preparing for the mission.

German Canteen

Renoir dissolves from Boeldieu's office to a German canteen after, as is soon revealed, Boeldieu and Maréchal have been captured. It's an ellipsis with a wicked punch. No dogfight, no plane in flames, no montage of conflict. This will be an anti-war film of a different stripe. It won't bludgeon the viewer with the horrors of war but, instead, will catch their side effects, with its anti-war theme suggested indirectly and made tangible, paradoxically, by rendering war invisible. Renoir might have reached this technical decision on his own, but the limited budget forced his hand, as he admitted.

The dissolve considerably strengthens the film's pacifist spirit. It is the first deeply cinematic flourish and a moment that is effective, implicitly, because of the negative space left between freedom and captivity, and because it carries the story forward easily despite being shockingly abrupt and unexplained.

Renoir, with this dissolve, also avoids the reductive strictures of melodrama and the intrusion of a heavily plot-laden scene. And sentimentality. Since Boeldieu and Maréchal had only been sketchily introduced, their engagement in the drama of a life-and-death struggle would have been without foundation and seemed thin, insubstantial. It would have gratuitously begged for our concern, even our empathy.

Think of those "thirty shots of airplanes, air fields, aerial combat" as indicated in the script. And think of the film mechanics needed in order to show the beginning, middle and end of a dogfight, and the melodramatic tensions involved in that kind of sequence. These are the stock-in-trade of countless films set during a war. But not this one.

In avoiding such theatrics, Renoir enables the slow and sustained development of emotional entanglement that distinguishes *La Grande Illusion*. A battle in the air would have severely altered this tone and thrown his film off course. Nothing as remotely intense happens until late in the Hallbach scenes and, by then, Maréchal's solitary confinement is a natural progression in his characterization and in the evolution of the plot.

The first shot at the German canteen, like the film's opening shot, is a long-held one (64 seconds). It begins on an open door with an indistinct sliver of the outside world beyond and, on the right-hand edge of the frame, the bell of a gramophone (reminiscent of the French base).

A German pilot, Captain von Rauffenstein (Erich von Stroheim), enters the canteen, smoking a cigarette, immediately after Boeldieu's image fades out as the dissolve ends. An aide behind him helps remove his belt and some flying gear, resonating with the previous shot in which Boeldieu discusses with Ringis, his aide, what coat he will use for the mission.

Rauffenstein, standing on the right side where Boeldieu had been during the dissolve, downs a shot of alcohol and clears his ear with his index finger. There's a rough-and-tumble quality to him and his swagger is more akin to that of Maréchal than to the fussiness of his counterpart, Boeldieu, who certainly would never twirl a finger in his ear or swig booze like some tough at a dive. Rauffenstein is a vigorous and confident warrior, the center of attention in this tracking shot; he will return, later in the film, broken and locked down in static shots like Boeldieu.

This first shot focuses on Rauffenstein's celebration after shooting down the French plane. Surrounded by his officers, he orders music; a Strauss waltz starts up on the gramophone. The shot ends, echoing the second shot at the French base, with a track to photographs of two women, apparently cabaret performers — as well as a poster warning of "DER FEIND" ("THE ENEMY"), a parallel to the French poster proclaiming the dangers of alcohol, both with their screaming capital letters.

These simple wooden structures, on either side of the front, are thus remarkably similar, though the music here is comparatively grand compared to the flippancy of "Frou-Frou."

The second shot at the German canteen also opens on the door and is almost as long as the first shot. The new prisoners, Boeldieu and the wounded Maréchal, enter and meet Rauffenstein, who gallantly switches to French in saying "Enchanté" ("Delighted") after Boeldieu introduces himself. It is all very civilized. Again the camera tracks back into the room, while Rauffenstein seats his guests for a shared meal. And, again, a waltz fills the air near the end of the shot.

Renoir then cuts to a two-shot of Boeldieu and Rauffenstein at the dining table, angled slightly upward, a faintly heroic effect. This is the first still shot in the sequence, reinforcing Boeldieu's staid character and also taming Rauffenstein within the frame. Behind them a picture of Field Marshal Hindenburg can be seen. Renoir further sets these two men apart from the others as Rauffenstein, after a bit, initiates an exchange in English, the language that will become their refuge against the creeping democratization around them.

The following two-shot of Maréchal and a German officer, also seated at the table, is pointedly different; the officers are flat to the camera, a simplified angle, and behind them are pinups. Renoir starts tracking to the right. Although now at a disadvantage with his left arm in a sling, Maréchal is presented in a fluid way — a man open to change. He brings camera movement with him to the other characters, while Boeldieu and (eventually) Rauffenstein bring it to a stop.

As the tracking shot continues, Maréchal finds common ground with the German

German canteen: Rauffenstein (left, Erich von Stroheim) greets Maréchal and Boeldieu (right: Pierre Fresnay) with "Enchanté" (*Photofest*).

officer, who cuts his meat for him; he had, like Maréchal, worked as a mechanic in France. The camera tracks around to include Boeldieu and Rauffenstein in the background. Maréchal looks up, interrupting himself mid-sentence, and everybody freezes, focusing on the same point off-camera, before getting to their feet.

Contrasted to the long tracks that have predominated so far, the next shot is held still and runs for only five seconds. A soldier steps into the room, holding a memorial wreath with two banners. It's a disquieting interruption and the wreath foreshadows the geranium, also held by a German, which will memorialize Boeldieu later. Renoir quickly cuts short the waltz music, as though cued by what Maréchal noticed in the previous shot. An odd connection beyond the mere realism of the scene that bolsters the moment. And this sound cut recalls the interrupted music at the French base.

Next comes a close-up of the wreath and, on the cut, even the rustle of room noise drops out as a deathly, unreal silence takes over; Renoir sometimes uses such gradations of sound levels to build an effect. The banners are in French, not German, and honor the death of a French pilot—an extravagant, and unlikely, fissure in national boundaries.

The scene continues with a two-shot of Rauffenstein and Boeldieu, again held still, that strengthens the controlled and emotionally cramped side of the movie associated with them. The German captain apologizes to his French visitor for the inopportune intrusion.

Then, in a medium long shot framed to take in the length of the table, Rauffenstein further acknowledges the feelings of his guests by offering a prayer in remembrance of the pilot. Everyone sits back down to the meal while the music resumes (as it had also returned in the opening sequence when Maréchal and Ringis left the bar). But, for all the parallels, the formal arrangement of this meal is dissimilar to the casual grouping of soldiers sharing food and drink at the French air base.

In the final shot of the scene, Renoir opens on the canteen's front door (for the third time) and a soldier enters to announce, in a workmanlike and dispassionate voice, that the prisoners are to be moved.

And so, continuing the film's emerging pattern, this introductory section ends as it began, with an interruption. But Renoir does not track back into the room (as in the first two shots of the scene) for goodbyes.

This shot also breaks the routine in other ways. Unlike the two elongated tracks that began with the same camera setup earlier (64 and 58 seconds), it lasts only eight seconds. And Renoir abruptly dissolves from the soldier to a traveling shot from a train, with background music added, ending the sequence awkwardly. This inelegant end to the get-together of "enemies" and particularly that of the new soul mates, Boeldieu and Rauffenstein, communicates more effectively the arbitrary way that war overwhelms whatever lies in its path than would the traditional (and ponderous) approach depicting somber farewells and reluctant exits.

Once again, Renoir puts more into his film by leaving more out. It is the difference between poetry and reportage.

4

The Film's Structure

> *"When I work I'm somehow incapable of understanding the meaning of a scene until it has taken on concrete form. I only discover its real meaning when the words have been materialized, so to speak, or when they exist, as Sartre might put it. Existence precedes essence; let us exist first and then we'll see what happens. I have to confront something that exists, and then I begin vaguely to understand its meaning. At heart I'm a profiteer. I expect other people to give me the basics, while I try not to contribute anything. I want everything to come from outside of me."*
> —Jean Renoir in *Jean Renoir* by Pierre Leprohon (Crown Publishers, Inc.; 1971; pp. 165–6); originally in *Cinéma 67* (June 1967)

La Grande Illusion falls naturally into four parts. These parts are coherent internally and feel almost comparable to separate movements in a piece of music, each with its own tone and rhythm. And each, in turn, develops further the film's themes and tightens the emotional pitch. This pace is dramatically accelerated in the last part, indicating a corresponding two-part structure: the building momentum through the prison camp sections, followed by release, if not quite resolution, during the threefold ending — on the run, the farm and, finally, the border.

The film opens with the neatly balanced overture (5½ minutes) featuring the parallel sequences in the two mess halls. These scenes, predominantly light in feeling, have repeating patterns and unexpected turns that dampen the proceedings.

After the connecting link of two documentary-like traveling shots from a train, the next part begins at the first of two camps that will make up the bulk of the film. This second movement at Hallbach (39 minutes) is a lively allegro, with sobering interludes set into it. The motivating principle becomes that of the ensemble. Though individual characters take turns in the spotlight, there are, significantly, twice as many group shots (four or more people) as all other shots combined in this part. Still shots (56) and moving shots (48) are close in number; this is an especially high percentage of tracks and pans, compared to the other parts, and reflects the sense of an interconnected group at Hallbach.

Some traveling shots, again from a train, lead to the third part, at the Wintersborn prison camp (40 minutes). This movement is slow and measured, an andante dominated by a series of duets, expressed mainly in two-shots or alternating shot/countershots; the ensemble is much less important. Also reversing the pattern at Hallbach, there are twice as many shots of characters alone or with one or two others than in a group. And there are almost three times as many still shots (108) as tracks and pans (39), suggesting a feeling of inertia, if not stagnation, at Wintersborn. Furthermore, although only a minute longer than the Hallbach section, it has 43 more shots; yet Wintersborn seems slowed down from Hallbach rather than sped up.

The last part (24½ minutes) is classically balanced, like the overture, though less cohesively distinct as a part. This grand finale begins and ends outdoors, in short, framing sequences set in uneasy freedom — from wintry landscapes in Germany at the start, to the final scene at the snow-covered border of Switzerland. In between is the *pièce de résistance* of the film, Elsa's farm.

Each episode in this last movement feels different, lending more tonal variety to this part: subdued and tense on the run; generally lyrical, even ecstatic, at the farm; and, finally, cautiously hopeful at the border. With only four characters of any significance, the last part escalates the gradual trend toward increasing intimacy. But Renoir also achieves a satisfying balance on the farm between individual relationships and the group (small as it is), making the dynamic there less extreme than the imbalance that is so marked in the two prison camps.

There are 373 shots (including the credits and end title) in the 113-minute version of *La Grande Illusion* that was released in 1999. A little over a full year of shots, but a modest number in film terms. In the film proper (354 shots), the average length of a shot is 18.8 seconds — a virtual eternity in movie time. This average begins dropping from part to part: from 25.8 seconds in the introductory section, to 22.5 at Hallbach, to 16.4 at Wintersborn. In the last part, the average shot length for the movie as a whole is more closely matched (19.8 seconds).[1]

La Grande Illusion is made up of short scenes that are sometimes symmetrically framed. Each scene becomes a building block, adding weight and solidity, and slowly, piece by piece, the whole takes shape. These scenes are usually condensed to a high degree, with little to provide context or make transitions smoother, as Renoir repeatedly cuts to the chase. But his film evolves naturally, making it less like collage than a fluid and unified work.

There appear to be 27 time shifts to a new day, though not necessarily consecutive days, signaled usually by a fade-out (and sometimes by a dissolve). And there are about twice as many distinct scenes. Dissolves more often represent a gap of time within a day, except when used to link the traveling train shots which, in leading up to Wintersborn, indicate many months in different camps.

Architecturally, then, there are two large blocks in the middle, framed by two shorter passages on either side. A classic balance. The opening and closing parts, unlike the middle ones, are composed of even smaller units — for a total of seven different "sections" making up the four parts.

What is noteworthy about these sections is that each one is set in a new locale. The film moves inexorably from location to location: French air base; German canteen; Hallbach; Wintersborn; the German countryside (in three settings); the farm; the Swiss border. At no point does Renoir double back and return to a previous location. Though this shift at the beginning of each new section may seem trivial, that structural characteristic helps drive the movie forward, and this movement ever ahead even mimics the passage of time itself.

These shifts are commonly marked by a new day. But the ellipsis between the French base and the German canteen, and then the first evening on the farm following the confrontation in escape, continues the day of the previous section — the first shift marking the loss of freedom and the second its preservation.

And a significant balance is also achieved at the end, with the relative freedom and security at the air base reached again, at last, in the final shot of the film.

5

Aspects of Style

"All technical refinements discourage me. Perfect photography, larger screens, hi-fi sound, all make it possible for mediocrities slavishly to reproduce nature; and this reproduction bores me. What interests me is the interpretation of life by an artist. The personality of the filmmaker interests me more than the copy of an object."
— Jean Renoir in *Film: Book 1—The Audience and the Filmmaker*, edited by Robert Hughes (Grove Press, Inc.; 1959; p. 57)

Perhaps what contributes most to the casually assured tone of *La Grande Illusion* is the steady and unrushed development of plot, characters, relationships, themes — in short, the film's leisurely evolving shape. As with someone who doesn't reveal too much too quickly and assume a closeness before earning it, Renoir slowly intensifies the hold of his movie.

There is a sense that, in not pressing his audience from the start, Renoir trusts that with time, as the film unrolls, its effect will coalesce more fully and be especially lasting. This maturity of expression, a hallmark of *La Grande Illusion*, makes possible the gradually earned, and well-earned, depths of feeling. It is a serious film, though also an entertaining one since Renoir carries its seriousness lightly and, among other things, tells a good story.

This approach provides a buffer against sentimentality. Renoir does not manufacture crises or tragedies for cheap effect right off the bat. No bombardment of close-ups and thumping music in the early reels, with people weeping, dying, facing traumas. He gains sympathy for his characters first, allowing them to become distinct and recognizable as the film progresses instead of thrusting forward stick figures to cry out for unwarranted attention. And he doesn't show and tell more than is needed, which can be all too easy in movies.

After establishing the main characters, Renoir lets *La Grande Illusion* meander a bit, as if feeling his way. But he also periodically ups the ante with strikingly expressive shots and sequences. And there are only a few times when the film takes a discernible "rest": the two brief sequences shot from the train; the digging of the tunnel; the musical revue; and, certainly, the diversion and chase of Boeldieu at Wintersborn. Many of those plot-heavy sequences are propelled by the theme of escape, which, in this film, is like one of Hitchcock's MacGuffins. As a motif, escape appears to be a major element in the story; in reality, it serves mainly as a sideshow while themes and characterizations develop.

But it would be a mistake to think that such sequences are extraneous and stand in the way of a leaner movie. They provide an important change of pace. The play of expressively charged shots against foils of mere plot details is especially evident at the prison camps. On the farm, by contrast, there are few foils of any kind and the resulting intensity is impressive.

In a similar way, the script only departs from its notably low-key dialogue in a few places where characters talk explicitly about issues: at Hallbach the prisoners share their reasons for escaping; at Wintersborn they talk about disease in relation to class; and Boeldieu and Rauffenstein discuss their life of privilege. These are exceptions to the more typically prosaic conversations in which larger implications can only be deduced. And each of these instances, as with the plot-driven scenes, has a purpose in the overall scheme. Renoir delivers cinematic jolts of power after lulling us with stretches of harmless patter.

Renoir's overriding strategy, contributing to the prevailing tenor of *La Grande Illusion*, is to achieve his effects through indirection. The director as "indirector." To some degree, he conveys nearly every significant moment obliquely and without weighted dialogue to announce it or prop it up. This is an open movie. Sometimes what happens beyond the edge of the frame, maybe even an off-screen sound, seems most relevant.

In line with this approach, the restraint of the camera is remarkable. Medium shots dominate, while long shots are less common and close-ups of the characters rarer still. The camera is usually placed flat to the subject or angled slightly from side to side; only occasionally are shots angled upward (at times for a bolstering effect) or, more unusually, angled downward. Renoir once wrote: "I think the best camera-angle is that determined by the height of an average human being. In a close-up the lens should be level with the performer's eye."[1]

It often appears as if nothing much is happening on the screen. Looked at with blinders, shot by shot, scene by scene, the narrative moves ahead simply enough and Renoir's intricate tracking shots seem to proceed naturally, without fuss. As he once wrote, his preference was "to avoid fragmentation" and he described the typical way he followed the movement of the actors:

> *La Grande Illusion* is perhaps the film in which I used the ... method most satisfactorily. Needless to say, if the technique is to be perfect it must be imperceptible—as is true of all techniques. The audience must not notice that the camera is positively dancing a ballet, subtly passing from one actor to another.[2]

Renoir developed this elongated and flowing style partly because, having a special fondness for actors, he felt it offered them a better opportunity to succeed. Without doubt, it worked here. There are many memorable performances in *La Grande Illusion*, not only by the five featured actors but also by the secondary ones. Rarely is there an alienating false note or broad appeal to break the spell.

And just as critics often take Maréchal for granted, Jean Gabin is not given enough credit for his subtle, even overwhelming, performance. He inhabits a range of emotions and stakes out a reassuring heft, and authority, to his presence. The change Maréchal undergoes is delineated finely, morphing slowly before our eyes. Gabin creates a role as layered as the movie itself, yet Erich von Stroheim is the one usually cited for his acting. Both are pitch-perfect, but Gabin helps hold the movie together and drives it forward; Stroheim stylishly crafts his performance, but the role is largely self-contained and his character remains aloof from everyone except Boeldieu.

Fresnay, Dalio and Dita Parlo (as Elsa) also fashion individualized characters and communicate gradations of feeling through slight gestures or eye movements—or absence of same. They seem as irreplaceable in their roles as Gabin or Stroheim. Julien Carette, in the critical supporting role of the music hall actor, similarly shines, but in an appropriately effusive way. And those playing the other prisoners (Jean Dasté, Gaston Modot and Sylvain Itkine in particular) complete the tapestry and make the acting all of a piece: understated, realistic and natural.

Jean Gabin, posing in Renoir's World War I uniform. Photograph: Sam Lévin (©*Ministère de la Culture/Médiathèque du Patrimoine/Sam Levin/dist. RMN-Grand Palais/Art Resource, New York*).

Only the little girl known as "la petite Peters" who played Lotte (unlisted in the credits) is sometimes self-conscious in looking directly into the camera, with excitement and curiosity, breaking the fourth wall and distracting from her performance; one needs, normally, to make allowances for children on screen. But she is also charming in her childlike enthusiasms and holds true in her crucial scenes with Gabin.

Renoir's filming style produced much more than this *tour de force* of acting. It goes deep into one's consciousness, under the apparently simple storytelling. There is a delicacy of expression, a poetic distillation that does not merely relay the film's humanism but embodies it. And, as in the works of great jazz artists like Louis Armstrong or Earl Hines, the ever-changing subtlety and forceful precision of Renoir's technique in *La Grande Illusion* is balanced by the ease of its expression. Complicated and yet restrained. At once expansive, but compressed. Indeed, a calm settles over a work of art whenever its very existence seems quietly inevitable while, at the same time, it is driven by a ferocious intelligence and creative force.

That is true of this film. *La Grande Illusion* moves along easily and Renoir quickly inspires confidence, as though he knows what he wants and simply goes out and does it. You can relax and take in the show. And what a show it proves to be. Renoir is almost continuously active in the cinematic sense—sometimes in small touches, sometimes at larger moments—and presents, in a bit less than two hours, a story that develops and changes so completely that he summons up a fully realized world.

Another factor is the varied technique. Like a skilled tennis player, Renoir varies depth (long shots and closer ones), speed (long-held and short shots), and angles (flat, sideways, up, down), maximizing his film's ebb and flow. He avoids the steady ticking of a metronome as the length and kind of shot vary, though many scenes open with long tracks or pans and close with shorter takes that are evenly divided between still and moving shots.

At times Renoir defuses a sequence by pulling the camera back at the end and changing the drift of the dialogue. This is a part of his style. But even his well-known tracking shots are just one element in the overall approach; they are not used to excess. And some key scenes end on a high note without any defusing at all.

There are contrasts too between long-held shots and sequences organized around brief countershots, and further contrasts between scenes heavy in dialogue and scenes of plot development or action. By not churning out tried-and-true patterns or depending on certain cinematic effects to the exclusion of others, Renoir infuses *La Grande Illusion* with an energy and freshness that remains strong even after many viewings. This carries the film along effortlessly, but one cannot assume the shape he will be adopting for it.

Renoir is also economical, as reflected in his judicious editing. Shots are cut short when appropriate, not to move on and mindlessly include more coverage or make sure that no element is left unseen or unexplained. And little goes wasted. No visual clutter drags down the film through an accumulation of needless changes in the point of view. He also uses very few quick cuts and no extended montage; only Boeldieu's escapade at Wintersborn briefly devolves into a deluge of shots.

Some critics, even ones favorable to Renoir, have pointed out that his editing can be awkward and choppy in places. At times, the story lunges ahead in spurts at a disconcerting clip; the farm is especially distilled. The narrative thread can sometimes even be tricky to follow right away, as in the first leap from one side of the war to the other.

There are also a number of slight jump cuts in *La Grande Illusion* as Renoir cuts to a new shot set at a slightly different angle, mismatching actions and disturbing the transition. And a few bigger jump cuts as well. But, to my eye at least, these do not disrupt one's suspension of disbelief. Nor do the many clashes on the soundtrack in cutting from one type of music to another. Often these disjunctions reflect the touch of a poet. And so much is going on that occasional breaks in continuity don't attract attention.

Renoir is a realist in the area of character and feeling, not necessarily of physical integrity and seamless narrative; his sensibility seems to overwhelm the mere mechanics of action. Perhaps the biggest challenge to the story's casual realism is the farfetched coincidence that Rauffenstein and Rosenthal each conveniently happen to turn up at Wintersborn, from diverse places, to be reunited with Boeldieu and Maréchal.

It's also certainly true that Renoir is known less for editing effects than for elaborately choreographed long takes and his panning or tracking camera, combined with depth of field — those cornerstones of his characteristic style developed during the 1930s. This helped make possible his seemingly "invisible" style.

Renoir's guiding instinct was to prolong the continuity of a scene, in time and space, rather than break it down into its constituent parts. As he put it:

> The farther I advance in my profession, the more I am inclined to shoot in deep focus. The more I work, the more I abandon confrontations between two actors neatly set up before the camera, as in a photographer's studio. I prefer to place my characters more freely, at different distances from the camera, and to make them move. For that I need great depth of field.[3]

This distinctive troika of long takes, tracking shots and deep focus (the Renoir signature) would reach its apotheosis in *La Règle du jeu* and, in the future, prove influential for the medium as an art form.

On another level, Renoir achieves structural and stylistic cohesion through his skillful use of reprise and leitmotifs — within shots, in the dialogue, on the soundtrack, in the editing. These strategic devices either draw similarities or establish contrasts. Alexander Sesonske, in his analysis of the film, puts it succinctly: "This use of parallels and repetitions, heretofore an important but subordinate element in the totality of a Renoir film, in *La Grande Illusion* becomes the organizing principle of the whole."[4]

As in variations on a musical theme, this has several ramifications. First, these repetitions anchor the film and have a structural purpose. Second, it is often pleasing to hear a line repeated or a musical phrase reprised, or see a similar kind of shot return, and recognize something familiar. And lastly, another affective component emerges as we are brought back to an earlier moment and reminded of the change that has taken place over time. The result can be somewhat like the effect, for example, when the "Aria" returns at the end of Bach's *Goldberg Variations*. This is the same piece of music as stated at the opening, but it makes a different impression when reprised, enriched by the 30 variations heard since its original statement.

Some of Renoir's repetitions resonate almost subliminally, like pictures on the wall or objects that reappear in a new setting. Others register more directly—perhaps a tracking shot, or a bit of music like "Frou-Frou," repeated in a different context to create a startling variation. And certain motifs that recur often in Renoir's films, such as meals solidifying a communal bonding or shots framing, and trapping, people in doorways and windows, denote states of mind that would be redundant if verbalized by the characters.

Another tonal element in *La Grande Illusion* is the sparseness of its sets. Renoir usually keeps the background in shots relatively unencumbered. The film technique is more efficiently clarified since the environment does not distract, in the analogous way that the black-and-white of the film helps keep images generally less diffuse compositionally than if they had been in color.

Renoir once said that, in making a film, he let the prop man fill up the set and then took away most of it. And he added: "To crowd the set and then to empty it."[5] This simplifies the look of *La Grande Illusion*. Renoir's stripping down of the set thus contributes to a concentrated focus on the characters in his film and heightens the effect, though still managing to seem real and true.

The cinematography of Christian Matras, classically composed and unassuming, also has a lyrical quality to it. Little distracts, even in the complex tracking shots, and yet Matras

Marcel Dalio, with crew member, on location during filming of the blowup. Photograph: Sam Lévin (©*Ministère de la Culture/Médiathèque du Patrimoine/Sam Levin/dist. RMN-Grand Palais/Art Resource, New York*).

provides a richness in his range of blacks and whites as well as in the evocation of characters and settings, almost painterly in feeling at times.

It is crucial that *La Grande Illusion* never degenerates into full-blown melodrama. The fortunate circumstances that prevented filming the dogfight and the rebellion of Gabin and Dalio against mouthing the luscious prose of the blowup helped, in those instances, to avoid undue bombast. More importantly, the understated script written by Renoir and Charles Spaak is a masterful combination of naturalism and psychological understanding.

Renoir's refusal to rely on the conventions of movie melodrama, spurning heavy doses of angled close-ups, dramatic lighting and hyped-up acting to telegraph big moments, was also critical. The nearest the film comes to being melodramatic is in scenes like the actor's near suffocation, Maréchal's solitary confinement, the chase of Boeldieu and his death, the blowup, and the final sequence at the border. But these scenes are prepared for sufficiently and are either fleeting moments or tempered by irony and Renoir's restrained technique. That approach lessens the chance of an overweening appeal.

There is also no facile pleading to the emotions by coating scenes indiscriminately with background "movie music." This avoids quick-fix editorializing. Except for the opening credits, the two short sequences from the train, and a brief musical comment on the actor's antics at Hallbach, there's no background music until 15 minutes into the Wintersborn section (more than halfway through the movie). By then, the characters have been fully established and Renoir has prepared for its introduction. And, shortly after the halfway point in the farm scenes, Joseph Kosma's catchy score is finally introduced into that section as well. A patience that again pays off handsomely.

On the other hand, incidental music is as prevalent throughout as background music, and it proves more essential. Renoir uses it to further the film's sweep and it plays a key role in the introductory scenes and at Hallbach. When Boeldieu and Rauffenstein assume central importance at Wintersborn, incidental music becomes literally "incidental" to the film, as Kosma's music more accurately reflects their formal personae.

In the last part, incidental music again is important, though the film ends (traditionally) with background music.

And hovering over *La Grande Illusion*, just as the war furnishes a steady undertone beneath, is a sense of tragedy, strengthened by the ongoing dynamic of interruption and separation that becomes most wrenching during the last part. A symphony of interruptions and separations. Having drawn his characters together, in league against restrictions of class and national boundaries, Renoir shows the inevitable rifts caused by war.

Much of the film's incidental music is also interrupted, cut abruptly and often left unresolved: "Frou-Frou" and the waltz early on; at Hallbach, "Frère Jacques" on the first day, "Le Pâtre des montagnes" soon after, "It's a Long Way to Tipperary" rehearsed by English prisoners, "Cadet Rousselle," a song-and-dance routine, and a diva's revue number; at Wintersborn, music played and sung by prisoners, and Boeldieu's tune in the ramparts; the children's song petering out during the blowup; and, finally, graphophone music at the farm's Christmas celebration. All broken off, incomplete.

The ending of each part reinforces this pattern. The introductory part closes with the German soldier announcing the transfer of prisoners, breaking up the meal shared by captors and captives. Hallbach ends with a guard ordering Maréchal to resume his place behind a restraining rope as the prisoners await removal to a new camp, having been interrupted in their escape plan. Rauffenstein memorializes Boeldieu's death (separation of a larger order) to end Wintersborn. And, as the final part nears its conclusion, the farm section closes with yet another lone German, Lotte, sitting at a dining table after Maréchal is separated from Elsa. With the insistent symmetry of these interruptions and separations, the film gathers a pent-up force.

Near the end of *La Grande Illusion* a dramatic inversion occurs. An interruption, for once, is fortuitous. Two German soldiers stand in the snows of a mountainside, having stopped shooting at Maréchal and Rosenthal in the valley below; one of them comments sarcastically on the fugitives they had, until then, been hunting down.

But that is not quite the end. The film does not close with Germans again having the last word. Nor does it close on this last interruption, or one more separation. It ends with two Frenchmen, together, walking single file through a field of snow. And Renoir, at least tenuously, brings us closer to the world that had opened *La Grande Illusion*.

6

Hallbach

[Action:] *"And then, of course, that segment where all of the men are in the window looking down at the marching band. It's effective to see their faces, their reactions.*
RENOIR: I think it's a way to have audiences participate in the making of the picture."
— Jean Renoir in "Directors Go to Their Movies: Jean Renoir"; interview with Digby Diehl (*Action*, volume 7, number 3; May–June 1972; p. 4)

The second part of *La Grande Illusion* is set in the Hallbach prison camp. After the intensity of the opening sequences, with their information-packed tracks and clever parallels, the first scenes at Hallbach are diffuse and somewhat ordinary. As Renoir begins one of the two large sections in his movie, he eases in slowly. It is a stretch where not much of critical importance happens.

The opening scene in the courtyard as prison regulations are read to the assembled prisoners, including Maréchal and Boeldieu, and the long tracking shot soon after as the two officers are processed and searched, point up their differences as well as the tension between French and Germans. And the next sequence takes place in an even longer and more digressive tracking shot as Rosenthal receives a package of provisions at the mailroom and, with his prison mates, discusses their fare and that of their jailers; in passing, he gives a packet of chocolate to a nearby guard.

Renoir follows with a slightly disjointed cut to a medium long shot of three German guards at a meal, sitting in a grimly lit room with a framed picture of Kaiser Wilhelm II above them and the shadow of window frames on the wall like prison bars. It has an even more constrained feeling to it than Rauffenstein's shared meal. Echoing the dialogue of the mailroom scene, the Germans comment on the national diets of prisoners, ending with one guard blurting out "plum pudding" (for the English) to the amusement of the others. Unlike the preceding sequences, the camera is held still. This fairly brief shot (17 seconds), which alone comprises the scene in full and is totally disconnected from the surrounding scenes (a rarity in the film), seems to come out of left field. But it also serves a purpose.

An immediate contrast is established by the tracking shot that follows, set in the quarters of the French prisoners; they gather for Rosenthal's feast in a more carefree atmosphere than in the previous scene or at the meal presided over by Rauffenstein. It is also set apart from the shot of the guards by its movement and length (56 seconds). The camera moves gracefully from character to character as they talk, twisting and turning, choreographed to end at an angle down the length of a modest table — in contrast to the long table at the German canteen — as they sit down.

This will be, already, the fourth meal in the film, and each one with a distinctly different tenor. But for all its casualness and small talk as the new prisoners feel their way, this shot

Hallbach: settling in for Rosenthal's feast; clockwise, from Rosenthal, standing at the head of the table, the engineer (Gaston Modot), Maréchal, the teacher (Jean Dasté), Cartier (Julien Carette), Boeldieu (*Photofest*).

gives the impression of a theatrical production about to begin, the players finding their positions.

The next shot pans up expectantly from the close-up of a place setting to a close shot of Rosenthal, beaming proudly as he announces his menu. And with that, the curtain is up.

Renoir partly conveys the ease and camaraderie of this meal, as the men talk about food and about Paris and its cafés, by a relaxed mixing of group shots and others focusing on individuals, as well as tracks mixed with still shots. Such a variety and balance is reached for the first time. A democratic occasion, with military rank of no great import.

The scene ends with a panning movement to the music hall actor, Cartier (Julien Carette), his mouth stuffed with food, singing "Frère Jacques" raucously as he focuses on Boeldieu. The actor plays jester to the French captain's royal presence. Maréchal calls Cartier "drôle" ("funny") at one point, the first appearance of a word repeated often in the film, and Boeldieu refers to "le jeu" ("the game") played by the irrepressible actor, understanding the theater at his expense. Boeldieu will, in time, enact his own version of a mischief-maker.

With this sequence, Renoir sets the tone for Hallbach, which is marked by a combination of broad joking around and good-humored teasing. A looseness informs this part, with comic playfulness coming to the fore. That tone is often set by the actor, a minor character but a central figure at Hallbach (he matches Maréchal in screen-time during this section). A jokester, he also has a major role in the other extended sequences: digging the tunnel; the reviewing and preparation of costumes; and, most prominently, as master of ceremonies during the musical revue, the focal point of Hallbach.

But Renoir does not reduce this part to an unmodulated lightness of spirit. The guards bark out orders and exert their authority over prisoners. And there are some crises: the actor nearly suffocates; a prisoner is shot, off-camera; the Germans put Maréchal in solitary confinement.

The actor's significance in the scheme of things reflects the primacy of the ensemble at Hallbach. The relationship of Boeldieu and Maréchal, at this point, is secondary to the dynamic of the group, though each character also has a chance to briefly strut his stuff. Maréchal remains a key player, particularly toward the end of Hallbach. But Boeldieu, without Rauffenstein as cohort, has a fairly minor role. And Rosenthal soon becomes a major figure.

Since it is the group that drives Hallbach, rather than the intimacy of relationships, two people are not often shown alone together in a shot. Instead, clusters of prisoners or of the guards are commonly placed in long-held tracking or panning shots, at times connecting French and Germans together. The community is preserved within its environment. This largesse, of unbroken time and intact space, offers a wider area of focus.

Within this close-knit group, the actor is so ubiquitous that, in the scene following the French at their meal, the camera opens on him, standing outside an open window and peering in as he tells the unseen engineer (Gaston Modot) that Boeldieu's request for an armchair cannot be met; behind him, prisoners play a game by pitching small objects (possibly coins). The camera then tracks backward into the room, past the frame of the window, to the kneeling engineer and Maréchal, sitting on a bed, having his feet washed — an image almost biblical in nature.

During this sequence Maréchal is brought up short about his illusions for the first time. When the engineer starts to confide in him about their tunnel, the camera is positioned closer, as if being let in on the secret, and it picks up the confidential exchange between them in close medium shots, ending in a two-shot. Maréchal doubts that the war will last more than a few weeks and the engineer scoffs at his "illusions"; Maréchal later voices a similar opinion in the gardening scene.

The sequence ends as Maréchal follows up a previous exchange about the engineer's field as a surveyor ("cadastre") by now revealing his ignorance of the word in asking curtly what it means, seeming to consider the engineer pretentious in his fancified vocation. Maréchal's scorn is emphasized as the camera tracks into him before he spits out the final word, "cadastre," raising his eyebrows while looking downward at the engineer, who is drying his feet. Gabin earlier lays the groundwork for this edgy tone by skillfully having his character pretend to understand the term "cadastre," and even turns his face away at that point as if, in pretending to understand it, he cannot look directly at the engineer.

Maréchal appears to be uneasy with anything he sees as affectation. All the same, his confrontational manner is not seemly, especially since he has accepted the engineer's kindness in washing his feet.

The extended tunnel-digging scene follows. After an introductory shot, Renoir tracks around the room as the men prepare for the task at hand; he introduces the motif of the theater (so important in his career) when the actor and Rosenthal theatrically hang a blanket over the window, with grand poses and mock self-importance.

This track is followed by the longest shot in the movie (117 seconds), which covers the preparation for digging and the actor going down into the tunnel. For a shot that is basically informational and plot-driven, its elaborate tracking motions and length seem peculiarly out of place. But it reflects Renoir's original plan to make an adventure movie based on a series of escapes.

It is not, however, only a vestigial reminder of an earlier concept of the film. The characters moving in and out of the shot, in counterpoint to the periodically tracking camera, reinforces the importance of the group, united together for a common purpose. No one person dominates, though again the actor hams it up, punning on the word "pattes" ("legs") to start a song about "le pâtre des montagnes" ("the shepherd of the mountains") and clowning around amidst the dogged efforts of the others. And stylistically the shot is elegant and complicated, though minimalist in effect since the digging of the tunnel remains essentially an insignificant development.

Compared to the concentrated energy of the film as a whole, the tunnel-digging sequence is a rare *longueur*. There are few undertones that will be echoed later, as is more normally Renoir's approach. *La Grande Illusion*, once again, seems a bit becalmed. Renoir provides little punch beyond the small melodrama that takes place as the teacher (Jean Dasté) finds that a prisoner attempting to escape has been shot, and then as the actor passes out in the tunnel; the alarm signal unluckily falls on a pillow before finally being noticed.

But the sequence presents a telling contrast, placed soon after the liveliness of Rosenthal's feast and before a series of powerful shots and scenes that builds the tension. As ever, Renoir, a master jeweler, sets off big scenes against humble surroundings.

There are intimations of things to come, I think, in a tracking shot of the actor and engineer that soon follows and which displays Renoir's deft instincts as a filmmaker. Though not meaningful in terms of the narrative, it begins to indicate something deeper and more serious in the works. And it's another one of his extremely long-held shots (59 seconds).

This medium long shot opens on an exterior within the prison grounds as the camera tracks along with some prisoners, including one in kilts (another nationality in the melting pot); the teacher and Maréchal talk about the exaggeration of military prowess by both sides in the war, the French and Germans linked again.

The shot settles on the actor and engineer heading toward the garden with tools. A marching song, sung by German soldiers, can be heard in the distance. The actor shuffles along to the music and then pokes his foot mischievously through a nearby barbed wire fence, pretending to escape; a German guard simultaneously shouts out a warning and motions him away. The actor draws back, feigning surprise, and reads aloud from a sign by the fence, comically elongating the word "weitergehen" ("go on")—which is set above "verboten" ("forbidden"), a word that serves as a leitmotif throughout *La Grande Illusion*. The singing of the soldiers is louder now.

The two Frenchmen continue walking left as the camera pans along with them. But as they exit the frame the camera becomes stationary, focused on German soldiers marching in formation behind the barbed wire, under the watchful eyes of three officers.

Renoir then turns the screw tighter. The shot continues to run for an unusually long time after the actor and engineer leave the frame (20 seconds), far more than is warranted by the plot, like eye contact lasting beyond a socially acceptable length.

In holding the shot so long, Renoir shifts the emphasis from the French, who are no longer on the inside, to the Germans outside who, in the changed context of the shot, are now the imprisoned ones, trapped behind the same barbed wire that had previously held in the French. Outside becomes inside, and the change is achieved without moving the camera or cutting to a new shot, making it especially effective. This is typical of Renoir's

![Photo] Cartier, carrying two shovels, and the engineer behind him — a mock escape (*Photofest*).

style, in which transitions often occur within an uncut shot. Without resorting to words or editing devices, Renoir communicates the common humanity of these enemy combatants as well as the relativity of wartime experience.

This throwaway shot moves effortlessly from light theater (the mock escape) to these larger themes, presented in visual terms (and also by the regimented rhythms of the marching song). And the shot closes with a poignant grace note when the soldiers exit left, as had the French prisoners before them, and the officers, in their unmatching coats and headgear, continue to walk idly toward the camera, out of step. Such a stark image of hierarchy indicates the distinction between those who must toe the line and those who are above it all.[1]

An inspired shot, it is quietly ironic, with the imprisoned Frenchmen ambling off to tend the garden while their German jailers are temporarily stuck behind, marching in cadence. It parallels a moment in the opening scene at Hallbach when the newly arrived prisoners walk out of the frame to the left, leaving German soldiers drilling in the background of the shot. Who exactly is prisoner and who jailer?

There is a key moment, also conveyed largely by an uncut shot, that contributes to the gathering momentum in an even more critical way. Soon after the barbed wire shot, the costume-reviewing scene opens with a shot of English prisoners in a rehearsal space, dancing in a chorus line and belting out the song "Tipperary" to piano accompaniment. The camera pans to the left and the singing is interrupted briefly but then starts up again.

Later, after the costumes pass inspection by a German guard named Arthur (Werner Florian), one of the French prisoners, Maisonneuve (Roger Forster), is sent off on a lark to model some women's clothes. He returns dressed as a woman, saying that it is "drôle" ("funny," or "droll"); the background noise of the shot drops out, increasing the tension, as he picks at his skirt and asks if it looks funny.

Then comes the significant shot. Renoir again pans left in a medium long shot that passes startled prisoners (and a German guard) and takes in the same setting of the opening pan across the English chorus line. But this pan is very different. Renoir brings the camera in slightly closer as he passes by these dumbstruck figures, posed as if in a frieze, and he begins the shot in dead silence, yet another shift on the soundtrack, far from the earlier tumult of the sequence and then the uneasy mutterings of Maisonneuve at the end of the previous shot. The absolute and sudden deadness in the air has a visceral effect, as if the film itself, not just the stunned prisoners staring at Maisonneuve, has sucked in its breath.

The pan widens out and comes to rest on a long shot of prisoners gathered around Maisonneuve in the distance, who again mutters, "C'est drôle," in an attempt to break the awkward silence, walking forward and primping himself nervously. The word "drôle" is at odds with the expression of these soldiers (French, English and the German alike). Touched by this makeshift version of a woman, they may feel a number of emotions—loss, sexual frustration, the boredom of prison life?

Nothing relieves the tension, nor does Renoir add a shot to defuse the effect before the scene fades out. The sea change imperceptibly taking place in *La Grande Illusion* is implicit in the difference between the opening and closing pans of the sequence. From here, Renoir ratchets up the emotional pitch, bit by bit.

"C'est drôle": Maisonneuve (Roger Forster) tries to break an awkward silence (*Photofest*).

A brief sequence of German recruits that immediately follows provides sharp relief to the costume-reviewing scene; it is much shorter (40 seconds as opposed to nearly three minutes) and its four shots are all held still (in contrast to the five tracking shots of the French prisoners going through costumes). This is the static and confining, or German, side of Hallbach.

Renoir begins the sequence with a shot aimed from within the prison gates as they are opened, revealing three women and a man outside, looking in. It's the first shot of flesh-and-blood women in the film and, in their dark clothes, they stand contrasted to the theatrical artifice of Maisonneuve parading in a ruffled blouse and skirt.

A closer shot of two old women in this group follows and one of them says: "Die armen Jungen" ("The poor lads"). She refers not to prisoners but to young German soldiers ranked in formation in the next shot (reversing the perspective, as in the barbed wire scene). Even in an insignificant scene like this, Renoir manages to suggest the relative nature of imprisonment and of war itself.

In the last shot, the soldiers are drilled by their officers and trot off in unison. A scene once more of regimented Germans.

Soon another searing image, set into the relaxed scene that follows as the French work on their costumes, raises the pitch again. And here *La Grande Illusion* fully turns the corner. A more substantial movie, even a grave one, is under way.

The sequence that sets up this moment begins with a medium shot of Boeldieu, in a room high up at the camp, as he looks out a window at the Germans drilling far below. The French talk about their reasons for wanting to escape and the camera follows the dialogue from one character to another, with some of them attending to their costumes.

Then, in a medium shot, the teacher tells about how his doctor ordered him to give up meat and, becoming healthy, he was sent to war; as he talks, the sound of marching soldiers outside begins to build. Following a brief two-shot of Maréchal and Boeldieu, the camera moves in closer to a medium close-up of the teacher as he continues his account, looking especially pathetic when a ruff is fitted around his neck by Rosenthal.

After another two-shot, with Boeldieu trying to reassure him and drums added to the soundtrack, Renoir cuts to a slightly closer shot of the teacher, alone now; the sound of fifes outside starts up toward the end of his monologue as he notes that he wound up cuckolded. It does not qualify as an important moment, and the teacher is a minor character, but this shot is one of the few full close-ups (of a person) in the film. By zeroing in, shot by shot by shot, closer to his face, and strengthening the effect with the sound of boots and military music, Renoir tightens the tension for an even closer shot of the group, which is soon to come.

The teacher's last close-up is followed by a medium shot of the engineer, who stands up and heads slowly toward the window, as if hypnotically drawn by the song of Sirens below. In a strangely theatrical and measured way, the other men gather with him. The camera tracks backward until it is outside the open window, looking in at the prisoners, who are now visually trapped inside the room; two side windowpanes form the flanking panels of a triptych, with them centered in the middle, the six men ranged formally like subjects posed in a Renaissance painting. Rosenthal lights a cigarette from the teacher's pipe at the right-hand edge of the central panel, then turns and joins the others in watching the Germans, off-camera below.

All is ready, another setting of the stage.

Renoir then cuts to the crucial shot, a beautiful pan in close-up across their faces as

A window high above Germans drilling; from the left: Maréchal, the engineer, Boeldieu, Cartier, the teacher, Rosenthal (*Photofest*).

they look out, starting with Rosenthal, smoke from his cigarette lightly wafting upward. This is the closest shot in the film. An intense shot — faces filling the screen one after the other, a sense of entrapment, the brutal tramping of boots. As the camera slowly pans left, Boeldieu and then the engineer comment on the scene below; the fifes and drums drop out after Boeldieu's comment, and the sound of marching boots becomes gradually amplified. It is momentous and startling, punched up by that closeness to the faces and the disturbingly magnified sound.

The close-up pan reaches Maréchal, who says pensively that it isn't the music or the instruments that grips him but "c'est le bruit des pas" ("it's the tramp of footsteps [boots]"). He snaps this phrase out, mesmerized, as the camera comes to a full stop on him and the thumping clatter of the boots continues on the soundtrack.

This final image is ambiguous, with the paradox that, though almost an extreme close-up, several meanings can be read into the shot. Is Maréchal attracted, or repelled, by the power of the sound? It's also relevant that his close-up is not an unadulterated one, since it appears at the end of a pan covering other characters and, even when the camera comes to rest on him, the engineer can be seen (out of focus) in the background. Maréchal remains connected to the group.

The fact that this is the largest close-up in *La Grande Illusion*, and Renoir uses it in a relatively unimportant scene in terms of the plot, gives it an elusive gravity. Why such a shot and why now? One possible explanation could be that it signals this will be a "large" movie. The war looms out there, still unseen, and this rare glimpse of Renoir's cinematic maneuvers, made fleetingly visible and spread broadly across the screen, reminds us that little is predictable in his film.

With the Germans remaining off-camera, but their presence made known by the ominous soundtrack, Renoir again distills a scene to its essence and leaves space for the imagination. And, as in the barbed wire shot, with its marching song growing louder, the soundtrack has a sobering effect.

Renoir defuses the scene by cutting again to the wider shot of the window (almost immediately after Maréchal's comment) and then tracking back into the room, reversing the movement that had established the setting for the window pan in the first place, as the actor discovers that an overheated iron has burned a hole in his costume. He starts a lively tune and goes into a frantic jig. His theatrics are interrupted by the entrance of an amused guard, pointing to his head as commentary on the actor's state of mind; a bit of triumphant orchestral music backs up the guard and mockingly fills the soundtrack.

Maréchal (with the engineer) and the sound of boots: "le bruit des pas" (*Photofest*).

This juxtaposition of heightened seriousness and low comedy is not an unfamiliar strategy in *La Grande Illusion* (nor in Renoir's films in general). And Renoir then flips back to serious matters with an abrupt cut to a poster announcing the fall of Fort Douaumont to the Germans. War is again thrust on us, with bells ringing in grating contrast to the excited orchestral music that had mocked the actor.

The high spirits at Hallbach return in full force, soon after the window pan, with the revue. Its sheer, amateurish exuberance brings Renoir's lifelong love of the theater to the fore, and he luxuriates, at length, in the show, filling it with slapstick as the music hall actor upstages everyone.

The complexity of the film, meanwhile, is temporarily put on hold during this *divertissement*, which Renoir leaves free to run its course. Theater for theater's sake — with Carette starring as the Chaplinesque figure leading the festivities. Its extravagance in length, uninterrupted for almost four minutes of real time, and its vaudevillian charm provides what has necessarily been missing in wartime.

After a long tracking shot opening on the actor, the shots are fairly short, a mixture of still and tracking shots. This amiable sequence sets in relief both the brilliant (and lengthy) shot that serves as its finale and the scenes that follow immediately afterward. For the moment, though, French and Germans escape the war and the backwash of tedium that has come in its wake.

The revue, with the camping around of the actor and the cross-dressing English chorus line and diva, is in direct contrast to the preceding scene in which German soldiers sing a plodding song of celebration at the taking of Douaumont. Once more, the French and English may be prisoners, and the war may not be going well for them, but they are at least capable of having more fun. Renoir communicates this difference by the sudden transition: German soldiers drinking mugs of beer (no French wine and cheese here) to the strains of a heavy-handed, patriotic song, "Die Wacht am Rhein" ("The Watch on the Rhine"), giving way, in a discordant clash, to the actor teasing out a French music hall ditty ("Si tu veux ... Marguerite").

There is also the gender play-acting in the revue. Similar undertones had been sounded earlier, especially in the buffoonery of the actor. During the gardening scene, he minces girlishly in anticipation when learning that women's clothes for the show have arrived. At the costume trunk, it's suggested that he model a dress and he reacts again with excitement. And when Maréchal explains that women, in the new fashion, are cutting their hair short, the actor eagerly exclaims that one must imagine going to bed with a boy, not hiding his titillation at the thought. Maisonneuve decked out as a woman and the Englishmen in dresses performing "Tipperary" on stage extend the motif. Later, near the end of Hallbach, Boeldieu needles the teacher about his passion for tulips by joking that he has "une âme de grisette" ("a soul of a girl").

The opening track of the revue ends on some German soldiers watching the actor, coyly flirtatious as he flounces around. Arthur whispers something in the ear of another and they all smile knowingly. Later, the actor sticks out his rear end, slaps his tails at one of the "girls" and playfully shouts out to Arthur; Renoir injects a cutaway of the same Germans, still enjoying the show (a doubling of compositions). And when the revue comes to an end the actor is lolling in the arms of the unshaven diva.

This hinting at homosexual possibilities adds to the general loosening of decorum at Hallbach, led by the actor, a consummate ham. It is still prison but a gaiety runs throughout this part, until the next turn in the plot.

And that twist comes suddenly when the diva's big number is interrupted by Maréchal, shouting to stop the show as he comes onto the stage (his arm not in a sling now). Then, in an extreme long shot, he announces the news that Douaumont has fallen to the French; the shot lasts only 5 seconds, a brief punctuation mark before the convoluted track that follows.

This tracking shot, among the most technically complicated ones in the movie, runs for 60 seconds and is often cited (justly) as a key turning point in *La Grande Illusion*. The shot opens on a 3-man orchestra, as it had at the start of the "Tipperary" number in the revue. Another doubling. But this time an English officer dressed as a woman enters the shot and says to the musicians, "'La Marseillaise,' please"; he removes his wig and an elaborately festooned hat. National lines again blurred — not to mention gender, resplendent as he is in a woman's gown.

The assembled prisoners begin to sing the French anthem with the officer, and then the camera tracks backward, angled slightly upward to the right, toward the stage above, past the performers singing and down to two Germans huddling together, pauses briefly before moving again (as the Germans leave), and then makes an oval pattern as it elegantly doubles back, angled to the left now, taking in the front row of the audience along the way and returning temporarily to the orchestra and the English officer, until it makes one last turn to the left, twisting to end with a head-on shot of the audience singing defiantly; the camera thus ends up at a 270-degree angle from the opening framing. And so the uncut shot expresses, compactly, the solidarity of English and French against the Germans.

Held still, the shot continues. This final framing takes in the front rows of prisoners, with others in the background, as they continue to belt out "La Marseillaise."

Renoir has shrewdly prepared for this camera position by the way in which he had previously presented the revue's audience. Earlier they were seen in the background of two shots filmed from the rear of the stage, a mass of faces below, with the figure of the actor in the foreground. When Maréchal stops the show to make his announcement, Renoir cuts to the back of the theater (with the camera aimed toward the stage beyond). He achieves here a distancing effect that keeps the focus on the French as a group and on the historical and military significance of the moment, instead of focusing on Maréchal individually. A faceless crowd, since only the backs of prisoners are visible.

But now, at the end of this long track, facing the audience for the last time, the camera is head-on and closer, the men fully seen for the first time as distinct individuals. The passion is personal and in keeping with a movie that pays little heed to larger events in the world outside.

Renoir draws attention to this newly personalized focus by letting the camera remain still for 14 seconds, though nothing further develops, as at the end of the barbed wire shot. The luxury of staying put, as the song plays out, imprints the scene in a haunting way. It also marks one of the few times that incidental music is not interrupted or cut off completely. And, after the last note is sung, the scene immediately shifts to a dark exterior shot, ending the sequence without the cushioning of a backward tracking movement, or a wider shot, and making the moment all the more effective.

But though clearly a signature moment in cinematic terms, this shot is a low point thematically in *La Grande Illusion* and runs counter to Renoir's apparent sympathies. It

"La Marseillaise"— the closing image of a convoluted and rich tracking shot (*Photofest*).

ranks as the most baldly nationalistic passage in the film — even more than an analogous shot shortly before when a guard flaunts his glee at the German capture of Douaumont in singing happily and strolling by the window of the French officers.

This final shot of prisoners singing fervently, their faces unyielding and stern, is as ambiguous as the window pan of the French prisoners watching the marching Germans. Though "La Marseillaise" is a stirring song, its use as a cry of victory, celebrating a battle won at the cost of many lives, sours the scene.

It indicates Renoir's breadth as an artist that he fills this intricate and sensuous shot, successively, with humor and contradictions (the Englishman in a woman's gown calling for the French anthem), anger (Maréchal glaring at the guards as he sings), national divisions (the Germans fleeing the scene) and full-throated patriotism (the ending). Renoir, throughout his film, leaves a trail of differently nuanced images but still manages to communicate, without making it too conspicuous, the triumph of irony over bitterness, brotherhood over nationalism. But the road is never a very straight one, as illustrated by such a shot.

At this important shift in the narrative, the catalyst is once again a sudden interruption, and a single, graceful track establishes the change.

Following Rauffenstein's capture of Boeldieu and Maréchal, there are five crises that can be seen as fortifying the impact of *La Grande Illusion*, and all are directly or indirectly caused by the war. The first one, the solitary confinement of Maréchal, paying for his insolence, follows the revue.

Renoir composes two powerful scenes in a few strokes; as in the blowup, he gets quickly to the heart of the matter. And once more Renoir prepares deftly for these scenes. After the singing of "La Marseillaise," he cuts to a brief shot of German guards in the shadowy night hustling out of a building. A pedestrian shot, on the surface at least.

But its fuller effect takes hold as Renoir opens the first scene in confinement with the close-up of a spoon being twirled listlessly and scraping a small dent in the wall. It is a shocking cut — to a shot that is abruptly silent (after the sound of hurried footsteps), fairly inactive (in contrast to the rushing figures), framed in close-up (as opposed to the long shot) and set in a brightly lit interior (played off against the dark exterior shot, which was faded to black). The cut is so visually striking that it almost makes one jump. And the seemingly commonplace shot of guards resonates, in absentia, with retroactive energy.

But that is only the beginning. The length of this new shot, 65 seconds, stands in distinct relief to the interlude of the guards (8 seconds). And its initial framing and camera movement perhaps subliminally recalls the opening shot of the film; only Maréchal's chest, arm and hands can be seen before the camera immediately pans up to his haggard face (the opening soundtrack will soon be recalled explicitly). The camera then pans to the right as Zach, a German guard, enters, and it tracks back with him when he heads over to the prisoner. Maréchal motions to the dent in the wall and explains unconvincingly that it's a hole through which to escape. This facetious explanation brings to mind the actor's mock attempt earlier to "escape" through the barbed wire fence, but the prisoner has an ulterior motive.

As Zach bends over to look, Maréchal shoves him aside and the camera tracks with him as he rushes out, slamming and securing the door behind him. The camera stays fixed on Zach, now trapped inside the cell, as he looks out through the grate in the door. We hear the sound of guards grappling with Maréchal, and his cries, but the struggle is not shown, just as Renoir cut the dogfight at the beginning of the film. The effect is particularly strong here since this struggle takes place at that very instant, on the other side of the door, and yet Renoir resists the temptation to show it, avoiding the mere spectacle of German guards subduing Maréchal—as well as his humiliation. And, by staying focused on Zach, Renoir again reverses the position of jailer and jailed.

Soon the door opens and the camera tracks back again as Maréchal, half-conscious, is carried to his bed by guards. The camera moves in and the tracking shot finally ends on him, alone, in a close shot, with the faint pealing of bells on the soundtrack. It is a harsh and disoriented ending, with Maréchal's head angled slightly downward in the frame (a unique composition in the film), which makes it hard to read his face or grasp his expression.

A brief scene follows, also in a single shot, as French and Germans alike comment on a poster announcing the German recapture of Douaumont; the bells ring loudly in celebration. The shot, and the soundtrack, is faded out.

The second scene of Maréchal's confinement is expressed in two exquisitely conceived shots packed with significant overtones.

The first shot begins on a small pot of lumpy slop (the sumptuous meals now over). Again, the silence on the cut establishes a somber tone. The camera tracks up to Maréchal leaning against the wall, worn out and grizzled; "ARTHUR" has been scratched in the plaster by his head.

With the sound of the door opening, the camera pans right to an old German guard entering the cell (as it had panned in the previous scene) and follows him as he goes over to Maréchal and tries a few pleasantries. After the guard solicitously places a hand on his shoulder, Maréchal, beyond giving a damn and not understanding German anyway, screams at him and lumbers around like a caged animal as he vents his frustrations in a full-out tirade. No holds barred. He yells that the cell stinks, that he wants to see light, and then lets out a distorted growl, his eyes still fixed angrily on the guard. It is an extraordinary moment, with Gabin at his most riveting, awful to watch yet impossible to look away.

Maréchal sits down and, in a defeated voice, says several times that he wants to hear someone speak French—the barrier of nations once more.

The shot continues. The guard settles next to Maréchal and again puts his hand on the Frenchman's shoulder as Maréchal says that he is "tout seule" ("all alone"). And he no longer looks at the guard. Now invisible to his prisoner, the old German produces some cigarettes from his pocket and offers them, as a grandfather might tempt his pouting grandson with candy, but Maréchal mumbles again that he never hears anyone speaking. He doesn't move. The guard puts the cigarettes on the bed and, determined, finds another gift, a harmonica. Maréchal continues to stare off into space. The old guard puts it down too, gets up, and walks off, shrugging his head. After a while, Maréchal glances down at the offerings. Casually, almost absent-mindedly, he picks up the harmonica, raises it to his lips, and makes a few desultory stabs at some notes.

And that ends the first shot, one of the longest in the movie (104 seconds), having moved from resignation to antagonism, to an attempted reconciliation, to separation and to, finally, possible connection. Renoir condenses the narrative trajectory even more than in the "Marseillaise" shot.

The second shot, on the other side of Maréchal's cell, begins as a medium shot with the guard peeking through the grate and checking to see if his bait will be taken. It echoes, and reverses, the first scene in solitary confinement when Zach had been looking out of the cell through that same grate (only three shots earlier).

The guard hears Maréchal begin to play "Frou-Frou" on the harmonica. He smiles and

Maréchal in solitary confinement (an unacknowledged gift) (***Photofest***).

closes the grate, a curiously contradictory motion, cutting off a source of light even as he takes pleasure in this tentative sign of revival. Singing along with the tune, he walks away. And so "Frou-Frou" returns, as a wistful version warbled shakily by an old German guard on his shift of duty rather than the spirited one sung by the dashing young French lieutenant looking forward to a night on the town as the film begins; Maréchal, on the harmonica, assumes the role of accompanist.

The gulf between Frenchman and German in the first shot has been bridged by an improvised duet, performed across a bolted door, in the second and last shot of the sequence. The international language of music breaks down national divisions, as it had during the revue enjoyed by both sides. And, by focusing on the guard, Renoir exhibits his usual tact. The tune, coming through the door, is far more moving than had he shown Maréchal playing it on the harmonica, and the chance of a sentimental appeal is minimized.

The shot ends with a nice bit of business (a Renoir topper again) as the camera follows the old guard passing another guard, who asks why the prisoner was shouting. The first guard replies that the war is too long. He climbs a few steps, turns and stands in a doorway, holding his rifle upright like a staff and with his upper body lost in shadow, the framing of the scene now rearranged as a long shot. A restrained composition, the guard in retreat, locked into his role as jailer in the gloom of the doorway as surely as Maréchal remains locked in his cell.

The gravity of this image, the slash of light across his lower body, the shadows, and the way that Renoir holds an extra beat on the old guard's unnaturally formal pose makes it a solid, if ephemeral, tableau, a Dutch painting come to life, a Vermeer — vivid, real, but also mysterious, unknowable. As with the window pan, much can be read into it. Renoir, having sketched a multifaceted scene in two quick strokes, leaves it open at the end.

This second shot completes the shift in a fleeting relationship: Frenchman and German at odds, united by a simple gift, and then separated again because, as with all the relationships in the film, war and its conventions separate the two sides. In this case, the comfort of the "enemy" is not directly acknowledged. No thanks or tears of happiness detract from the scene; the strains of "Frou-Frou" are gratitude enough. And this moment also reverses the antagonistic nationalism of the "Marseillaise" shot.

There is another unusual, if minor, characteristic of the shot: it's the only significant one in the film, either thematically or cinematically, that has no featured (or even secondary) characters. These two guards are thoroughly peripheral figures. And only one other time is a shot held at least this long (40 seconds) without featuring any of the main characters (a slightly longer shot of two officers at Wintersborn). This marks a noticeable change in a film so concentrated on the central protagonists. *La Grande Illusion* often surprises in this way. It's difficult to dig in and find the pattern, as with a batter in baseball trying to outguess a seasoned pitcher by looking for a particular kind of pitch. Be ready to scramble.

Maréchal's ordeal in solitary confinement extends the growing intensity at Hallbach from the slight overtones of the barbed wire scene, to the shot of Maisonneuve in a dress and the close-up window pan, to the singing of "La Marseillaise." With the scene between Maréchal and the old guard, there is now decidedly a true depth to this film.

The Hallbach section soon comes to a close. The last day opens with a still shot of the prisoners in their room as they pace anxiously back and forth, waiting to put their escape plan into effect. As when preparing to dig the tunnel, the characters walk in and out of the frame. But this time the camera is still and the characters crisscross like the choreographed members of a marching band, confined by the locked-down frame. They are all business — and frayed nerves. No playing around now.

Their plans are interrupted when Arthur enters and brusquely announces a roll call and that the officers are to be transferred to other camps (as in the last shot at the German canteen).

With the French gathered in the courtyard, Arthur is genial as he jokes and winks at the actor, who gaily responds, "Au revoir, Arthur." It is the actor's farewell; he disappears from the movie after this scene.

Hallbach ends in separation, as do most of the other sections of *La Grande Illusion*. And, as it began in the opening courtyard sequence, Hallbach closes with a German guard barking out orders, directed here at Maréchal after his failed attempt to tell an English officer about the tunnel, with the ironic twist that it may not be found. Maréchal withdraws. On the final dissolve, the German guard remains alone in the frame.

The high spirits at Hallbach are over. A major shift in tone is imminent.

7

Wintersborn (the Opening)

"What was good about Von Stroheim was that he understood that he should act in contrast with Fresnay. A big part of the picture deals with the contrast between the two men. The story is many things, but most of it is the story of Von Stroheim and Fresnay."
— Jean Renoir in "Directors Go to Their Movies: Jean Renoir"; interview with Digby Diehl (*Action*, volume 7, number 3; May–June 1972; p. 5)

Renoir undervalues his singular achievement, and is too limiting, in this 1972 statement. Modesty may have been one of his endearing qualities, yet he could also be crafty and even appear disingenuous. A charming raconteur, in interviews and filmed introductions to his movies, he was never at a loss for words but sometimes made pronouncements that may have relied too much on the pleasing effect of a cleverly turned phrase.

If *La Grande Illusion* is seen as being mostly about Rauffenstein and Boeldieu, according to Renoir, it's curious that the film does not end with the death of Boeldieu. Or with Rauffenstein, afterward, shattered and wandering around, alone in his prison fortress.

Boeldieu's death is in some strange way unexceptional. The scene certainly provides a climactic moment, but seems memorable more as an elegant, if sad, occasion than a time of great tragedy. The most wrenching separation, allowing *La Grande Illusion* to end, occurs later on the farm.

Following Hallbach, the next part, at Wintersborn, opens with symbols of death and Rauffenstein's fractured body, and it ends with death itself. This section becomes an extended memorial, formal and elegiac. It feels grayer, slower, more weighted than the rest of the movie.

And though *La Grande Illusion* takes place largely in winter, it is especially desolate at Wintersborn, aided by the harshness of stone walls and a name resonant with the season's chill. Scarves proliferate, though Boeldieu doesn't indulge, being far too aware of his appearance to muffle its precision of effect. Instead, in one scene he wears his bulky fur coat, which is more in line with Rauffenstein's excesses.

But Renoir does not simplify. In spite of a Prussian rectitude and his grisly war wounds, Rauffenstein is at ease with his prisoners, hands out French rules of conduct in place of German ones, and goes only so far as to decide on a roll call in response to the prison disturbance.

At Hallbach characters throw themselves into the present, but Wintersborn is more rooted in the past. It also reverses field in being driven by individual relationships, particularly the one between Boeldieu and Rauffenstein but also Maréchal's relationships to both Boeldieu and Rosenthal; the other prisoners at Wintersborn play only minor roles and are barely introduced. And any ambience of togetherness is often undermined. Lieutenant Demolder (Sylvain Itkine), the scholar of Greek literature, is dubbed "Pindar" and mocked several times by the others; Maréchal snubs the Senegalese officer (Habib Benglia) in one scene; and the other officer in the room has only a few lines and no specific identity (Georges Péclet).

The crucial scenes at Wintersborn take place between two people: adjoining tête-à-têtes between Boeldieu and Rauffenstein; a shot of Maréchal and Rosenthal confiding in each other; two scenes of Maréchal and Boeldieu alone together, as well as their parting; and, most critically, the confrontation of the two superior officers and the deathbed scene.

Renoir contrasts the central relationships visually. When together, Boeldieu and Rauffenstein are most often isolated apart into short, still shots; they are individualists and become increasingly at loggerheads despite their obvious affinities. Maréchal, though more frozen into still shots during this section, continues to bring some movement to his scenes with Boeldieu, and he appears mostly with others, rather than alone.

Wintersborn seems, to me, the least emotionally charged part of the movie and also the least cinematically expansive. And Boeldieu's escapade in the ramparts is the longest sequence presented almost purely as action melodrama.

The film technique during the Wintersborn scenes is distinct in other ways, further marginalizing the ensemble. Unlike Hallbach, the tracking shots are not predominantly choreographed group shots but quite often follow only one or two people. There are also many more still shots of characters alone and the shots are shorter, on average. In fact, the long track that opens this part (73 seconds) is unusual, both in terms of movement and length, in this quieter and more fragmented section of *La Grande Illusion.*

That first shot at Wintersborn quickly establishes a changed dynamic. It opens on a huge crucifix in an officer's quarters, a converted chapel, with the sound of a military trumpet call soon replacing the last notes of music that cover the preceding traveling shots; the camera pans down past a picture of Hindenburg behind another cross (God and country), a bed, and then some personal possessions (a potted flower, a champagne bottle in a silver bucket, a book labeled "CASANOVA" with a pistol on it, a woman's photograph, more pistols, riding crops, swords). The long tracking shot then settles temporarily on a German orderly blowing into a pair of white gloves; a wooden airplane propeller is propped against the wall behind him. The trumpet refrain is interrupted and, off-screen, a voice barks out, "Fenster aufmachen!" ("Window open!"), and the speaker complains that it stinks enough to make you vomit (a subdued echo of Maréchal's rant in his cell). The trumpet call resumes as the camera pans slightly and the orderly opens the window.

A measure of decay is already palpable in this shot, down to the white gloves being prepared as if for a corpse. And the command to open a window is shouted with such disgust that it extends the motif of Germans trapped inside their own prison.

The opening shot continues as the orderly points out that only two pairs of white gloves are left. The trumpet call ends and the camera draws back as he comes forward to offer coffee to the still unseen officer. A gloved hand in the foreground puts down a cup and raises a monocle as the camera, from behind, partially reveals the familiar figure of Rauffenstein.

The track comes to rest as a two-shot angled from farther behind him after the orderly pours the coffee. This return to the movie, at first as a disembodied voice and then in an obscure composition, aptly brings back the broken-down Rauffenstein. He's not all there. Rigid in a chin brace and moving stiffly, he appears to be a changed man, even from the back. Only in the next shot is he shown full-face at last.

The opening shot also suggests Rauffenstein's adjustment to a state of entrapment and

7. Wintersborn (the Opening)

Wintersborn: return of the broken warrior — Rauffenstein and his orderly (*Photofest*).

stasis in another way. This aristocratic officer has not only been reduced to mundane things like the quality of air he breathes and a glove shortage, but he's linked visually to a mere orderly. And the propeller as décor, a relic from the old days, recalls his initial appearance as a self-assured aviator.

These quarters are more mausoleum than bedroom, dominated by the crucifix. Other types of crosses had been in evidence at Hallbach; in the opening and closing scenes there were military crosses on German helmets, and at one point a medical team carrying a stretcher wore Red Cross armbands. But at Wintersborn religious crosses are introduced and, in the last scene, crosses multiply exponentially as death finally takes hold. And the bed and potted flower will play roles as well in that final scene.

It's a different atmosphere than the one established by the tracks at the two canteens and at Hallbach, which indicated vitality and community. In further contrast to those settings and their communal meals, Rauffenstein eats breakfast alone while his orderly, instead of taking part, waits on him, and the small, exclusive table stands in his bedroom, not in a dining area that could include others.

So begins Wintersborn, with a flourish. And though often absent from the action in this part, Rauffenstein, and his influence, dominates. But more extraordinary, generating greater depth to *La Grande Illusion*, is that Boeldieu begins to pull away from Rauffenstein while reaching an accommodation with Maréchal, who, in turn, unexpectedly exhibits characteristics of Boeldieu.

Though still at times expressive in film terms, Wintersborn is more driven by the narrative than Hallbach, and its scenes are powered by the twists and turns in the relationships of the main characters. To better understand this part it helps to look at how Renoir develops those relationships throughout the film and, in the process, orchestrates his grand themes to such an unresolved pitch that only during the scenes on the farm is some resolution possible.

8

Themes and Relationships

"My chief aim was the one which I have been pursuing ever since I started to make films — to express the common humanity of men."
— Jean Renoir in *My Life and My Films* (p. 148)

"Everything interests him. In Paris, watching a newsreel with me once, he was touched and tenderly amused by a sequence showing the back view of a plump Olympic girl solemnly running with a torch. 'I am against great themes and great subjects,' said this maker of two of the world's greatest films. 'To me, a theme is exactly like a landscape for a painter. It is just an excuse. You can't film an idea. The camera is an instrument for recording physical impact.'"
—*Jean Renoir: Essays, Conversations, Reviews*
by Penelope Gilliatt (McGraw-Hill; 1975; p. 9)

Themes

One measure of Jean Renoir's moviemaking genius is that he communicates the themes in *La Grande Illusion* mainly through the filming of "physical impact." The dialogue does not overtly convey the humanism of this humanist film *extraordinaire*, nor can his film be discussed solely in terms of an explicit philosophy. The themes are indeed "excuses" and can only be made out somewhere in the reverberations caused by the impact of images — a French prisoner sticking his foot through a barbed wire fence; an old German guard singing to the strains of a harmonica; two men dueling with verses of a children's song; a war widow announcing that coffee is ready. One could argue that, reversing the myth of Medusa, themes looked at directly become heavy as stone. Renoir steers well clear of that pitfall.

La Grande Illusion, first and most importantly, tells a story. Renoir certainly hints at larger issues, but they emerge naturally from the narrative. The themes are merely undertones, having some peripheral effect perhaps but coming into focus more in retrospect, thinking back over the film. Experiencing the movie firsthand, one's initial reaction is not, I think, that this is a film so much about brotherhood and class, but that it is, more elementally, a film about men in prison camps and refuge on a farm.

Renoir himself, in his memoir, emphasized the importance of the plot in *La Grande Illusion* as a springboard:

> My story was a banal one of escape. I maintain that the more banal the subject of a film, the greater are the possibilities it offers to the film-maker ... it means a simple canvas affording scope for the imagination.[1]

Critics have often reduced the film by focusing on its themes. The implication is left that Renoir props them up as part of a didactic scheme. But themes are more than understated. They are barely stated at all — if even that.

A danger in diverting the focus onto those themes is that they will assume a kind of solidity, which in reality must be deduced. But they need at least to be delineated.

Renoir's basic humanism, and the respect and affection one comes to have for the characters, emerges in several ways. First, his unforced development of characters is critical; we get to know them fully through the slow, even novelistic, revelation of details. Second, Renoir strengthens the depth of these characterizations through his use of repetition (and reversal) — repeated or revised compositions, actions, objects, music, words; this cinematic manipulation brings out the differences and likenesses between the players in his piece. Finally, an impression of possible brotherhood is established as Renoir often connects the French and Germans, visually and through aspects of language, apart from its use as dialogue. And he also bolsters a feeling of comradeship with a string of character reversals in Maréchal and Boeldieu as they draw closer, despite their backgrounds.

With these cornerstones in place, there are two major themes that run throughout: the barriers created by both nationalism and class division. Alongside them, less pervasively, run the theme of anti–Semitism and, more broadly, the issue of gender.

These themes are gradually integrated into the story. In the opening scene, the references to Josephine in the first shot (and the pinups) introduce gender immediately. Class surfaces with the appearance of Boeldieu in the next sequence. At the German canteen, nationality is added to the mix as Rauffenstein makes his grand entrance. And anti–Semitism becomes a factor at Hallbach with sarcastic barbs directed at Rosenthal by the actor and Maréchal (enjoyed by Boeldieu).

La Grande Illusion can be seen, on this level, as a movie about the way in which the bonds of brotherhood, built up so carefully by Renoir, challenge those obstacles to solidarity.

National identity is the omnipresent barrier from beginning to end. Language, its handmaiden in the art of divide-and-conquer, causes problems until decisively engaged at the farm, and, in a neat trick of inversion, it helps unite the lovers across national lines.

The barrier of class is the division least resolved by the end of the film. Boeldieu, though drawing closer to Maréchal, chooses to side with him not in some attempt to break down class distinctions but primarily because of his duty to France and to the rules of war, fulfilling his obligation as the commanding officer.

Thus *La Grande Illusion*, to a certain extent, illustrates Renoir's most quoted aphorism that the world is divided "horizontally" rather than "vertically." National lines are breached often but the horizontal division of class, though weakened, remains largely intact at Boeldieu's death, despite the developing friendship of Maréchal and Rosenthal across their differing class backgrounds.

Meanwhile, divisions of gender and anti–Semitism simmer uncomfortably until, like the rhythm of the film itself, these themes gather strength in the last part and obstacles that separate characters are overturned.

But, in this apparently all-embracing movie, other divisions are not confronted at all. Anti-intellectualism, for instance, is ingrained in Boeldieu and Rauffenstein as well as in Maréchal (strange bedfellows, to be sure); they take turns deriding the Greek scholar, Demolder. And, during a room search, the binding of his beloved edition of Pindar is ripped by a German soldier, against Demolder's protests. Another figure of the intellect, the teacher at Hallbach, is portrayed as something of a sad sack as he recounts his cuckolding, and is unmanned further by the ruff placed around his neck in preparation for the revue.

When some of the Russian prisoners at Wintersborn burn a crate of technical books by setting fire to the straw packing material, angry that the Czarina had not sent more useful provisions like vodka or caviar, the moment resonates eerily (this is still "only" World War I after all). Boeldieu, Maréchal and Rosenthal are somewhat amused by the inappropriate gift of books. Only Demolder, the intellectual scorned by the others, eagerly picks up a volume to leaf through — this is his vodka, his caviar. He decries the conflagration and calls the Russians "sauvages" ("savages") after being pushed out of the room by an angry Russian prisoner, with fire raging beyond.

And racism is implied in an awkward moment when the Senegalese officer proudly shows a drawing he has just completed to Rosenthal and Maréchal; the latter rudely shrugs him off, without making eye contact, revealing perhaps his philistinism (and possible prejudice) and obviously stinging the Senegalese. Yet, in the next scene, this same officer warns his cellmates that guards are coming to search the room, and later he wraps a jury-rigged rope around Rosenthal as the escape plan moves into high gear. The underclass often has little choice but to turn the other cheek.

La Grande Illusion can of course be viewed from several perspectives. Brotherhood, pacifism, nationalism, class, gender, religion, race. Or repetition, reversal, inversion, interruption, separation, and continuity of space (the long tracking and panning shots).

But one can more fruitfully look at the interaction between those themes and aesthetic strategies. The themes are not presented in essay form; one feels and senses them. The film exists rather than represents, and seems open, not closed. It becomes completed by the viewer when, as in Wordsworth's theory about the basis of poetry, emotion is "recollected in tranquillity" and transforms the experience.[2] But only because Renoir has provided the breathing room to do so.

Relationships

The themes of *La Grande Illusion* are steeped in the relationships of its characters. And the waxing and waning of these attachments keeps the film fresh — and unpredictable.

Renoir builds an effective structure of overlapping entanglements, pivoting around Maréchal as the central figure. In the first half, Maréchal interacts with Boeldieu, and their connection continues into the second half, at Wintersborn, while the parallel relationship of Boeldieu and Rauffenstein takes off and, simultaneously, Maréchal draws closer to Rosenthal (despite having had little interaction with him at Hallbach).

This budding relationship of the junior officers, in turn, continues to the very end — with another overlap as Elsa appears at the farm. That third, most vital, connection for Maréchal, like the Boeldieu-Rauffenstein bond earlier, ends abruptly. But once again, as he had after Wintersborn, Maréchal carries the movie onward with Rosenthal to the last shot.

These overlapping connections keep the momentum going and emphasize Maréchal as the pivotal character. And, except at Hallbach, the relationship between two people (in various combinations) is critically important.

As the film opens at the French air base, Maréchal and Boeldieu unquestionably belong to different worlds. This is the only section, short as it is, in which the featured characters remain emotionally distant. But the central relationships during the rest of the film, including that of Maréchal and Boeldieu, fluctuate considerably, always with an element of conflict and, in the end, some resolution. During the scene at the border, in a reversal, the key figures, Maréchal and Rosenthal, are close to one another throughout the sequence. And this contributes to a sense of optimism and driven energy at the end, even in the face of uncertainty inherent in the final image.

This intense focus on relationships generates a feeling of intimacy. And it is unrelenting. Aside from the credits and the two brief sequences shot from a train, there are only 52 shots with no featured or supporting characters (mainly at Wintersborn), which amount to just 9 minutes in total length, including only four shots with no people at all (31 seconds).

Each character is clearly defined, covering a range of society's strata, but the characters are not just symbols locked into a fixed scheme. Maréchal and Boeldieu, in particular, change greatly, and Rosenthal and Elsa are substantially enriched by their attachments to Maréchal. Rauffenstein, though diminished physically in the course of the film, alone stays basically unchanged and ends up unfulfilled.

Maréchal is the only one to appear in all seven sections, and he plays a major role in each of them, though in the two largest sections the actor (Hallbach) and Boeldieu (Wintersborn) are at least equally relevant. The leading characters, like instruments in an orchestra, take turns assuming center stage and then draw back to become supporting players. Maréchal

Some of the crew, at home in Rauffenstein's quarters: Carl Koch (1), Marguerite Renoir, holding a dog (2), Renoir (3), and Françoise Giroud (4). Photograph: Sam Lévin (©*Ministère de la Culture/ Médiathèque du Patrimoine/Sam Levin/dist. RMN-Grand Palais/Art Resource, New York*).

is the first among soloists, but also an accomplished sideman; in over half his shots he appears in a group of four or more people.

Though duets predominate, at times larger combinations develop. At Hallbach, Maréchal and Boeldieu are supported by those around them. But only at Wintersborn do two characters often appear alone together, apart from the group, as duets play off each other, shifting and recombining (Rauffenstein/Boeldieu; Boeldieu/Maréchal; Maréchal/Rosenthal).

MARÉCHAL

It is Maréchal, more than any other character, who overcomes barriers — of class (Boeldieu), of religion and class (Rosenthal) and of nationality, language and gender (Elsa). That is a measure of his journey and featured place in the film (151 shots); he appears physically on the screen for 52 minutes of screen-time at some point during those shots.

Opening the movie as a swaggering man of action, Maréchal wears his kepi tilted at a cocksure angle. And he starts by being ill at ease with class privilege, mocks his German captors and then smiles condescendingly at Rosenthal's Jewish background and family estates.

From there, his life takes surprising turns. He closes the movie having come to respect the aristocratic Boeldieu, fallen in love with a German woman, and escaped with Rosenthal, his comrade now. With this changed mind-set, he acquires gravitas and becomes a more serious person, attuned to those around him.

Maréchal's growth most vividly reflects the humanism of *La Grande Illusion*. But his overcoming of divisions is not as a representative of the working class, or a Frenchman, or a reformed anti–Semite.

On the contrary, he helps influence Boeldieu's unexpected breaking of class ranks, for instance, not because of class consciousness but because he confronts and engages Boeldieu as a person, not as a man of privilege — and because Boeldieu, in turn, comes to appreciate Maréchal's integrity. Despite this rapprochement, their class differences remain, even as Maréchal is able to cross less distinct lines in bonding with Rosenthal.

But what is notable about the pace and structure of the movie is that the other barriers, which are challenged and sometimes momentarily breached, are only finally shattered in the last part. The walls come tumbling down, and Maréchal does the toppling.

At the beginning of the final part Maréchal faces his anti–Semitism. But, even here, though his prejudice slips out and is an explicit part of the scene, his attempt at atonement indicates, I think, more an embarrassment at deserting a comrade in need than shame at his anti–Semitic slur. It is Rosenthal as a friend, not as a Jew, which brings Maréchal back. The undermining of anti–Semitism is simply a by-product of their friendship.

Maréchal's relationship with Elsa then overcomes the divide between genders and the gulf of competing languages. And nationality, which threatens everything in *La Grande Illusion*, is fully upended at the farm. There had been other forays. Arthur and the old German guard briefly reach out to the French at Hallbach; Boeldieu and Rauffenstein begin by skirting national allegiances, but nationality ends up trumping class. It stays in place until Maréchal and Elsa fall in love.

And again this is not a dry, thematic resolution of national divisions. There is instead the usual interplay of physical attraction and empathy that comes with falling in love, which naturally makes mincemeat of those divisions.

Boeldieu and Rauffenstein

Boeldieu is, in some ways, the second most prominent character in the film (107 shots — though only 28 minutes of screen-time). He changes more than anyone, excepting as always Maréchal. Boeldieu lingers on the periphery of the ensemble at Hallbach, not even attending the revue; but, though still superior to the others, he begins to waver. And as he moves into his principal role at Wintersborn he practically wilts. After renewing class connections to Rauffenstein, he reverses himself and sides with his fellow countrymen.

Rauffenstein, due partly to Stroheim's charismatic screen presence, seems to be the equal of Boeldieu in the film. But he is decidedly a secondary character, though important as a catalyst (64 shots; 18 minutes on the screen). And he remains essentially passive and narrow in his class-bound beliefs, in contrast to Boeldieu. The gap between them, at the end of Wintersborn, is a wide one.

Rosenthal and Elsa

The first appearances of Rosenthal and Elsa, unlike those of the other main characters, are oblique and unceremonial. Rosenthal's entrance at Hallbach is especially offhanded — he is merely one member of a group in a medium long shot, his back to the camera for a few seconds; in the next shot, again part of the group, he helps warn the new prisoners to hide their valuables. And Elsa makes her appearance at the barn ushered in by a cow.

Both Rosenthal and Elsa largely act as catalysts in the narrative. They are providers and caregivers. In touch with their feelings, they are also the only ones to shed tears.

Rosenthal is on the screen more than anyone except Maréchal (107 shots; 33½ minutes screen-time). With the backstory that he comes from a banking family and has a fashion house, he supports the others by providing meals and cognac at Hallbach. He also plans the escape route at Wintersborn and, later, acts as translator and unofficial baby-sitter on the farm. And of course he proves instrumental in facing down Maréchal's anti–Semitism.

Elsa is decidedly a secondary character (37 shots) and appears on the screen a little over 11 minutes, which is even less than the music hall performer, Cartier. But Elsa's importance is far out of proportion to her time on screen and arguably makes her as critically integral to the film as the other catalytic characters. Overcoming obstacles of gender and nation, with Maréchal, she ignores the accepted protocol of things as they have always been. And their unusually well-balanced relationship exhibits both strength and vulnerability.

The hold of *La Grande Illusion*, emotionally and intellectually, evolves and intensifies as the film unfolds. This steady sweep is nearly unbroken. By contrast, the central relationships generally move from wariness to acceptance to a feeling of affinity (or love) and, crucially, to separation. Beyond their affective impact, these separations have a structural function. Each one leads to the burgeoning of another attachment and foreshadows the last, and most difficult, separation at the farm.

With this motif of blocked and severed relationships, the ultimately tragic nature of the film emerges from a steady flow of mini-deaths — characters separated, scenes broken off, music cut short.

At the end, like so much else in this changeable film, that unsettling pattern is reversed. *La Grande Illusion* ends on a tentatively triumphant note, though the haven reached in the snows of Switzerland leaves many questions hanging in the balance.

9

Maréchal and Boeldieu

> *"As a matter of fact I carry my ideas for years. I am no good at telling a new story ... I am fascinated by the influence, the importance of caste in the world.* Grand Illusion *is a story of caste.* The Rules of the Game; *that's also a story of caste. All of my pictures are more or less the story of milieu."*
> —Jean Renoir in "Renoir: A Progress Report" by Alexander Sesonske (*Cinema*; Vol. 6, No. 1, 1969; pp. 17–8)

Maréchal and Boeldieu are of course fundamentally divided by distinctions of class. At the air base, their dissimilarities are pronounced. Rauffenstein later receives Boeldieu as a fellow career officer while Maréchal connects with the German who had, like him, worked in France as a mechanic.

The opening part, then, closes with little in common between the two men except that they are prisoners of war—and French. That, in the end, will be enough to make a difference.

Typically, at Hallbach, Boeldieu is self-contained and preoccupied with his own concerns, while Maréchal finds himself at a disadvantage; his wounded arm remains in a sling until the revue. And Renoir initially shows Boeldieu most often talking with the actor, the engineer or Rosenthal. Only toward the end of this part does he begin to interact more with Maréchal.

During the first shot, on line in Hallbach's prison yard, Boeldieu discreetly covers a slight yawn with his gloved hand and then Maréchal yawns full-bore and at length; Boeldieu regards him with some disdain.

When Maréchal is searched, he jokes that he regrets not having brought money. But Boeldieu complains about the roughness of the search; following rules is serious business to him and a matter of good form. Later at the roll call, distinguishing himself from the other men whose names are also read without rank, he calls out, "*Capitaine* de Boeldieu," as a corrective.

At the communal meal, when Boeldieu talks about going to Maxim's in Paris, Maréchal coolly says, without looking toward him, that he prefers a simpler kind of place. Yet, even at this point, Boeldieu is a somewhat different person. When the actor makes fun of Boeldieu's haughtiness, expropriating his monocle and teasing him that he is "difficile" ("difficult"), the captain takes it in good humor (while maintaining his distance). This couldn't have happened at the French base, as he was not one, back then, to suffer fools lightly.

During the following scene, the engineer asks Maréchal if Boeldieu can be trusted. Maréchal reassures him that he is a good guy despite his odd airs, with the word "drôle" appearing again, now in the sense of being strange. Maréchal has begun to see through the facade of class mannerisms to the man within, while the engineer, suspicious of the aloof officer, is, on the other hand, ready to assume that Maréchal, a man of the people like himself, can be trusted.

The disintegration of the relationship between Boeldieu and Rauffenstein is already in the works; it will not be a Valhalla of upper-class officers when they meet again. Exposure to another world has begun to take its toll on Boeldieu.

In the next scene, he does not disappoint. At the start of the tunnel-digging sequence, Boeldieu sits cross-legged on his bed playing solitaire, a fitting card game for him and in contrast to the group pitching game in the previous scene. But he soon joins the others when he makes room on his bed and helps place the unconscious actor on it. Cartier, barely escaping death, is revived by swigs of cognac (Rauffenstein will later down a stiff drink when Boeldieu dies).

And when the engineer explains it is the captain's turn to dig next, Boeldieu cavalierly proclaims crawling good exercise. The engineer smiles in appreciation of his brave manner, but Maréchal looks on blankly, unable to make sense of this disengaged character who seems above it all.

In the gardening scene, Maréchal stealthily dumps dirt from the tunnel, concealed by his coat, and sings a song to cover his actions; Boeldieu ostentatiously empties his bag and then folds it in full view. And with the news that costumes for the revue have arrived, Boeldieu declines to go with the others, explaining to Maréchal that he is a realist. They exit on opposite sides of the frame — Boeldieu off to another game of solitaire, Maréchal to see the costumes, though earlier he had shared Boeldieu's dislike for theater, belittling it to the actor as too serious.

Later, in the costume-making scene, Boeldieu, at the window, having observed troops drilling below, delivers one of his pronouncements and, in the process, connects Frenchmen and Germans again: "D'un côté, des enfants qui jouent au soldat — et de l'autre, des soldats qui jouent comme des enfants" ("On one side, children who play soldiers — and on the other, soldiers who play like children"). He memorably reverses his superiority to child's play at Wintersborn.

During this scene Maréchal and Boeldieu are coupled visually, for the first time, apart from the others. The actor goads Rosenthal by insensitively joking that he was born in Jerusalem, which amuses Boeldieu. Soon, in a medium two-shot, with Boeldieu at the lower left of the frame, Maréchal joins in and teases Rosenthal meanly and with hints of the fuller anti–Semitism that will seep out later, mocking Rosenthal's defensive pride in his naturalized Danish and Polish parents: "Vieille noblesse bretonne, quoi!" ("Old Breton nobility, what!"). Boeldieu also looks skeptical. They are united in prejudice by now, if little else.

Maréchal's snide remark spurs Rosenthal to detail the material achievements of his family; he gets more and more exercised, building up a head of steam. An uncomfortable moment, perhaps indicating a history of similar slights in the past.

Toward the end of the scene there are two more shots of Maréchal and Boeldieu together, again isolated apart. First, Maréchal expresses surprise that the teacher got into the army because he was a vegetarian, and then Boeldieu, in another two-shot, reassures the teacher that he was able to do his "devoir" ("duty") — a word, like "verboten," that returns at critical moments to different effect. These are minor shots but significantly link Maréchal and Boeldieu.

News of the war soon follows with the poster, divided in half with a communiqué in German on one side and a French translation on the other, announcing the German victory at Douaumont, accompanied by bells ringing in celebration. The two sides are further brought up against each other by the tracking shot of the German soldier singing triumphantly as the camera then moves off him and up to the French prisoners at their window, looking out grimly; the shot nearly matches the wide shot toward the end of the costume-making scene, but from a lower angle. Maréchal is most prominent in the composition, thrust forward and the center of attention. When the actor raises doubts about putting on the show, Maréchal insists that, especially now, they should go ahead and even invite the camp commandant and his officers.

Boeldieu is impressed and, though excusing himself from taking part, offers his congratulations. He adds a last tribute, continuing to look directly at Maréchal with some admiration: "C'est très chic" ("That's very stylish"). This marks a tipping point. For Boeldieu to find, and admit, something stylish in Maréchal represents a concession. And for such a realist to admire a gesture of defiance is not a small step. They are at least intellectually joined, if only out of nationalistic pride in opposing the common enemy. And it's a switch from their initial meeting at the base when it was Maréchal who deferred to Boeldieu and looked toward him.

They are soon connected emotionally as well. With Maréchal still in solitary confinement, and the tunnel almost finished, there's a medium shot of Boeldieu, again playing solitaire. He finds it painful that Maréchal won't be with them as they escape. But he catches himself, saying, in another of his bromides, "C'est la guerre, les sentiments sont hors de

Hallbach: the show must go on, as Maréchal (lower left) impresses Boeldieu (clockwise, from Maréchal: Rosenthal, the engineer, the teacher, Boeldieu, Cartier) (*Photofest*).

question" ("That's war, feelings are out of the question"); Arthur, in defending the search on the first day, also used that phrase, "c'est la guerre." Renoir then creates an effective moment as Boeldieu looks up from his cards and smiles, having seen Maréchal, off-camera, at the door. Once again, an interruption. And Boeldieu's dispassionate words are instantly contradicted by his smile.

Renoir cuts to a shot of the weakened Maréchal walking into the room, supported by another soldier. Boeldieu enters the shot and welcomes him back, affably calling him his pal ("mon vieux"). Since Boeldieu was at some distance from the door in the previous shot, this appearance, condensing the time frame a bit, connects him more closely to Maréchal. Their relationship will never quite be the same.

In the final scene at Hallbach, as the French wait to be transferred, Boeldieu suggests that perhaps they should warn the new English prisoners about the tunnel. It is Maréchal, however, who takes action and slips under the restraining rope. But he's unable to communicate with the befuddled English officer who speaks no French. Boeldieu of course speaks English, but does nothing; despite the thaw in his demeanor, he remains detached.

All this changes at Wintersborn. Maréchal and Boeldieu reverse character traits at an escalating rate and reach an unexpressed appreciation of each other, strengthening their growing solidarity across class lines, even though the relationship of Boeldieu and Rauffenstein dominates the narrative.

While Rauffenstein lectures them in his office, having handed out a booklet of rules, Boeldieu and Maréchal exchange conspiratorial glances and a few smirks. In league against the pedagogue, they have already forged something of a bond, presumably cemented by sharing the experience of two camps since Hallbach (indicated earlier by prison camp signs).

Soon afterward, Maréchal gets upset when a German soldier inspects his kepi and he angrily struggles to grab the hat back. This complete turnabout from his nonchalance during the search at Hallbach is more in keeping with Boeldieu's insistence on civility from the guards.

The two men also react similarly in disdaining Demolder's obsession with Pindar. Boeldieu is annoyed when the translator's books crowd his game of solitaire, and Maréchal follows by making fun of Demolder, snapping out the Greek name that he finds unfamiliar: "Je m'en fous, mais qu'est-ce que c'est ton Pindare?" ("I don't care, but what is your Pindar?"). It recalls his needling of the engineer in derisively enunciating the word "cadastre." Maréchal's gibes are not pretty and imply an insecurity about matters of the intellect. And he had also made no effort to conceal his boredom with Demolder's impromptu lessons on architecture during the tour of the castle, looking uninterested and saying little.

Though his relationship with Maréchal has changed, Boeldieu continues to assume the role of patriarch at Wintersborn. When their room is about to be searched, Maréchal and Rosenthal scurry about, not knowing where to hide the rope they have been making. Coming to the rescue, Boeldieu calls their feeble attempts "enfantin" ("infantile") and calmly attaches the rope to a drainpipe outside a window. Father knows best.

Later, when Boeldieu, with Maréchal and Rosenthal, realizes that the book-burning by Russians has diverted the guards, he notes that the Germans have been kind enough to stage a "répétition" ("rehearsal") for them. He proposes an escape plan, saying it would amuse him, and asks when they want to leave. Rosenthal objects it would be unfair for them to escape without him, and Boeldieu replies impatiently: "Qu'est-ce qui est juste dans une guerre?" ("What is fair in a war?"). In league now with his prison mates, he seems to have a more relaxed view of the rules governing warfare.

But Boeldieu retains his schoolmarm's correctness as he ends the discussion by asserting coldly that he is not asking for advice and, turning his back on them, declares he has made his decision. Father still knows best, and his subordinates meekly follow his lead.

The next scene (consisting of a single shot) begins in their prison quarters with a close framing of a caged squirrel, the camera pulling back to include Maréchal and Boeldieu on either side. The shot visually underscores their changed relationship since this is the first time, without others around, that they are seen alone together.

Though the symbol of the cage is a bit trite, Renoir does not belabor it as Boeldieu immediately starts talking about a neutral subject, music. When Maréchal shows little interest, Boeldieu says that he adores the flute — a far cry from his "horreur des fifres" ("horror of fifes") conveyed with distaste at Hallbach during the window pan.

After Boeldieu outlines his escape scenario, Maréchal haltingly tries to express embarrassment about his captain's generous role in the plan; he has become similar to his commanding officer in revealing feelings only tentatively. True to character, Boeldieu cuts him off.

In the following scene Boeldieu, washing some white gloves, is definitely in command as Maréchal, playing his servant now, pours water over his gloved hands. It recalls the opening shot at Wintersborn when the orderly prepares Rauffenstein's gloves. In putting on such formal attire, Boeldieu is ironically linking himself with Rauffenstein even as he has decided to challenge him. When Maréchal again tries to articulate his unease, Boeldieu once more rebuffs him and says he's doing nothing for him personally. Another attempt by Maréchal — and again he is interrupted and shut down. Then, in a visual reminder of their relationship, Boeldieu leaves the frame first and Maréchal follows.

In the second shot of this scene, Boeldieu hangs up his gloves to dry. The camera tracks around the two men. Behind them and out of focus is the Senegalese officer, probably working on another drawing; they continue to talk as if he didn't exist (the invisible man). Boeldieu then walks off and Maréchal, the obedient schoolboy, trudges after him again, pointing out that after eighteen months together Boeldieu still uses the formal "vous" ("you") with him. Reframed into a two-shot, Boeldieu attempts to reassure him by saying that he uses "vous" with both his mother and wife (and not the more intimate "tu"). A curious fact, reinforcing this revelation, is that Boeldieu and Rauffenstein also use "vous" with each other, despite their friendship; Maréchal and Rosenthal, by contrast, use "tu" throughout, even during their blowup in the mountains.

And then, following Boeldieu's reassurance, comes one of the few false notes in *La Grande Illusion*'s dialogue. As Maréchal sits down, Boeldieu offers him an English cigarette, which Maréchal refuses, adding: "Ah, décidément, les gants, tabac — tout nous sépare" ("Ah, definitely, the gloves, tobacco — everything separates us").

The line is unworthy of such a consistently understated script, and Gabin only manages to bring out the last three words woodenly, without conviction, as if not sure what to do with them. The sentiment had already been expressed implicitly throughout the movie and now, in this scene, is indicated also by the choreography — Boeldieu twice departing the frame before Maréchal. Then, at the very end of this second shot, the camera draws back slightly to emphasize their isolation from each other in space. These cinematic effects are weakened by the direct verbalization of their relationship.

The two tête-à-têtes follow one after the other, as did tête-à-têtes between Boeldieu and Rauffenstein earlier. It is also significant that Renoir places Maréchal and Boeldieu together in long takes — the single shot in the first scene (58 seconds) and the two shots (37 and 50 seconds) in the next—instead of separating them into a series of countershots, flitting one to the other, as Boeldieu and Rauffenstein are most often presented, set in their places.

Though Maréchal and Boeldieu are still separated by class and manner, they have at least reached some degree of accommodation as they go over the escape plan together. And these shots are distinguished by a tracking camera and the movement of the characters; once again Maréchal brings movement with him.

Their final scene together takes place at the end of another lengthy tracking shot, running 67 seconds, that is richly packed and doubles back on itself. This shot especially stands out since it follows a prosaic series of comparatively short, stationary shots of prisoners and German guards during the disruption.

The shot starts at the door to their quarters. The camera tracks to the right across the prisoners, some of them banging pots and singing, including even Demolder liberated from his scholarly activities, before it temporarily stops on Boeldieu putting on his gloves. Behind him on the wall are reproductions of paintings, mainly featuring women, including Venus's head in *The Birth of Venus* by Botticelli, which had previously appeared behind Maréchal and Rosenthal, and could also be seen at Hallbach next to Rosenthal opening a tin for Maréchal after his return from solitary. Boeldieu, in alliance now with the others, is no longer stuck in his corner with pictures of stiffly posed racehorses.

The noise in the room subsides and the camera tracks back again to the left, coming

Wintersborn: the parting of Maréchal and Boeldieu (*Photofest*).

to rest at the front door on a German guard, who then announces a roll call. The French start to file out; Demolder exclaims boisterously that he understands his students at last and has never had so much fun. This is in counterpoint to an earlier scene when a German officer questioned Rauffenstein's loose command of the prison, noting that he knew better than his commandant how to deal with prisoners since he was a schoolmaster; he later orders bread and water as punishment.

The shot finally settles into a two-shot of Maréchal and Boeldieu, alone together at the door. As Maréchal prepares to frame his goodbyes, he says, "Alors..." ("Then..."), and uneasily eyes Boeldieu who, taking control, challenges him: "Quoi?" ("What?"). An awkward pause. The captain's unflinching eyes establish the ground rules and Maréchal, sensing a need in him to part on his own terms, simply says "au revoir" and accepts an offered handshake, assuming again Boeldieu's reserve.

After Maréchal leaves, Boeldieu smiles slightly, turns, and attends to his gloves. A quiet ending to a shot that opens in such turmoil.

On the farm, Rosenthal teases Maréchal during Christmas Eve by referring to Jesus as "mon frère de race" ("my racial brother"), slyly recalling their earlier confrontation. Maréchal replies: "Une pierre dans mon jardin, comme dirait ce pauvre Boeldieu" ("A stone in my garden, as poor Boeldieu would say"). At Wintersborn, Boeldieu had used the same aphorism in responding to an ironic barb directed at him by Maréchal.

Rosenthal wonders if Boeldieu is still alive. Maréchal, eyes shifted away, tells him not to talk about it and adds that "ça vaut mieux" ("it is better"). His uneasiness may signify guilt at Boeldieu's sacrifice though, of course, he doesn't know about his death.

Maréchal's freedom has come at a cost. In shunting aside Rosenthal's concern, Maréchal avoids facing his acceptance of the escape plan and resulting dependence on Boeldieu or, at the least, his debt. Despite having grown as a person, he remains a complicated and flawed character.

At the border, Maréchal tells Rosenthal that the war must be finished up — an unconscious assimilation of Boeldieu's commitment to "duty." Bowing to the rules of war once more.

Something of Boeldieu thus lives on in Maréchal, tenuous as it may be. And it is one of the wellsprings of this film that Renoir manages to find the shared humanity in his characters. Superficial differences hide more than they reveal.

A similar formulation could be made about *La Grande Illusion*. There is a complexity not necessarily apparent at first glance.

10

Boeldieu and Rauffenstein

> *"RENOIR: I felt that this friendship between this German and the Frenchman was a kind of love affair.*
>
> [Action:] *I get the same feeling when Von Stroheim comes back and says, 'I beg you to come back, I'm going to have to shoot you.'*
>
> RENOIR: *I asked him to give it the feeling of a lover begging his mistress not to leave him."*
>
> — Jean Renoir in "Directors Go to Their Movies: Jean Renoir"; interview with Digby Diehl (*Action*, volume 7, number 3; May–June 1972; p. 4)

When Rauffenstein meets the captured French aviators at the German canteen, he directs his attention to Boeldieu (who salutes before shaking hands) and then perfunctorily shakes Maréchal's hand. Boeldieu is the superior officer but Rauffenstein also knows class when he sees it.

Later, seated next to Boeldieu, Rauffenstein raises a monocle to his eye, as his counterpart had done at the French base. And after establishing that he knew Boeldieu's cousin, he says in English, "He was a marvelous rider"; Boeldieu responds, also in English. The remembrance of this coincidence from the past, in a shared foreign language, eloquently indicates their appreciation of class. Boeldieu returns to French and Rauffenstein remarks, "...that so?" in English, as if loath to withdraw from their common ground high above the others.

At Wintersborn, a change is noticeable when they meet again. In a long shot, toward an impressive crypt-like doorway leading to his quarters, Rauffenstein seems entombed in the chapel beyond as he sprays himself with perfume, extending the sense of decay from the opening shot at the castle. This long shot develops into a medium tracking shot; Rauffenstein walks into his office to greet the three new prisoners in his self-possessed way, smoking a cigarette as in his first shot in the film, but now with the added stiffness of a battle-scarred body. He focuses on Boeldieu, pleased to see him, and on the wall behind is a map, as at Boeldieu's office.

The shot continues as the camera comes to a stop when he reaches the French officers who await him. Echoing their first encounter, in opening with the same word, Rauffenstein says, "Enchanté de vous revoir, Boeldieu" ("Delighted to see you again, Boeldieu"), pointedly marking out his friend for himself alone; their matching monocles again separate them from the others. Boeldieu salutes, but he hesitates before accepting Rauffenstein's offer of a handshake, unlike their first meeting.

Renoir designs the shot to further suggest a shift in their relationship when Maréchal interjects himself into the conversation and Rauffenstein, reminded now of his presence, moves to the right in order to be in front of him (with Demolder next in line), but he deliberately looks leftward back at Boeldieu and asks the French captain if they will be seated. It is Maréchal who nonetheless declines the offer, assuming Boeldieu's role as ranking officer. Rauffenstein appears somewhat taken aback that this mere lieutenant, this mechanic of the bistros, has taken charge; Demolder is too far off his radar to be even acknowledged.

The pleasantries clearly over, there's nothing left for Rauffenstein to do but conduct the business at hand, and he settles down to review with the prisoners their escape attempts. Renoir presents the sequence in a series of opposed shots in which Rauffenstein sits at his desk while the prisoners stand, visually fortifying his supremacy. He is also shot at a slight angle upward, as in the two-shot with Boeldieu at the canteen, which similarly strengthens his position; pictures of Kaiser Wilhelm II and Kaiserin (Empress) Augusta Viktoria, seen as well at Hallbach's canteen, hang on the wall beyond, backing him up. The occasion is hardly like the sociable gathering after his capture of Boeldieu and Maréchal.

In these shots, Renoir uncharacteristically presents Maréchal alone in the frame. And, rather than Boeldieu, it's Maréchal who interacts most with Rauffenstein. He even displays Boeldieu's kind of irony when he banters with the commandant about his disguise as a woman during an escape attempt. Rauffenstein muses: "C'est drôle"—the same words used by Maisonneuve in impersonating a woman. Maréchal responds that he didn't like it when someone tried to pick him up (another wink at homosexual possibilities). Rauffenstein raises an eyebrow after asking, "Vraiment?" ("Truly?"), as if questioning his manly outrage, and Maréchal teasingly assures him of his feelings. Rauffenstein allows himself a brief smile. Such an exchange between them would have been inconceivable when they first met.

Rauffenstein informs his prisoners that he will use French rules and regulations to avoid charges of German barbarism, blurring national lines again and countering the opening scene at Hallbach where prison regulations are read out sternly, punctuated by the phrase "streng verboten" ("strictly forbidden"). For all its oppressive grayness, life at Wintersborn has a civilized veneer, due mainly to Rauffenstein's old-world style.

On the tour of the castle that follows, undertaken to discourage any idea of escaping, Rauffenstein stops by a group of older soldiers. In the next shot, he quips that they are not young but "ça les amuse de jouer aux soldats" ("this amuses them to play soldiers"), paralleling Boeldieu's remark at Hallbach.

The tour continues with a shot angled up at Rauffenstein as he leads the way down stone steps, with Boeldieu behind him, followed by Maréchal and Demolder. But the relative strength of their positions is casually, and artfully, reversed when they stop to talk, leaving Maréchal a few steps above the two other men, who are face to face on the same step together. He follows their conversation, looking down at them from his perch with a slightly bemused expression, as though observing exotic birds.

Rauffenstein refers to a mounted gun on the steps and asks Boeldieu if he knows this Maxim model. Maréchal again jumps in ahead of Boeldieu, pointing to his wounds, and jokes: "Personnellement, je préfère le restaurant" ("Personally, I prefer the restaurant"). Here again is a curious reversal. At Hallbach he had specifically disdained Maxim's, after Boeldieu had talked about going there, but now he favors it for the sake of making a joke. And he aims this witticism not at Rauffenstein but looks instead at Boeldieu, who good-naturedly accepts the ribbing.

Seeing himself disadvantaged, Rauffenstein slips into English with Boeldieu, their language of exclusion, saying that he knew a girl at Maxim's named Fifi. But he only momentarily restores the balance of power. Boeldieu coldly responds in English: "So did I." Then, seemingly bored, he looks upward to cut the conversation short.

Maréchal prefers the restaurant named Maxim's to the machine gun; from the left, Rauffenstein, a German guard, Demolder (Sylvain Itkine), Maréchal, Boeldieu (***Photofest***).

Rauffenstein, not Boeldieu, is the one who usually initiates their exchanges in English, especially in public. He plays the suitor, ever trying to bring Boeldieu back into their charmed, but weakening, circle. Further, since Boeldieu apparently does not know German, Rauffenstein must accommodate him by using French as their primary means of communication.

In the next shot, Rauffenstein doesn't understand Maréchal's question, phrased again with an irony and circumlocution more familiar in Boeldieu: "Cette villa ... elle a été construite exprès pour le capitaine de Boeldieu et pour moi?" ("This villa ... it was built purposely for Captain Boeldieu and me?"). Boeldieu, standing behind Rauffenstein, cuts in to interpret and takes a direct, Maréchal-like approach: "Sommes-nous vos seuls pensionnaires?" ("Are we your only boarders?"). Rauffenstein is obliged to turn around, chuckling politely, and ward off their thrusts. But the match is on.

At the tour's next stop, Boeldieu and Maréchal again gang up on Rauffenstein, alternating jabs. After Rauffenstein puts his monocle in place, Boeldieu imitates him by doing the same and thanks him for his tour as their "landlord" (slowly stretching out the word "propriétaire" sarcastically); Maréchal calls the fortress "un bien joli château" ("a very nice castle"), as though it was no more than some glorified country club.

The German commandant receives another jolt at the last stop, the anteroom to his office, when he says to Boeldieu that he regrets being unable to offer him a room of his own and the French officer replies that he would not have accepted it. This isn't what Rauffenstein would have expected from the old Boeldieu. But, respecting this reserve, he salutes Boeldieu, who returns the salute. The camera tracks around and ends on the French officers watching Rauffenstein walk off in the distance, framed by the doorway, constraining him much as when he perfumed himself in his quarters.

In the background of the next and last shot of the tour, which faces the French head-on, is the poster headed "DER FEIND," seen also at the German canteen. A taste of the war raging outside. And more salvos are directed at Rauffenstein. Maréchal points to the departing commandant (off-screen), overdressed in his fur muff and collar and with a sword at his side, and mimics Demolder's earlier architectural history lessons on the twelfth, then thirteenth, century details of the castle; he remarks to his tutor, "Quatorzième" ("Fourteenth"). Boeldieu does not miss a beat: "Pur style gothique" ("Pure gothic style").

And the sense of German soldiers playing for their amusement, as noted by Rauffenstein at the beginning of the tour, is exemplified not by guards but by some prisoners in the next shot, as Demolder ambles down a snowy slope oblivious to a lively snowball fight behind him.

In the two tête-à-têtes of Boeldieu and Rauffenstein at Wintersborn, the continuing upheaval in their relationship is signaled in part by the varied delivery of a single word, "Peut-être" ("Perhaps") — a word that could serve as the film's mantra. So much in *La Grande Illusion* seems conditional.

These conversations are preceded by a scene that begins as the French talk about the relationship of disease to class, leading soon to the put-downs of Demolder. Maréchal and Rosenthal then go over plans for an escape. Like the sequence at Hallbach in which escape is discussed, these leisurely digressions help etch the critical scene more firmly by providing it with a bland relief.

The first tête-à-tête takes place in the prisoners' quarters during a routine search of the premises. To frame this exchange, Renoir constructs a cleverly balanced scene. He opens with a dissolve into a close-up of the escape rope, wrapped around legs of a stool, and then moves the camera back to take in Maréchal and Rosenthal; the scene comes to an end, after the search, as the camera reverses this motion and moves into a close-up of Maréchal in the same spot, untangling the rope, ending the scene back where it had begun.

Rauffenstein enters the room in the middle of this search. He stops his men from their rummaging of Boeldieu's corner, though the French captain had ignored the invasion, in contrast to his indignation when searched at Hallbach and more like Maréchal's indifference in that scene.

In a two-shot, the captains salute each other, with pictures of racehorses on the wall behind (their shared interest). Rauffenstein, sporting a monocle, unlike Boeldieu, asks for his word of honor that there is nothing in the room against regulations. Boeldieu hesitates for a moment, having hidden the rope from the drainpipe outside the window. He could either be making up his mind to give his word falsely or rationalizing that the rope is not technically "in the room." In either case, when he gives his word of honor he allies himself with his French cohorts and, to a degree, breaks the code of conduct so dear to him. Boeldieu then asks why his word should be accepted rather than that of the others, a rhetorical question and a bit pointed, if not malicious, forcing Rauffenstein to come up with a diplomatic answer.

Renoir cuts to a close-up of Rauffenstein, splitting him off visually from Boeldieu and emphasizing the struggle between them (though Boeldieu's profile can barely be made out at one edge). Bobbing uncomfortably and adjusting his monocle in looking off-screen, part of his face at one point exiting the frame for a moment, Rauffenstein communicates reservations by his halting delivery and intonation: "La parole d'honneur d'un ... Rosenthal?" ("The word of honor of a ... Rosenthal?"). For him, the mere mouthing of that name is proof enough of Rosenthal's unworthiness, preceded by the pause and, afterward, attached to a question mark in his voice.

There is a cut to a medium close-up of Boeldieu as Rauffenstein includes Maréchal in his skepticism. Boeldieu then twists the knot tighter, saying that such a word is as worthy as their own and thus challenging Rauffenstein, visible on the left of the screen, to scramble and again find a riposte in this battle of wits.

Renoir returns to the previous close-up framing of Rauffenstein, who looks once more around the room, his discomfort seemingly matched by disappointment in his friend. He lowers his eyes briefly, then fixes them on Boeldieu and responds enigmatically: "Peut-être."

It is a stunning moment. This last close-up in the quick succession of close framings gives weight to a simple, ambiguous word and indicates, as does Stroheim's delicate expression of distaste, not ambiguity at all but the unmistakable implication: No — their word could never be worth as much as ours. It's also effective because Renoir uses close-ups so sparingly in the film. The disjunction between the equivocating word and Stroheim's expression, as well as between the inconsequence of that word and the significance inherent in a close-up, typifies *La Grande Illusion*. A word does not mean what it usually means, transformed by its context in the dialogue and enhanced by a particular cinematic setting. And the close-up also isolates Rauffenstein to stew in his sense of superiority, even more removed from Boeldieu.

This moment, like the window pan at Hallbach, turns the mood and shifts gears at Wintersborn toward a greater weightiness in the offing. But this grand moment supplied by Rauffenstein occurs much earlier in the Wintersborn scenes than had the similarly crucial pan at Hallbach. A further acceleration.

Renoir defuses the intensity by returning to a two-shot as the officers again salute, a formal and unspoken acknowledgement of the rupture in their class-bound solidarity. For the moment, they have reverted to their roles as German commandant and French prisoner of war.

"Peut-être": Rauffenstein's unequivocal slur (*Photofest*).

Their second tête-à-tête follows immediately, in Rauffenstein's quarters. It marks the only time that they are completely alone together. With the crucifix that opened Wintersborn hovering above them, the scene begins as they walk in unison toward the camera in a long shot, swamped by the chapel's luxurious dimensions. Boeldieu smokes a cigarette for the first time in the film, joining Rauffenstein in his pastime of choice. Ambling along and smoking in their elegant and dandified style, they are once again at ease. And as if to recapture that convivial time at the German canteen, Rauffenstein asks about Boeldieu's cousin, Edmond. They pause, engaged in talk, and then resume their synchronized stroll, smoking now in mirror image of each other.

In a closer shot the camera tracks slightly into a window bench as they settle onto it and exchange a few lines in English. Boeldieu remembers that Rauffenstein had won a horse race in Liverpool before the war. This return to the language, and sport, of privilege temporarily cements the balance they have restored.

Renoir follows this two-shot with a shot of Rauffenstein as he starts to share what is most on his mind, in French. It's a noticeable jump cut as suddenly he is now leaning a bit forward with his right hand extended (pulling an ashtray nearer), that hand having been held close to his chest in the previous shot.

Then, in a loose series of reverse shots, their conversation continues. But it doesn't conform to the standard practice of 180-degree matched compositions in a reverse-shot sequence. And only some of these shots, shifting from speaker to speaker, shot and countershot, have the identical composition. In fact, there are 9 different camera setups among the 19 shots, in a little over two minutes. A dizzying and messy profusion, bordering sometimes on more jump cuts and crossing that line at one point.

This is the film's first sustained shot/countershot sequence. Until this scene, there had been only brief flurries, a few matched pairs at a time, so this common movie convention hits freshly and with more force here. And Renoir creates a deft visual and rhythmic metaphor for their growing separation. Shot versus shot.

In the longest-held shot of the sequence, angled from the side, Rauffenstein reminisces about his past as a combatant, lamenting that he has been reduced to the position of a prison official and pointing to his wounds, as Maréchal had earlier. The introduction of somber background music, scored by Joseph Kosma, provides greater emphasis and is the first time that Renoir extensively uses non-incidental music in the story proper. And, from here, background music assumes an important role throughout the rest of *La Grande Illusion*.

After a shot of Boeldieu, Renoir cuts to Rauffenstein, who clearly is no longer sitting but, instead, appears to be half-kneeling on the window bench as he leans forward (though he could not physically have made such a shift in that short time). This obvious jump cut visually breaks the pattern of shots.

The camera returns to Boeldieu. Playing innocent, he asks why an exception was made to receive him in these quarters. Posing the question forces Rauffenstein to repeat his performance in the previous scene, and again it is almost mean-spirited to put him through his paces. In a closer shot of him, and now leaning against the wall (another shift), he notes their comparable positions as career officers.

A series of rapid-fire shots between them follows. Boeldieu is also framed in a closer shot and replies, in a new term for him, that his "camarades" ("comrades") are also officers. Rauffenstein then adds venom to his earlier dismissal, not just impugning their words of honor but now not even accepting them as true officers: "Un Maréchal et un Rosenthal ... officiers?" Boeldieu defends his compatriots. Rauffenstein bows facetiously and refers to them as a gift of the French Revolution. But his friend doesn't join in the fun and says that neither of them can stop the march of time.

Now a larger break is imminent. Renoir cuts to Rauffenstein moving to put out his cigarette. In the next shot of him he holds scissors to prune his geranium, which is between them — a foreshadowing of the final scene at Wintersborn. With attention focused on him, he pontificates that the end of the war will also be the end of the Rauffensteins and the Boeldieus of this world; at one point Renoir intercuts a wider shot of Boeldieu, listening.

In countershots, Boeldieu replies that they may not be needed and Rauffenstein asks, "Et vous ne trouvez pas que c'est dommage?" ("And you do not find that it's a pity?").

Then, in the wider setup again, Boeldieu, undoubtedly remembering Rauffenstein's response to a different question, immediately answers: "Peut-être." Before the word punctuates the scene so adroitly, a slight hiatus in the music briefly lets it slip in — once more the soundtrack as a framing device.

This verbal reprise demonstrates the relative nature of language and links the tête-à-têtes even as it divides the two men, as does the fact that, again, only Rauffenstein sports a monocle. For Boeldieu, "peut-être" implies he at least has some doubts it is a pity; he exhibits none of the disdain, or hesitation, that had been shown by Rauffenstein. And the wider shot befits his lighter tone, as he teases with his contrariness, in contrast to the tight close-up of Rauffenstein when he brought out the same word. They are more separated, one from the other, than at any time up to this point.

Boeldieu allows "peut-être" to linger in the air before changing the subject by admiring Rauffenstein's care of his potted geranium, the only flower in the castle (a change from his ridicule of the teacher's passion for tulips).

Renoir further defuses the scene in the next shot. He pulls away from Rauffenstein, his back turned while pruning the plant, and brings the skirmishing officers together in reconfiguring them into a wider two-shot as Rauffenstein takes his seat and indulges in small talk. The reframed shot closely matches the opening composition of them on the

"Peut-être": Boeldieu's ambivalent response (*Photofest*).

bench. Another pair of bookends. The music fades, its main theme the same as the one that had covered the opening titles and will return both at Boeldieu's death and the first shot of Maréchal and Rosenthal in Switzerland — music associated with being free (at the beginning and the end) and with the one who will die to make that freedom possible.

Despite its formal qualities, the scene is somewhat problematic, a rare time that characters openly discuss a major theme in the film. Previously, such discussions were harmless sidetracks. This sequence is meatier. And it might be cited to make an argument that here *La Grande Illusion* deals schematically with class divisions.

But still, even with this drawback, the scene has a lovely, nostalgic feeling to it, fitting Rauffenstein's persona. And the compelling use of brief countershots to express the split between them, and Boeldieu's teasing repetition of "peut-être," with Renoir magnifying its impact by placing it after such explicit dialogue, is far more typical of the movie as a whole.

The next scene, partly through its cinematic expression, communicates the gulf between the relationship of Boeldieu and Rauffenstein on one side and (in a single, still shot) that of Maréchal and Rosenthal on, decidedly, the other side of the tracks. And no music is thrown in to elevate the scene, letting a simpler and more relaxed conversation develop.

The opening composition foreshadows the framing of the reconciliation after the blowup, with positions reversed. Maréchal is sitting, looking down, and only the lower half of Rosenthal can be seen as he stands next to him, before also sitting. Like Boeldieu and Rauffenstein, they smoke, but in a plebeian and casual way. And they too talk about big issues — the wall between Boeldieu and them (though they respect him), Rosenthal's generosity, and his Jewish background. Maréchal says he doesn't give a damn what people say about Jehovah since Rosenthal has been a pal; this will of course come back to haunt him.

Huddled together in the two-shot, they are equal in importance and closely connected, not like the sparring upper-class dandies in their separate shots, facing each other on the window bench. The closeness of Maréchal and Rosenthal is also emphasized by the unblinking length of the shot (65 seconds); it lasts half as long as the combined times of all 19 shots in the previous scene's conversation. In comprising the whole scene, this is a shot that endures, in sync with the relationship it chronicles, unlike the scattershot scene of Boeldieu and Rauffenstein that has shots bouncing from angle to angle — three seconds here, six there, five here. And not only is it among the longest still shots in the movie but to see either Maréchal or Rosenthal tamed within a still shot for so long is unusual.

Renoir establishes yet another parallel sequence later, just before the prison ruckus, with the long-held shot (50 seconds) of two German officers, who also smoke casually together as one lectures the other about their superior, Rauffenstein. But, unlike Maréchal and Rosenthal, he has contempt for his commanding officer.

As with the tunnel-digging at Hallbach, both the sequence of the prisoners creating a diversion (3½ minutes) and that of the roll call and Boeldieu's escapade before his confrontation with Rauffenstein (5 minutes) are plot-driven and directly related to the theme of escape. It is another relatively dry patch in the film, relieved only by the weightier tracking shot of Maréchal and Boeldieu parting company that bridges the two sequences. But the groundwork for Wintersborn's climax begins to take shape with the theatrical game of run-and-duck, strung out by Boeldieu in the upper nooks and crannies of the fortress.

When his name is called out during the roll call, Boeldieu makes himself known by playing a children's song on his pennywhistle, sitting on a railing high above the ground, one leg dangled nonchalantly in the air. He tootles "Il était un petit navire," as did the other prisoners during the disruption, first on flutes and then singing the song while banging on pots.

Again he has set himself apart, as during the earlier roll call at Hallbach. But it is also a radically new pose for this gentleman officer who was responsible for setting off the movie's chain of events for no better reason than his obsession with the smudged photograph. A prankster now acting out in the parapets, Boeldieu takes on his role in spotlights, occasionally playing the pennywhistle and far removed from his earlier contempt for theater, having taken his cue from the "rehearsal" provided by the book-burning Russians. A Pied Piper leading on a horde of guards.

For the first time in *La Grande Illusion*, he is seen alone in tracking shots as the central and most active character, not locked down in still shots or simply one amongst others in tracks or pans. He has become a sort of civilized Pan; his name, in one version of the script, is a play on "Bois-le-Dieu" ("Woods" and "God"). In a strange reversal, this refined career officer acts like the Greek god of the natural world, playing his pipe and losing any claim to propriety.

There is also the odd twist in the narrative that Rauffenstein drops out of the action during the diversion and then during the pursuit of Boeldieu. Another German officer makes decisions about the disturbance. This does not make sense since Rauffenstein is, after all, in charge of the prison camp. But by not showing him undertaking his duties, Renoir avoids diluting the focus on his relationship with Boeldieu, preserving its centrality for their struggle when Rauffenstein, at last, returns to the story.

The chase of Boeldieu has some undertones that give it more depth — Boeldieu as performer, the incidental music used later to great effect, the terrible irony that Maréchal and Rosenthal owe their freedom primarily to ties of national identity — but this sequence is a perfunctory, hide-and-seek adventure. From Boeldieu's last notes on the flute, after musically announcing his presence, to Rauffenstein's return to the courtyard, nothing is spoken beyond the general hubbub and a few commands in German. It's the longest time without dialogue in the film (4 minutes). And background music continues through the escape of Maréchal and Rosenthal, which marks the most extensive stretch of uninterrupted music without accompanying dialogue.

The chase is also the most substantial sequence to be composed mainly of short shots, often held still as well. But despite the rush of activity, in the plot line and profusion of shots, this is a prolonged lull in the narrative. Both the development of characters and the film's intensity are at a standstill. There is a little bit of old-fashioned suspense instead. For instance, after Rosenthal slips out a window, Maréchal hears guards nearby and hides anxiously before slipping away. Such suspense is rare in the film.

And nothing else particularly distinguishes the chase sequence. Only a small but expressive moment near the beginning adds some spice. Renoir cuts to a shot of German soldiers hurrying down steps in an archway as Rauffenstein, deflated by Boeldieu's baffling prank, walks slowly upward in the background, in counterpoint to the rushing soldiers but consistent with the Frenchman's movement, though in tired resignation here.

Other than that moment, blandness largely takes over. Even after many viewings of the chase, it's impossible to remember the exact sequence of shots; they meld together, a potpourri featuring guards and the fleeing Boeldieu. Renoir's economical precision, in which every shot counts, seems on hold.

An effective transition on the soundtrack sets up the final confrontation. The stirring chase music ends after Maréchal and Rosenthal land outside the prison walls and scurry off.

Renoir cuts, in shocking silence, to a tracking shot of German soldiers poised on the ramparts. The calm before what will be a deadly standoff.

Then, after hearing gunfire, Rauffenstein returns to stop his men from firing again at Boeldieu (an interruption only momentarily fortunate). He engages him as an adversary, making his initial plea in French. But after that attempt the exchange is wholly in English — once again instigated by Rauffenstein. It is their longest retreat into English as a refuge. Rauffenstein desperately carves out this intimate space for them, standing in the courtyard with a soldier at his side and other soldiers still aiming, presumably, at his friend. The contrast between the private and the public is striking.

Their thrusts and parries lead nowhere and Rauffenstein fails to lure Boeldieu away from his defiance. It's a brilliant touch that this language of class elitism, shared by these like-minded officers, ends up as the language of discord and separation. Rauffenstein pleads in a soft voice; Boeldieu responds harshly, not conforming to the rules of genteel behavior.

This confrontation is the second (and last) extended shot/countershot sequence in the film, a series of quick shots that are unusually short for *La Grande Illusion*. Renoir's restraint again heightens the effect. He also strengthens the scene by framing the first shot of Rauffenstein from an angle above, which diminishes him as he arrives in the courtyard. In the next shot of him, with the camera even farther removed, Rauffenstein looks almost comically small; he's at a clear disadvantage, straining to look up and reduced as if caught in the wrong end of a telescope. This startling angle and composition, at such a height, is unique in the film and aptly establishes the tone, as does the fact that the shots are held still to the end of the sequence.

These first two shots of Rauffenstein include a soldier nearby. Once the crosscutting begins in earnest, and Rauffenstein switches to English, he is at first alone but, after two matched pairs of shots with Boeldieu, the soldier is again shown at his side for the rest of the sequence. Two against one. Two guns against the defenseless Boeldieu. Two Germans, one Frenchman — and the critical dialogue between like souls, though safely encoded in English, polluted by an eavesdropper. And, at that, a common soldier.

This sequence, made up of shots angled slightly up at Boeldieu and leveled at Rauffenstein, separates them even more and indicates who has the upper hand, until a single bullet ends all that in the German's reluctant favor.

After a flurry of 9 extremely brief shots, Renoir settles, for emphasis, into a longer shot on Rauffenstein (18 seconds), pleading in English still and ending: "I beg you ... man to man ... come back." Boeldieu defies him again and snaps out, in retort: "It's damned nice of you, Rauffenstein — but it's impossible" (spitting out the last word in derision). And then 5 more brief shots as Rauffenstein fires his pistol and Boeldieu falls.

Moments later Rauffenstein finds that Maréchal and Rosenthal are missing. He seems crushed. Understanding Boeldieu's behavior now, he realizes how far apart they have drifted and any illusion he may have had about their relationship is shattered. But, like a good soldier, he switches back into his role as commandant, barking out orders for a search party.

The death of Boeldieu is the next crisis in *La Grande Illusion*. As with Maréchal's solitary confinement, the nature of war, and the rules of that particular game, precipitate this crisis. And empathy between supposed enemies again lessens the gulf. Bringing the mortally wounded Boeldieu to Rauffenstein's quarters to die is, in itself, a sign of friendship and respect.

Renoir does not dissolve or fade out the confrontation to indicate a major time gap, unlike the usual pattern in the film. The deathbed scene instead comes smack up against the shooting that preceded it, despite the mechanics obviously needed to get Boeldieu settled into those quarters.

This last scene in the former chapel brackets the first one at Wintersborn. The camera again tracks in the opening shot, but this time it moves from a close-up of a small crucifix and other accouterments in a priest's valise (instead of the huge crucifix) and continues up to Rauffenstein, who helps the priest with his overcoat. Last rites have presumably been administered, and Rauffenstein's orderly holds a lit taper as subdued music fills the soundtrack until the end of the scene, music that recalls the earlier tête-à-tête at times.

The intimations of death that opened Wintersborn are magnified here in an impressive array of crosses. The attending priest is laden down: a cross on his collar and a larger one hanging around his neck; an Iron Cross, like Rauffenstein's, on his chest; and two Red Cross armbands.

After the priest and orderly leave, and a soldier updates Rauffenstein, the opening shot continues as the camera tracks with Rauffenstein past yet another photograph of a woman to, at last, a full-blooded woman, a nurse with Red Cross insignias on her coif and arm, sitting by Boeldieu; she gets up and remains in the background as Rauffenstein replaces her at his dying friend's side.

Renoir cuts to a closer two-shot and Boeldieu tries to comfort Rauffenstein: "Français ou Allemand, le devoir, c'est le devoir" ("French or German, duty is duty"). And, as in their other exchanges, they talk mainly in broad, historical terms, distancing themselves from their feelings and giving the scene an elegiac air. A realist, as ever, Boeldieu analytically goes over the sequence of events, trying to reassure Rauffenstein that it was an accident.

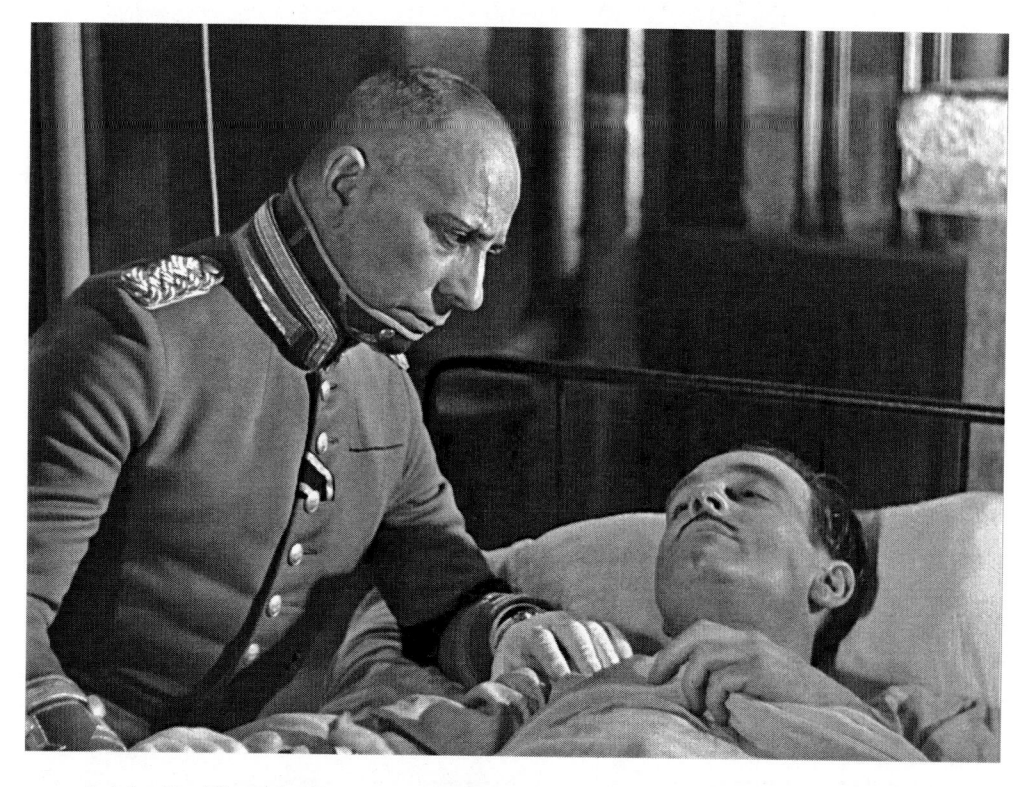

A dying Boeldieu (abed) comforts Rauffenstein: "Le devoir, c'est le devoir" (*Photofest*).

10. Boeldieu and Rauffenstein

When Boeldieu says that he is not the one to be pitied since he will soon be gone, Rauffenstein responds by musing about himself: "Pas fini de traîner une existence inutile" ("Not finished dragging out a useless existence"). Here is one of those few lines that lectures too much and Stroheim handles it awkwardly, trying unsuccessfully to sound natural. For Rauffenstein, it lacks his usual safety net of irony and detachment.

Boeldieu gallantly welcomes his own death: "Pour vous et moi, c'est une bonne solution" ("For you and me, it's a good solution"). He has satisfied his personal code of honor; after being hit, he had raised his hand toward his head as if attempting to salute, in recognition of a duty fulfilled. And though resigned to a democratized society, Boeldieu knows he would not fit into it easily. His admission to Rauffenstein that death provides a good solution, as he lies dying, brings them closer and counters their polite disagreement during the tête-à-têtes.

This shot runs for 105 seconds; it is the second longest in the movie, befitting the scene's importance. To be held together for such a long time in a two-shot reinforces their reconciliation by contrasting it with the fragmented confrontation in the courtyard, presented in quick cuts. Renoir returns here to the long takes that distinguished Hallbach and lends greater support for their renewed solidarity.

This is their final time together as soul mates but, as with the soldier at Rauffenstein's side in the courtyard, again they are chaperoned, this time by the nurse. She interrupts them, warning that Boeldieu needs rest; Rauffenstein gets up and leaves. And they are separated.

In the next shot, Rauffenstein stands by a cabinet, poised to drink a shot of spirits, when he hears the nurse's voice from behind him, calling out softly: "Herr Major." Rauffenstein understands. He downs his drink, ramrod straight, as he had at the German canteen. Back then he celebrated the downing of Boeldieu's plane; now he marks his death. The reappearance of that gesture defines the arc of the film to this moment. And insignificant words again signal a large occasion.

Renoir reprises the opening track of the scene in the next shot, though closer now, as Rauffenstein heads to the bed once again and the nurse looks at a watch pinned to her uniform and shuts off the transfusion tube. This camera movement makes the death of Boeldieu more palpable by paralleling that track, only three shots earlier, when he was alive; now his corpse is the still point at the end of a similar tracking movement. The camera pans down and Rauffenstein's gloved hand, with his wristwatch visible, passes over Boeldieu's face to close his eyes. Those gloves, which first appeared in the opening shot of Wintersborn, connect the two men one last time.

But before the end of Wintersborn — a frozen frame. Time out.

In *La Grande Illusion*, time seems to be a minor factor. In the opening shot, Maréchal, eager to leave the air base, asks Halphen when he will be going to Épernay and finds it will be in a half-hour. But time is most often associated with more urgent forms of escape. Maréchal asks the time at Hallbach as he waits for the escape plan to go into effect. At Wintersborn there's a close-up of a clock before the diversion. Later, a French prisoner checks his watch to resume the noisemaking. And Boeldieu, after being shot, looks at his watch to be sure Maréchal and Rosenthal have had enough time to escape. Then the nurse recording the time of death and Rauffenstein's wristwatch in this scene.

The other clocks and watches in the film are less central to the plot. At Hallbach's reception area, the English officer (Jacques Becker) drops his watch on the floor and defiantly crushes it with his boot. At the farm, a grandfather clock stands in the background.

There is nowhere to go at Hallbach or Wintersborn and, on the farm, the idyll is all the more an oasis for being outside of time. Only at the end of the prison camp sections does time become increasingly relevant, and pressing. But, underneath the surface, the passage of time has an influence in *La Grande Illusion*. Renoir's use of reprise allows the earlier selves of the characters to haunt the movie, and time is being regularly marked.

Time in. The shot continues.

As Rauffenstein leaves the deathbed, his clenched fist, with the wristwatch now more visible, accidentally bumps into the transfusion tube, bringing it to life. The tube still jiggles in the shot after his exit, next to the corpse. A memorable moment, held fast. And a moment illustrating the truism that it's all in the details, those quirks and oddities sprinkled throughout a narrative that enliven a film. That which is original and specific. As in any art form.

This reprised tracking shot, which starts on Rauffenstein and ends on Boeldieu, alone and dead, is sharply in contrast to the scene's opening track on Rauffenstein that bustled with the priest, the orderly and the reporting soldier, and which finally ended as a three-shot with the nurse standing behind the two officers. All that life and activity in the initial shot is drained in the reprise, except for the animated tube.

In the final shot at Wintersborn, the camera tracks with Rauffenstein as he walks toward the window and settles a knee on the bench, above which stands a saddle mounted for display. A suggestion of the riderless horse in military funerals? The camera movement toward the bench is larger than the one in the opening track of the private tête-à-tête with Boeldieu, and this time Rauffenstein is alone. The track develops into a close-up and Rauffenstein cuts the potted geranium by the window.

The largest misstep in *La Grande Illusion* is perhaps the banal symbolism that underlies Rauffenstein cutting the only flower in the fortress. It might be defended as a natural reflection of his grief but, in movie terms, especially in a movie that is evocative and expressive rather than merely realistic, it seems too explicit as a symbol.

A plaintive variation of the tête-à-tête music plays over the shot and this traditional use of background music to ramp up emotion also weakens the scene. And outside the window, snow falls for the first and only time in the film—a somewhat egregious metaphor, though at least preferable to rain streaking the panes.

Further, Rauffenstein first holds up the cut geranium in his left hand, then shifts it to his other hand and holds the flower still, as if posing for the camera ("I'm ready for my close-up"), before he removes it. The artificialness of that pose belabors the symbolism, unlike the use of crosses at the beginning and end of Wintersborn, which are incidental to the action and more effectively work as overtones.

On a less obvious level, Rauffenstein's gesture for his fallen friend recalls the memorial wreath at the German canteen, though the tone is darker here.

Yet, for a movie taking place during war, death has been largely absent. There is first the written, and symbolic, reference to death (the wreath with its banners). Then, at Hallbach, the teacher comes upon the German guards carrying the stretcher with a prisoner (who is probably dead). Now, for the third and last time, death returns, and with a familiar face.

But Boeldieu's death is also a bit absurd. He could have remained hidden in the upper reaches of the fortress, or else surrendered without fear of anything more than the mildest questioning. The shooting makes little sense since there was no rush to capture Boeldieu; the guards might have simply followed his route to catch up with him. There was also no reason for him to expose himself to gunfire and then defy Rauffenstein.

One can perhaps see these actions as those of a man bent on suicide, consciously undertaken or not. At one point in the chase, for instance, he mockingly plays his pennywhistle and guards stop in their tracks, turn, and fire on him.

His death, in any case, is only partly the consequence of an act of heroism. Yet, with Rauffenstein, Boeldieu appears to have accepted the pretense of a tragic imperative that ended in the fatal shooting (the "solution") as he gamely plays out the scenario. Also part of the game is that Rauffenstein accepts the responsibility of trying to wound Boeldieu superficially; only an officer of equal caliber would take on such a task.

And so Wintersborn closes. A crucifix opens this part and Boeldieu's Christ-like sacrifice ends it, with death embraced, at least in some measure, for the sake of others. And for the first time there is a fade-out instead of a dissolve between sections. Renoir makes a cleaner break to the wildly different part that follows, set outside the prison camps.

An almost subliminal effect flickers briefly in the last few seconds of the final shot when Rauffenstein's shadow passes over the cut plant, as he leaves, and the shot begins to fade out. The shell of his former self had marked the passing of an era—and here, now, is the shadow of that shadow of a man, similar but on a much smaller scale than Renoir's magnificent closing shot of *La Règle du jeu* when shadows of equally outmoded characters flit along the walls of the country chateau.

There is also a moment in this final scene at Wintersborn that resonates immediately in the next part. It's the abrupt, and somewhat shocking, appearance of the nurse, who, though subordinate, is the first woman seen alongside men (unlike the old women outside the gates of Hallbach). This nurse provides care and, with the cross on her headpiece, can be seen as an angel of death. Solemnly, after Boeldieu dies, she notes the time and writes it down in a little book. A recording angel of sorts.

The nurse establishes a small foothold in the world of men, a record-keeper who is a trained professional. Renoir extends this foothold in the first shot of the next part. And, soon after, Elsa makes her entrance.

Hallbach and Wintersborn are over, though war will yet claim dominion.

11

Elsa's Farm

> *"If a French farmer should find himself dining at the same table as a French financier, those two Frenchmen would have nothing to say to each other, each being unconcerned with the other's interests. But if a French farmer meets a Chinese farmer they will find any amount to talk about. This theme of the bringing together of men through their callings and common interests has haunted me all my life and does so still. It is the theme of* La Grande Illusion *and it is present, more or less, in all my works."*
> — Jean Renoir in *My Life and My Films* (p. 280)

The last part of *La Grande Illusion* opens in the German countryside with a woman leading a workhorse along a deserted road — a riderless horse now up on the screen, after the empty saddle at Wintersborn in the previous shot. This opening signals a new world, far from the drab interiors of the prison camps or the thoroughbreds remembered by Boeldieu and Rauffenstein. The silence on the cut, except for the tramp of the horse, makes a sharp contrast with the lush orchestral music over Boeldieu's death. This will be a simpler world.

The camera tracks down to Maréchal and Rosenthal hiding by the side of the road, wearing civilian clothes; at last, no military uniforms are in evidence. And the gender confusion that began with the androgynous voice singing "Frou-Frou" at the start of the film, and which continued at Hallbach, surfaces again when, in the next shot, closer to them, Rosenthal mistakes the figure leading the horse for a man.

There is an important psychological aspect to this opening since it not only features French characters, as at the beginning of the film, but a provisional freedom exists. Along with the natural setting, this gives the impression of something different under way and detoxifies *La Grande Illusion* of the constraints that had characterized the camps. No national antagonisms or competing allegiances. That is a thing of the past. For the moment.

The blowup on the mountain road occurs shortly afterward. This crisis, coming so soon after the death of Boeldieu, quickens the tempo considerably. And that screaming match between Maréchal and Rosenthal, unlike the war of civilized words in the courtyard of Wintersborn or the subsequent truce forged in the chapel, is more a bludgeoning than a point-counterpoint debate. It also has a more satisfying resolution. Some of the pent-up frustration that festered throughout the prison camps is vented as Maréchal and Rosenthal manage to draw on what they share in common and move on. With the boil burst, healing can begin.

The first evening on the farm follows this reconciliation earlier that afternoon. By not beginning these farm scenes on a new day, the cohesiveness of this last part as a discrete unit is indicated; the sequence in escape serves not simply as a connecting link between larger parts, like the documentary train shots, but is conjoined with the farm.

Then, all at once, when Elsa enters onto the scene, national background as a fact of life returns, within the modest confines of her home—and with a twist. At Hallbach and Wintersborn there were periods of relief when the French were alone in their pursuits, apart from the guards. But, at the farm, there is less chance to avoid the other side.

This last part acts as a finale and, especially with the fresh start provided by the outdoor scenes, Renoir makes it complete enough to seem almost like a self-contained movie. There's also a distinctive casualness to it. The details of ordinary life and the bantering dialogue, freed now of the prison camps, creates a new feeling, as if starting from scratch, though appropriating two familiar characters from the previous narrative—a narrative which has run its course and been left in the chilly rooms of Wintersborn.

After a relatively slow development of the action at the prison camps, suddenly, in rapid fire—bang, bang, bang—comes the countryside, farm, border. And the pace speeds up, condensed and heightened.

These intensely distilled sequences unfold in spectacular, though understated, fashion. In a little over 24 minutes this finale moves fitfully, back and forth, between connection and separation, as Renoir sorts out some of the film's strands. Although it is only about one-fifth of the movie in length, divisions of religion (the blowup) and gender and nationalism (Elsa) are undermined. There is also perhaps the greatest crisis in the film (the parting of Maréchal from Elsa) and the greatest triumph (their love). As well, a large array of shots and sequences are charged with deep feeling.

The sting is definitely in the tail.

Renoir, then, accomplishes a nifty sleight of hand. After applying a kind of misdirection in focusing so heavily on the camps, he makes this final part, seemingly a mere appendage, unexpectedly profound, and laces it with powerful scenes packed with little filler. And *La Grande Illusion* takes off as it nears its close.

Following the lengthy preoccupation with imprisonment and escape, what proves most crucially important takes place on the farm. Indeed, had the narrative ended with Boeldieu's death, it would have been a great movie with some memorable highlights, but hardly a masterpiece. The last part, instead, transforms the film as each of its sections, unlike in the introduction, features a significant crisis, adding to the emotional impact.

Maréchal and Rosenthal, escaping through the countryside, first in Germany and at the end in Switzerland, open and close the neatly balanced finale; Maréchal and Elsa are the focus of the middle section. These parallel relationships grow, and change, more than any others in the movie, contributing to a headlong rush of momentum to the final shot. But there still remains the counterweight of an ensemble at the farm, reduced now to a chamber group of four people (Lotte included) playing off each other.

The farm section, though only 17 minutes long, is the most complex, varied and cinematically creative section of *La Grande Illusion*. In a film so rich and substantial, the scenes on the farm are especially layered. And Renoir provides a synthesis of what has gone before. Though the farm, unlike Hallbach and Wintersborn, is a peek into the future (a world apart from war), it also recalls the past (a German soldier at a window, memories of Elsa's loved ones and of Boeldieu). But it is primarily rooted in the daily farm life of the present. From the wholehearted engagement of life at Hallbach, through death at Wintersborn, and, on Elsa's farm, a sort of rebirth.

There are several shifts in tone during the farm section. It opens with the tension of the first evening as Maréchal and Rosenthal encounter Elsa. Short shots, often of characters alone, mark the sequence and Renoir usually holds the camera still—a change from the long takes and tracking shots during the escape.

But in the first shot following that evening, which begins with a pan across photographs of Elsa's husband and brothers, Renoir introduces a different, freewheeling approach. The camera begins to move more easily, the takes are longer and Renoir uses more group shots. During this part of the farm, there is the heaviest concentration of tracking shots in the movie. This change of pace contributes to the sense of ease and connection that culminates in the embrace of the lovers and the Christmas morning scene.

The final day and evening on the farm, which follows that Christmas scene immediately, shifts back to a feeling of unease, as Maréchal and Rosenthal must leave. The camera becomes stationary once again.

The farm is also the most intimate section of *La Grande Illusion*. Aside from a single shot of the farmhouse, at least one of the four characters is in every shot, and only one other person (the soldier at the window) temporarily appears on the periphery of this small group as the narrowing of focus from Hallbach to Wintersborn further intensifies.

There is, as well, a synthesis stylistically. Renoir combines tracking shots of the group (Hallbach) with still shots (Wintersborn), making a relatively balanced distribution of these shots at the farm (though not as evenly as at Hallbach).

And although the farm seems to be diametrically opposite to Wintersborn in spirit, it has a similar focal point: the central relationship is between a Frenchman and a German (and, to a degree, both are love stories). Also like Wintersborn, Renoir sometimes uses background music under key scenes. That can be a sign of weakness in a film, but it's not rushed into or overused on the farm and at least serves to place Maréchal and Elsa squarely at center stage, where they belong, celebrated by this traditional use of movie music.

In a pronounced change, Renoir has almost as many shots of Maréchal alone in this section (7) as in the rest of the movie (8). Until the farm, he was most often seen with others, but now he seems his own man and in his element.

Another change is his physical condition. For a large part of the movie, Maréchal struggles along in a weakened state (the broken arm, his solitary confinement). He has also been passive, relying on others; he doesn't take part in the musical revue and at Wintersborn acquiesces to Boeldieu and his escape plan. Once he escapes, he becomes a man of action — returning to Rosenthal after their confrontation and leading him onward. But Maréchal again is physically depleted.

On the farm, he becomes hearty and active. Rosenthal's ankle, instead, must be attended to by Elsa, with shades of the engineer washing Maréchal's feet. And another irony of the film is that this twisted ankle, which frustrated Maréchal during their escape, gives him a reason to stay on the farm, allowing his romance with Elsa to blossom.

The farm section begins in an offhanded way, with the only quasi-surreal moment in the film. After an introductory shot, in which the escaped prisoners become aware of someone outside the barn, Renoir cuts to a medium long shot as Maréchal waits anxiously with Rosenthal and keeps a club ready; the door opens — enter a cow, followed by Elsa (Dita Parlo). A fleeting bit of comic relief.

But most striking about this opening sequence is a sudden burst of shots that separate Elsa visually from each man. Two brief crosscutting sequences, first between Maréchal and Elsa and then between Elsa and Rosenthal, like the shot/countershot sequences at Wintersborn, distance the characters from each other. The camera remains still as the three protagonists are locked into their separate shots. In fact, an uncommonly large number of consecutive still shots of characters alone (9) are compressed into a short timespan (48 seconds). When

11. Elsa's Farm 83

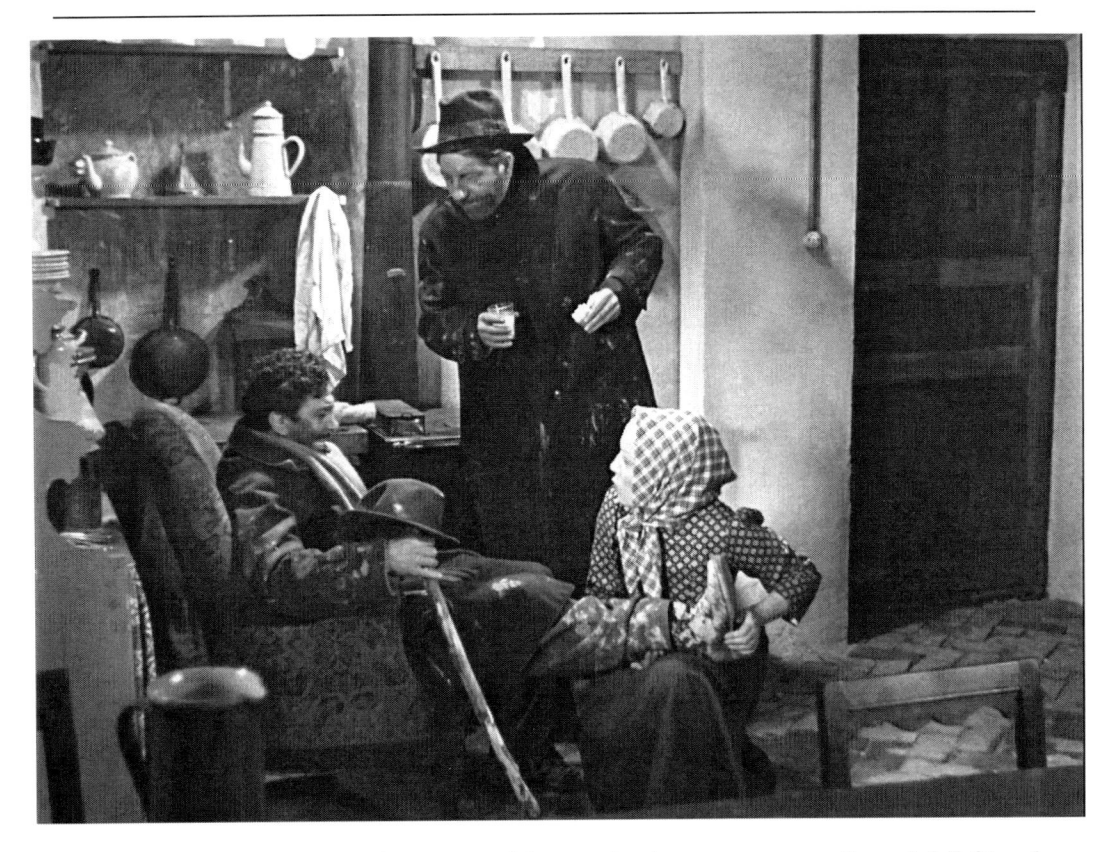

Elsa's farm: the first night, as Elsa (Dita Parlo) opens her home to strangers Rosenthal (left) and Maréchal (***Photofest***).

Maréchal and Rosenthal become more comfortable and follow Elsa into her house, the camera loosens up and Renoir begins to connect them together in longer-held tracking shots.

The appearance of Elsa changes the movie dramatically. Everything that went before establishes a foundation, but her presence signals a new dynamic.

She is, of course, the only three-dimensional woman in *La Grande Illusion*. From the first shot, with Josephine mentioned in the dialogue, women have been peripheral to the film. Other names are also brought up, loaded with affection or longing: Fifi (of Maxim's), "Marguerite" (in the actor's erotically coy showpiece), the Czarina (with hopes for her gift).[1] In addition to these disembodied names, there are other women: the pinups and pictures in the canteens and camps, including at Wintersborn an odd cardboard cut-out of a woman from the shoulders up swiveling on a string; the comments about women preceding Maisonneuve in a skirt; the three (real) women at the prison gates; the men in dresses during the revue; the nurse at Boeldieu's deathbed; and, finally, the woman with the horse, opening the final part.

Not a lot to build on, as Elsa arrives on the scene. Quickly she becomes not just a player but, in some ways, a dominant force. There are more shots of Elsa alone than of either Maréchal or Rosenthal alone on the farm. She has strength of character in seeming to run the farm by herself and will undoubtedly be running it again, after Maréchal and Rosenthal leave.

Elsa is also a mother—and a protective one. In the last shot of the opening scene, Rosenthal cries out when Elsa raises his injured ankle to bathe it; she warns him harshly not to wake her child. Lotte appears in the next shot and becomes the other significant female in the film, though only as a catalyst for the drama around her.

After the more traditional crosscutting and plot elements of an escape story at Wintersborn, all hell breaks loose cinematically on the farm.

This development is bolstered by a greater stylization, in contrast to the essential, though enhanced, realism of the prison camps. The farm seems strangely disconnected from the world at large. In the rest of the film Paris (and its pleasures) is recalled many times, and other places come up as well: Berlin, Lyon, Bordeaux, Jerusalem, Vienna, Amsterdam, Liverpool, and Douaumont (the war) and Switzerland (the safe haven). The outside world, though unseen like the women who are mentioned in passing, is also, like them, lovingly remembered or endowed with expectations.

But not so much at the farm, which seems a world of its own. And at times unreal, as in a dream or fairy tale. It is extraordinary, in the first place, that Elsa invites the escaping Frenchmen into her home so readily and with little hint of anxiety or fear. And apparently no attempt is made to hide Maréchal and Rosenthal. Where, it could be asked, are Elsa's neighbors? And how about the road nearby on which German troops can be heard marching on the first evening?

The farm appears to transcend the nitty-gritty of any "real world" concerns. It remains fresh and unto itself, and Renoir fools around with technique more, as if himself freed from the restraints of the prison camps.

A shot out of the ordinary and relaxed in execution, for example, is a close shot of Elsa walking with Lotte, after waking her at midnight on Christmas Eve to see the crèche. The camera pulls out of focus for a few seconds as they walk, then back into focus, creating a documentary-like effect; there are only a few other pull focus shots in the film but, instead of being on characters, they are more often used in adapting to a distant landscape.

There is also a startling exterior panning shot, after Elsa leaves the barn with her visitors on the first night. As they walk toward the front door of the farmhouse, an eerie and strong glow washes over her and the wall behind them. It has the chiaroscuro effect of a Caravaggio or film noir. Elsa holds a small lamp but, given the extended range of the lighting and the intense shadows as they move, that lamp cannot be the light source, though it is the only possible source from within (or without) the shot.

This flooding of the scene with artificial light from outside the frame, moving along with the actors, assaults the film's generally naturalistic lighting. Another bit of poetic license that, all the same, maybe because of its vividness and brevity, does not attract untoward attention.

Renoir's expansion of his cinematic repertoire continues with the first shot after the opening night and indicates the shift to a growing ease and intimacy. The shot opens on the photograph of a soldier, with Elsa's off-screen commentary that her husband died at Verdun; this is the only time in the film that a character's voice provides narration over an image. Renoir then pans to a group photograph and the camera begins to settle on Elsa as she introduces her brothers by pointing to them, one by one: "Lüttich ... Charleroi ... Tannenberg." A rare acknowledgment at the farm of the outside world. She gathers herself and coldly refers to Germany's "größten Siege" ("greatest victories"). Elsa's bitter irony, uncharacteristic of the film, is unlike the ironic tone of Boeldieu and Rauffenstein, which had been displayed more for amusement.[2]

The pan develops into a track, Elsa walking toward a seated Rosenthal. The camera then pauses before panning to the dining table and coming to rest on Lotte (played by a girl known as "the little [girl] Peters"); she eats alone, with a cross on the wall beyond and

*Elsa pointing out a great victory for Germany: "Tannenberg" (**Photofest**).*

two chairs upended on the table. This ending composition has been weakened, however, by Elsa's explicit statement that the table is now too large, just before the camera pans to illustrate her observation more effectively (and indirectly).

Renoir makes an inversion of technique in this tracking shot. At the French base and German canteen, the camera moves to photographs and posters at the end of tracking shots, mainly as decorative touches to close the shots. And, at Hallbach, Renoir tracks to pictures of the Kaiser and Kaiserin as Germans celebrate the capture of Douaumont. But here Renoir reverses the movement of the camera, investing the scene with poignancy. These photographs have pride of place — for Elsa, and for the camera. They open the shot, as they are commented upon with rueful dignity, and then are connected directly to Lotte (the daughter and niece of the pictured soldiers).

Like Hallbach's window pan, and Rauffenstein mouthing "peut-être" at Wintersborn, the shot is a turning point in this section of the film. The momentum picks up from here, with the action compressed, and Elsa's cheerless manner will, at the last, return on the final day and night at the farm.

In the next shot, Maréchal, now at home on the farm, becomes something of a provider (a role more fitting for Rosenthal or Elsa). He carries hay in the barn for the cow and jokes about their similarities despite being from different countries, wryly crossing borders not only of nationality but of species. Maréchal even refers to himself and the cow as "copains" ("pals"). Near the end of the shot, as he leaves, church bells start ringing and the cow, now alone, turns her head and moos. Again Elsa's cow gets the laughs.

This comedic tone is unusual. With all its qualities, there is not much outright humor in the film, except for the joking around of the actor, Rauffenstein's desiccated barbs, and the amusing scene at Hallbach as English prisoners incongruously pick up their tennis rackets before heading off to new quarters. Otherwise, the ironic wit and teasing is more a subterraneous humor, for an inward pleasure.

Renoir follows with a slightly skewed long shot outside the barn; the bells continue ringing on the soundtrack — a linking of shots, as with the bells marking the recapture of Douaumont during Maréchal's confinement. The slanting angle indicates an easing and relaxation, a switch from the squared-up framing that Renoir usually prefers. And Maréchal yawns, stretching out his arms toward the edge of the frame, chickens in the distance. Time is also stretched, unhurried. No rush. The camera tracks with him as he idly sings a tune he had sung at Hallbach in the gardening scene; then, after burying an ax in a tree stump, he heads into the farmhouse. Uncommon shots like this casually tilted one help set the farm apart.

The farm is also unusual, certainly, in that people go freely about their daily lives. Dialogue is never about class and rarely about war, and the characters are not defined by their roles as prisoners or jailers, French or German.

In this concentration on civilian life, Elsa and Lotte become the only developed female characters in *La Grande Illusion* and are, significantly, known solely by their first names. Such informality emphasizes this mother and daughter as people, above anything else.

Oddly, throughout the film, men are known by their ranks and last names (except for Arthur, the German guard). We also learn a little about their professions, stressing their roles in society. At Hallbach the roll call does not include the engineer or teacher and we never even learn their names; the actor is identified as "Cartier" in two bits of off-screen dialogue, but the name never becomes firmly attached to him.

It is especially curious and not realistic that, on the farm, and even after Maréchal and Elsa become lovers, the first names of Maréchal and Rosenthal are still not used and remain unknown. This bolsters the impression that they are merely visitors at Elsa's home and must eventually return to that other world of rank and serial number back at the front. The farm will only briefly be a refuge.

A basic transition occurs on the farm. Maréchal starts the movie as part of an urban world — staring at the gramophone record and listening to the recorded voice of a cabaret singer. At Hallbach the prisoners talk about the theater and Paris bistros, as well as bike races and fashions, and they put on a sophisticated, if amateurish, revue. And the dumping of dirt from under the floorboards onto a restricted plot of land has a covert purpose instead of being a sincere attempt at gardening. Wintersborn continues that isolation from nature (the lone geranium).

Further, domesticated animals are evident at the camps. In Hallbach's courtyard, military horses prance around and a team hitched to a cart brings in crates; pictures of dogs and horses are on the prison walls. Soldiers patrol the grounds at Wintersborn with large dogs on leashes, and the pet squirrel is confined to its cage.

Maréchal must adapt to farm life in a cottage surrounded by open space, harbored by a woman and far from the clannish gathering of men, as barnyard life takes over. The cow and the chickens in the yard solidify this change. During the Christmas celebration, Maréchal affectionately says to Lotte as he puts her to bed, "Bonsoir, grenouille" (literally, "Good evening, frog"), and in the next shot he picks up a donkey from the crèche (which includes an ox) before saying goodnight to Elsa. Even though he must leave the farm, at the end he is immersed, knee-deep, in the snows of a wide valley. The natural world prevails.

Renoir also inverts other patterns at the farm. The earlier scenes in the film are filled with men smoking, almost incessantly; the engineer and the teacher puff on pipes while others indulge in cigarettes. Alcohol is evident as well, from drinks placed on the table behind Maréchal in the film's opening shot — to wine, cognac and beer at Hallbach — to Rauffenstein's glass of spirits in remembrance of Boeldieu.

At the farm, there isn't any drinking or smoking. A traditional man's world no more. Smoke drifts up lazily from a pot on the stove and from celebratory candles blown out on the Christmas tree, in contrast to the extinguished candle as the actor starts to pass out in the tunnel and the single taper preceding Boeldieu's death later.

Meals, too, are of course lavish before the farm. At Wintersborn, though a more Spartan environment than Hallbach, an elegant silver service, with sausage and bread, has been set before Rauffenstein in the opening scene. Healthy food even has negative connotations for the teacher at Hallbach, who bitterly recounts how vegetarianism led to his conscription.

Elsa's food is simple and sustaining: milk and bread on the first night; bowls of soup for Lotte; a plate with an apple and sweets by the Christmas tree and more apples hanging from it, in the tradition of Père Noël; potatoes used to make the crèche, with Lotte taking Joseph to eat in bed; apples on the table in Maréchal's room; even the cow's hay. When Maréchal leaves, Elsa presents him with a small package of food, no doubt the wholesome fare of country life.

And coffee appears, at first, in a new light on the farm. At Wintersborn, Rauffenstein had branded his morning brew "Jauche Kaffee" ("slurry coffee" or "liquid manure coffee") in disgust. On Christmas morning, by contrast, coffee is an indication of love; it will later be offered listlessly by Rosenthal as the lovers face separation. Then, with the table set for a final meal together, Elsa slowly pours coffee but, overcome, rushes away. This last meal interrupted like the one at the German canteen, and with a similar outcome — Maréchal leaving for his next adventure, forced on him by the realities of war.

Pots and pans, crockery, and cutlery are plentiful and put to use on the farm. By contrast, at the prison camps, pots and cans of food serve merely as décor or are mobilized to facilitate escape: an empty can as the alarm signal; others fashioned into the actor's candlestick and his communication tube in the tunnel; and, at Wintersborn, pots and pans banged to force the roll call.

As opposed to the crucifixes and crosses at Wintersborn, Elsa has a modest crucifix on her wall and an Iron Cross draped over the photograph of her husband. And instead of pictures of the Kaiser or Hindenburg, there are ones of common soldiers (her husband and brothers), religious figures and children. In addition, military boots give way to slippers and wooden clogs, as Elsa removes her clogs on the first night and Maréchal clunkily takes off his pair, coming in from the barn later. Uniforms, and the coats and hats during the escape, are replaced by more casual civies, probably the clothes of Elsa's husband.

Extending this atmosphere of domesticity, there are luminous shots in the opening farmhouse scene that have a Vermeer-like quality: Elsa's simple gesture in pouring milk (his painting, *The Milkmaid*?); the tableau formed as she bends over, tending to Rosenthal's ankle; and, especially, the first shot of this scene when she walks away from the camera to the back of the house through two doorways, turns on a light, and disappears around the corner, briefly leaving an empty interior in the distance flooded with mystery — again, a motif of Vermeer's work.

Another characteristic of the farm is the varied nature of its night scenes. The prison camp sequences that take place at night involve theater, of one sort or another, and end disastrously. At Hallbach, the play-acting at the window and the actor's theatrical bravura are followed by his near suffocation, and Maréchal stopping the musical revue leads to his confinement. Boeldieu of course acts out his doomed role in the glare of spotlights.

At the farm, the opening evening is fraught with the danger of Elsa coming upon the two fugitives and the German soldier's appearance, but it ends without further incident. The Christmas celebration at midnight, with the homemade crèche and graphophone music, qualifies as a kind of theatrical production and ends with the embrace of the lovers, fully reversing the harsh denouements of night scenes at the camps. And this gathering marks the birth of Jesus, not his death as commemorated by the crucifix at Wintersborn.

The farm sequence closes, as it began, at night, but this time there is the pain of Maréchal and Rosenthal leaving. And their safe house at the farm comes to an end.

There are a striking number of inventive moments on the farm. One of the most graceful and expressive shots ends on the embrace of Maréchal and Elsa, with the interweaving movement of camera and characters demonstrating Renoir's *legato* style.

In an oddly choreographed, and long-held, panning shot in the main room immediately preceding this shot, the three characters say good night and Maréchal walks to his room in the background, opens the door, and reaches in to switch on the light inside; he then returns to the foreground, blows out the Christmas tree's candles and gently says good night again to Elsa, who is frozen in place, and heads off, curiously, not to his own room but to Rosenthal's adjoining room.

Renoir then cuts, from within Maréchal's room, to a medium shot of the doorway that opens onto the adjoining room as Maréchal enters through it into his own room, with Rosenthal briefly visible in the background. It's an offhanded beginning for what will become a climactic shot, and Rosenthal is included; the group remains intact, even during a shot that will end with the embrace, in private. Maréchal closes the door behind him and, from a bunch of apples spread out on a table, picks one up and takes a bite. The camera shifts position as he starts to close the door to the main room beyond, at which point he notices Elsa still standing by the crèche.

So, what has happened to this point? The contrived choreography of the previous shot has allowed Maréchal the opportunity to see Elsa through the open door. It would have been more natural in the earlier shot for him to blow out the candles on the way to his room and then shut the door behind him. There was no need to turn on the light in his room, leave the door open, and then double back to blow the candles out and enter Rosenthal's room (instead of his own). His circular route seems unnecessarily elaborate and awkward. In particular, it is cinematically elaborate, arranged that way in order to set up the next shot. That first shot is, in effect, the beginning of a staged dance in which Maréchal, the principal dancer, will eventually complete a 360° turn as his ballerina remains stationary.

Now, in the shot of the embrace, Maréchal has come full circle, back to his doorway onto the main room, but facing outward this time. When he sees Elsa through that doorway, one's mind perhaps unconsciously remembers the unnatural convolutions embarked upon by Maréchal, and by the camera, conspiring to get his door open so that he can now see her. This contributes to a sense of anticipation since Renoir, in cold blood, has maneuvered it so Maréchal can finally connect with Elsa under the ruse that it all happened by apparent chance (the open door).

The stylization of movement in the first shot, which prepares for the coming together of the lovers in the second, exemplifies the nonrealistic approach that Renoir, at times, so unobtrusively applies in *La Grande Illusion*.

11. Elsa's Farm

And it's a provocation in itself that Elsa has not moved. A restrained eroticism informs this figure of a woman encased in black up to her neck, standing rock still and wearing a small cross around her neck, eyes fixed blankly ahead. A religious picture of a bearded patriarch holding a baby child hovers above her head in the background.

Elsa must know what she is doing by remaining in full view through the open door — and the innate voyeurism of movies puts the viewer in Maréchal's place, watching over his shoulder. She makes no direct appeal to him; there is simply the telling fact that she has stood in the same spot where she had bidden him good night in the previous shot, as though waiting for him to reach the point where he is able to see her again.

Maréchal slowly starts to move his body through the doorway; finally Elsa raises her eyes to him. He is clearly not predatory and his ambling shuffle bears no resemblance to the cocky gait at the French base with which he set out on his journey. Maréchal's body momentarily blocks out Elsa as he moves and, in a wonderfully gentle gesture, as if being careful not to bruise it, he places his half-eaten apple on a nearby bureau. The camera stays fixed in place and the music continues its crescendo as he eases closer to Elsa, seeming to gauge her reaction, with her eyes fixed on him.

When he reaches Elsa, the religious picture beyond is blocked out. She moves deliberately into Maréchal's shoulder, the crèche by their side. Seen in the distance, framed by the doorway, they embrace, gingerly, reduced to moving in slow motion. An unshaded light bulb hangs above them. There is no kiss, nor will they ever kiss (on-screen) in their short time together.

This final framing in long shot typifies the film's understatement, even here in a classic

End of a dance — the lovers embrace (*Photofest*).

movie moment in which, since the kinetoscope, a close-up has seemed practically an obligation.

As soon as they embrace, the shot is quickly faded out. Renoir, who rarely lingers, cuts to a sunny exterior shot of the farmhouse in the distance, set in a wintry countryside. A clashing shot of documentary objectivity. He also creates a jarring clash on the soundtrack as lively music cuts short the ecstatic strains covering the embrace, similar to the effect at Hallbach in shifting dissonantly from the patriotic German song to the actor's cabaret number. The sound cut is particularly abrupt here, even for *La Grande Illusion*, and the effect is almost disconcerting as Renoir unceremoniously dumps the romantic music for a tune that skips along cheerfully.

Likewise noteworthy is the concision of the shot ending with the embrace. The relationship of Maréchal and Elsa changes from friends to lovers within a leisurely shot, rather than cutting to a new perspective to present them more intimately. And the change is also suggested metaphorically as Maréchal crosses the threshold of his room.

Perhaps the symbolism of the apple, bitten into by Maréchal, flaws the shot slightly. True, the farm conjures up a kind of paradise and Maréchal's voluntary expulsion later is especially painful. Even so, the pointed nature of the symbol is questionable, though at least a broader sense of fecundity and sensuousness, with the table full of apples, dilutes the pointedness to some degree. As well, a depth of feeling and an innocence that is not often found in Renoir's work pervades the farm. The relationship of the lovers seems to be based as much on a mature understanding, and mutual empathy, as on physical attraction. Love is never as wholesome for him as in *La Grande Illusion*.

And the important role played by a child in the love story, as it develops, is also unusual in his films. It possibly expressed something deeply nostalgic, even sorrowful, in Renoir's makeup. In *Renoir, My Father* (published in 1962) he wrote movingly about the death of his beloved surrogate mother, Gabrielle Renard-Slade, regretting that there was no one left to remember the old days "or to open a window onto the past which seems to me much as the Garden of Eden must have seemed to Adam after he tasted the fruit of the Tree of Knowledge."[3] Such a Proustian passage captures not only longing and nostalgia but also an awareness of the fall that, at least in the mythology of the Bible, comes with sexual knowledge.

Soon, a real window will be opened and then closed, and Maréchal, too, must leave his Eden — and his Eve.

The recurring motif of windows in *La Grande Illusion* provides some memorable moments. Renoir makes this metaphor for escape effective by keeping it incidental to the action. And, at the farm, a reversal occurs in its use.

The window as a dividing point between outside (the Germans) and inside (the French) is first established at Hallbach when the prisoners hang the blanket over their window to hide the nightly digging. But it comes to the fore in the close-up window pan and, later, the shot of them looking out the window as German soldiers celebrate the fall of Douaumont.

At Wintersborn, windows are associated with escape: Boeldieu hides the rope outside a window, and Maréchal and Rosenthal later shimmy down that rope, hung through another opening. And when the prisoners begin their diversionary noisemaking, one of the German officers gossiping about Rauffenstein gets up and opens a window; as the shot ends, he listens to the cacophony coming through that window, clearly unsettled by this development. The prisoners are temporarily the ones with the upper hand, on the outside.

But Renoir reverses this use of the motif at the farm, on the first evening, as the farmhouse becomes a shelter for the fugitives and it's the outside that poses a threat, as at Hallbach. During a three-shot on Maréchal, Rosenthal and Elsa in the kitchen, the sound of German soldiers marching and singing begins to build ominously (recalling the soundtrack over the window pan). There's a nice touch when they freeze in place and Renoir tracks around Maréchal and Elsa standing together, with Rosenthal sitting to the side in an armchair, as though the camera is circling a group of statues. The three of them are united for the moment as they hold still and wait silently, unsure of each other and of what lies ahead. After a few knocks on some shutters, Elsa heads to the window.

In a closer shot, she opens the shuttered window to reveal a fresh-faced German soldier (Carl Koch), who smiles at the peacefulness of her home. He says, with resignation, he would rather stay there but "Dienst ist Dienst" ("duty is duty"). This reprises the phrase Boeldieu used on his deathbed, bridging not only nationality but class.

The appearance of this soldier is something of a shock, a reminder of the prison camps that seem already to have existed in another lifetime. But Elsa closes the shutters on that world, and the sound of soldiers fades away as she returns to Maréchal and Rosenthal. This is the last time that the two sides will be linked by Germans singing or playing music in the background — from the barbed wire sequence, to the window pan and the Douaumont celebration, to this moment. Always with the Germans free and on the outside, and the French, on the defensive, inside.

This sequence presents Elsa with a difficult test of loyalty to her country. Though it would have been safer to give up the strangers in her kitchen, compassion proves stronger than the cold logic of war. Harboring these two men is a brave act and a truer strengthening of the bond across nations than the comfortable relationship of Boeldieu and Rauffenstein.

Renoir makes his most expressive use of the window motif in two shots toward the end of the farm scenes. The first shot takes place on the Christmas morning after the embrace. In a medium shot, his back to the camera, Rosenthal leans out a window, enjoying the landscape beyond; bouncy music fills the soundtrack. As he turns and starts to leave, the camera moves gently outward, passing through the window, pulling focus on the distant landscape and coming to rest when that landscape is alone in the image.

By eliminating the confining edges of this window, Renoir allows the unbounded movie frame to fully embrace the countryside. He frees the camera itself, letting it float high in the great outside. It is an expansive movement, the tracking shot in the film that most fully expresses a feeling of liberation.

Once again, Renoir's tact has paid off. This specific camera movement is masterful here since it has been held back, only to be let loose near the end to encompass a brief moment in the sun.

It also inverts the dollying movement at Hallbach that sets up the close-up window pan, in which the camera also moves out a window but faces inward and traps the prisoners inside; this time the tracking camera both moves and faces outward. And it reverses the direction of the track opening the feet-washing scene, which moves from the actor outside their room to the engineer and Maréchal inside, restoring the window frame along the way and establishing a sense of enclosure.

Until the last part, *La Grande Illusion* is relentlessly closed-in and claustrophobic, as in those tracks. After the traveling shots from the train, the outside world can only be seen obscurely through doorways or openings — the shots aimed out the doorway of the German canteen with indistinct scenery beyond, the landscape outside Hallbach as the old women watch the recruits (with a few farmers in the distance), the surrounding countryside at Wintersborn glimpsed through an archway during the tour, and later Maréchal and Rosenthal scrambling outside the castle's walls. But even the beauty of the natural settings as the last part begins is sullied by the blowup in the mountains.

Rauffenstein had called out to his orderly to open the window. Renoir, finally, does just that — and then dispenses with the window itself.

But in tapping into the tragic nature underlying *La Grande Illusion*, Renoir upends the effect of this track only five shots later. In a much lengthier medium shot, standing in front of a closed and curtained window, Rosenthal tells Elsa that he and Maréchal must leave. She heads off and he opens the window, revealing Maréchal in the middle distance as he leans against a cart. Rosenthal calls him in, saying without enthusiasm that there is some hot coffee; this comes soon after Elsa's excited announcement that coffee was ready, days before perhaps but only moments earlier in film-time.

Maréchal exits the shot and Rosenthal closes the window. No music and no camera movement this time. And no encompassing landscape, or pull focus to feature it — only a slight pull focus off Rosenthal as he opens the window and then a focus onto him again in closing it. This curtained window, set within the film's restricting frame, shuts in Rosenthal (and the camera) before he leaves the shot. At the end, all three characters have exited, briefly leaving the scene emptied of life.

This still shot caps a terse, but vivid, exposition of plot since it takes Renoir less than two minutes to move convincingly from the liberated camera moving through the window to this very different moment.

The motif of doors and doorways is also adjusted on the farm. At the German canteen, its doorway provides a backdrop for scenes of captivity (three times). At Hallbach, doors, like its windows, divide the French inside from the Germans outside. The diversion at Wintersborn is shown largely through open doors, with Germans rushing in and out; there's even a playful shot where two prisoners furtively exchange rooms, anticipating the arrival of guards, as if playing a game of escape from one room to another while the actual escape plan is under way. And Rauffenstein is sometimes framed in doorways or arches, as if trapped in his own cage like the pet squirrel of the prisoners.

But, at the farm, doorways signal change and connect people more closely. Elsa enters the barn, changing everything, and then welcomes Maréchal and Rosenthal into her home through the front door and, ultimately, into her life.

Most noticeably, the Christmas celebration is structured around doorways. The doorjambs of her room frame Lotte in bed as she is awoken by Elsa before being led toward the crèche, a doorway opening onto the festive setup; Maréchal later carries Lotte back through it to her cozy and safe room beyond. The long tracking shot as the adults say goodnight begins with Maréchal, and then Elsa, exiting Lotte's room and ends as he enters Rosenthal's room. And of course the intricate shot of the embrace starts and ends on doorways.

The last shot on a doorway, as Maréchal and Rosenthal leave Elsa, breaks this pattern, making it more comparable to the setting of Maréchal's final scene with Boeldieu at Hallbach.

One of the most original aspects of *La Grande Illusion* is the way that Renoir makes use of language. At the most basic level, the fact that several languages are spoken has led to one more way that the film is sometimes undervalued. In addition to French, German and English, there are brief snatches of Russian. It can be all too easy to forget, or at least not acknowledge, that Renoir strengthens his film's realism by having the characters speak in their native tongues.

Renoir does not expropriate language and impose French on the world he portrays. At the time of *La Grande Illusion*, such respect for the diversity of people and nations was notable. By embracing the appropriate language of the characters, Renoir draws attention to national barriers and yet, in a paradox, undermines those divisions by honoring the integrity of disparate cultures.

Still, in terms of language, an imbalance, and a chasm, between the two warring sides essentially remains intact throughout the prison camps. French, naturally, dominates the film, and there is only some crossover. Among the Germans, Rauffenstein and Arthur speak extensively in French, and the mechanic at the canteen and two Wintersborn guards try a bit; the actor, Rosenthal and Maréchal manage to muster a few words of German. But on the farm French and German are more equally spoken and a balance is reached.

On a much deeper level, making use of language apart from its meaning, Renoir shows that it can be as relative and ambiguous as anything else in his film. Language first comes into play, in this sense, in the relationship of Boeldieu and Rauffenstein. English affirms their solidarity but, at the end, becomes a measure of how far apart they have drifted.

In counterpoint to them, minor characters also speak English. The British officer at Hallbach taunts his captors by asking, "What do you want, my watch?," and stomps on it. Later, the Englishman in the revue certainly breaches national lines by asking in English for the French anthem.

And Maréchal futilely tries to warn another British officer about the tunnel as the two men talk over each other in their own languages, to cross purposes, one desperate and the other bewildered. The irony that the completed tunnel may go to waste, because of this inability to break through the language barrier, is only intensified by the officer's apology that he doesn't understand French, adding a few words he knows: "Bon voyage, bon voyage." The attempt to reach across the divide, done for the sake of good manners, delineates this gulf more precisely. The officer then reverts to English: "Thank you. Thank you."

Language as a foreign tongue assumes critical importance at the farm. The developing relationship of Maréchal and Elsa, in particular, can be traced by the way that French and German, irrespective of the words spoken, act as an obstacle or bridge, reveal despair or express love. Beyond meaning.

When Elsa first discovers the two men in the barn, Maréchal tries out some German words and she asks if he understands German; he responds: "Nein — nein." Rosenthal, understanding German, interprets for Maréchal, who remains suspicious of Elsa and says he doesn't trust her when she invites them into her house. He stays on guard until she gets water for Rosenthal's ankle and asks Maréchal if he is hungry. He then answers in French and assures Rosenthal, who interprets needlessly, that he understands. This first step indicates a beginning.

Soon after the first night, there is a two-shot of Rosenthal sitting with Lotte as she happily counts off numbers for him in German; the camera tracks up to Maréchal, who has come in from the barn and, in disjunction with this innocent scene, stares intently at Elsa (off-screen). Taking no notice of the math demonstration, he instead remains zeroed in on her, mesmerized and dazed. It is the first erotic charge in the movie. Behind his head, silver spoons and a fork in a rack shine luminously, linking Maréchal to this domestic paradise. An incandescent, and quietly expressive, shot.

Renoir then cuts to Elsa, on her knees as she scrubs the floor. Though hardly a romantic scene, there's an intimate vulnerability to it. Embarrassed by Maréchal's clear attraction to her, she stands up and asks him to get water.

In a wide shot, with Elsa on the other side of the frame from him, and Rosenthal and Lotte in the background, Maréchal struggles to translate: "Moi ... chercher ... Wasser ... huh?" He laughs at this polyglot attempt to form a sentence and they smile at each other. For the first time, French and German words have been joined together in a single phrase. The progress of their love is measured by such incremental improvements in the manipulation of language.

The Christmas Eve celebration brings a larger change. The opening shot in the scene is a close-up of the crèche with its straw roof—that material more constructively put to use here than the straw packing for the Russian books at Wintersborn. Renoir then tracks to a wider shot of the grownups. On the wall behind them, the photograph of Elsa's brothers and the one of her husband draped in black are muted reminders of death hanging, literally, over them. The shot ends with Rosenthal winding up the graphophone, its slender bell recalling the first shot of the film, which is soon recalled in another way.

In the next shot, as Maréchal turns to put out the light, getting ready for Lotte, he gallantly holds Elsa's hand aloft and nearly bumps into her as she stands beside him; they pause briefly, relishing their physical proximity. But this evening is for Lotte, and Renoir does not extend their moment together.

During the gathering at the crèche, Lotte wants to eat the baby Jesus and Maréchal laughingly warns her, "Streng verboten" ("Strictly forbidden"), adding an endearment in German.

"Moi ... chercher ... Wasser": Maréchal reaches out to Elsa, with Lotte ("la petite Peters") and Rosenthal in the background (*Photofest*).

A deft reprise of the familiar words. At Hallbach, prison regulations are twice read aloud to the prisoners, and both times Maréchal mocks the severity of "streng verboten" by sarcastically parroting the phrase; later, "verboten" is on the sign near the barbed wire fence and even on another one seen from a train, after Hallbach. Maréchal trots the phrase out again, at Wintersborn, as he surrenders his pennywhistle to the angry guards. But now it comes back as a light-hearted joke and connects him affectionately to Lotte.

Elsa and Maréchal are soon more firmly coupled by language. In a medium group shot, Maréchal carries Lotte toward her room and the music from the graphophone wobbles as the machine starts to run down.

Then, in a closer group shot, the music comes to a stop and all is quiet for the stunning exchange that follows. Maréchal holds Lotte in his arms and asks Rosenthal how to say, in German, "Lotte a les yeux bleus" ("Lotte has blue eyes"). Rosenthal tells him and Maréchal looks at Lotte as he repeats the phrase, "Lotte hat blaue Augen," clipping off the words like a drill sergeant; Elsa watches intently from the side (her turn to gaze on the loved one) and gently smooths out his pronunciation: "blaue Augen." Music returns on the track and Maréchal turns his attention to Elsa as he repeats the two words, wistfully and with a softer delivery, easing them out as if searching for something deep within himself.

Thus the identical words return, in the same shot, spoken by the same person, but with a different meaning. The second time around is his declaration of love, filtered through the innocuous words, and Elsa gives him a knowing look. In such a simple way, under cover of this little group, Renoir indicates their mutual attraction.

Maréchal's second attempt at "blaue Augen," but his first words of love (*Photofest*).

The punctuation provided when music returns to the soundtrack, after Elsa corrects Maréchal's pronunciation, strengthens the shot. However, unlike the musical sequencing in the film's opening shot, instead of the lively incidental music from the graphophone returning, it is subdued and romantic background music that plays over the scene.

This framing by the soundtrack highlights the dialogue as a critical moment, but there is also something haunting about the way that the graphophone derails (as could happen in the real world) and then, before Maréchal repeats "blaue Augen," the way that Kosma's music comes up rather than the incidental music (as happens in a movie or stage musical). In this subtle way, Renoir heightens the effect by forging a somewhat disjointed transition to the artificially added music on the soundtrack.

And, by covering Maréchal's repetition of "blaue Augen" with romantic movie music, Renoir directly links the loving exchange between Maréchal and Elsa to their embrace a few shots later since the music continues through that shot, making a seamless progression.

Typically, Rosenthal, ever sensitive to others, distracts Lotte by playing tug-of-war with her during the shot, sticking a piece of straw out for her to grab. And the shot ends as the camera tracks a bit and Maréchal puts Lotte into her bed, framed by the doorway, with everyone enjoying the scene.

The French and German languages are connected even more closely in the next shot when the two men bid good night to Elsa, each shaking her hand and saying, in German, "gute Nacht." Then, after blowing out the candles, Maréchal softly says "bon soir" to Elsa. She responds in kind, using French for the first time and timidly looking downward, barely getting the words out. This stronger connection through language, Elsa responding to French with French, essentially seals their love. The embrace, in the following shot, confirms what is already obvious.

I think that the climax of *La Grande Illusion* takes place on the next morning, in a scene of five shots lasting only 51 seconds, as Renoir manages a breathtaking concision of effect.

The sequence opens on the exterior long shot of the farmhouse, seen at the end of a field with a snowy mountainscape beyond; the skipping, dotted rhythm of the music on the soundtrack continues to trip along throughout the rest of the scene. As one of the four shots in the film with no people in it, this shot is, in itself, a shock. And its brief length (4 seconds) after the preceding tracking shot of the embrace (43 seconds) is also striking. A quick jump-start for this Christmas morning sequence, further energized by the suddenly energetic music and this detour into documentary mode with the insertion of a standard-issue country setting.

Renoir follows with the shot of Rosenthal at the window as the camera moves out and takes in the landscape. The viewpoint thus shifts from the camera's placement outside to a position within the farmhouse looking, and then moving, outside. The exuberance of that image of release and liberation sets the stage.

The third shot is a medium shot that tracks slightly, from a vantage point behind Rosenthal walking into the main room; he surprises Maréchal and Elsa, who are standing by the window, as Maréchal drops his hand from her shoulder. Framed by the doorway, the scene is objectified, like the shot of the embrace, and with a similarly voyeuristic slant. A moment of embarrassment takes hold and the lovers move forward decorously; Maréchal looks down as if guilty, while Elsa looks to Rosenthal, who joins them to form a full-length three-shot.

Almost absurdly proper and sensitive to their discomfort, Rosenthal shakes hands with them, reprising the handshaking with Elsa the night before when they had all said their good nights. He greets Elsa in German and Maréchal in French, the languages returned to their usual niches. But even though they are on different footing now, shaking hands with Maréchal is plainly ridiculous, and slightly comical.

This formality, bolstered by the framing effect of the doorway, sets Rosenthal apart from the couple, as properly as the archangel Gabriel separated from the Virgin Mary by a column or some other obstruction in paintings of the Annunciation. And for a similar reason — to circumvent the delicate subject of sexual contact (or no contact, as the case may be). Maréchal stands beyond, between Elsa and Rosenthal, a further separation visually. It is another little improvised dance choreographed by Renoir and Christian Matras, preparing for the last two shots in the scene.

Renoir then cuts to one of the closest shots in the movie, a shot of Maréchal looking triumphantly gallant and self-assured. He is seen up close and alone, finally, unlike the close-up shared with the engineer during the window pan. A new man — the romantic lead.

Yet nothing is quite that simple (again). Maréchal, at his time of greatest happiness and contentment, still shares the spotlight. His close-up begins with Rosenthal's voice on the soundtrack trying to put the lovers at ease and regain neutral ground by offering to make coffee, and it ends with Maréchal replying that the coffee is ready and, turning his head, leaving him in profile, he directs his attention (and soon, ours) to Elsa and asks her to tell Rosenthal in French. His voice, laced with a lover's warmth and the pride of a teacher in his prize student, infuses the shot with a gentleness that spins off to Elsa.

This is the only exclusive close-up of Maréchal in the movie, but he remains connected to the others around him and is eager, in modest profile, to pass his close-up on to the woman he loves.

Renoir then cuts to the fifth and last shot in the sequence, a close-up of Elsa. It is not quite as close as the one of Maréchal and it begins with her facing to her left, as she perfectly mirrors his profile facing right in the previous shot. She eagerly receives his invitation and then turns full-face to the camera. This is also, as with Maréchal, her first exclusive close-up and she looks at Rosenthal (off-camera) slightly to the left, again mirroring Maréchal.

These parallel close-ups are notable in several other ways as well. They are held still and are short takes (6 and 9 seconds), making a contrast to the longer tracking shots that have dominated the previous scenes at the farm. Also, for the only time, Renoir places full close-ups in succession. They have a formal quality, in the manner of paired portraits, side by side on separate canvases. Maréchal and Elsa are linked cinematically by these two head-on shots, with temporarily matching profiles; they are presented to us as a couple.

Maréchal prepares Rosenthal for Elsa's triumph (*Photofest*).

In this final shot of

Elsa in the sequence, with these underpinnings in place, Renoir brings release from all the pain and confinement and struggle in his film as, in close-up, haltingly, and ecstatically, Elsa repeats to Rosenthal the French phrase she has learned: "Le ... café ... est prêt" ("The ... coffee ... is ready"). Elsa is further linked to Maréchal as his voice on the soundtrack proudly adds, "Et voila," and she laughs, innocently and more fully than she has allowed herself until then. Or will allow herself again. And Maréchal also lets out a small laugh, off-screen — another lovely grace note as the shot fades out.

For me, this is the most emotionally charged moment in *La Grande Illusion*. All that preceded the morning scene seems to disappear. The film soars and feels suddenly weightless as Elsa, in relief, after working hard on the first two words, fairly exhales the last two in a rush — the first isolated, staccato words followed by those final ones rushing to hang onto the solidity provided by a period at the end, as if like a child taking its first tentative steps and then letting loose and flailing into the arms of a waiting parent.

A transcendent moment. And the film itself seems to let out a cathartic sigh, having earlier caught its breath in the hushed silence at the sight of Maisonneuve in a skirt and blouse.

Like Maréchal's "Lotte hat blaue Augen," Elsa's insignificant words imply, rather than announce, their love. The scene is enhanced by that echo, this doubling of these simple statements of fact, newly learned four-word phrases which become expressions of love, the one offered earlier in German by a Frenchman and now the other tried out in French by Elsa. In each case, the translated phrase is fed to the speaker in a bland tone — matter-of-factly by Rosenthal and, here, equally without emphasis by Maréchal.

Renoir has not overplayed his hand. He presents, at last, two of the closest shots in the movie and the faces of Gabin and Parlo fill the screen. The concentration is exhilarating. And he also achieves a reversal. For the first time, full close-ups, as well as adjacent still shots of characters alone in the frame, communicate intimacy and love instead of unease and outright confrontation (as at Wintersborn) or wariness (the first night in the barn).

A substantial part of the scene's power comes from the fact that Renoir does not promiscuously use this close-up framing. There had only been a few full close-ups of characters before: the teacher in his ruff, the French during the window pan, and Rauffenstein twice (finally muttering "peut-être"). Our sensitivities have not been dulled by overexposure.

The close shots of these lovers are also enhanced by the contrast to the medium shot of the three characters, confined by the doorframe, which preceded them. Furthermore, these brief, still close-ups are almost an anomaly in terms of the other crucial shots in the film — in their brevity, lack of movement, and number of characters. They are capstones, distinct and fresh.

Elsa: "Le ... café ... est prêt" (*Photofest*).

These images of Maréchal and Elsa transform the film. An ordinary French phrase, spoken by a giddy German war widow, overwhelms the separation and loss that has marked *La Grande Illusion*.

After fading out Elsa's shot, Renoir creates a skillful effect on the soundtrack when he drops the music and fades slightly into the tense scene of Maréchal and Rosenthal discussing their plans to leave. And by not defusing the Christmas morning scene with another shot or additional dialogue, as he does at the end of some sequences, Renoir generates an even greater impact. Nothing, after all, can decently follow that climactic shot of Elsa, laughing in appreciation of her small triumph in communication.

Soon afterward, Maréchal comforts Elsa, after she has learned that he must leave. They sit together by a closed window. A feeling again of entrapment. She talks in German about her pleasure hearing his footsteps (unlike Hallbach's threatening clatter of boots) and he responds in French, promising to come back after the war if he is still alive to take her, and Lotte, to France. These monologues in different languages may not be understood, but it's a matter of no great consequence. They know each other by now.

This final time alone, before parting, parallels the two-shot of Rauffenstein and the dying Boeldieu. A grieving German is once again reassured by a Frenchman. Rauffenstein expresses his grief by cutting the geranium; Elsa cries openly.

And Renoir underscores their union as a couple by dissolving from this shot of the seated lovers into a shot of them standing, facing each other, as they prepare to say goodbye on the last night at the farm. Their positions on the screen are reversed in the second shot so that the dissolve briefly causes Maréchal and Elsa to be partially superimposed, one on top of the other, on opposite sides of the frame—an effective doubled linking.

The realities of war, again, precipitate the penultimate crisis of *La Grande Illusion*, the parting of Maréchal from Elsa. One last separation. This motif seems especially cruel here, coming after scenes of a more normal life.

The leave-taking of Maréchal and Rosenthal is shown, appropriately, in static and relatively short takes. The opening shot, which begins with the dissolve of the lovers, continues as Elsa holds back from Maréchal's attempt to embrace her, urging him to leave quickly, with Rosenthal and Lotte beyond, out of focus. Renoir thus denies the couple a goodbye kiss or even an embrace, either of which would have been natural, either in real life or in the conventions of a movie. A thwarted expectation, and another connection stymied.

The shot is reconfigured into a wider group shot and Maréchal goes to pick up Lotte, as at the Christmas celebration, moving the focus off Elsa. Then, in a two-shot, Maréchal holds Elsa's little girl. But this time, with a glazed look, he bypasses Lotte and, in a velvety tone, directly addresses her mother, who is off-screen: "Lotte hat blaue Augen."

A close-up of Elsa follows (nearly as close as her Christmas morning shot), and she again lovingly corrects his pronunciation of the last two words.

Renoir then cuts back to the wide group shot, with all four of them together as in the first "blaue Augen" scene, making the camera an expectant participant, poised to record Maréchal repeating the words again. Everything is ready. But he only smiles slightly in recognition of his mispronunciation and kisses Lotte on the cheek, as he had kissed her at the end of the earlier scene when putting her to bed. The pain inherent in separation is pent up in the silence enveloping those unrepeated words, expressed implicitly by that break in the pattern.

There are other broken patterns in the scene. For the first time since the opening night on the farm, Maréchal and Rosenthal wear the clothes they had worn during their escape.

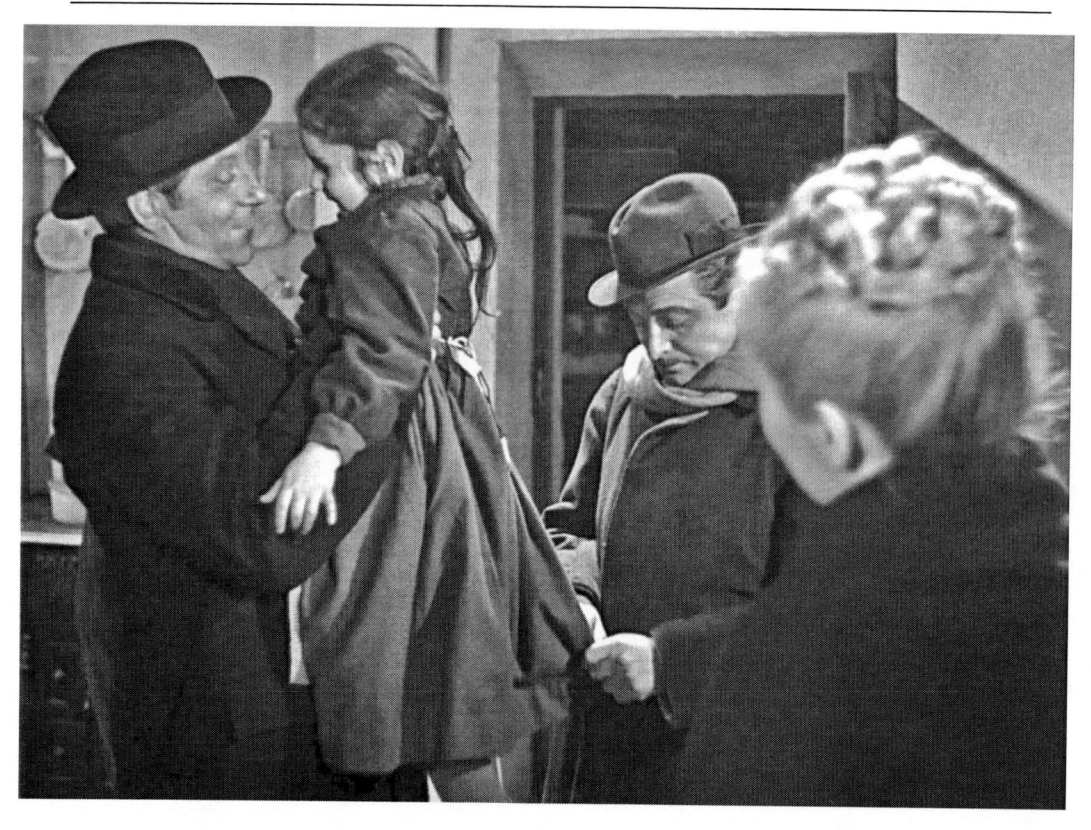

The group together one last time — the unrepeated words of love (*Photofest*).

They are in flight mode — one foot out the door. And, unlike the earlier "blaue Augen" scene, where Lotte alone separated Maréchal from Elsa, in this group shot Rosenthal also stands between them (in the background) and Elsa is removed even further, her back to the camera in the foreground, fuzzy, and her face unseen. The group already fractured.

This is the most complex reprise, and reversal, in the film, using not only the repeated words but also breaking down the cinematic expression. Rather than a single tracking shot of 38 seconds keeping the group together, Renoir uses three still shots (totaling 29 seconds) to break it apart: the two-shot of Maréchal and Lotte, the close-up of Elsa, and finally the group shot, which then disintegrates into a two-shot at the end after Maréchal and Rosenthal leave. That ending configuration of mother and daughter alone is in stark contrast to the earlier "blaue Augen" shot that ended with the cozy and familial scene of Lotte being settled into bed by Maréchal and Elsa.

The happiness and buoyancy of the previous scene is recalled, but not replicated — lost in the empty space left by those two unspoken words. And in comparison to some of the language in the prison camps, where discussions of escape and Maréchal's illusions touch on themes of war and peace, these small, neutral words carry the greater weight. Even without being spoken. This effect is strengthened by the fragmentation of the group and by wrenching apart the shot itself. A last disruption of attachment and community.

Later, in the final shot at the farm, the camera pans on Elsa and Lotte as they go to the dining table. Elsa removes some dishes and Lotte sits alone, the photograph of her father on the wall beyond. This panning shot recalls the earlier track that had started, not ended, on that photograph and had introduced Lotte sitting in the same place at the table. But this time the image is left without commentary.

The similar movement of this shot also indirectly connects the absent Maréchal to Elsa's husband (his photograph in both shots), with the man in the house again gone, the war again crimping the communal meals, and the table once more too large.

The stage has been cleared. No Elsa, no Maréchal. And Renoir fades out the scene on Lotte, instead of dissolving into the next section. It is a cleaner break, as at the end of Wintersborn. The idyll on the farm comes to an end; the war was always lurking in the wings, ready to deal another blow.

Near the Swiss border, Rosenthal asks Maréchal, "Tu l'aimes?" ("You love her?"). Maréchal replies, "Je crois qu'oui" ("I think so") — not exactly a ringing endorsement. Little is fixed or certain in this movie, not even the early stages of romantic love. That too may be relative and open to question.

In this film with such a humanist bent, only in the waning moments is "love" mentioned. Intimations of sex dominate instead, with the names of women bandied about, starting with Josephine, and the boys-will-be-boys talk in the camps — the teacher cuckolded, Rosenthal discussing venereal disease, Maréchal reading aloud about a woman named Louise who refers to twenty-two nights of lovemaking. There are also hints of "the love that dares not speak its name," though Boeldieu and Rauffenstein's relationship is not sexually infused, despite the advice given by Renoir to Stroheim for the confrontation.

Perhaps the ones who most appreciate "love," as Maréchal comes to know it, are the two intellectuals — Demolder, with his adoring and even infatuated encomium to Pindar ("le plus grand poète grec"), and the teacher, who says his wife is the only one for him, provoking the actor to unkindly suggest that that was why she cheated on him.

Maréchal never tells Elsa that he loves her. It remains unspoken and understood. The verb "aimer" ("to love" or "to like") is used quite often in the film but always in terms of "liking." Rosenthal, as amateur psychologist at the border, probing Maréchal's feelings, finally uses the verb in the sense of "loving."

Rosenthal had also been a catalyst for the relationship of Maréchal and Elsa, serving first as translator and then agreeing to tell Elsa that her guests must leave and giving the couple a last moment alone, discreetly shuttling Lotte outside to say goodbye to the cow (about to get another earful from that strange other species). And so, at the end, Rosenthal acts again as confidant, asking Maréchal directly about Elsa, a post-mortem on their lost time of refuge.

Maréchal pledges to return to Elsa. Many critics see this as one more illusion. Possibly, but not necessarily. It serves, at least, as a Rorschach test for the viewer. Will he return, or not? It may be hopelessly unrealistic to believe that Maréchal will find Elsa again. But this is also not the same Maréchal who sang "Frou-Frou" to himself at the French air base. He has grown, as a man and as a man of action, and his love appears genuine. A less naive, perhaps cynical, reading would see war as too overwhelming and that, even with the best intentions, people change or fall short.

But whatever the case, pipe dream or realistic promise, it remains open to interpretation. Whether, beyond the time frame of the movie, there is hope for the characters in *La Grande Illusion* or only tragedy, or some combination of outcomes, seems, in the end, hardly relevant. There will always be questions and always a number of possible answers.

And none of them easy.

12

FIN
The Swiss Border

"'And, you know, the film changed so much in the shooting that I didn't know how it should end. I didn't decide how to do the last scene until the exterior shooting was almost all over—maybe I had even edited some. It was only then that I saw how the end should be.'"
— Jean Renoir in *Jean Renoir: The French Films, 1924–1939* (p. 285)

"In 1916 he [Carl Koch, the technical advisor on La Grande Illusion] was in command of an anti-aircraft battery in the Rheims sector.... As it happens, in 1916 I was flying in a reconnaissance squadron in the same sector, and we were the main target of a German battery which gave us a lot of trouble. Koch and I concluded that this was his battery: so we had made war together. These things form a bond. The fact that we had been on opposite sides was the merest detail. Indeed, as I come to think of it, it was even better—a further instance of my theory of the division of the world by horizontal frontiers, and not into compartments enclosed in vertical frontiers."
— Jean Renoir in *My Life and My Films* (p. 161)

The last section of the film, near the border of Switzerland, begins with a pan from a long shot of mountains down to a snowbank. This is the only one of the seven sections in *La Grande Illusion* that opens with background music filling the air. With the final unrolling under way, there's no need for a slow and steady development of the narrative at this point. It starts full speed.

Renoir then cuts to a long-held shot of Maréchal and Rosenthal; this neatly balances the opening shots of the last part, the pan down to the embankment where they were also hiding and on the run, and the closer two-shot that followed. As they survey the landscape in front of them, Rosenthal checks his crumpled map, confident they are near the border. This map, which they had studied at Wintersborn, is never seen, unlike the maps of Boeldieu and Rauffenstein displayed on their office walls.

Maréchal talks about finishing "cette putain de guerre" ("this fucking war" or "this whore of a war"—grating language, in either case, for such an understated film). And when he adds, "en espérant c'est la dernière" ("in hoping it is the last"), the worldlier Rosenthal, like the engineer at Hallbach, chides him for having "illusions." That Maréchal had thought, near the beginning of the movie, that the war would be over in a few weeks was a trivial misconception. But his hope, here, that it will be the war to end all wars is without doubt his greatest, but also his grandest, illusion—grand because a degree of nobility tinges his naiveté. "Be reasonable. Demand the impossible!" as students proclaimed during the 1968 uprising in France.

The title of *La Grande Illusion* perhaps makes most sense in terms of Maréchal's illusions at the border; Renoir himself acknowledged he had that in mind. But it can mean other things too and its meaning has been much discussed. War itself, surely, is based on illusions. The barriers that Maréchal challenges throughout can also be seen as illusory. Differences between French or German, aristocratic dandy or mechanic, even a man or woman, often prove as immaterial as the unmarked transition between Germany and Switzerland in this last scene. And the oasis on the farm also proves something of a mirage.

Further, the make-believe of theater, in its many guises during the film, comes up against hard realities to demystify it. Much else turns out not to be what it seems as well, or at least appears ambiguous: that smudge seen differently by three officers, the Hallbach garden serving more as a dumping ground, men in dresses, the contents of the crate at Wintersborn, the woman leading a horse on the country road. And now the border.

The film could have been titled "*Les Grandes Illusions*," in the plural form. But the ambiguity of "*La Grande Illusion*" is appropriate, even though Renoir's movie is not as overtly philosophical or concerned with abstract concepts as its title might imply.

Rosenthal's reprise of the word "illusion" at the end is the final telling repetition of a particular word or phrase, in a movie anchored throughout with such leitmotifs — from the opening "frou-frou" to "streng verboten," "c'est la guerre," "devoir," "peut-être," and to the children's song distorted in the mountains and the indirect declarations of love on the farm. This airing of Maréchal's "illusion," like those other landmarks, strengthens the film's structure and pleases with its familiar repetition.

The shot continues as the two men prepare to cross the border. They embrace warmly and tease each other; Maréchal addresses his friend as "sale juif" ("dirty Jew"), and Rosenthal repeats the actor's affectionate tag when Maréchal returned from solitary confinement, "vieille noix" ("old nut"). It's a fantastic twist, this upending of anti–Semitism, with Maréchal using the pejorative in jest rather than anger, recalling also Rosenthal's teasing reference to Jesus as "mon frère de race," and it is a measure of how close they have become. Words, again, are relative in Renoir's world. During a screening at UCLA in 1951, Renoir was greatly offended by the mistranslation of "Au revoir, sale juif" in the subtitles as "Goodbye, old pal"[1]— political correctness rearing its ugly head.

Maréchal kisses Rosenthal on both cheeks and they say goodbye in case a border patrol comes upon them and they are forced to separate. There is thus a chance that this relationship may also end in separation. And they scramble up the snowbank, as they had scrambled up to the road in the opening scene of the last part.

A pan in long shot, on a group of German soldiers following the footprints in snow of the escaped prisoners, opens the final sequence of *La Grande Illusion*. The incongruity between the beautiful mountain setting and a patrol bent on hunting down fugitives is chilling. The soldiers stop in their tracks and, conveniently, some of them step into deep footprints dug into the snow on either side of the trail (undoubtedly left over from previous takes of the shot); a few of them fire into the distance.

Then, in a medium shot of two soldiers, angled slightly upward, one of them raises his rifle to shoot again. The orchestral music that runs throughout the border sequence drops out portentously as the other German tells him to hold fire since their quarries, off-screen, are in Switzerland; the first soldier, after dropping his gun, replies contemptuously and with eyes staring coldly ahead, "Es ist besser für sie" ("It's better for them"). The music immediately returns full blast, providing a perfect frame and punctuation mark for the exchange, with the main musical theme of the film now restated a final time.

It is the film's last Handelian pause — and its most affecting one. As a monumental work, *La Grande Illusion*, like Handel's *Messiah* for instance, evokes a range of moods and emotions,

"Es ist besser für sie": a German gets the final (sarcastic) words (*Photofest*).

brought out by choruses of characters and by smaller ensembles. For Handel, his signature pause at the end of a movement creates a false ending with its sudden silence. A harbinger of the final silencing to come, followed by the last flickering of notes. That rekindling after the pause is poignant, as if raising the music from the dead before it passes away for good.

La Grande Illusion also has a series of pauses on its soundtrack (starting with the opening shot). After this last pause at the border, and with the resumption of the orchestral music, it is reaffirmed in the next shot when the camera pans to them that, like the music, Maréchal and Rosenthal are alive. The reprieve provides a momentary lift. But the movie must finally end, and a last chord sound.

This brief sequence of the border patrol is significant far beyond the game of escape and pursuit. For only the second time in the movie shots are fired with an intent to kill. The final crisis. And Rauffenstein's earlier order to stop his guards shooting at Boeldieu has foreshadowed this command by the German soldier.

The other soldier's response, so laced with a contempt at odds with the literal meaning of his words, is one of the harshest sentiments expressed in the film, and it comes soon after Maréchal's expletive about the war. Two splashes of cold water bracing the proceedings.

Think of the journey taken, from the first lyrics we hear, sung in French, "frou-frou, frou-frou," to the abruptly dismissive German words. The film begins in a frivolous tone and yet Renoir slowly and painstakingly establishes, at last, a sense of the human spirit ascendant, only to end his film with words of sarcastic derision, whose meaning (as so often) is changed by the context in which they are spoken and the intonation of the speaker. "Better for them." But more like: "So much the better for them, the lucky bastards." Nothing is easily settled.

It's also an inspired touch that Renoir closes the film's dialogue with a German phrase — this movie that seems so quintessentially French. The balancing act of nation against nation that teeters throughout ends as the pursuer, the "enemy," gets the last word (and a bitter one at that). Orchestrating this sudden turn of events, Renoir returns to the mechanisms of war and conflict just as the movie is about to end. These dazzling reversals inject some of war's grim reality, as Maréchal and Rosenthal themselves will probably soon return to active duty and face again that reality.

This final interruption balances the disruption of Maréchal's leave in the opening shot that led to his capture. The decision by the patrol to stop its pursuit allows him to be free once again. The circle is joined, and an interruption now fortuitous. Lives spared, freedom secured, and the characters still together.

There is the further irony that Maréchal and Rosenthal are saved by an artificially created border. Nationalism, which had been undermined throughout, saves them in the end. And this odd development is compounded by the arbitrary nature of it all since, as they realize, nothing particularly distinguishes the border. Without a clear marker it could be an illusion to the naked eye. Only a map reassures them that it lies somewhere ahead in the snow. Such is the power of rules, made by men, to divide a snow-filled valley into two opposing halves and make the resulting division a matter of life and death.

In the film's next-to-last shot, Renoir pans from the German patrol to the valley below where the tiny figures of Maréchal and Rosenthal walk along in single file, far away in the distance. And so the warring sides are connected a final time in this continuing *pas de deux* that the camera has recorded nearly from the outset.

Renoir here presents one of the widest shots in his movie. After extended exposure to the close quarters of prison camps and the intimate scenes in Elsa's farmhouse, the world outside is fully embraced as it had been in the Christmas morning shot. Although almost as liberating, there is at the same time the constraint of the camera, remaining so remote from Maréchal and Rosenthal. It marks the beginning of our separation from them (and from the film).

The final image of *La Grande Illusion* is a shot of the two men struggling unevenly through the deep snow, heading away from the camera. Again a remote long shot, though closer than the previous one. It's clearly dissimilar from most of the other critical shots in the film — relatively short (18 seconds), held still, framed as an extreme long shot, and covered by Kosma's score.

The two characters are swamped by the snowy landscape. Following such warmth and engaging movement, Renoir's film closes with an objective viewpoint at a clear remove, and a stationary one. Maréchal and Rosenthal seem to be in Switzerland (if the patrol is correct in its assumption) but the camera stays behind enemy lines in Germany, as the point of view remains that of German soldiers.

And the orchestral music has the insistent beat of a simple, repeated phrase, notes walking evenly, which Kosma then pares down to the opening pitch of that phrase, stuck in uneven beats now, struggling, and slowing down — ending on a single, higher pitch held to the very end. A hint of optimism? But the music also has the feeling of a military march, closing this film steeped in pacifism.

So many disjunctions, suddenly, at the end.

Thus contradictions and ironies continue to swirl around the film in its last moments. Yet this shot is calm, even meditative — a cleansing of the palate after a rich and satisfying meal.

The closing image: the fugitives in Switzerland (perhaps) (*Photofest*).

    The last shot also has three unusual (though minor) technical oddities that may add to its powerful, even hypnotic, effect. For whatever overtones provided by them, they are at least worth noting.

    First, rare for *La Grande Illusion*, the cut to this last shot is a huge jump cut. The previous long shot shows Maréchal and Rosenthal on a direct line toward a large house nearby and, to the right, a curving path broken deeply into the snow and, farther to the right, what looks like railroad tracks. Even accounting for a different lens and a new angle, still from behind but closer and slightly from the left of them instead of the right, this final shot disturbs the continuity; no house is in evidence and the landscape in front of them is a wide expanse of pristine snow, with only unbroken snow and trees to the right. Despite spells of choppy editing, there are no jump cuts as blatant as this one in the film. That clash of images, then, makes its mark.

    Second, the shot has a telephoto lens effect, flattening out the perspective and drawing added attention because of the specifically movie-like quality of the image. This device is rarely used in the film and, as with the jump cut, registers more firmly.

    Lastly, the final shot is unusual in an inconsequential, and largely subliminal, way: it drifts very slightly to the left as it unrolls. Other shots are adjusted somewhat as they end, but nothing so gradual and almost imperceptible as this one; it has to be looked for carefully to be noticed. Nevertheless, this physical attribute is recorded somewhere in the brain and may contribute further, in its minuscule way, to the uncertainty of these final moments in the film lives of Maréchal and Rosenthal. Duly noted.

It is a brilliant ending, classically rounding out *La Grande Illusion*. The first and last shots of any movie, of course, are crucial — the first to set the tone and generate confidence, the last to leave a strong impression. Renoir does not fail on either count.

In the first shot Maréchal strolls off to report for duty, setting the narrative in motion as Renoir establishes thematic and aesthetic motifs that are developed later. It's a modest and casual shot, yet a complex one, and within it lies the genetic code that will mature into the full-grown movie.

The final shot, though much simpler and shorter, also carries great significance. At the end of this film there is nothing casual about the movement of Maréchal and Rosenthal; their steps are purposeful, and a bit tortuous. Also in contrast to the opening, this shot is writ large, with a heroic feeling in their Sisyphus-like struggle as they hobble along in the snow, breaking through fitfully.

A tentative sense of triumph prevails. After all the tragic separations in the film, this last relationship endures, against the odds, though as Maréchal and Rosenthal slip and punch through the snow they cannot be sure if they have reached Switzerland. But at least they end the movie together. The many interlocking relationships in *La Grande Illusion* have been reduced to two men trying to make it out of the movie alive.

As in a piece of music that returns, at the end, to the tonic key established in the beginning, there is a similar resolution here. After all the major and minor keys sounded throughout, the ups and downs, Renoir comes back to the original key at the air base: Maréchal as a free man. So the film, in closing, can be resolved, at least to the extent that it harmonizes with its opening.

Jean Renoir on location for *La Grande Illusion*, with a cameraman. Photograph: Sam Lévin (©*Ministère de la Culture/Médiathèque du Patrimoine/Sam Levin/dist. RMN-Grand Palais/Art Resource, New York*).

And, as Alexander Sesonske has perceptively written, Renoir achieves an intriguing asymmetry in this final shot:

> The first image of *La Grande Illusion* is of a phonograph record, the last, of a field buried in snow. Tone changes from black to white; perspective, from close-up to extreme long shot; movement, from a spinning in place to the slow forward progress of two men moving together. These changes might be seen as symbolic of the distance covered in the film, in the life of its hero, in the world portrayed.[2]

In common with many profound works of art, Renoir's film closes while it is opening up. We are left with the possibility of more illusions. How can there be a war to end all wars? Will Maréchal return to Elsa?

The last shot fades out and, on the final title card, "RAC," the acronym of the production company, is replaced by "FIN."

And *La Grande Illusion* ends.

The image of Maréchal and Rosenthal, soldiering on gamely and perhaps starting to enjoy their freedom at last, ends this film of intense intimacy with a cold eye cast on two floundering specimens of the human race, vulnerable and seemingly insignificant in the larger picture of things. But we have seen the movie, and we know better.

In the end, as throughout, the poetry of *La Grande Illusion*, rather than flaunted openly, is submerged in its final image. This time not the sound of marching boots that stirs the blood but, instead, as observed from a great distance, the feel of snow, slightly crusted and yielding to silent footsteps, the sound of which can only be imagined by Renoir's newest collaborators, who are now us, the audience.

Rest in peace, Jean Renoir.

Part II
AROUND THE FILM

13

La Grande Illusion
A History

> *"In the end, we went all over Paris. Luckily Gabin liked the idea, and we were also really good friends. That's how I shot* Grand Illusion, *thanks to Gabin.... All the distribution specialists, the big names in the commercial end of the industry, all adamantly rejected the script. I was able to shoot it only because of Gabin's influence."*
> —Jean Renoir in *Renoir on Renoir: Interviews, Essays, and Remarks* (Cambridge University Press; 1989; p. 91); originally in *Cahiers du Cinéma*, Second Interview by Jacques Rivette and François Truffaut (Christmas 1957)

The making of *La Grande Illusion* was marked by some fortunate circumstances. But, at the start, in attempting to get his film off the ground, Renoir spent over two years trying to find a backer. As he later recalled:

French, Italian, American, British producers saw nothing in the project. They wanted a villain. They said the German to be played by von Stroheim was not sufficiently a villain. I said the villain was the war. "The public won't understand that," they said.[1]

In early 1936, Alexandre Kamenka, whose company was producing Renoir's *Les Bas-Fonds* (*The Lower Depths*), showed interest in the proposal and made an estimate for its production. But Kamenka withdrew support when Renoir refused his suggestion to add a liaison between the hero and a nurse, to be played by the actress, Annabella.[2]

It was the involvement of Jean Gabin that helped secure financial backing (star power has its quiet charm). Renoir remembered how he waited with Gabin and Charles Spaak, his co-scenarist, in the anteroom of a possible producer, while his friend Albert Pinkevitch acted as negotiator. Even after Renoir agreed to cut costs by not filming at a chateau, the producer extracted one last concession as Renoir accepted plated silver, instead of sterling, for a proposed dinner service.

The true nature of *La Grande Illusion* is reflected in the fact that the credits note its production company rather than the individual producers, Pinkevitch and Frank Rollmer, a banker who had successfully invested in the stock market and backed Marcel Carné's first film, *Jenny* (1936). Rollmer staked 3 million francs on Renoir's film, but this was no Hollywood studio product, with the moneyman given billing next to the director.

In any case, Renoir finally signed a contract with Réalisations d'Art Cinématographique on November 9, 1936.

The series of lucky breaks and chance encounters that helped lead to the movie as we know it began twenty years earlier, during World War I. Renoir had enlisted and, in 1916, was assigned to air reconnaissance, like Maréchal. During one mission, his Caudron, an

Mid–World War I: (left to right) Georges Rivière, Paul Cézanne, Jr., Jean Renoir; Jean-Pierre and Aline Cézanne in front (ca. 1916) (*UCLA Charles E. Young Research Library, Department of Special Collections, Jean Renoir Collection*).

old-style airplane, was attacked by a German Fokker. A French fighter plane shot down the attacking Fokker and saved him; his rescuer turned out to be Captain Armand Pinsard, an acclaimed ace in the French air force.

A champagne dinner at their canteen celebrated the occasion (a bit of Rauffenstein) and they became friends. During their time together, Pinsard talked about horses he had trained (Rauffenstein or Boeldieu, perhaps).[3] They were separated when Renoir's squadron transferred to another area.

Years later, in 1934, while Renoir was filming *Toni* in the south of France, planes from a nearby airfield flew overhead, disrupting his sound recording. He went to the base and found that the commanding officer was Pinsard. The planes were rerouted and the two veterans renewed their friendship, dining together often, with Pinsard recounting his wartime adventures, many of which had already been publicized in a 1917 magazine article.

Pinsard had been shot down a number of times and once succeeded in tunneling through a thick prison wall to escape captivity. Renoir made an outline that covered his exploits, "Les Évasions du Colonel Pinsard" ("The Escapes of Colonel Pinsard"), and thought it might be the basis for a good film some day.

In addition, Spaak, who sketched out a treatment for the movie about a year later (based on Renoir's outline), had spent two weeks in a World War I prison camp and shared his firsthand experiences. Renoir and Spaak also interviewed veterans and read accounts of the war; the scene at the German canteen, for instance, was inspired by the memoirs of the famous Baron von Richthofen. And Renoir's German friend, Carl Koch, the technical advisor on the film and a war veteran, kept the German side of the story accurate. Renoir, for his part, did not want to inflame patriotic bias by perpetuating myths that had grown up about the war.

A less heralded influence was a novel by Jean des Vallières called *Kavalier Scharnhorst*, published in 1931. Des Vallières, a contemporary of Renoir, had served a comparable military stint in World War I. The plot of his autobiographical novel is similar to the original scenario of *La Grande Illusion*; even some details, like the catch phrase "streng verboten," appear in it. Renoir and Spaak were sued. Although the court ruled against plagiarism and the case was settled, it left bitter feelings.

In several letters at the time, Renoir claimed that the stories told by prisoners of war were in the public domain and belonged to history rather than to any one individual. And he rejected what he felt was petty nationalism in *Kavalier Scharnhorst*. But there are enough scenes in common that some acknowledgement has to be made, though the plot of *La Grande Illusion* is not what distinguishes it as a movie.

Other fortunate breaks, during preparation for shooting, also changed the film a great deal. Originally, Renoir wanted his brother, Pierre, to play the commandant at the fortress. Though Pierre Renoir was a gifted actor, it would have significantly lessened the film's authenticity if he had played a German. But a theater engagement forced him to bow out.

Even more fortunately, Erich von Stroheim, the renowned silent film director, had arrived in Paris to appear in a film by Raymond Bernard, *Marthe Richard au service de la France* (also known as *Marthe Richard*). Renoir admired Stroheim greatly. As a young man, before starting his career, he had been spellbound on seeing *Foolish Wives*, which Stroheim had released in 1922. Later in life, Renoir noted that he had gotten into film mainly because of his love for Stroheim's work.

There are several versions of how Stroheim became involved in the film. The most convincing one is that by mid-January 1937, shortly before shooting began, the role of the German commandant was still an insignificant one when the director of production, Raymond Blondy, offered Stroheim the part. His presence in the cast led to a major transformation of the role, and he quickly agreed with Renoir to avoid stereotyping the German officer as a martinet.

Françoise Giroud, the script girl on the film who later became a noted writer and public figure (credited as "Gourdji" in the titles), recalled that, when Stroheim joined the cast and crew at Colmar, Renoir rented an empty theater to show him work done in the previous few days. The lights were turned off and the sound of marching boots, louder and softer and louder, went on for twelve minutes. Nothing else, no images:

> "There," said Jean Renoir to Stroheim, "that's all that I have to show you."
> "I think that I am going to have a fancy for working with you," responded Stroheim.[4]

One artist recognizing the quirkiness of another. And this description of the sound certainly jibes with the soundtrack during the window pan at Hallbach.

Stroheim, after years in Hollywood, was not fluent in German and ironically had to work on his lines. And in helping to create "Captain von Rauffenstein" he suggested, among other items, the chin brace and white gloves. In spite of Renoir's concern for realism, the uniform worn by Rauffenstein was more flamboyant than typical of the time. Renoir wisely accepted this bit of poetic license.

Erich von Stroheim, posing in his costume for *Foolish Wives* (1922). Photograph: Freulich 108 (*Photofest*).

Stroheim and Renoir developed a good relationship, despite their different temperaments. While Stroheim was mercurial and cultivated an image often, if not largely, based on myth, Renoir tended to be a patient and modest man.

Early in the filming they argued over Stroheim's idea to incorporate prostitutes into the opening scenes at Wintersborn. As he later related his version of the story, Renoir was so distraught that he burst into tears and said that, rather than quarrel with someone he respected so much, he would give up directing the film. This sounds like a liberal dose of Brer Rabbit psychology, but it worked. Touched by the gesture, Stroheim agreed to follow Renoir's direction. The collaboration went smoothly thereafter.

Koch, who also admired Stroheim, quarreled with him as well when Stroheim wanted to add elaborate details to the nurse's costume; Koch insisted on the reality he had experienced during the war. Renoir recalled how Koch, who was a pacifist, finally lost his temper and threw a glass at the retreating Stroheim as he left the room. Stroheim returned, smiling, and offered his antagonist another glass. Their differences were resolved over a bottle of wine.

Renoir relied on both these foreigners, as he admitted, the one to express a strain of poetry in his film, the other to strengthen its realism. And the innately collaborative nature of movies was reinforced throughout the production by his patience and apparent absence of false ego.

Similarly, Renoir expanded the role of Rosenthal in talking with Marcel Dalio; another actor, Robert Le Vigan, had originally been in Renoir's mind for the part. Pinkevitch, in addition to being a producer, also became instrumental in shaping the character, suggesting most critically that he be Jewish. It possibly led to another detail that, according to Renoir, his friend's eyes would fill easily with tears, like Rosenthal, when making an appeal to someone.

Furthermore, Pinkevitch, who loved puns and word play, helped Renoir develop the distinctive dialogue of Cartier, the music hall actor at Hallbach. Renoir later gave tribute to his friend: "Without him there would have been no *Grande Illusion*."[5]

The casting for the role of Boeldieu also hit snags. Louis Jouvet, like Pierre Renoir, had a previous commitment and Pierre Richard-Willm declined the offer. Fresnay was third on the list. Yet one more circuitous route to such a perfect fit, in this case, that any other actor as Boeldieu is almost inconceivable.

To establish the time period of the action in *La Grande Illusion*, it's useful to look at certain clues within the movie. The wreath in the German canteen is mistakenly dated "19 March 1916," an anachronism since later at Hallbach the poster announcing the capture of Fort Douaumont by the Germans is clearly dated "26 February 1916," which is historically accurate. The date of the German recapture of Douaumont ("17 April 1916") can be seen on the second poster. Therefore the year on the wreath (set at an angle and hard to read in any case) should have been "1915."

Near the end of the Wintersborn section, Maréchal mentions that he has been together with Boeldieu for eighteen months, which would make it September 1916 at that point. It can be assumed that the Christmas on the farm occurs later that year. The film, then, must take place between March 1915 and the end of 1916 or early 1917 (at the border).

Renoir put some of his own war experiences from that same period into the film. Even the name "Maréchal" resonates with Renoir's original position as a sergeant in the mounted dragoons ("maréchal des logis"). The French bar in the opening shot is a recreated version of his canteen during the war, and Gabin wore Renoir's own Flying Corps uniform in that shot and throughout the prison camp scenes. Also, the first meeting of Maréchal and Boeldieu was based on an encounter Renoir had with a haughty air force Captain.

And just as Maréchal wants to return to action, Renoir himself returned to the front, even after having been wounded. On a deeper level, the camaraderie that he found between soldiers from different classes certainly became a central theme.

Renoir is so much in his movie that a minor exchange during the costume-reviewing scene was lifted from a dark moment in his life. As he recuperated from his wound in a military hospital at Besançon during the summer of 1915, Véra Sergine, his sister-in-law and a well-known stage actress, came to break the news of his mother's death. Sergine showed up with short hair and a short dress to match. This was especially startling since she was in mourning and it caused a sensation. The outraged comments of fellow soldiers (perhaps mixed with a measure of prurience) are reprised in *La Grande Illusion* when an older French officer is unhappy with Maréchal's news of shortened dresses and bobbed hair on the home front.

Unlike the prison camp scenes, there is no specific source material for the farm sequences. This may help explain why those scenes have a different feeling to them; Renoir and Spaak seemed to have fashioned them out of whole cloth. Based not on real events, or reminiscence, the farm has almost a dreamlike quality at times.

The film's working title, "*Les Evasions de Capitaine Maréchal*," is an early indication of Maréchal's importance in the story. It also reflects Renoir's initial plan to make a straightforward adventure film, featuring air combat and prison escapes based on Pinsard's stories.

On location for the farm scenes of *La Grande Illusion*: back row, Carl Koch (3rd from left), Jean Renoir (5th from left), Dita Parlo (7th from left); center row, Jean Gabin (4th from left), Jean-Serge Bourgoin (far right); woman in front of Gabin, Françoise Giroud; front row, white arrow, the mysterious Marguerite Renoir. Photograph: Sam Lévin (©*Ministère de la Culture/Médiathèque du Patrimoine/Sam Levin/dist. RMN-Grand Palais/Art Resource, New York*).

"*La Grande Illusion*" was listed as the title throughout production. Though *The Great Illusion* was the name of a 1910 book by Norman Angell, an Englishman who won the 1933 Nobel Peace Prize, there is no link to Renoir's film, despite some accounts. Possible translations of the title into English could be "*The Great Illusion*" or "*The Big Illusion*," or even "*The Great Delusion*," and not the more evocative *Grand Illusion*, as the film is known in English-speaking countries.

Renoir on at least one occasion noted that the title refers mainly to Maréchal's illusion at the border that World War I could be "the last war," as Renoir remembered soldiers naively talking about it.

Jean Renoir was 42 years old in November 1936 when he started to scout locations for *La Grande Illusion*. His method, typically, was to rehearse scenes at length before filming, partly to prepare for the long and intricate tracks he planned to use.

With his crew, Renoir began shooting in the Alsace region on January 30, 1937. The Hallbach exteriors were filmed at military barracks in Colmar while Stroheim finished his acting assignment in *Marthe Richard* and, coincidentally, as Renoir waited for that film's studio sets in Paris to be freed for his own interiors.

The Wintersborn exteriors were staged near Colmar at Haut-Koenigsbourg, a medieval castle that had been restored by Wilhelm II, the Kaiser whose picture appears throughout the film. Renoir used local inhabitants, many of whom had been in the German army, to play soldiers in the prison camps, helping to keep his budget down. In 1972, Renoir estimated the movie had cost about $500,000 (in 1972 dollars).

It was decided not to film the interiors on location since it was technically easier to use a studio stage and would allow Renoir more freedom. To film the shot of Rosenthal opening the window on the farm, set designer Eugène Lourié ingeniously brought the wall of the farm set to an exterior location at Tibremont; he put up the freestanding wall on a hillside so Renoir could shoot through the window, creating the illusion of a complete house surrounding it. Lourié used the same trick at Colmar to film some shots in the costume-making scene that required exteriors in the background.

After exterior shooting was completed toward the end of February, the crew returned to shoot interiors, mainly at the film's headquarters at the Tobis studios in Épinay-sur-Seine, a suburb northeast of Paris. The interiors were shot in a little over a month, even with an interruption to show rushes to the nervous producers.

The first day of interior shooting covered the opening scene at the French bar. After filming the sequence at Boeldieu's office, the crew returned to the set of the bar, which had been rebuilt as the German canteen. From then on, the project continued to be filmed only roughly in sequence. Needing more space, Renoir moved to the nearby Éclair studios to shoot the musical revue (set in a stable) and the farmhouse scenes; some farm shots were filmed by his friend and assistant, Jacques Becker. Renoir then completed the Wintersborn interiors on a set built with real paving stones to avoid having to later dub in the sound of boots on stone.

The final scene at the border was to have been filmed after the studio schedule, but Gabin had a competing engagement and could not return for location shooting. Renoir solved the problem by filming Gabin's final dialogue with Dalio in a fake snowbank on the set and then used a double on location in snowfields near Chamonix for the last long shots. So the movie ends, in reality, with an uncredited actor leading the way across the border. One last behind-the-scenes illusion spun by Renoir.

Filming was completed in about two months, on April 2. It took only two more months

Renoir and Dita Parlo on the barn set. Photograph: Sam Lévin (©*Ministère de la Culture/Médiathèque du Patrimoine/Sam Levin/dist. RMN-Grand Palais/Art Resource, New York*).

to edit the film at the Billancourt studios for its gala premiere on June 8, 1937 at the Marivaux cinema in Paris; the film opened to the public the next day.

Such a timetable for such a film is astounding — a little over four months from initial filming to completion (*La Règle du jeu* was to have an equally impressive history). Whatever one's feelings about the film, the sustained concentration and resulting depth of expression achieved in a short period of time is an extraordinary accomplishment.

It's also remarkable, and a testament to the contradictions in human nature, that Renoir began to write a weekly column on March 4 in *Ce Soir*, the Communist Party daily, dealing with a variety of subjects, while still shooting *La Grande Illusion* — a film antithetical to the conformism and authoritarian hierarchy of communism. Renoir continued the column until November 4, 1938.

La Grande Illusion was almost universally praised by the critics, unlike many of his films, and it became Renoir's most popular and financially successful movie. He felt that its reception by the public as an escape film changed with time and that the relationships of characters then came to the fore.

Renoir also seemed somewhat conflicted about his film, and he once told Roger Viry-Babel in an interview that he had made better ones; he cited, in passing, *La Règle du jeu*, *La Chienne* and *Toni* as examples.

Notwithstanding its success, Renoir continued to have problems raising money for other projects. But he never compromised his principles:

> That blessed *Grande Illusion*! I probably owe my reputation to it, and I also owe it a good many misunderstandings. If I had made a bogus *Grande Illusion* I should probably also have made a fortune.[6]

The film was favored to win the top prize at the Venice Film Exposition in July 1937 but it seems likely that Mussolini intervened to block its victory (though, oddly, he liked the film and owned a copy). Julien Duvivier's *Un Carnet de bal* proved a safer choice and *La Grande Illusion* was designated the best artistic ensemble as a consolation prize.

It did well in the United States too. The film opened in New York at the Filmarte on September 12, 1938 for a 26-week run. It was also the first foreign language film to be nominated for the Best Picture award in the Oscar sweepstakes but lost out to Frank Capra's hokey film, *You Can't Take It With You*, with its annoyingly lovable eccentrics — an embarrassing choice, even for Hollywood. Letting foreign films compete in the top category, as if they would be considered legitimate contenders, allowed Hollywood to toss in a token entrant for the art-house crowd. That *La Grande Illusion* lost in such an exercise measured its stature more truly.

The film was shown at the White House in October, for Eleanor Roosevelt's birthday. Later, in accepting the 1938 New York Film Critics Circle award for the best foreign film, Renoir called this special showing an honor. And President Roosevelt was alleged to have declared: "All the democracies of the world must see this film." According to Olivier Curchod, however, an American journalist made the remark and the phrase only belatedly became attributed to Roosevelt.

Equally a confirmation of its humanist appeal was an epithet coined by Joseph Goebbels: "Cinematographic Enemy No. 1." The film was banned in Italy and Germany, where prints were destroyed, and banned also in Belgium by the foreign minister, Paul-Henri Spaak, who was the older brother of Charles Spaak — politics proving thicker than blood. In an ironic twist, the musical revue at Hallbach was based on the elder Spaak's own experience as a prisoner of war, as told to his brother.

When the Nazis entered Vienna, Renoir took pride that his film, playing in theaters, was immediately shut down. And Louis-Ferdinand Céline, the novelist, wrote an anti–Semitic pamphlet, "Bagatelles pour un massacre," in which, at one point, he attacked the role of Rosenthal in the movie.

With World War II, *La Grande Illusion* was withdrawn from exhibition in France. The Vichy government judged the film demoralizing. It probably did not amuse them that the German commandant was played by an actor whose parents were Jewish, though Stroheim, with his fictitious "von," hardly wore his heritage proudly on his sleeve. Further, pictures of Marcel Dalio were displayed on propaganda posters in Nazi-occupied France depicting him as a supposedly "typical Jew."

The film had generated an enviable list of enemies. Nevertheless, to appease a new set of naysayers after the war was over, many cuts were made before it was rereleased in a butchered form in August 1946. The name of Dita Parlo (who was German) was removed from the credits; her demure embrace of Gabin and the scene in which German soldiers celebrate the fall of Douaumont were also cut. Too pro–German, apparently. The arrival of Rosenthal's well-stocked food package was scrapped as well. It seems that Jews could not be seen as prosperous (or generous). Maybe also the authorities in charge did not appreciate Rosenthal fraternizing with the enemy by giving chocolate to a guard.

Even in this diminished state, most critics hailed the film's reappearance and again it was a success. But, in the post-war climate, there were bizarre charges of anti–Semitism and criticism that it was too kind to Germans, even without the offending embrace or the misguided gift of chocolate.

Despite the cuts, Renoir did not yield to the hysteria of the day and refused to cede to Hitler and the Nazis all things German. As he once wrote: "I owe a great deal to the Germans. I owe them Karl *[sic]* Koch, without whom *La Grande Illusion* could not have been what it is."[7]

In 1956 Renoir and Spaak bought the commercial rights to *La Grande Illusion* in order to restore the film to its original version. When they found that some lines of dialogue on the soundtrack during Boeldieu's deathbed scene were unclear, Renoir wrote Stroheim to ask if he would re-record them. Stroheim was very ill but offered to do the recording from his bed; he died before it could be arranged.

A nearly complete version of the film was reconstructed by Renée Lichtig, assisted by Ginette Courtois-Doynel, under the direction of Renoir and Spaak. It opened on October 6, 1958 at the Studio Publicis for its third Parisian run. Afterward, the co-scenarists spent months touring Europe with the film. Critical acclaim again greeted its appearance on the scene.

An English-subtitled version of the film was released in 1959 as *Grand Illusion*; the French title sequence had been replaced by credits in English on a cloth background, with a short statement about the World War I setting.

The version of *La Grande Illusion* released forty years later in 1999, based on the 1958 restoration, ran 113 minutes and, unlike the earlier version, was crafted from the original camera negative. The main improvement, besides the print quality, was the restitution of the original credits, which are superimposed on layered rings of stone (or slate) formations.

The backstory of this reincarnation of *La Grande Illusion*, according to various accounts, seems almost like a fanciful film plot. It was thought that the camera negative had been destroyed in a 1942 Allied bombing raid that had hit a major laboratory outside of occupied Paris. But Frank Hensel, a Nazi who headed the German Reichsfilmarchiv, was secretly collaborating with Henri Langlois and other film enthusiasts to help preserve some films from destruction. At one point, the camera negative had been removed to Berlin. Luckily, perhaps because of some archival mania lodged in the Nazi madness, "Cinematographic Enemy No. 1" escaped obliteration.

The German film archive in Berlin happened to be in the future Russian sector and, after the war, the camera negative was shipped with other films to the Soviet Gosfilmofond in Moscow, without having been identified. As a consequence, the prints that went into circulation in 1958 were not of the highest caliber.

In the mid–1960s, the Russians transferred the camera negative with other films back to France, its significance still unappreciated, as part of an exchange between the Soviet archive and a new Cinémathèque in Toulouse. It was only properly identified in the early 1990s when archivists found that 50 cans of picture and sound were, in fact, the original camera negative and soundtrack of *La Grande Illusion*.

After an odyssey of a half-century, the original filming and recording materials were safe, leading to the 1999 reissue of tonally rich and sharper prints. A turn of events as unlikely, and fortunate, as the gestation of the movie itself in the 1930s.

At the Brussels World's Fair of 1958, *La Grande Illusion* was voted the fifth greatest film of all time by a panel of 117 film historians (for whatever dubious interest such a parlor game merits). The four films ranked above it were, in order: Sergei Eisenstein's *Bronenosets Potyomkin* (*Battleship Potemkin*), Charles Chaplin's *The Gold Rush*, Vittorio De Sica's *Ladri di biciclette* (*Bicycle Thieves*) and Carl Theodor Dreyer's *La Passion de Jeanne d'Arc* (*The Passion of Joan of Arc*). *Citizen Kane* only garnered ninth place in the beauty contest; *La Règle du jeu* had not yet been revived and didn't make the list of 12 films.

Since then the pendulum has swung and, until 2012, *Citizen Kane* remained solidly first in the most long-lasting Top Ten poll, the *Sight & Sound* critics listing that comes out every ten years. *La Grande Illusion* has never made the listing, while *La Règle du jeu* was ranked no lower than third in any of those polls.

With its 1958 reincarnation, after twenty-one years, Renoir's masterpiece had been preserved in its original form for posterity. *La Grande Illusion* was, at last, secure — physically and historically.

14

The Road Not Taken...

"In the beginning, the picture was for me just an escape story. While I was working on the script, and shooting it, I discovered more about it."
— Jean Renoir in "Directors Go to Their Movies: Jean Renoir"; interview with Digby Diehl (*Action*, volume 7, number 3; May–June 1972; p. 4)

Movies, even some great movies, teeter on the edge of disaster. Because a film involves many different craftspeople and draws upon a number of disciplines, and because the potential for literal representation in a film can be seductive and, when succumbed to, make obvious what might better be left implicit, it is no mean feat for a director to end up with a movie that works, let alone one that soars.

Though Renoir once said that he made *La Grande Illusion* because he was a pacifist, he seemed to have begun his project in a different spirit altogether. The word "pacifist" might not come readily to mind.

An early, undated treatment of *La Grande Illusion* reveals how much had to change, in many ways, to turn the film around.[1] This typed synopsis, probably completed in late 1935, has a signed notation by Charles Spaak designating it the first version of the film. It's a startling document and an object lesson in the mysterious process that manages to bring sketched-out ideas finally to the screen.

The treatment primarily outlines the plot, including many elements that appear in the completed film. Although there is little indication of the form it will take, clearly Spaak and Renoir envisaged an adventure movie instead of a film about relationships and larger themes. They focused on the cruelty of wartime life rather than on common bonds that unite people. Most notable is an explicit presentation of those old standbys, violence and sexual liaisons. And even if their treatment had been shot with some restraint, the resulting film would probably have been a routine melodrama at best.

Between the opening scenes at the French base and German canteen, which are recognizably similar, the capture of Boeldieu and Maréchal is described in detail: their plane rises into the air; the engine fails and the enemy shoots at them; the plane crash-lands; they are knocked out with clubs. A German officer reproaches his men "for their pointless brutality" (even the indicated dialogue is heavy-handed). Thus the two sides are established as enemies and a conventional war film settled into place.

Later, when prisoners defiantly interrupt the revue and sing "La Marseillaise," the treatment describes a far different scene from the one in *La Grande Illusion* as armed guards arrive to quell a possible uprising: "the Germans advance, clubs raised, among the dancing, howling madmen."

But the French cannot so easily be tamed. German women occupy the other wing of the prison, preparing food for the camp. One woman with attractive legs regularly adjusts her garter in front of a vent that opens onto their quarters. At first this is a joke, but soon the frustrated prisoners must "get back at the bitch," a phrase unimaginable in terms of *La Grande Illusion*:

> They wait. She comes. Her usual merciless display. She is seized. Everyone dashes to grab hold of the leg sticking through the vent.... The men take off her shoes, tear off her stocking. Everyone wants to touch the fresh, gleaming skin. And Maréchal, cruelly, bites her. The woman screams. The men retreat, and her friends pull her out. "Now she'll leave us alone!" cry the men.

This might evoke the Marquis de Sade more than Renoir as we know him, and this early Maréchal is far from becoming Jean Gabin's Maréchal. And the sarcastic tone of these men occurs only once in *La Grande Illusion*, to telling effect, in the final words of the German soldier at the border. In the treatment, sarcasm develops into full-fledged cynicism.

The escape of Maréchal and Dolette, the prototype of Rosenthal, also lends itself to knock-em-out melodrama. The prison is a "hell-hole" in which "a frightful discipline reigns." Boeldieu creates a disturbance by hitting a guard and a gunfight follows in which he is shot and killed. No confrontation or rapprochement with an enemy officer here. The struggle is strictly along national lines, Germans against French.

At the Swiss border the fugitives come up behind a lone guard. A noise startles the German soldier who grabs his gun before being shot by Maréchal. It may be self-defense, but it's hard to picture the Maréchal of *La Grande Illusion* even handling a gun.

Eugène Lourié (standing hatless at center, coat and tie) with some of his unsung crew on the set. Photograph: Sam Lévin (©*Ministère de la Culture/Médiathèque du Patrimoine/Sam Levin/dist. RMN-Grand Palais/Art Resource, New York*).

Once in Switzerland, Maréchal and Dolette meet a little girl carrying a loaf of bread:

> They steal it from her. And the girl, astounded, looks on through her tears as these two bearded, filthy, unsightly men bite ravenously into the golden crust.

The treatment, in keeping with its pulp adventure plot, seems never at a loss for just one more choice adjective or adverb.

The two men pledge to meet again at Maxim's next Christmas. The final scene takes place on that day and the cynicism of the treatment is played out: a shot of an empty reserved table amidst the bustle at Maxim's. A nice touch, but more fitting for a different sort of movie.

With the appearance of a woman on a farm, near the end, the treatment diverges even further from the completed movie. Her entrance, at least, resembles the final version. She comes upon the two escaped prisoners in a stable, with a lamp in her hand.

But not much else seems familiar. She is described as "one of those German blondes made to bring beautiful children into the world." We have reached a nation of Aryan super-mothers breeding pureblooded Siegfrieds. And no Lotte inhabits this alternative world to put some kind of damper on the farm sequence.

What follows sounds like a dime-store romance:

> She is calm; she moves slowly. She looks at Maréchal, and he thinks her beautiful. She removes her shawl, blows out the lamp, and lies down in the warm hay beside Maréchal. And Maréchal listens to her passionate, foreign tongue as she whispers, "It has been over a year since all the men left."

Shades of the promiscuous Josephine rather than Elsa. The "foreign tongue" is there, but sex with a stranger overcomes the language barrier, not the appreciation of a child's blue eyes.

Unfortunately there's a topper:

> Dawn. Maréchal comes out of the barn and looks for eggs in the yard. Meanwhile, soft and beautiful, her long hair in lovely disarray, the German woman lies in the arms of the sleeping Dolette.

The men leave the farm, bidding goodbye "to the woman they shared," and "she has the same smile for both of them." A knowing smirk, no doubt. Not surprisingly, the temptress does not get a name.

Much more is missing. A Rauffenstein-like character appears as "General van der Winter," to whom the captured Frenchmen are brought. He engages in a similar conversation with Boeldieu but then disappears from the movie for good.

The role of Rosenthal is also far less important. He doesn't appear until the last prison camp, as "Dolette," and is not identified as Jewish. Instead of an argument and reconciliation during the escape, Dolette, suffering from his injured foot, "insists that Maréchal abandon him and continue on his own."[2] But this particular Maréchal, having been trained in the Hollywood School of Manly Etiquette, drags Dolette to the providential stable, soon to be rewarded for his good deed with the nameless woman's favors. Nothing so complicated as anger between friends.

Maréchal is a different type of person in the treatment (brutalized and insensitive), with no illusions. During his first day in solitary confinement he thinks to himself: "The war to end all wars; that's a good one."

In line with this approach, the treatment does not cotton to anything infected by the slightest hint of ambiguity. Yet François Truffaut, no slouch as either a critic or filmmaker, wrote in his introduction to the treatment that "most of the essentials of the final film are here"[3] (a nose there, an eye here, part of an ear over there, you've basically got the *Mona Lisa*). But those "essentials" of the plot are meaningless without developed characters or themes and without an indication of something beyond sensationalism.

When Spaak saw the final cut of *La Grande Illusion* he barely recognized the film from earlier versions and even suggested to Renoir that his name be removed from the credits. Who (or what) was responsible for this transformation? It makes sense that the dynamic of so many people coming together at various stages of its development and filming could have resulted in some of these changes, with Renoir expertly guiding the enterprise, making decisions and adjustments along the way to turn down the volume on his project and get it under control.

In a filmed introduction to the 1959 English-subtitled version, Renoir strangely devalues his own film. He describes it as based on the escapes of Capt. Pinsard, and he shows two photographs of World War I planes, giving the impression that they are somehow especially germane to the finished film. Renoir cites the participation of some actors, bringing out photographs of Gabin, Fresnay, Modot, Stroheim, and Parlo. Shockingly, he does not show a still of Dalio, thereby downplaying his major role, not to mention Rosenthal's significance as a Jewish character.

And he condescendingly refers to Parlo as "so sweet, as a German country girl" who "will bring so much love to Jean Gabin,"[4] reducing her to the treatment's more limited characterization. Maybe he thought this pitch would best sell *La Grande Illusion* to an American audience (better to have let the film stand on its own).

More strangely, in a later interview, Renoir boasted that what he "observed of the Jews is absolutely real" and, contrary to the image of them as stingy, Jews often say of themselves that they are vain.[5] Here this master filmmaker, having made a complex work driven by basic humanist principles, including the scourge of anti–Semitism, managed to stereotype Jews and displayed, in some measure, an insensitivity of another sort — if not exactly anti–Semitism. Rosenthal's reference to the sin of pride, at Wintersborn, is a charming and modest reflection. But it's hardly to be taken as claiming the trait of some universal "Jew," even though he talks about Jews as a group at one point. Maréchal, in any case, summarily dismisses his notion.

Movies are a mystery. It sometimes seems a miracle that anything good ever gets made. But despite such an unpromising treatment, Renoir was able to right himself and turn his film around as completely, and gracefully, as one of his pirouetting tracking shots.

15

...and the End of the Journey

> *"Well, what matters is the action, not the target. Of course one needs general ideas, but they must be so deep-rooted, so profound, that one hardly knows one has them. You have to start out in a certain direction, and keep to it, but in the way that migratory birds follow a line instinctively, without knowledge. I believe the artist ought to be like that. And then the conscious part of his mind goes into the detail, into action, into doing.... It ought to be done for the pleasure of the moment, the pleasure of working well."*
> — Jean Renoir in "Conversation with Jean Renoir"; Louis Marcorelles (*Sight & Sound*; Spring 1962; p. 103), used by permission of the British Film Institute

The last, typed version of the scenario, with shots detailed, was completed in November–December 1936, dated in Spaak's handwriting.[1] It is curious that, contrary to Renoir's later explanation that the reprise of "Il était un petit navire" was adopted only when on location, in this draft Dolette, because he is dragging them down, urges Maréchal to leave him, and singing the song gives them courage. They part amicably, exchanging verses, and, as in the finished film, Maréchal returns. This earlier, sentimental sequence was eventually replaced by its darker inverse, and Renoir's story at least partially holds true.

By comparing the last scenario to the finished film, some of the changes that came late in the process become clear. As well as cutting out the dogfight, other scenes were scrapped: the German woman's leg stuck in the grate; a scene of English prisoners digging a second tunnel; the fabrication of a key at Wintersborn; a long conversation between two guards pursuing the escaped prisoners; the gagging of a frontier guard (toned down from Maréchal shooting the guard in the treatment); and a new scene that had been added at some point in which the two fugitives are arrested in Switzerland, suspected of involvement with the Germans.

These deleted scenes dealt mainly with the theme of escape and thus the emphasis was changed considerably at the eleventh hour. But perhaps more importantly, Rauffenstein's scenes, with the engagement of Stroheim, were expanded beyond recognition and, also critically, "Dolette" became "Rosenthal." In addition, the friendly parting of the fugitives developed into their blowup instead, and the German patrol at the border was added.

Other scenes at Wintersborn were yet to be created: Rauffenstein at breakfast; the tour; the room search; the conversation of the two captains, and the following one of Maréchal and Rosenthal; and Boeldieu's deathbed scene.

Prior to these changes, which probably were made in early 1937, the film was far from reaching its final form and would still have been primarily an adventure movie.

As with the treatment, it is not clear how, and why, changes occurred — except for the few instances that Renoir discussed. Movies morph into existence through competing pressures. But Renoir's genius was to help keep the film on course and in an inspired direction,

Location shooting of Maréchal and Rosenthal on the run. Photograph: Sam Lévin (*BFI Stills*).

step by step. And though *La Grande Illusion* did not simply spring directly from Jean Renoir's brow, it could not have sprung from a different source. Nor, for that matter, could have lesser movies like *Les Bas-Fonds* and *La Marseillaise*.

A published scenario (1965), based on the completed film, is only roughly accurate.[2] But it helpfully notes bits of dialogue that were dropped, indicating small adjustments made after the larger changes from the treatment and the November–December 1936 scenario — presumably either just before, or during, filming.

In the shot of Maisonneuve dressed as a woman, the 1965 version of the scenario indicates both Maréchal and Rosenthal call the sight "drôle." It is far more effective to leave them speechless, as in the film, while Maisonneuve nervously repeats the word.

At the end of the window pan at Hallbach, after Maréchal says that what gets him is the sound of marching soldiers, a qualifying phrase was cut: "le même dans toutes les armées" ("the same in all armies"). Removing direct verbalization that might imply the antiwar theme allowed it to be communicated more eloquently through metaphor (the sound of boots) and the image (Gabin's ambiguous expression).

Later, when Boeldieu proposes his escape plan, a line by Maréchal was also cut, before he says that he cannot accept the plan: "Vous risqueriez votre vie pour nous" ("You would risk your life for us"). Again, better left unspoken.

And when Maréchal asks Rosenthal to tell Elsa that they must leave, he was to have added, according to the scenario: "Fais-le pour moi.... Je n'ai pas le courage" ("Do it for me.... I don't have the courage"). Big words like "courage" do not appear often in *La Grande Illusion*, especially not from Maréchal's lips.

There is, then, a directly ascending line, in subtlety and indirection, from treatment to typed scenario to the published transcription and the final film. Crucial scenes and key characters were added piecemeal, while many scenes centered on the mechanism of war and of escape were ditched. And the dialogue became less highly charged and explicit. Perhaps the actors felt uncomfortable saying certain lines, or perhaps Renoir realized, on the set, that scenes would be stronger if left uninflected by self-analysis.

As Renoir once said:

> I don't improvise. I build up a very solid ground. I want to be safe. But while I'm shooting, I discover things I didn't see while I was writing. When you see a piece of acting, it becomes different. You see what's bad is wrong, what's good is good, and you can modify and give better shape to the film. It's the same thing with the scene on the mountain in *The Grand Illusion*. The thing that was unexpected was better than what was planned.[3]

Much indeed was unexpected, before and during the making of the film. And the original plan quickly faded away.

Renoir's suspicion of targets, as expressed in his conversation with Marcorelles, is evident in *La Grande Illusion*. His "general ideas" are so deeply buried that one is not, usually, aware of them. The strength of the film lies, instead, in leading us "into the detail, into action, into doing." The arc from treatment to completed film traces that process graphically.

16

An "Anti" Anti-War Film

"Because I am a pacifist I made 'Grand Illusion.' To my mind a true pacifist is a true Frenchman, a true American or a true German. Among right thinking men the day must come when there will be a common ground of understanding.... In 'Grand Illusion' I attempted to show that we in France really have no hate for the Germans.... I was an officer during the war and I have kept a vivid memory of my comrades. We had no hate for our opponents; they were just as good Germans as we were Frenchmen."
—Jean Renoir in "M. RENOIR SPEAKS OF WAR"
(*New York Times*; October 23, 1938)

When *La Grande Illusion* was being made in 1937, with Nazi Germany a threatening world power, pacifism hardly qualified as a popular cause. After some anti-war films following World War I, the climate had shifted. But Renoir, even in the face of Hitler's growing menace, held to his belief that nations shared a common humanity, foolish as that may have seemed at the time. He once noted that he had made a film in the cause of peace, which became a success, and then, a few years later, came war. Out of step with his time, he was also far ahead of it.

And what a different kind of anti-war film *La Grande Illusion* turned out to be. In some ways it reflects Renoir's lifelong attraction to military uniforms and the code of honor practiced by World War I's officer class. In his memoirs, for instance, he remembered Capt. Pinsard. "He remained faithful to pre-war uniform. It was a pleasure to me to look at him in his tight black tunic and red breeches."[1]

Furthermore, on the surface, the premises for war are never challenged. Naturally, Boeldieu and Rauffenstein, as career officers, accept the protocols of combat. Rauffenstein shoots Boeldieu and, conversely, the border patrol stops shooting at Maréchal and Rosenthal because, in both cases, the rules of this game are obeyed to the letter. The Germans guard, the French try to escape, Elsa is caught in the middle. This is the way war works, and "duty is duty."

More significantly, Maréchal, the central (and generally sympathetic) character, though hoping this will be the last war, never questions it directly; his stated objective is to gain his freedom so he can fight again. And though the old woman outside the gates of Hallbach shows concern for the young German recruits, it is Elsa who comes closest to expressing reservations when she ironically catalogues the deaths of her loved ones in German victories. She also chooses to hide the escaping prisoners and, in her way, stand up to the accepted demands of war.

What makes the movie a powerful anti-war film is that Renoir goes against the genre. He rejects the usual strategy of assaulting the viewer with atrocities. Instead, he shows the possibility of relationships set amidst, and against, the divisions caused by war, diverting his story from the cause to the effect. This sort of indirection and understatement can even be seen as analogous to the film's very technique.

16. An "Anti" Anti-War Film

Jean Renoir in uniform, World War I (*UCLA Charles E. Young Research Library, Department of Special Collections, Jean Renoir Collection*).

La Grande Illusion is an "anti" anti-war film. Renoir attacks war by not attacking war and shows its horrors without specifically showing its horrors. The anti-war feeling lies in his development of the characters, rather than in any ideas they might harbor. Maréchal, and Elsa too, despite her pointed commentary over the photographs, epitomize this approach.

Renoir refuses to give the devil his due. And there is nothing left for the devil but to slink away before such largeness of spirit. He establishes this tone immediately by the dissolve from freedom to captivity, indicating war's arbitrary nature. It could just as easily have been Boeldieu, instead of Rauffenstein, swaggering into his canteen to host a meal for a downed enemy pilot.

Still, the influence of war runs like a *basso obbligato* throughout the film. It provides the skewed culture in which the narrative unrolls and is implicit in the film's title — the grandest illusion being war itself, as well as the idea that the end of this particular one might mean the end of all wars.

Though usually called an anti-war film, it is more accurately a pacifist film. The ends are the means. Renoir makes his case not in a dying soldier coughing up blood but through the love affair on the farm. As the political activist A.J. Muste put it in a well-known quote: "There is no way to peace — peace is the way." Renoir shows the triumph of brotherhood and adopts this idealistic end as the way of the movie itself. A model, not a sermon — "Do as I do" rather than "Do as I say." In his most specific reference to pacifism, the 1938 *New York Times* article, Renoir wrote about "an ideal of human progress,"[2] with the French and Germans sharing much in common. By caring so intensely for the characters, on both sides of the conflict, it becomes only natural for one to find war unthinkable.

In contrast, the typical blood-and-guts, anti-war movie can be dehumanizing. No matter how noble the intention of the filmmaker, that type of film almost invariably exploits or sensationalizes violence to one degree or another, like the mayhem ghoulishly detailed on local television's evening news, appealing to the worst instincts of its consumers. Though bearing witness is important, a film that honestly displays the brutal slaughter of war, whether or not a documentary, exposes victims who have been horribly degraded. We, the captive audience, become voyeurs of that debasement. And a part of it.

There are exceptions, of course, that belie the typical. For instance, Francesco Rosi's little-known and thus underappreciated *Uomini contro* (*Many Wars Ago*, or literally, *Men Against*), made in 1970, is a great anti-war film. Rosi assaults the senses in a nearly unwavering campaign of attrition. But he perhaps manages to avoid sensationalizing war and degrading its victims because of his unusual mixture of neorealism (capturing the chaos, randomness, brutality, the mess of war) and an operatic, even rococo, grandiosity (a stylized removal from that realism). Rosi's highly theatrical neorealism makes of war a tactile sensation and its visceral horror seeps under your flesh — a horror less "real" visually than real emotionally.

But Renoir, in *La Grande Illusion*, takes the tack that the most convincing pacifism is not the pacifism that curses war and holds up its atrocities as exhibit A. He shows the beauty of life, and its pain, as if to say: let's make the most of this fragile, and brief, existence. For almost two hours, he expresses that fragility. We are left to imagine the *Sturm und Drang* that has been cut out, swirling somewhere beyond the confines of the frame, and we can draw our own conclusions.

War, of course, has never been out of style. It simply changes fashion, now and then. In confronting that reality, Renoir's pacifism may be unarticulated but it is not unexpressed. That makes his film timely and, sadly, ever relevant.

17

The Art of Collaboration

"I've never tried to influence anyone at all. In effect, when I make a film I'm asking other people to influence me."
— Jean Renoir in "Interview with Jean Renoir"; Rui Nogueira & François Truchaud, interviewers (*Sight & Sound*; Spring 1968; p. 58), used by permission of the British Film Institute

The careers of most film directors seem, in general, more inconsistent than those of artists in other fields. The stars (of the celestial kind) are rarely aligned. I think the problem, again, lies partly in the vagaries of collaboration on two very distinct levels: the precarious combination of different arts and disciplines into one transmuted art; and, on the interpersonal level, the collective nature of the filmmaking process.

In the first instance, those disparate specialties must be meshed seamlessly with the cinematic expression of them and not supersede or make irrelevant that expression by showing, or explaining, too much. A balance needs to be reached, which is not easy.

Secondly, the director relies on men and women in a number of areas to produce accomplished work while making a movie together as a group. Is that to be expected across the board? The chances for human fallibility are multiplied and things can fall apart. A film director, at this point, bears little resemblance to a musician facing blank staves on a sheet of music or a painter in front of a canvas.

It is hardly surprising, under these conditions, that even the greatest filmmakers may make only one or two masterworks, to my taste at least, along with some good (or perhaps great) films and a slew of middling ones.

Film, then, demands the gifts of a synthesizer and organizer as well as that of a creative artist. And Jean Renoir, for one, dealt shrewdly with the fact that he was not on his own as a filmmaker. From his earliest movies, he brought friends together into a trusted core group. On *La Grande Illusion*, some of his collaborators were part of an informal repertory troupe, working with him regularly during his career: Jacques Becker (assistant), Joseph de Bretagne (sound engineer), Joseph Kosma (music), Eugène Lourié (set decorator), his nephew, Claude Renoir (camera operator), Marguerite Houllé-Renoir (editor), and the actors Gabin, Carette and Modot.

Renoir felt that moviemaking should be fun and welcomed collaboration: "I'm a sort of opportunist. I ask others to give me all the ingredients. For my part I contribute nothing."[1] But such modesty, whether false or genuine, shortchanged his talents. It should not be forgotten that he was the one who made everything come together, and his films clearly bear his mark, despite their unevenness.

In addition, Renoir was adaptable, in conjunction with his collaborators, and sometimes went with developments on the set rather than what he imagined ahead of time and then

Some of the cast and crew of *La Grande Illusion*: Julien Carette (1), Jean Dasté (2), Jean Gabin (3), Gaston Modot (4), Pierre Fresnay (5), Jean Renoir (6), Werner Florian (7). Photograph, Sam Lévin (*courtesy Taschen*).

attempted to replicate. Though his films were planned in advance, he often quoted a remark made by his father, Auguste Renoir, the painter:

> "You should be like a cork, drifting this way and that. You must not resist it, or you will die. It is to push it a bit to the left, or to the right in order to adapt. The other direction to which you are yourself."[2]

Being receptive to experience "the other direction" indicates an acceptance of chance (or fate) that was also in keeping with his interest in Eastern religions.

Satyajit Ray, when he was not yet a director, got to know Renoir during his time in India making *The River* and quoted him as saying: "Each time I make a new film, I want to feel like a child who is learning about the cinema for the first time."[3]

After acting in *La Grande Illusion*, Erich von Stroheim wrote a gracious appreciation of Renoir's qualities, "My First Meeting with Jean Renoir." Given Stroheim's tempestuous reputation, it is a measure of the charisma and quiet self-confidence of Renoir that he was able to help bring out a remarkable performance in his fearsome counterpart.

Stroheim described the experience of filming in Alsace. It began snowing for an extended period and Renoir had to change the script. But the sun came out after five days, melting the snow. He didn't panic, calmly ordered materials to simulate snow, and then waited. Stroheim's account further gives a sense of how Renoir related to his crew:

He is incredibly patient. Without ever raising his voice, he asks over and over again until he gets what he wants. His politeness towards everyone he works with was a source of endless amazement to me, especially as I personally cannot say three words in succession without swearing in whatever language I am using.

Jean Renoir could have been an excellent diplomat as well, for he has far more finesse and ability in his little finger than any professional has in what he calls his brains.[4]

Renoir sometimes referred to a director as *le meneur de jeu*, "the ringleader of the game," who sets up the play but remains apart from it. And Lourié once wrote that "Renoir compared the functions of a film director with those of a chef in a restaurant." He later continued:

Renoir knew how important his collaborators were to his work, and being a truly great director, he did not deny their influence but tried to assimilate it to reinforce his own point of view. The feeling of being an intimate collaborator with Jean made my work with him exhilarating. He sometimes called me his "accomplice." I consider Renoir's accomplice to be a title of nobility in the film world. After *Grand Illusion* was finished, it was hard for me to adjust.[5]

But this could also be Renoir's undoing, having placed himself somewhat at the mercy of others. In particular, the risky intersection of collaboration and openness to change can lead to uncertain results.

In making *La Grande Illusion*, chance obviously played a significant part in the casting. It was also Renoir's good sense to make use of such happy accidents as not having money to film the dogfight and his actors rejecting the florid dialogue written for the blowup. When, on another occasion, Renoir found that Fresnay and Stroheim both spoke English, he used this discovery to work English exchanges into their conversation.

Other critical details also came from his accomplices. The book-burning sequence was based on an incident, related to him by Lourié, in which Czar Nicholas II had shipped icons to his hungry and depleted troops during the Russo–Japanese War of 1904–5.

Lourié also suggested setting Rauffenstein's room in the chapel with its imposing crucifix; Stroheim loved the idea and made a list of props he wanted (they appear in the opening track at Wintersborn). And Lourié further asked Renoir if he could add a geranium pot to the chapel set, which he had seen in the janitor's room at the Haut-Koenigsbourg castle. Renoir agreed, saying he could make use of it (indeed).

The reluctance of the producer to film the German canteen in a chateau proved fortunate as well. Lourié and Renoir paralleled the sequence at the French bar by filming the canteen in a similar prefab location, using the same set; the producer's cost-cutting unintentionally led to this nice effect.

One doesn't think of its sets and props as integral to the success of *La Grande Illusion*. But considering how different the film would be without some of these minor details and expanding that principle to more crucial aspects, it's possible to see how unsteady the balance can become, and how quickly it may be undermined.

Think of what can go wrong in a movie. Take Maréchal. To start, Jean Gabin is at his peak playing the role. But Gabin's performance does not single-handedly define the character. There's the naturalistic dialogue that Renoir and Spaak wrote for Maréchal. And his clothes, his broken arm, his renewed health on the farm. And then, too, the images of Gabin as filmed by Christian Matras — at times worn out, at times radiant, and as part of a group or, in other scenes, gloriously alone.

"Maréchal" is a name on a piece of paper made solid by these collaborators working together to make him Maréchal. To have taken away or changed any single element might

Gabin on the Wintersborn set of Rauffenstein's bedroom (wearing his sling from Hallbach) with two unidentified colleagues in the production. Photograph: Sam Lévin (©*Ministère de la Culture/ Médiathèque du Patrimoine/Sam Levin/dist. RMN-Grand Palais/Art Resource, New York*).

have made him a less believable character. Or conceivably, though not likely, a more vivid one. And that would affect the movie around him, as in the parable of the detail altered in the past causing large changes in the future. No man is an island. No prop, no fleeting image without its effect. When something is missing and things don't fit together smoothly, a film can spiral out of control and be like the nightmare world of Capra's *It's a Wonderful Life*, transformed by an alteration to the overall scheme.

In *La Grande Illusion* there was, as in any film, a tenuous progression from the original idea to the final script (as shepherded by Renoir and Spaak), to casting and directing the actors (the nearly flawless performances), to filming (a transparent and yet expressive style), and to editing (the classic structure and natural flow). Decisions had to be made and people coaxed along or given free rein, at every turn.

Françoise Giroud remembered Renoir on the set as "*le patron*":

> Respecting only one heirarchy [sic], that of professional competence, he gave us all the chance to understand how fifty individual efforts could fuse into a collective effort and give each one the pride of having fully participated.
>
> Is that a grand illusion? It is his, and I must not be the only one to whom he has communicated it.[6]

Yet Renoir, despite embracing collaboration, on one occasion referred to himself as a tyrant and wrote that his "tyranny extended into every field," including props and music.

A bit of tongue-in-cheek may have been involved here, but he went on to define his role, as a director, in terms of getting collaborators to do what he wanted in a way that convinced them it was their own idea. Renoir concluded: "I got nearer and nearer to the ideal method of directing, which consists in shooting a film as one writes a novel."[7]

Simple enough for him to say perhaps, but the reality facing a film director is a good deal more complicated than that.

18

Other Takes, Different Angles

"'The thing about Renoir was that he was extraordinarily friendly and jovial, remarkably unpretentious, extremely accessible,' recalled Malle. 'It seemed at the first meeting there was no generation gap of any kind. He was terribly curious and interested in our work. He was enthusiastic about our enthusiasm. He was very modern.... We recognised that the generosity he had as a man was evident in his films. Renoir was the inspiration for our generation when we started making our own films. You could say he was the father of the New Wave. There was something about his cinema which was so inventive and spontaneous. Somewhat ignoring the rules and inventing the rules.'"
— Louis Malle in *Jean Renoir: Projections of Paradise*
by Ronald Bergan (The Overlook Press; 1995; p. 293)

In 1937 the initial reviews of *La Grande Illusion* in France, and the following year in the United States, were generally enthusiastic, hailing the film as a great work. Most critics stressed its anti-war theme, the class divisions, the relationship between Boeldieu and Rauffenstein, its realism and understated technique. To a large degree, that has been the pattern ever since.

There were also left-wing critics in the 1930s who identified *La Grande Illusion* as a Popular Front movie, in the spirit of that political coalition of leftist parties. But it is notable, reflecting the film's open-ended nature, that others condemned it as nationalistic; they claimed Renoir had embraced patriotism and exhibited nostalgia for the aristocracy.

Conversely, some right-wing reviewers praised it for the same reason. And Lucien Rebatet, under the pseudonym of François Vinneuil, wrote a repugnant review in which he made an obscurely framed argument that Rosenthal's valor as a soldier represented an exceptional case only (?) and that Renoir, therefore, served the anti–Jewish cause (??).

That Roosevelt and Mussolini both liked the film is an illustration of this strange division of opinion at the time. "*Chacun à son goût,*" but to see this film simply as a political statement is patently reductive.

In response to the *Kavalier Scharnhorst* affair, Renoir once wrote: "I did everything possible to make a film which, by being totally national, would be absolutely international."[1] This fairly assesses a paradox that marks his film. Renoir was true to the culture of France, but not at the expense of other cultures and peoples, and thus was able to transcend national boundaries.

On its rerelease in 1946, Georges Altman, a French journalist, added to the controversy by attacking the movie as "pacifisme sentimental" and seeing racism in the relationship of Maréchal and Rosenthal. He also expressed indignation at the friendship between Germans and Frenchmen, as seen in hindsight after the Nazi horrors. "Le sang est trop proche" ("The blood is too near").[2] Other critics came to the film's defense and Altman's hysteria, misguided even in 1946, seems thoroughly dated now. The truth of the film was, and always has been, beyond the genocide of the Nazis.

Yet the narrow politicization of the movie continued. Marc Ferro, in *Cinema and History* (1977; 1988 translation), took exception to its favorable German characters, the effeminate English soldiers, the mocking comments directed at Rosenthal and at intellectuals, and even what he saw as a "resentment against women" (true of some Renoir films, but not this one). He went so far as to call it "a perfect model of a virtual apology in favor of Vichy" though oddly noting that this is done "without the director's knowledge or desire."[3]

In *French Cinema* (1985), Roy Armes praised the acting and the lessons in solidarity, and then threw in a series of "buts": that the film doesn't see class differences as unjust; that it offers "a nostalgic look back at a now vanished world"; that it is "almost too benign a view of war" since atrocities are not shown and the Holocaust was soon to come. He condescendingly suggested that maybe because of this approach it was popular, although there is "only a partial view of Renoir's complex talents."[4]

These fulminations miss the obvious point that *La Grande Illusion* is primarily about people and relationships, rather than politics and broad theses, but critics often treat it as if the characters are merely stand-ins for the stereotype of a German or Frenchman, an aristocrat, a workingman. As well, the film is about the pall cast by World War I's carnage, not the carnage itself. And there are clearly no rules set by the film gods ordaining that a movie must show the atrocities of war directly to be morally, and politically, correct.

When critics reduce Renoir's film to designations like "left-wing" or "patriotic" or "reactionary," *La Grande Illusion* disappears and the politics of the critics in question take over. Such diatribes do a disservice. There is no "for" or "against," no pros and cons to be weighed. The characters are not even necessarily consistent, nor can they be pigeonholed to make a point. The film is "pointless" in the best sense of the word.

A great deal, naturally, has been written about *La Grande Illusion*. Taking only a cursory look at the literature on the film in French, two names stand out: Roger Viry-Babel and Olivier Curchod. And Daniel Serceau has also published interesting analyses.

Viry-Babel's *Jean Renoir: films/textes/références* (1989) supplies a useful filmography and reference for written works, and *Jean Renoir: Le jeu et la règle* (1994) is an informative review of all his films. Though I haven't read it, Viry-Babel also completed a university thesis in 1973 that, according to Curchod, includes a second volume on the film with a scenario that corrects errors in the published version.

Curchod's critical study, *La Grande Illusion: Jean Renoir* (1994), is part of a series called "Synopsis" devoted to individual movies. This valuable little book provides a solid understanding and appreciation of the film. Curchod makes original observations about the structure and Renoir's technical approach. He also presents a meticulous history of the film's production and the development of the scenario, from treatment to final version. And a fascinating (and lengthy) discussion of the cinematic qualities underlying the second tête-à-tête of Boeldieu and Rauffenstein.

But this brief summary, of course, does not even begin to characterize the many works in French that deal with *La Grande Illusion*.

As for works published in English, an extensive and insightful appraisal of the film is Alexander Sesonske's 41-page analysis in *Jean Renoir: The French Films, 1924–1939* (1980), a worthy homage that appropriately honors the subject with its lyrical style. Sesonske makes intelligent connections through a kind of stream of consciousness, darting here and there, and he has an eye for the telling detail. Though very strong in analyzing characters and themes, and though he quotes the dialogue at length, he also makes some perceptive points about the technique as well, at least more than most other critics have attempted.

The work done by Christopher Faulkner is also important in studying Renoir, particularly his exhaustive and scholarly *Jean Renoir, a guide to references and resources* (1979) and his beautiful, oversize book with many photographs from the films and from Renoir's life, *Jean Renoir: A Conversation with His Films 1894–1979* (2007). But in another book, *The Social Cinema of Jean Renoir* (1986), he diminishes *La Grande Illusion* at times to the level of a Popular Front film that is politically driven. Though Faulkner eloquently cites the emotional intensity of the farm scenes, he reduces them as a whole to a commentary on war and class.

Martin O'Shaughnessy's *La Grande Illusion (Jean Renoir, 1937)* (2009) is the longest analysis of the film, up to that date, and contributes some cogent analyses of particular shots and scenes (especially his take on the two canteens). He also furnishes a full account of its reception through the years and adds further to Curchod's chronology of the various scripts, including the hitherto unexplored outline by Renoir.

In expanding on observations in his earlier book, *Jean Renoir* (2000), O'Shaughnessy applies an explicitly political interpretation and calls the film "a classic example of political cinema."[5] Hitching Popular Front politics to the film can become forced, as when he metaphorically imagines Maréchal and his comrades, during the window pan, staring down into Germany under the Nazis. But the militarism in 1916 was enough of a horror to warrant Maréchal's expression.

Another 2009 book, Julian Jackson's *La Grande Illusion*, is slimmer (about half as long) and presents an introduction to the history and basic dynamics of the film, with only a few side excursions into its cinematic technique and with large chunks of dialogue cited in English. It can be quite unreliable in places and Jackson, like O'Shaughnessy, yokes the film to the politics of its time; he too imagines an implied reference to storm troopers under the window at Hallbach.

A key piece in the literature is an article by James Kerans, "Classics Revisited: 'La Grande Illusion'" (1960). Its idiosyncratic style and high tone of seriousness make it an early groundbreaking text. At one point, for instance, he poetically calls Boeldieu a "mathematician of behavior" in working out his escape plan as a "good solution." Kerans offers insights that provide a different perspective on a movie that too often gets the same predictable treatment, and he persuasively develops an intriguing concept of "the polarity of ceremony and instinct" in the film.[6]

Stanley Kauffmann's succinct analysis in *Living Images* (1975) makes a number of salient points and looks at the film as a cinematic achievement. He captures the effect of the confrontation in the mountains and appreciates the farm scenes. And Colin Davis in *Scenes of Love and Murder: Renoir, Film and Philosophy* (2009) also does honor to the farm, and he discusses the film in terms of the strength found in differences as well as the fragile balance between separateness and community.

Most of the other critical writing on *La Grande Illusion* is sketchier and deals less extensively with Renoir's technique. As in the first reviews of the film in 1937, its themes are noted and the focus usually falls on Boeldieu and Rauffenstein.

Their relationship becomes the exemplar for Renoir's often-expressed idea about the world being divided horizontally rather than vertically. His film, however, only partially illustrates this old saw, since Boeldieu ends up rejecting the demands of class loyalty. Does that make him a class-breaker, or a patriot giving his life for his country? Maybe a mixture of both, though weighted toward patriotism. But critics frequently minimize the complexity of the relationship forged between Boeldieu and Rauffenstein to a discussion of plot and dialogue.

And a major focus is the anti-war "message." Many critics cite this element with admiration, but some find fault with Renoir, calling his film dated and claiming that he made World War I into a "gentleman's war" (Renoir didn't help by sometimes using that phrase).

Many critical assessments present the farm sequences as an afterthought, if they are mentioned at all. Only a handful of critics emphasize the importance of these scenes; some even dismiss them as a weakness. At times, they are excluded from the simplest description of the film. The blurb in a 1973 Janus Films catalogue, the bible for foreign film rentals in the 1960s and 70s, leapfrogs from Boeldieu's death to the final shots in Switzerland.

Strangely, the pervasiveness of Maréchal's presence, impelling the film forward, is also often downplayed. His solid, dependable demeanor exudes a certain unhurried serenity and, like Poe's purloined letter, can be overlooked. As well, the roles of Rosenthal and Elsa as irreplaceable players are similarly marginalized in much of the criticism.

Beyond themes and characters, there is a recurring pattern in the discussion of specific shots and scenes. This limited selection, because of so many omissions, allows the inference to be made that only at rare moments does *La Grande Illusion* rise above the level of a thesis film. The shots most often noted are panning and tracking shots: the pan to Maisonneuve in a skirt, the circular track during the singing of "La Marseillaise," the opening track at Wintersborn. Also noted are the window pan at Hallbach, the matching tracks in the French and German canteens, and the scene of Boeldieu's death.

But these shots are usually analyzed not so much for their cinematic attributes as for their relevance to the plot and the film's themes. Some critics, for instance, have mentioned the similar singing of "La Marseillaise" in *Casablanca* (1942) and others even cite *Stalag 17* (1953) and *The Great Escape* (1963) as comparable escape movies. But none of these later films have anything in common with *La Grande Illusion* beyond minor plot similarities; it is absurd to mention them in the same breath as Renoir's film.

There are also some sequences not covered to the extent they deserve: the opening shot, the two scenes in solitary confinement, the blowup in the mountains, both "blaue Augen" sequences, the embrace of the lovers and the Christmas morning scene, the border. Or even the barbed wire sequence at Hallbach, despite its inconsequence in terms of the plot.

These oversights indicate a striking lack of technical analysis in the literature. But Renoir's subtle technique is a way of life in *La Grande Illusion* and not just a collection of momentary flashes of inspiration orchestrated into "big moments."

Yet Peter Harcourt, in *Six European Directors* (1974), after praising the film for its "immense warmth and humanity," astonishingly adds: "But it also seems to me to be a film that requires very little comment." And, though he cites the power of the romance on the farm, he writes that the film has "an element of thinness, as if everything is too neatly resolved by the end."[7] These sentiments reflect, again, the old canard that *La Grande Illusion* is less a cinematic work of art than a humanitarian thesis thoughtfully bundled for the viewer, and enough said.

A problem exists at the heart of any appraisal of film technique. Very simply, shots flit by so quickly that it becomes hard to recall their exact details.

I've been humbled on this score. After 20 theatrical viewings of *La Grande Illusion*, and many more times watching bits and pieces on videocassette and DVD, I found, nearing completion of this book, that certain nuances had been inaccurately described.

These discoveries sent me scrambling to review other sequences, playing shots over and over to pin down when exactly the camera moves or a certain word is spoken. It was a chastening experience, and I found more mistakes. A few errors were even significant enough to affect the point being made. And now I would not be so foolhardy as to guarantee that no errors remain in my description of shots in any of Renoir's movies.

Shots are difficult to transcribe on a first or second (or sometimes an umpteenth) viewing; incorrect images get stuck in one's memory. Using a DVD to move back and forth in a film can take some maneuvering to correct a mistaken reading. As in checking for typos in a manuscript, the eye keeps repeating the same error, tricked by an initially false imprinting.

The easy way out for critics is to write about the story and characters, and perhaps the

Marguerite Renoir and Jean Renoir joking it up with Jean Gabin (in character) on location for the blowup. Photograph: Sam Lévin (©*Ministère de la Culture/Médiathèque du Patrimoine/Sam Levin/dist. RMN-Grand Palais/Art Resource, New York*).

director's philosophical point of view, and then add a summation to cover things like editing, cinematography, even direction, as if they can be divorced from the mechanics of the film. For lesser movies, where not much happens cinematically, that kind of approach is at least serviceable; I use it myself for some of Renoir's weaker films. But for films of more substance, it represents a fatal sacrifice on the altar of convenience.

Published scripts don't always help critics since they can be inaccurate in important ways. It is imperative, however, to get it right, or analysis becomes meaningless and counterproductive. Yet a cavalier attitude prevails in some film criticism about the sequence or composition of shots, as though it's enough to be roughly accurate (horseshoes and grenades). Even extravagantly produced coffee-table books can contain major gaffes in simple plot summaries, let alone shot descriptions. Publishers in other fields, it is safe to say, would never tolerate a reversed image of a painting or print the wrong order of words in a poem.

Also noticeable is that production stills are often not distinguished from frames reproduced directly from *La Grande Illusion*. But the posed stills on the set can be quite different from the actual shots.

And there is also sloppiness in using translated dialogue without citing the original French, at times without even listing the source of the translation. Hardly a respect for Renoir's insistence on the appropriate language in the film itself.

For many years, the published scenarios of *La Grande Illusion*, as in the wider literature, also had a skewed emphasis. Certainly Rauffenstein, and more specifically Erich von Stroheim, served as the meal ticket for the publishers, with stills of him dominating their covers. Stroheim's fame as a director, his outrageous personality and his low-key but nonetheless scene-stealing performance help account for this emphasis. It shows, as well, the bias toward the Boeldieu-Rauffenstein axis. And the photographs within these publications usually failed to indicate the relative importance of the characters, with Maréchal barely pictured more than Boeldieu.

An encouraging shift was signaled by the cover of Curchod's book (1994), with Maréchal in a group at Hallbach, and was cemented by those of the 2009 books, with Maréchal bidding goodbye to Boeldieu (O'Shaughnessy) and playing the harmonica (Jackson). And in these later books Maréchal is best represented in the photographs inside.

The restored version of *La Grande Illusion*, released theatrically in 1999, made Renoir's film a bit more current. The elegant and sturdy Paul Davis poster accompanying its release features a large portrait of Maréchal, with Jean Gabin's name placed first in the list of actors below; at the bottom is a smaller portrait of Rauffenstein. Though a bit incongruous that these two men, who don't often interact together, are pictured in the same layout without others, Maréchal is at least prominently featured.

When Jean Renoir died, *The New York Times* cited *Grand Illusion* in its headline but felt compelled to identify it as a film (February 14, 1979). The obituary had a still of Rauffenstein in the courtyard with his soldiers, and the caption incorrectly noted that the movie was shot in 1939. *The Rules of the Game* is referred to as being often considered his greatest achievement (fair enough). New York's *Daily News*, in its account, cited *Grand Illusion* as one of the great films but only mentioned *The Rules of the Game* among other films.

Despite many appreciative notices like these obituaries, *La Grande Illusion* is not universally admired. That certainly does not make it unique among great films. But there are more critics cool to this film than one might expect, given its acknowledged status as a classic of the cinema.

It bears looking into the critical writings of François Truffaut because his attitude toward *La Grande Illusion* typifies this strain of lukewarm, if not sometimes hostile, criticism. The well-known director admired Renoir and made a memorable splash in 1959 with his first feature, *Les Quatre Cents coups* (*The 400 Blows*), an important film of the Nouvelle Vague. Truffaut appeared to have found in the older director a mentor, friend, even something of a father figure. During that same period, Renoir's renaissance was in full sway with the rerelease of *La Grande Illusion* and most particularly, in 1959, with the restoration also of *La Règle du jeu*.

In 1958, Truffaut joined the sideshow that had started with the reissue of *La Grande Illusion* twelve years earlier. He wrote that the film was "passablement démodée" ("fairly old-fashioned") because of the Nazis and even designated it "un film historique, c'est-à-dire en retard sur son temps" ("a historical film, that is to say, late in terms of its time") since, soon afterward, Chaplin thrashed Nazism in *The Great Dictator* (1940).[8] But that simplistic

François Truffaut and Renoir, Beverly Hills (1973). Photograph: Roger Corbeau (©*Ministère de la Culture/Médiathèque du Patrimoine/Roger Corbeau/dist. RMN-Grand Palais/Art Resource, New York*).

film, released after war had begun, appallingly reduces Hitler to a buffoon; Chaplin may have had his heart in the right place but not much else was so well positioned.

Truffaut later edited André Bazin's unfinished study of the director, *Jean Renoir* (1971; 1973 translation). He wrote in the introduction that he was hardly detached in his passion, feeling that "*Jean Renoir* by André Bazin is the *best* book on the cinema, written by the *best* critic, about the *best* director." The superlatives start raining down harder as he installs Renoir on an auteur's throne and cedes any interest in critical judgment by writing that "I am not far from thinking that the work of Jean Renoir is the work of an infallible film maker" and that he created "the most alive films in the history of the cinema."[9]

At the back of Bazin's book, a number of writers present thumbnail analyses of Renoir's films. Truffaut himself contributed a one-page appreciation of *La Grande Illusion*.[10] He opens: "I will not be so perverse as to belittle the one Renoir film which has been understood and loved by audiences all over the world." He then proceeds to do just that, as a modern-day Mark Antony who reverses the con in claiming to praise, not bury, the film: "I think simply that *Grand Illusion* is just as good a film as *Toni*, or *The Lower Depths*, or *The Southerner*." A case of damning with faint praise.

It can be hard at times to tell whether Truffaut, as with other *Cahiers du Cinéma* critics of the time, is merely exhibiting the bluster of an *enfant terrible* or also making a polemical point based on deep-rooted convictions. And perhaps it's unfair, and certainly futile, to argue about something that can be explained as a matter of taste. But his dictum seems akin to saying that *Citizen Kane* is as good as *The Lady from Shanghai* or *Mr. Arkadin* or *The Trial*. Down such a road one quickly loses bearings.

Part of the bias against *La Grande Illusion* may be due to its popularity. According to Truffaut, Renoir's talents served "a patriotic theme, and everyone knows that movies about the war, the resistance, and prison escapes succeed automatically." (Hmm). Truffaut further claims that excesses, for which Renoir was often criticized in his career, are "permitted" when found in this genre. But it is ridiculous to characterize *La Grande Illusion* as a patriotic movie. The singing of "La Marseillaise" is a scene of intense nationalistic fervor, but not a triumphant moment. One doesn't leave the theater with an image in one's head of the French tricolour waving heroically.

Most bizarrely, Truffaut writes that "Renoir explains very clearly that the idea of class should remain, all the more since certain classes disappear on their own." And that boundaries "should be abolished." But Renoir explains little — that's one of his endearing characteristics. And where does he make known this alleged embrace of class? He had a romantic affection for the chivalric code, but nothing in the movie lends support to Rauffenstein's nostalgic monologue about the passing of his kind from the world's scene. One may feel empathy for Rauffenstein and Boeldieu as people, though not necessarily for their views on class.

Truffaut ends his piece by stating that *La Grande Illusion* is an unusual Renoir film in that "psychology takes precedence over poetry" and that it remains "perhaps the least eccentric of all of Renoir's French movies." A restrictive observation, blind to the poetry embedded in its cinematic language.

One can agree that the film may not be "eccentric" but is, instead, classic and balanced; this is no work of an Angry Young Man. But "eccentricity" doesn't provide a guarantee against banality. It can often be a pose that wears thin. True eccentricity in a conformist world involves originality of self-expression, not the mannerisms cloaking self-promotion. Under that definition, *La Grande Illusion* qualifies as an exceedingly eccentric film.

It may be pertinent that Truffaut's *Jules et Jim*, released in 1962, is squarely in the mode both of *La Règle du jeu* and many other Renoir works. *La Grande Illusion* differs from most of those movies in dealing seriously with mature relationships and that dreaded "L word" (Love). No casual affairs, no multiple lovers, and no murder spurred by jealousy. *La Règle du jeu* captures the glamour of sexual byplay, indulged in by wisecracking sophisticates. But that is not what makes it eccentric and original.

In looking at Truffaut's assessment of *La Règle du jeu*, also in Bazin's book, he chronicles its failure on release and how the film "for decades was appreciated only by film buffs."[11] This possibly gets closer to what drives him — the ones in the know understand more than the ignorant public, which was duped by *La Grande Illusion* and missed the subtleties of Renoir's later masterpiece. The proponents of this brand of criticism stand up to conventional wisdom and patronize *La Grande Illusion*, for example, by acknowledging it the equal of an undistinguished film like *The Southerner*.

Truffaut continues that, after *La Grande Illusion* and *La Bête humaine* (*The Human Beast*), Renoir "tired of psychology in movies" and now needed "to show instead of to analyze, to move instead of to touch." Again, taste cannot be argued. But just looking at the evidence on the screen, the characters in *La Règle du jeu* analyze their loves, their shortcomings, and their psyches more than do the protagonists in *La Grande Illusion*.

Responding to a question asking which films on peace and war are most effective, Truffaut wrote in 1962: "war films, even pacifist, even the best, willingly or not, glorify war and render it in some way attractive: *La Grande Illusion* (which I admire) makes one want to be a prisoner."[12] Allowing for a healthy dose of mischief, as he also notes that Howard Hawks's *Sergeant York* makes him want to be a war hero, this reaction to Renoir's film seems extraordinary. Is the enforced male bonding of prison camps really so much fun? And is that why the French are always trying to escape? If anything, the film might encourage the idea of retreating to a farm in some secluded spot.

Elsewhere, Truffaut wrote that "*La Grande Illusion* is a film precisely about chivalry."[13] And he emphasized the adventure and sport of war, in further minimizing its scope.

But Truffaut, in these pieces, does not write about either Elsa or the farm. In a much longer 1974 essay in a combined scenario and photographic version of the film, he presents the uncontroversial party line — how hard it was to produce, its success, the autobiographical elements, class divisions, its anti-war theme, the movie's realism and its censored state until the restoration of 1958.[14]

The lengthiest analysis in this essay is devoted to Boeldieu and Rauffenstein. Truffaut writes that their relationship is such that, even if the character of Elsa did not exist, one could say there's a love story in the film. He elaborates on this thought by describing the relationship of Boeldieu and Rauffenstein as "l'histoire d'amour qui court tout au long de *La Grande Illusion*" ("the love story that runs throughout *La Grande Illusion*"), parallel to the story of Maréchal, Rosenthal and the actor. It's strange that he cites the actor, who appears in a section of the movie in which Rauffenstein is absent, like Elsa, but whose relationship to Maréchal and Rosenthal, unlike her relationship to them, proves inconsequential. Truffaut only mentions Elsa, in fact, to posit her absence.

Most revealingly, Truffaut writes that if one considers the film divided into "trois parties" ("three parts"), the middle part is devoted to the musical show. Given the math of that particular characterization of the structure, unless one somehow manages to lump together the farm with Wintersborn, the farm becomes non-history. In this revisionist version, only the men exist, boarding in prison heaven with their own love story. And the farm ends up on the cutting room floor.

Truffaut also notes that the most beautiful moment in the film occurs when the English officer at Hallbach starts up "La Marseillaise"— the sendoff for the shot that, with its nationalistic slant, is in sharpest contrast to the farm sequences.

This relegation of Elsa, and to a degree Maréchal as well, to the dustbin of film history, along with the canonization of Boeldieu and Rauffenstein and the "Marseillaise" sequence, could serve as an example of the traditional approach to *La Grande Illusion*. And it can also serve as a measure of how seriously the film has been underestimated.

Whatever the reason for this large sector of the literature dealing with Renoir's classic film, psychological or aesthetic, it is shortsighted and needs correction. The resurgence of *La Grande Illusion* in 1999, with Maréchal featured on the film's poster, was a step forward and boded well for its future.

Part III
THE DIRECTOR

19

Jean Renoir
A Biographical Sketch

Jean Renoir (September 15, 1894–February 12, 1979)

Jean Renoir was 25 years old when his father, Pierre Auguste Renoir, the Impressionist painter, died on December 3, 1919. The young Renoir, a veteran of World War I, was making ceramics without much success, though also beginning to have an interest in the relatively new medium of movies.

The father, as a famous painter of the period, is certainly far better known than the son — an indication in part that film is still not generally accepted as an important art form. In any case, rarely do both a parent and offspring become such major figures in the arts.

Jean served as a model for some of his father's paintings, achieving a small measure of immortality before he would earn it more significantly as a moviemaker. But, in some ways, he remained swamped by Auguste Renoir's fame despite being known as one of film's greatest directors.

A fair comparison of them as artists is difficult, of course, partly because there are far more acknowledged masters and distinct eras in painting than in film. Still, Renoir, the director, has a central role in film history as one of its most influential figures; Renoir *père*, it could be argued, though a great painter within a specific movement, exerted only limited influence beyond his era.

In December 1919, Jean Renoir's life was on the verge of a dramatic change. And two pivotal events helped him begin to escape Auguste's long shadow, as a person and as an artist.

First, in 1920, he married one of his father's favorite models, Andrée Heuschling, known as Dédée. Renoir's own mother, Aline, had also been a model for the painter before her marriage to him.

Then Renoir saw Ivan Mosjoukine's *Le Brasier ardent* (1923), an experimental film made in France by a charismatic Russian actor. Along with Stroheim's *Foolish Wives*, it impressed upon Renoir the possibility of creating an authentic French cinema far removed from the academic and theatrical films popular at the time. He abandoned ceramics, a profession his father had encouraged him to pursue, and began making movies; Dédée starred in his early ventures.

With this quasi–Oedipal challenge to his famous father, he took his first steps toward becoming Jean Renoir, the filmmaker, and not merely a son of the painter. To his death, however, he honored the memory of his father, writing a loving biographical reminiscence and applying some of Auguste Renoir's aesthetic principles to his own works.

Childhood

Jean Renoir was born in Paris on September 15, 1894 at the Château des Brouillards, the family home in the Montmartre section. His birth was witnessed by Gabrielle Renard, his mother's 16-year-old cousin, who became his principal caretaker during childhood and also a strong presence throughout Renoir's life. He ended his 1974 memoir, *My Life and My Films*, written only a few years before his death, with a touching plea to the woman who had died in 1959: "'Wait for me, Gabrielle.'"[1]

Her importance to him can be traced back to the time of his birth. In *Renoir, My Father*, the revealing biography-cum-memoir of his father, Renoir reported the various reactions to his arrival, as most probably provided by Gabrielle. His mother exclaimed: "'Heavens, how ugly! Take it away!'" (notice the impersonal pronoun). His father commented: "'What a mouth; it's a regular oven! He'll be a glutton.'" Renoir, in an aside, added: "Alas, his prediction was to come true." But Gabrielle's reaction was different, saying, "'*I* think he's beautiful.'" Renoir noted: "Everyone laughed."[2]

Complicating this mixed reception to baby Jean's entrance onto the world's stage, Auguste, according to Renoir, "was terribly worried" about Aline, who had had an earlier miscarriage; "he accused himself of selfishness," putting her at risk for the momentary pleasures of sex.[3] It seems that, even at his own birth, Renoir was not assigned the leading role, upstaged by his father's self-pity and protestations of compassion for Aline.

The pattern was set. Renoir's relationship to his parents, especially to his mother,

Gabrielle Renard, Renoir's beloved surrogate mother, with paintings of Auguste Renoir (ca. 1910) (*UCLA Charles E. Young Research Library, Department of Special Collections, Jean Renoir Collection*).

remained conflicted. Though he glorified his father's place in art history, Renoir wrote little about his mother and what comes out is equivocal. He saw her as an uncomplicated woman who liked the comforts of an orderly life. The stout Mme. Renoir closely resembled her son and had, like Jean, a large appetite.

His world, as he put it, became divided into two parts. His mother made him do the things he had to do, while Gabrielle was the one with whom he had fun. And she carried him around, unlike Mme. Renoir. That he should think of Gabrielle as he neared the end of his life is hardly surprising. As he once described her, she embodied "the criterion of everything that was good."[4]

Renoir grew up in a protected and privileged environment, revolving around Auguste and his artist (and writer) friends. Jean's older brother, Pierre, became a respected actor, not only in some of Renoir's films but also in his own right; Claude (Coco), his younger brother, pursued a career in film and television production, and he later moved on to make ceramics.

Auguste Renoir was clearly ruler of the roost. In the area of child rearing he ruled largely by proxy. He believed in spankings, feeling they were good for both the child and the parents (not unusual for the time), though he never administered them himself and left the dirty work to his wife.

Renoir's father also had an eccentric attitude toward women. He professed love for them and wanted women surrounding him, claiming they were superior to men because they did not make judgments but simply experienced life. This didn't prevent him from joking about their demands for education and independence. He instead valued the simple virtues of motherhood and held the traditional view that women were not fit for men's work.

It also appears that the son doth protest too much in referring to his father's nudes as being "of a purity unequaled in the whole history of art."[5] And it is odd that, at one point, after having mentioned that his parents slept in separate rooms, he felt the need to bring up their sexuality "to stress how normal Renoir was in everything, including sex,"[6] even as he apologized for bringing it up.

The choice of the word "normal" is a peculiar one. Auguste was, at the least, quirkily original and well beyond fitting norms. A man of many opinions, he made pronouncements on a range of subjects. One of his theories was that women needed the exercise provided by housework in order to enjoy making love. He also rationalized the need for prostitution in a patriarchal society and even, according to his son, envied pimps.

With his father's models around the house (including Gabrielle), Renoir grew accustomed to nudity and was surprised that classmates were excited by pictures of nudes. But this bit of worldliness seems to have been overwhelmed by ambivalent feelings about gender, stimulated by a love-hate relationship with the long hair he had as a little boy.

Renoir's obsession with his hair is a notable leitmotif throughout his childhood. In the first 26 pages of his memoir he refers to these luxurious tresses four times. And, though his biographical study of Auguste Renoir has only tangential references to himself in the second half of the book, he manages to bring up four more anecdotes about the shame, even trauma, inadvertently caused by his hair.

His father loved Jean's long curls. He delighted in painting them and, in one of his maxims, believed they protected his son in falls and from damage caused by the sun. They were "'real gold,'"[7] according to the painter in a phrase repeated by others, and were, initially, a source of pride for his son. Perhaps they served as a welcomed connection to his father. But the curls also led to difficult moments.

In one incident, Auguste insisted on painting him and his reddish golden hair, even as Jean resisted and started sobbing. He pretended to have a bad leg, limping around (later in life he limped for real, from his war wound). Gabrielle suggested that he sew a coat for his toy camel while sitting for his father, and the little boy was placated. On another occasion, Auguste wanted to dress Jean in a velvet costume with lace collar to achieve a Little Lord Fauntleroy effect; Gabrielle remembered him kicking as he was forced to dress up in the suit.

Not surprisingly, Jean developed a liking for clothes he saw as masculine. He envied his brother's school cap in particular, because of its manly air. But when given a similar cap, which offended him since it didn't have some important features, he lost his temper, was called a spoiled brat, and then was spanked by his mother.

Another memory stemmed from a scene in a train car. Renoir was holding a smelly cheese on his lap and fellow passengers thought that the "girl" with the long red locks had messed her underwear. Doubly insulted, he pulled down his pants to disabuse them of their misconceptions. His mother wanted to get rid of the cheese, but his father was amused by the whole affair.

And one of Renoir's most poignant memories involved an incident when traveling with his parents on another train. An English woman in their compartment referred to him as:

Auguste Renoir, *Child with Toys — Gabrielle and the Artist's Son, Jean* (1895–1896), oil on canvas (*courtesy National Gallery of Art, Washington*).

"'Such a sweet little girl, such pretty hair!'" At the same moment, by coincidence, Renoir's pet lizard popped its head out from his shirt. The woman screamed and his father tried to soothe her. But she got a guard on the train to throw the offending reptile out the window. Renoir was in tears. And he closes his anecdote: "The English lady, relieved, settled back in her corner and, indifferent to my sobbing, began to read the Bible."[8] It is the sort of vividly cinematic detail that graces many of his movies — and, significantly, the lady's indifference plays a bigger role in the retelling than the apparent lack of comfort or outrage from his parents.

Renoir was 7 years old when his hair was finally cut so that he could attend school, though he turned out to be neither a disciplined student nor a happy one. His father had resisted cutting the curls and Renoir himself was unsure, though he felt relieved after the fact. He hated being mistaken for a girl on the street, but at least there was value attached to this "real gold" at home.

Paralleling Renoir's struggle with his long hair was a fascination with the pageantry of soldiers and their uniforms. Writing about this attraction, he noted an ecstasy that was "more physical than spiritual." He described becoming a different person, and added: "I forgot about my long hair, although I hated it to the point of weeping."[9]

At 10, he discovered Alexandre Dumas: "The Musketeers restored the dignity of long hair — it is impossible to imagine d'Artagnan with a crew-cut."[10] At one stage he wanted to be a Napoleonic grenadier and he loved toy soldiers, a passion shared with his father.

One day the young Jean was glad to be sent on an errand to get cigarettes for his father (the boy on a man's excursion). But, preoccupied with his distinctive accent and how it made people laugh at him, he absentmindedly ended up walking too far. He ran back, worried that his parents would be anxious, ever sensitive to their psyches.

When he arrived home, his father had indeed been concerned and scolded him angrily, "'Did you ever see such a muddle-head! You'll never be any good.'" Renoir burst into tears. Auguste, reversing roles with his son, went into a sulk but soon began painting. "When I heard him begin humming to himself, I forgot my own wounded feelings and got out my lead soldiers to play with."[11] No aggrieved inner child getting revenge in this dispassionate account, except maybe in reading between the lines.

Renoir's honesty is admirable in relating a candid picture of his childhood, whether from his own memory or that of Gabrielle. It's also intriguing that he usually refers to his father as "Renoir" in his biographical study, instead of by his first name or "my father," identifying him more as a historical figure than a parent. Yet he managed to escape from Auguste Renoir's legacy without outward bitterness. It was a noble odyssey, and indicative of an innate generosity, combined perhaps with his disdain for psychological probing.

Renoir's first exposure to movies, ironically, proved a frightening one. Gabrielle recalled the event for him. In 1897 she took him, when he was 2 years old, to a free showing of a phenomenon known as "the cinema" at the Dufayel department store. Renoir began to cry, startled by the beam of light cutting through the dark, the piano playing, the noise of a projector and the flashing images. Gabrielle, sensibly, removed him from the scene.

The small child was nearly contemporaneous with this new medium. The Lumière brothers first showed one of their films on March 22, 1895, only six months after Renoir's birth, and their first public showing took place later that year on December 28.

Though Renoir a few times teasingly called himself a coward and had felt overwhelmed at the Dufayel showing, the 2-year-old child had not reacted unreasonably. In any event, this was an inauspicious introduction to a medium that, within 50 years, he would master and help develop into a major art form.

Gabrielle not only introduced him to his future métier but also to theater and, by extension, elements that would become integral to his films. At the age of either three or five (according to Renoir's differing memories), she took him to Guignol, the traditional puppet show. Gabrielle remembered how little Jean was sometimes so excited that he wet his pants as the curtain went up. And Renoir wrote that he felt the same thrill, throughout his life, waiting for a curtain to rise.

The devoted Gabrielle also took him to the Théâtre Montmartre. The experience started his informal education in aesthetics, instilling in him a preference for simple melodramas and what he called "a profound mistrust for what is generally called psychology."[12]

The young Jean further encountered movies, as a 9-year-old, when he went to Sunday film showings at school. He especially liked the films of a slapstick comedian, Automaboul, who often had to deal with the balky mechanisms of a car.

Movies were beginning to make their mark on him.

The Young Man

Renoir's infatuation with the trappings of military life gained an outlet when, as an 18-year-old, he enlisted in the First Regiment of Dragoons. He particularly loved horses and was attracted to the elegant dragoon uniforms.

World War I broke out the next year and he joined an army battalion. As he noted in his memoirs, he quickly learned the harsh truth about war. But, while Renoir lost some of his romantic notions, he treasured meeting people from different walks of life and social classes. It was an education for a young man coming from a rarefied world.

The war would also leave its scars, physically and emotionally. Wasting no time with pleasantries, Renoir begins his book about Auguste Renoir with the following lines:

> *I*N APRIL 1915 a Bavarian sharpshooter did me the favor of putting a bullet through my leg. As a result of the wound I was eventually transferred to a hospital in Paris, where my father had been brought so as to be near me.

The opening sentence has the bravado and Boeldieu-like irony of the soldier class. Renoir's red badge of courage. But that second sentence, noting his transfer to the Parisian hospital, is a jump cut in time that upends the chronology of his life.

Something else had happened in the interval between these events, and it only limps in, out of order, with the third sentence of this montage that opens Chapter I:

> The death of my mother had completely crushed him and his physical condition was worse than ever.[13]

Why did Renoir construct such a sequence, dropping his mother's death to a position after his reunion with his father? And why did he report her death in terms of its effect on her husband and not on himself as well?

The fuller story can perhaps be gleaned from a paragraph in the book's last chapter. After Renoir was wounded, his mother came to see him at the hospital in Besançon. When told that doctors planned to amputate his left leg because of gangrene, she objected and a specialist was summoned. He cured the infection by circulating distilled water through Jean's leg. Mme. Renoir was told that her son would not have lived through the proposed amputation. Renoir closes the paragraph: "As soon as my mother saw that I was out of danger, she went back to Cagnes and died."

This abrupt announcement is followed immediately by another flash-forward in time with the shift to a new paragraph and the next sentence: "At the beginning of 1916 I was a pilot in a reconnaissance squadron."[14] And we are off and taking flight, his mother's death diminishing into the past as rapidly as the landscape under an ascending Caudron.

For someone who was able to write honestly about his fears and weaknesses, this is a flat and unemotional account. The passage on his mother's death in his memoir, written years later, indicates a possible explanation. After recalling that the doctors attributed her death to diabetes, Renoir continued: "but I knew that she had died of the nervous strain of a journey to the front after I had been seriously wounded and conveyed to a hospital close behind the lines."[15] A biographer, Ronald Bergan, speculates about "a feeling of profound guilt within the young man, an emotion that lingered for the rest of his life, and surfaced from time to time."[16]

Whatever the case, Renoir displayed a certain aloofness from his mother. It may be significant that her name is missing from the index of his memoir, though he mentions her a number of times in the text—and six other Renoirs who appear in his book are indexed. A curious oversight. And though elsewhere he recalls his mother's gaiety, a portrait emerges of a remote woman who disciplined him but didn't seem to share many other memorable moments with her son.

In the opening chapter of *Renoir, My Father*, Renoir relates how he went back to his father's house to convalesce from his wound and had the opportunity to learn about the painter's life, gathering information for the book he eventually produced. He writes:

> For the first time I felt, in my father's presence, that my childhood was over and I had become a man. My wound gave me an added sense of being on an equal footing with him. I could not move about without my crutches. We were both cripples, more or less, confined to our chairs.[17]

The little boy with curls of real gold, at the service of Auguste Renoir's art, now saw himself finally equal to his father, if mainly in sharing physical weakness—though there is perhaps a teasing quality to this passage, written from the perspective of an increasingly famous filmmaker.

Further, near the end of this first chapter he produces a cheerfully bland sentence: "I had good reason to be grateful to that Bavarian soldier for bringing my father and me together again."[18] This welcoming of a French-German connection, so reminiscent of *La Grande Illusion*, appears in a remarkable context here. Renoir seemed to have felt so strongly the benefit of getting closer to his father that he temporarily put aside his feeling that the cause of their reunion had also led to Mme. Renoir's death.

This detachment is evident later when he recalls talking to his father about "an incident connected with the wound which had restored me to him" (another telling characterization). It was the story of his sister-in-law's visit, with her bobbed hair and short dress, to break the news of his mother's death. He reports that his father "was much struck by the anecdote"[19]—a cool assessment indeed.

Once able to return to action, Renoir joined air reconnaissance. But a bad landing in 1917 put an end to his military service. In order to become a pilot, he had dieted to bring down his weight; as he acknowledged, he often found it hard to resist good food and wine. And though in his youth Renoir had a somewhat trim figure, he was a large, heavyset man as an adult.

During the war he also went to Charlie Chaplin movies with his brother, Pierre. Soon he fell in love with film for good and became a fan of American movies, which were then more inventive than many productions being turned out in France.

The vivacious Dédée, meanwhile, livened up Les Collettes, the family's summer place, and Auguste enjoyed her singing of popular songs. As Renoir wrote: "Dédée adored my father, who returned her love."[20] She had a full figure, and her big eyes gave her at once an innocent and yet seductive air; she also shared Renoir's enthusiasm for movies.

Still floundering in his life, Renoir took up pottery in 1918. His father had a studio built for him and Coco. Dédée was included since Auguste felt she was talented and that they would all work well together. So the son became a potter by default, spinning along in his father's orbit while becoming entranced by the painter's muse.

Winter 1919 — and the death of Auguste Renoir.

Lionizing his father as ever, Renoir once wrote that his painting had reached the level of great artists like Titian, Rubens and Velazquez. And, in the last pages of the biography, after referring to the popularity and public acceptance of Auguste Renoir, he added:

Jean Renoir in convalescence during World War I with his father, Auguste (1915–6) (*UCLA Charles E. Young Research Library, Department of Special Collections, Jean Renoir Collection*).

> He has molded the crowd in the image of his ideal, just as he molded his wife, his children and his models. The streets of our cities are now filled with Renoirs: young girls, children with wide, candid eyes and skin that takes the light.[21]

Even taken metaphorically, this is a strange attribution of godlike powers.

He also uses this conceit when writing about parents who showed their children to him and asked if he thought them "perfect little Renoirs." He continues:

> And the extraordinary part is that they are! Our world which before him was filled with people with elongated pale faces has since his time seen an influx of little round, plump beings with beautiful red cheeks. And the similarity is carried further by the choice of colors for their clothing. He is responsible for that too.[22]

This discussion of genetics and fashion is made especially preposterous by crediting Auguste Renoir in both areas, however ironically intended of course. One imagines a horror movie populated with clones of his models.

But, idealized or not, the king was dead. Renoir, with greater financial independence from his inheritance, would soon make his own way. And less than two months after Auguste's death, Jean and Dédée were married. His only child, Alain, was born in October 1921.

Early Films

Renoir continued to be fascinated by movies, even as he struggled along making ceramics. Seeing *Le Brasier ardent*, a few years later, helped inspire him to try his hand at film. And Stroheim's *Foolish Wives* made him realize he could make films in a similarly realist, and expressive, fashion. He would perhaps repay his debt by giving Stroheim his most illustrious role.

The choice of such a profession can be interpreted as an implicit, if not explicit, rebellion against one of his father's cherished principles:

> In my father's view it was impossible to do anything good under the system of division of labor. A picture, a chair, a tapestry interested him only if the different stages of its creation were an expression of one man's personality.[23]

Embracing a militantly collaborative art form was fraught with danger. Though Renoir was able to express his personality, with time, and within the constraints of the fledgling medium, the end result still depended on a successful "division of labor."

Movies also posed a possible challenge to another tenet espoused by Auguste Renoir — that the subject matter, or theme, was not important in art. Only form mattered. Film provides the filmmaker with a seductively easy opportunity to develop themes and make grand statements. Renoir avoided that temptation in his greatest works, but his embrace of the new medium was nevertheless risky and an assertion of artistic independence.

Renoir broke into moviemaking in 1924 with his screenplay for *Catherine*, released in 1927 as *Une Vie sans joie* (*A Life Without Joy*). It starred Dédée, now known as Catherine Hessling, and was directed by Albert Dieudonné, who later played the title role in Abel Gance's epic, *Napoléon* (1927). Renoir took part in directing the film, but relations with Dieudonné were chilly and he ended up without a credit as co-director.

Renoir, nearing 30, went ahead and directed his first film on his own, *La Fille de l'eau* (1924), and Dédée starred again. In his debut, he was less concerned with the plot than in experimenting with movie techniques and special effects. There is also an assured and tactile sense of nature in all its radiance — his father's son, clearly. Though heavy on melodramatic effects, and his natural style undeveloped, he had set out to be original and personal.

La Fille de l'eau was a failure and Renoir decided to open an art boutique. Again he sputtered along. But a friend, Jean Tedesco, soon afterward showed a fanciful dream sequence from the film to a theater audience. Renoir and Dédée attended the showing and the appreciative reception helped persuade him to stay in movies.

In 1926, influenced in part by *Foolish Wives*, Renoir made *Nana*, based on an Émile Zola novel. He was pleased with the results but, like so many of his movies, it failed commercially.

Nana has some of the perverse elements of a Stroheim movie, with an attention to gritty details and a compelling (and twisted) upstairs-downstairs subplot, as well as lively theater and dance sequences integrated into the story. It is an impressively conceived film, especially for a neophyte, and moves along briskly despite intertitles and a limited number of Renoir's patented tracking movements.

The biggest flaw of *Nana* is that Hessling manages to overact even in a role that begs for some measure of overacting; as the theatrically callous Nana, she drives two men to suicide and humiliates another for her own amusement, accompanied by histrionic gestures and mugging. But the film survives her excesses and holds up as a convincing melodrama.

Around this time, Renoir reluctantly sold some of his father's paintings to pay off debts incurred by his films. In spite of this reluctance, he was shedding a reminder of Auguste Renoir while, paradoxically, becoming indebted to him. Through the years, many of the paintings would be sold.

Bergan, in his informative and entertaining biography, *Jean Renoir: Projections of Paradise* (1995), notes an unusual confluence in 1927 on the set of *La P'tite Lili*, a short film by Alberto Cavalcanti. Renoir, Dédée and their son appeared as actors. The editor, Marguerite Houllé, soon became the next woman in his life. And Dido Freire, who also appeared in the film and whose family was close to Cavalcanti, later became Renoir's second wife and would share his last years with him.

On the set of *Nana* (1926): from the left, Pierre Lestringuez, Catherine Hessling, Werner Krauss, Jean Renoir (***The Kobal Collection at Art Resource, New York***).

Renoir developed some close collaborations with women. But his movies reflect a marked uneasiness in the battle of the sexes. Love, as opposed to falling in love, is not generally a factor — nor are children, or families, often featured. There is a relaxed and non-judgmental approach to sex, but also a stereotypical imbalance in relationships. A disturbing occurence in many films is a man pouncing on a resistant woman; in many plots two or three men lust after, and become jealous over, a single woman who proves elusive (as in *Nana*).

The most fulfilling relationships, instead, are usually the friendships between men. And the most notable performances are mainly by male actors.

Renoir also displays a misogynistic belittlement or mistrust of women in some of his films. They are reduced in these movies to being either promiscuous or, at the other extreme, passively buffeted around by the men in their lives. There's an idealization of women (a yearning love or a lust) but also a sense that true love is impossible, with men often predatory. And women in these films, even those who are not prostitutes, gain what personal power or financial stability they have through sexuality, either by their actions or their allure. Rarely are they strong and positive characters in their own right.

In this respect, *La Grande Illusion* is an anomaly, as on so many other levels, though its male friendships fit the more usual pattern. *La Règle du jeu*, conversely, serves as something of a paradigm. But it is more balanced than many of his films, with men and women equally duplicitous and strong-willed.

Renoir's only substantial acting role in his movies, as Octave in *La Règle du jeu*, is perhaps revealing. The admiration of Octave for Christine's father, a well-known orchestra conductor, echoes the way Renoir was in thrall to his own father. Octave is a self-proclaimed failure, though a witty conversationalist and raconteur. And when Christine says that he needs someone to take care of him and, later, instructs him to kiss her on the mouth like a lover, one feels pangs for this awkward man-child. Christine embodies an uncomfortable mixture of a mother figure, as Renoir had found in Gabrielle, and a possible sexual partner (briefly). Something of Jean Renoir seems to be in Octave — much as Orson Welles, in many of his films, played decidedly Wellesian figures.

Amused by stories of romantic intrigues and great passions, Renoir admired friends like Pierre Lestringuez and Jean Gabin who were successful ladies men, and he enjoyed Michel Simon recounting his sexual adventures.

In his memoir, Renoir also wrote movingly about his longtime assistant and friend, Jacques Becker, whom he considered both a brother and a son. They shared an apartment during the filming of *La Grande Illusion*. Renoir noted that their friendship was so close some might have suspected a sexual relationship. Referring to Becker, he further pointed out: "I am a firm believer in loving friendships in which there is no sexual element." His free association then leads him to mention that the relationship between Boeldieu and Rauffenstein was "simply a love story."[24]

Renoir, in his life and particularly in his movies, keeps coming back to this theme of men who bond more easily with each other than with women. And certainly the intimations of homosexuality in *La Grande Illusion* indicate a natural curiosity, which might originally have been complicated by his childhood experiences with his hated long hair. In an aside, Renoir once recalled, in *Renoir, My Father*, how the family rented a farm in Normandy one summer at which Oscar Wilde had lived during the previous winter. When his father noted that Jean had slept in the same bed as Wilde and joked that it was fortunately in a different season, Jean found out about homosexuality.

Renoir's "surrogate son," Jacques Becker, and only son, Alain Renoir (with fishing rod), on location for *Partie de campagne* (1936). Photograph: Eli Lotar (*CNAC/MNAM/dist. RMN-Grand Palais/Art Resource, NY*).

An important development in his career was a short 1928 film based on a Hans Christian Andersen story, *La Petite Marchande d'allumettes* (*The Little Match Girl*), which Renoir made in a small, improvised studio with Tedesco, exploring different aspects of filmmaking techniques in the process.

This stylized fairy tale, with a clever dream sequence turning into a nightmare, features some of the tricks he had been using in his earlier films, and again it starred Dédée. The death of the match girl, for instance, is poetically evocative; her face in profile against a white background with flower petals falling (the end of the reverie) dissolves to the same profile against black with snow falling on her lifeless face (the real world).

Once again, the film was not successful, despite its charms. Renoir continued along, unremarkably, with several more low budget films. But he was on the verge of breaking through and asserting his distinctive style.

The Classic Years

With the coming of sound movies, Renoir made *On purge bébé* (1931), a bathroom-humor farce, to show that he could handle the new form. His trial run worked well enough to gain backing for *La Chienne* (*The Bitch*—though almost never identified by that title).

Renoir thought that *La Chienne* (1931) was his first truly accomplished film and felt he came close to achieving "poetic realism," the term sometimes associated with him. It also marked a change in his personal life. The producers insisted on using Janie Marèse, instead of Dédée, for the title role. Renoir accepted the proviso, ending the partnership with his disappointed wife.

By this time he had already begun a ten-year involvement with Houllé, an editor on the film; although they never married, she took his name, without objection, and became known as Marguerite Renoir. But she is a puzzling figure, not often mentioned by Renoir, or even by film historians, despite her long career and association with his films and those of Becker.

La Chienne was one of the first French sound movies to be filmed on location and exhibits a refreshing naturalism. Michel Simon stars as a henpecked husband, Maurice Legrand, in a story of lust and murder. Although there are some very effective touches, it has an awkward and clunky pace (as in many early sound films) and some broad acting by both the wife and a hapless pimp.

Renoir shot the film his own way, slyly not showing the producers what he was doing. At one point they took the movie away, but he was able to regain control over the final cut. And though *La Chienne* was a modest success, he became saddled with the reputation of being a "difficult" (read "original") director.

The film marks the beginning of Renoir's classic period. His movies in the 1930s are, without question, the ones for which he is best known, though critical opinion varies as to their relative significance (except in the case of *La Règle du jeu*).

La Chienne has some narrative features that recur in a number of Renoir's movies — the love triangle, a fickle woman, and a murderer who gets away with murder. There are also certain details of plot and dialogue which reappear in *La Bête humaine* and *La Règle du jeu*, and even in his last film, almost forty years later; such reprises are common in Renoir throughout his career.

The title character is Lucienne ("Lulu"), a prostitute who loves her abusive pimp and, in turn, deceives the clueless Legrand, both sexually and financially. She pays for her duplicity by being murdered, after mocking Legrand to his face. In the mold of Hessling's Nana, though much less flamboyant, Marèse's Lulu is one of the more *fatale* of Renoir's *femmes fatales*. And one of his more flawed women.

Though Renoir earned the reputation of being a warmhearted, lovable bear of a man who celebrated the joy of life, his movies often reflect that jaded view of relations between the sexes found in *La Chienne*. He was, above all, a man of contradictions.

His films also reflect, during this period, a somewhat nihilistic attitude toward murder, as in *La Chienne* where Legrand not only goes free but the wrong man is executed. In *Le Crime de Monsieur Lange* (*The Crime of Mr. Lange*), *La Règle du jeu*, and possibly *La Bête humaine* murderers also get off scot-free. The exact circumstances of the climactic murders in *Les Bas-Fonds* and *The Diary of a Chambermaid* are unclear, since they are the result of mob vengeance; whatever the legalities, no one pays much for the crimes.

The cynical ending of *La Règle du jeu*, however, as the marquis covers up André Jurieux's murder to avoid scandal, beautifully rounds out Renoir's depiction of a withering (and decadently withered) social class. By contrast, in *Le Crime de Monsieur Lange* and *Les Bas-Fonds*, murder is rationalized as a political means to combat the suppression of poor people and workers. These progressive sentiments may be noble, but the vigilante justice of the oppressed is, still, disquieting. The elitism of the righteous remains elitism nonetheless.

In 1932 Renoir made *La Nuit du carrefour* (*Night at the Crossroads*), a moody and expressionist Inspector Maigret mystery starring his brother Pierre. Renoir created a mysterious ambience, with darkly atmospheric exteriors, rather than a perfectly formed (or even comprehensible) plot. And some scenes were never filmed, because of budget concerns. But the film has its ardent supporters.

Renoir followed it, in the same year, with *Boudu sauvé des eaux* (*Boudu Saved from Drowning*), his exuberant farce that stars Michel Simon as an anarchic tramp wreaking havoc on a bourgeois household. It is one of Renoir's better films, unencumbered by much overt psychology or philosophizing and no insistent background music. But, like *La Chienne*, it has that awkward pace of the early sound period.

The contemporary fable is allowed to unfold naturally, driven by incidental music throughout, including a flute-playing man who acts as Greek chorus and sustains the theme of Pan introduced at the start. For Renoir, it's his first extended use of a satyr-like Pan figure to magically excite the sexual tensions of the characters.

Simon engagingly upstages everyone as the vagabond unfettered by social mores. A child of nature. One can't help thinking that Renoir perhaps saw in the character an alter ego — a fantasized self, an uncivilized and regressive Octave who acts instinctively on his desires. The bravura performance by Simon, mannered and all out, dominates the film.

Boudu sauvé des eaux is also distinguished by vivid documentary-like footage filmed in Paris at a park, along the banks of the Seine, in the streets and, at the end, on the river again. These compelling evocations are in contrast to the staid and confined interiors. Renoir often called his movies "documentaries" of the time and *Boudu* can be seen as a prime example. That documentary eye never deserted him, even in his more banal films, and, if he had chosen that path, Renoir might have become a great documentary filmmaker.

In 1933 Renoir shot *Madame Bovary* (released in 1934), which the distributors drastically cut by more than an hour. Unfortunately the original version was lost. But judging by what remains of the film in a shortened version (100 minutes), Flaubert's novel has almost been reduced to a potboiler, with much hysteria, especially in the portrayal of Emma Bovary. Her death is particularly drawn out to an absurd degree. The exteriors, however, are again filled with a lovely lyricism — at odds with the talky melodrama indoors.

Renoir shifted into another gear with *Toni* (1935). Though at times a pedestrian movie, it was unusual for that period in film history as Renoir hired some non-actors, encouraged improvisation, shot on location, and only used incidental music, including catchy guitar songs, instead of background music. There are wonderful exteriors, the Renoir documentary effect again, and the film has frequently been cited as a precursor of Italian neorealism. But self-conscious dialogue underlines the psychology of its characters, and a melodramatic story line detracts greatly.

There are certainly some arresting moments where words give way to the action. But there's also the tiresome motif of an open season on women, with the heroine pursued by three men and pounced on, and later battered, by one of them.

An interesting sidebar is that Luchino Visconti was an assistant on *Toni* and acknowledged that Renoir had been an important influence in his career. Renoir suggested to him that James M. Cain's *The Postman Always Rings Twice* would be good film material; Visconti adapted it for the screen in 1942, as *Ossessione*, one of the first neorealist films of the period.

There are some outstanding performances in Renoir's movies, perhaps aided by his patience and geniality. Gaston Modot once described a rehearsal in which Renoir reacted enthusiastically to an actor's performance and then casually suggested a slightly different tack, over and over, without being critical, until he got what he had secretly wanted from the outset.

He ran his rehearsals in what he called "the Italian fashion," crediting Louis Jouvet and Simon for his conversion to this method. The actors initially read their lines without any expression, as if reading a telephone directory (as Renoir put it). In that way they avoided falling comfortably into clichéd interpretations. Gradually something new would come out of the readings, at which point the roles began to develop. This improvisatory way of finding an interpretation was true to Renoir's concern not to control or intellectualize the filmmaking process.

Also at this time, and partly under the influence of his companion, Marguerite, who was a militant radical, Renoir became involved in the leftist politics of the Popular Front. He attended Communist Party gatherings and grew close to a radical theater company, Groupe Octobre. Its members included some of Renoir's future colleagues on *La Grande Illusion*—Jean Dasté, Sylvain Itkine and Joseph Kosma.

Another member of the company was Jacques Prévert, the poet and writer, with whom Renoir wrote the screenplay for his next film, *Le Crime de Monsieur Lange* (released in 1936). After filming was completed, Renoir traveled to Russia for ten days.

When he returned to France, still sympathetic to communism, he collaborated with Groupe Octobre, becoming the supervisor and a co-director of *La Vie est à nous* (1936), a film promoting the Communist Party for the 1936 elections. Renoir followed it with a stretch of films that includes his highest levels of achievement: *Partie de campagne* [*A Day in the Country*] (1936); *Les Bas-Fonds* (1936); *La Grande Illusion* (1937); *La Marseillaise* (1938); *La Bête humaine* (1938); and *La Règle du jeu* (1939).

Interlude in Hollywood

La Règle du jeu premiered in July 1939 and was a terrible failure. Renoir's career, and his life, dramatically changed again. He had already given up his column in *Ce Soir*, and his relationship to Marguerite (who remained committed to communism) was ending.

In August, Dido Freire, as his assistant, accompanied him to Italy, where he had been invited by the Italian government to make a film version of *La Tosca*. Renoir gave varying reasons for accepting this assignment—his curiosity about Italy, the chance to make *La Tosca*, the poor reception of *La Règle du jeu*, and disillusionment with his career in France. Whatever the rationale, it indicates an unsettling malleability that he would accept the invitation of Mussolini's government only a few years after making *La Vie est à nous* and movies like *Le Crime de Monsieur Lange* and *La Marseillaise* that reflected his left-wing politics.

Some people criticized him for going to fascist Italy, with some reason. But it is fair to say that Renoir did not seem to think through his political passions carefully. As a leftist, he was naturally horrified by fascism, even in accepting the *Tosca* project, though he was evidently slow to see communism's own brand of centralized repression and terror.

In addition to working on *La Tosca*, Renoir gave film lectures attended by, amongst

Jean Renoir and crew on location for *La Règle du jeu* (1939) — a picnic on the grass, as if in one of his own films: (right to left) Roland Toutain (foreground, white sweater), Renoir (in a fedora), Henri Cartier-Bresson (checked jacket), Gaston Modot (dark turtleneck, facing camera). Photograph: Sam Lévin (©*Ministère de la Culture/Médiathèque du Patrimoine/Sam Levin/dist. RMN-Grand Palais/Art Resource, New York*).

others, Visconti and Michelangelo Antonioni. Genuinely interested in the next generation of filmmakers, he influenced, often on a personal level, many future film directors.

Renoir renewed his friendship with Visconti, who showed him around Rome and was an assistant director on the film. But when anti–French sentiment escalated, he returned to France. Carl Koch, his German friend, completed *La Tosca*; it starred another friend, Michel Simon, who was Swiss and could stay in Italy.

With World War II and the Germans nearing Paris, Renoir fled to Les Collettes in the south with Dido and his close friend, Paul Cézanne (the son of the painter), and with Cézanne's family. One day some functionaries came to him, on behalf of Nazi cultural institutions, and suggested that he make films for them. Renoir realized it was time to leave France — somewhat as Fritz Lang had earlier fled Germany after the Nazis made overtures to him.

Robert Flaherty, the documentary film pioneer, arranged a visa for him and he reached Portugal in December 1940 via northern Africa. From there, the Renoirs got passage to the

United States with the help of Charles Boyer (then working for the British government). On board an American liner, Renoir shared a room with Antoine de Saint-Exupéry, the French writer and aviator, who later briefly lived with the Renoirs in Hollywood.

Renoir's career got a second life in the United States. But many of his films after *La Règle du jeu*, even with some signs of brilliance, reflect his admitted weakness for melodrama and show a startling inability to rise above it.

His bias in that direction may have stemmed partly from an avowed suspicion of intellectuals and big ideas, despite his own considerable erudition. Whatever the case, in contrast to the approach in his two great films, Renoir often does not bother to develop the characters in these films and yet seems to want genuine feelings felt for them. He throws in emotionally hyped situations in early scenes; this sentimentality is sometimes juiced up with background music and close-ups. And dialogue becomes the primary means to communicate both the inner make-up of characters and the themes.

In short, he sustains these movies with the kind of technique he rarely applied in *La Grande Illusion*, and then only after carefully building up a foundation in support.

It's true that a banal plot can provide the means for invention, as Renoir once argued. Genres such as the western and film noir certainly qualify on that count. But the cinematic technique of a great genre film, even when perhaps melodramatic, is used creatively and lifts the form. Renoir, however, sinks many of his post–1939 films with an approach that reduces and trivializes, rather than elevates, its subject. He accepts the easy laughs and cheap tears of melodrama, instead of using that setting as a jumping-off point for something subtler.

In 1941, Renoir and Dido settled into life in Hollywood. He signed a contract with 20th Century-Fox to make two films, but his movie ideas were routinely shot down, including a proposed version of Saint-Exupéry's classic, *Terre des hommes* (known as *Wind, Sand and Stars*).

The studio assigned him *Swamp Water* (1941) but it was not a happy experience. Darryl F. Zanuck exercised control over the film and, though Renoir put up a fight to shoot on location, the studio only allowed him to film briefly in the swamps of Georgia. The Hollywood system, with its devaluation of the director, its artificial sets and, at times, cliché-ridden stories, was antithetical to his way of working, despite his penchant for melodrama. He soon became known as a director who went over budget and worked too slowly (the man who made *La Grande Illusion* in four months).

Renoir once wrote about an incident during the shooting of *Swamp Water* in which he had filmed an argument between a father and son in a single shot, his usual filming technique. The studio objected and he reshot the sequence, breaking it into several shots. And Renoir added: "This was my first surrender to Hollywood."[25]

But the film represents surrender of a larger order. Renoir submitted to Hollywood's romanticized version of poor folk dialogue, with characters saying things like "I heard tell" and the heroine being called "young-un." He further surrendered by fashioning a cornball plot that features lessons in psychology, backed up by intrusive movie music and a happy ending. This brand of declarative cinema only periodically plagued Renoir's earlier movies but infects much of his later work.

The location shooting, with Renoir's eye as a documentarian, is effective but also in disjunction with some crude rear projections and other substitutes for the swamp. And it doesn't save the film that there are familiar stylistic touches, like shots framed by doors and windows to indicate people trapped in their lives.

It's astounding that the director of *La Règle du jeu* would next make *Swamp Water*, only two years later. The gap, from the sublime to the ridiculous, can not be ignored. Certainly the conditions under which he worked were horrific and, literally, alien to him, and Renoir was out of his element. But filmmakers like Fritz Lang, or even Robert Siodmak and Jacques Tourneur, managed the transition better, especially in their film noirs.

Yet Jean-Luc Godard claimed that *Swamp Water* "revolutionized Hollywood" because of its location shooting. And he also wrote:

> If *The Rules of the Game* was not understood in its time, it was because it burned, destroyed, *The Crime of M. Lange*. And *Swamp Water* because it consumed in its turn *The Rules of the Game*.[26]

Godard's hyperbole sheds no light. The idea of *La Règle du jeu* being consumed by *Swamp Water* is a bit like trying to imagine Jonah swallowing the whale.

Renoir's relationship to Orson Welles began, obliquely, during the location filming of *Swamp Water*. While Renoir was away, Robert Flaherty stayed in his home. Renoir recalled meeting Welles later at a party and found that Flaherty had often invited the new hotshot director to the house, and Renoir added: "I had just seen *Citizen Kane* and was flattered by this indirect link between us."[27] At another point, after noting his principle of using a single take for scenes, in his confrontation with the studio, Renoir wrote that "Orson Welles had done the same in his magnificent *Citizen Kane*" (also released in 1941).[28]

The admiration was mutual. When Welles saw Dita Parlo in *La Grande Illusion* he wanted to cast her in his projected film of Joseph Conrad's *Heart of Darkness*. Later, after *Renoir, My Father* was published in 1962, Welles wrote that it showed some of the "inspiration" behind Renoir's films and called him "one of the four greatest directors this century."[29] Their lives intersected one last time in 1971 when Welles invited Renoir to make a short film with him about movie directing; Renoir declined because of his health.

Like Welles, Renoir struggled unsuccessfully within the studio system. He at least was cheered up when joined in the United States by his son Alain, who enlisted in the U.S. Army. Gabrielle also moved to California and settled near the Renoirs with her husband, Conrad Slade, an American painter.

At this time Renoir developed a close friendship with Charles Laughton. Their relationship led to Renoir's second American movie, *This Land Is Mine* (1943), which he wrote with

Orson Welles, 1962. Photograph: Sam Lévin (©*Ministère de la Culture/Médiathèque du Patrimoine/Sam Levin/dist. RMN-Grand Palais/Art Resource, New York*).

Dudley Nichols. Laughton stars as a timid schoolteacher in a Nazi-occupied, unnamed country in Europe, though the locals (and Germans) speak English very nicely. Renoir wanted Stroheim to play the German villain but commitments prevented him from accepting the role; it went to Walter Slezak instead.

Renoir and Nichols had control over the production but, despite this advantage, the film is one of the worst misfires in Renoir's career. It comes off as counterfeit and didactic, relentlessly driven by the dialogue. Trite characters are propped up as symbolic figures, including a domineering mother, and there are maudlin speeches about resistance and freedom, with rapt and teary onlookers intercut for good measure.

On the set of *La Règle du jeu*: (left to right) Dido Freire, Paulette Dubost, Henri Cartier-Bresson (obscured), Renoir, André Zwoboda (far right). Photograph: Sam Lévin (©*Ministère de la Culture/Médiathèque du Patrimoine/Sam Levin/dist. RMN-Grand Palais/Art Resource, New York*).

This Land Is Mine, in brief, conveys a conventional anti–Nazi tract in the guise of an ordinary story about people. Political messages take precedence over character and feeling, with only glimpses of a more familiar Renoir in the process.

Renoir continued to have trouble financing his projects, including a proposed remake of *Les Bas-Fonds*. David O. Selznick offered him *Joan of Arc*, with Ingrid Bergman in mind, but Renoir declined because he greatly admired Carl Dreyer's 1928 masterpiece, *La Passion de Jeanne d'Arc*; it would have been hard to follow that extraordinary film.

In February 1944, Renoir married Dido at the home of Elsa Lanchester and Laughton, who served as best man. Gabrielle was again present at a key moment in his life.

Renoir then worked on a film produced by the Office of War Information to be shown to American troops as part of the war effort. In some books he is credited as the co-director, with Garson Kanin, of *Salute to France* (1944); a few others list Renoir as the sole director.

The film is straightforward propaganda, whatever the chain of command, and an outright glorification, in places, of war. This broadside, with its mindless nationalism aimed directly at Germany, mixes documentary footage into the fictional story to inject a sham sense of reality. The English version was drastically cut and Renoir never saw the final French version, which has since disappeared. The slight film that remains cannot be judged in terms of a coherent work; as Renoir once said: "There is little of me in the film."[30] But his name stayed attached to *Salute to France*.

Renoir next made *The Southerner* (1945), which was a success and is often cited as his best American film. The original scriptwriter, Hugo Butler, admired *La Grande Illusion* and stepped aside to let Renoir rewrite the script to fit his needs. He also got advice from Nunnally Johnson and William Faulkner about the story, which takes place on an impoverished farm.

The film was made on a low budget, without major stars in the leading roles (Zachary Scott and Betty Field), and this time Renoir was able to shoot on location. But, despite these promising conditions, he subverted the naturalism of the landscape with oppressive music and phony, "aw shucks" dialogue as in *Swamp Water*; "reckon," for instance, proves a popular word in the facile patois of these country folks.

The Southerner starts off, tugging hard quickly, with the death of Uncle Pete in a cotton field, backed by music and a cute little dog to mourn him as well. Not a reassuring way to set the tone. Beulah Bondi as the crotchety grandmother especially hams it up. Meanwhile Scott and Field radiate Hollywood glamour and their presence undermines any attempt at a realistic edge. Renoir instead concocts a strained melodrama, with improbable twists and some silliness in its exposition. The film is standard fare, in spite of the relief provided by the location shooting.

The next year he made *The Diary of a Chambermaid* (1946), with Eugène Lourié doing the sets to recreate France in Hollywood. But this time the film did not do well. Renoir felt it reflected his concerns in *La Règle du jeu*, though it seems overwrought and overacted. The triteness persists, with painted skies, syrupy music and much self-reflection. Telling counts more than showing, and caricature replaces embodiment. Another declarative film rather than an experiential one. In trying to emphasize the setting's artificiality, to make theater of life, Renoir only managed to be banal and ring false.

He was, in any case, delighted to make the film with his friends, Burgess Meredith and Paulette Goddard. It added a certain *frisson* that Goddard had once been married to Renoir's early idol, Chaplin. She is charming in the lead role, showing some restraint in her performance, but Meredith flails around in a manic state and chews up the scenery as if he hasn't had a square meal in weeks. And many others in the accomplished cast act to the typical, not the individual.

Early in 1946 Renoir shot his last Hollywood film, *The Woman on the Beach* (1947), a strange movie loosely in the film noir genre. Though one of his most obscure films, and greatly cut and re-cut after a poorly received screening, I feel it's his best American film. There is little of the blatant psychology that mars the others, though at one point Scott (Robert Ryan) does say, pensively: "the hard thing is to know yourself." But that stands out for its baldness. In Renoir's other American movies, such lines become more the norm.

The Woman on the Beach is a cat-and-mouse story of suspected lovers, a film noir filmed in daylight, a ghostly story shrouded in foggy beach scenes and a sandstorm. A kind of morality tale, with a modernist feeling of open-endedness to it. The heightened setting is complemented by generally low-key acting and hard-bitten dialogue, though there are also some fake settings and fuzzy rear projections. And there is the usual swagger of its noir characters, with music helping to make some easy points.

Renoir's final American film, however, does not make you cringe at the sort of hokeyness that detracted from his other films in Hollywood — and some of his later ones in France. It's a limited movie, but an entertaining one.

Even so, excessive claims have been made for it. Jacques Rivette once wrote that the

The Woman on the Beach (1947). Joan Bennett and Renoir on the set (with Harry J. Wild, cinematographer, and unidentified woman) (*Photofest*).

film is a masterpiece and summoned up Johann Sebastian Bach in an attempt to elevate the film beyond its constricted dimensions:

> Must one prefer the great *Passions* to *The Well-Tempered Clavier*? Perhaps, but if there is such a thing as pure cinema, it is to be found in *The Woman on the Beach*.[31]

There's a problem in any discussion of this film posed by its different versions, and Rivette makes reference to the original one, but the idea of purity is plainly a strained one. *The Woman on the Beach* is not some Dreyer or Bresson film floating in a parallel universe of its own. Though an intriguing disconnect from reality and a touch of otherworldliness haunts some scenes, the film remains grounded in Hollywood, even if a Hollywood when going well and modest in its aims. In fact, going well because of that very modesty. Renoir wisely did not try to escape the conventions of the story and pretend to some purer state beyond.

The Woman on the Beach was released in 1947 and had little success on any level. And has largely been forgotten.

During this period Renoir obtained dual citizenship, but his American career, such as it had been, was over. As he reported, Zanuck had said about him that he "'has a lot of talent, but he's not one of us.'"[32] No more pertinent confirmation of Renoir as an artist could have been spoken; Hollywood was hardly a club to which one would have wanted to be accepted as a member, to mangle Groucho Marx.

Clearly Zanuck's backhanded compliment was a reminder, if not a warning, that it would be difficult for Renoir to finance another project in Hollywood. Though he was never officially blacklisted, it is no surprise that, with the rise of the House Un-American Activities Committee, he could not find work.

The Final Period

Renoir's career took another turn in 1949 when he went to India to research a film based on Rumer Godden's novel, *The River*. Without Hollywood backing, the film was produced independently. Satyajit Ray, then a 27-year-old book illustrator with an interest in movies, served as a guide. Ray often watched the filming and Renoir later encouraged him to make his first film, *Pather Panchali*, launching his brilliant career; as with Visconti and Truffaut, Ray cited Renoir as an inspiration.

The River (1951), Renoir's first production in color, was influenced by his growing interest in Hinduism and is graced with chunks of Indian music and dance. The documentary parts make up a good portion of the film and offer a slice of Indian life, shot in beautiful color, with a narration by the now adult heroine, Harriet, providing lectures on Hinduism.

It is an episodic film, with a reversal of Renoir's usual formula as three young girls pursue the same man. A film about the loss of childhood innocence, it's hampered by pointed dialogue and schematic scripting of ideas. At times *The River* borders on the ludicrous, particularly when the stilted plot and acting intrudes on the effective documentary sequences.

Near the end, the strains of a recorder played by Harriet's little brother, fascinated by a cobra, leads to his off-screen death (unlike the life-affirming effect of Renoir's much favored Pan motif). This, in turn, leads to a painfully florid toast by a neighbor, Mr. John, beginning: "I drink to the children. We should celebrate that a child died a child, that one escaped." And then he lists a catalogue of ills foisted on children as they grow up. Again Renoir can't resist a high-flown rumination on life, saccharine or specious as it may seem.

Back in California, his proposal to make a film of an Albert Camus novel, *L'Étranger* (*The Stranger*), fell through because the rights were too expensive. Renoir's former assistant, Visconti, would later make *Lo straniero* (1967), based on the novel.

In another twist, Renoir replaced Visconti on a project that became *The Golden Coach* (1953), known also as *Le Carrosse d'or*, his light comedy in the consciously artificial style of *commedia dell'arte*. Renoir filmed in Italy (in English) and elegantly suffused his film with the music of Vivaldi.

This was the first of three films in a row that signified a shift. After having largely been devoted to naturalism, Renoir used make-believe sets and locations (as in *The Diary of a Chambermaid*). Again he aimed to reach an internal truth beneath the theatricality of the surface and to blur the line between theater and life.

The opening and closing curtains of *The Golden Coach*, on the same set, gracefully connect real life (at the start) to, finally, the acting troupe using that set, for their performance, at the end. And though the bits of theater are captivating and the parallel story appropriately stylized, the acting is wooden (except for Anna Magnani), with the dialogue and philosophy hackneyed. Toward the end, proclamations take over, dragging down another Renoir film that features three men after the same woman.

During filming, Renoir had serious problems with his old war wound; his leg became infected and he was briefly hospitalized. But he returned to finish the film.

Though he continued to live in California, his career was soon revived in France. His reputation also received a boost. André Bazin wrote a profile of Renoir and the influential film magazine, *Cahiers du Cinéma*, championed his films, with whole issues devoted to him in January 1952 and September 1954. He became, too, an important figure for young critics like Truffaut, Godard and Rivette before they started their own careers in the late 1950s.

Given Renoir's lifelong passion for the theater, which figures so prominently in his movies, it is odd that he never directed a play until offered the chance in July 1954 to stage *Julius Caesar* in the Roman arena at Arles. This one-time performance became a major event for the young cinéastes of the time. Truffaut, then only 22, served as an assistant to Renoir. And key figures from the past and future history of French cinema made the pilgrimage. The actor Jean-Claude Brialy drove down to Arles with Claude Chabrol, Godard and Rivette; Bazin, Eric Rohmer and Michèle Morgan also attended.

The cast was uneasy as it gathered for the performance since there had not been a full rehearsal. Renoir calmed them by leading a discussion of Hinduism. And when the sound system didn't work properly and the audience grew restless, Renoir, ever the astute psychologist (for all his belittling of psychology), suggested to the actor playing Casca, who had had trouble with his costume earlier, that he trip over his toga on purpose. With this improvised shtick, he broke the tension and won over the audience.

Renoir next directed his own play, *Orvet*, with Leslie Caron in the role of a poacher's daughter. Caron became a close friend and confidante.

In 1955, Renoir made his first French film in 16 years, *French Cancan*. Jean Gabin stars in this recreation of La Belle Époque, memorable for a colorful cancan in the finale. It's an inoffensive *bonbon* of a movie, as Renoir seemed content to indulge in the costumes and dances and cabaret life of the period, even giving Edith Piaf a turn. Gabin takes over the movie, which is always a pleasure, but his climactic scene revolves around the arch cliché of a driven artist eaten up by his art and giving everything to it (in so many words). The beleaguered life of artistes underlined for us.

French Cancan is another intentionally artificial film. Renoir mainly films in long shots, with painted sets and primarily stationary tableaus, but he invests it with little of the subtlety of his earlier films. And there's the motif again of women reduced to sexual beings, for the benefit of men, with three men after one woman (two examples of that, in fact)—and the mirror-image pursuit by three women of Gabin. Almost laughable, this multiplicity of intrigue.

The following year Renoir got the chance to make a film with his old friend, Ingrid Bergman. Their relationship had solidified after Bergman left her husband in 1949 to live with Roberto Rossellini; her daughter, Pia Lindström, stayed for a time with the Renoirs. Now Bergman reminded him of his promise, made years before, that they would make a movie together when she was in need of work. This was the time.

As an admirer of Rossellini's films, Renoir made sure it was all right with him; the formidable Italian director admired Renoir as well, and the film was on. In a recurring pattern, he seemed awed by other directors (Chaplin, Stroheim, Dreyer, Welles, Rossellini) though he was surely, at least, their equal—and they generally admired him in turn.

Renoir shot *Elena et les hommes* [1956] (*Elena and Hermen*) in French and English. Another look back to his father's milieu and the 1880s. A romantic comedy, the film has some plot elements resembling ones in *La Règle du jeu* and Renoir tries to recapture its sexual sophistication. But, midway through, the lame variation on that film's final evening of mayhem is played merely as silly slapstick instead of farce devolving into tragedy. And then Renoir goes off on another binge of dragged-out inanities at a country inn.

The film, even with Bergman enchanting in the title role, is broad and heavy-handed. And this time Renoir throws five men after Elena, who is nearly as unattainable as Christine in *La Règle du jeu*.

Renoir then took time to write his engaging book, *Renoir, My Father*. Honors, also, continued to be bestowed and helped build his position as a seminal figure in the film world. *Cahiers du Cinéma* devoted another issue to him (Christmas 1957), and in June 1958 the Renoirs attended the Brussels World's Fair, where *La Grande Illusion* was so highly honored.

La Règle du jeu was shown at the 1959 Venice Film Festival in a new, longer version and became a sensation. And the young French cinéastes, who had embraced him as a patron saint, burst onto the scene, generating the movement known as the Nouvelle Vague.

On a personal level, Renoir suffered some losses. Bazin died in 1958. On February 26, 1959, Gabrielle Renard-Slade died. The loss of his surrogate mother was followed, the next year, by the death of Jacques Becker.

Working out a new mode of production for himself in 1959, Renoir used television techniques to shoot *Le Testament du Docteur Cordelier*, his loose adaptation, in black-and-white, of Robert Louis Stevenson's *Strange Case of Dr. Jekyll and Mr. Hyde*. Renoir rehearsed the cast for weeks and filmed in long takes, using multiple cameras. This was a natural progression for him, concerned as he always had been that actors be able to explore their roles fully.

The end result, though, is an airless and lethargic film, with even the room noises seemingly sucked out of it. Only Jean-Louis Barrault brings relief through the marvel of his twitching and loose-limbed impersonation of the Hyde part of his character (Opale). Unleashed animal nature, a Boudu without his saving innocence. Otherwise, it's a pinched film of men and science and philosophy. Women once more are reduced, (off-screen) to a patient sedated by the Jekyll side of the character to be raped and a prostitute terrorized by Opale — and (on-screen) to a little girl attacked, hysterical maids and available mistresses at several offices.

Renoir followed that film with *Le Déjeuner sur l'herbe* (*Picnic on the Grass*) in 1959, set in the south of France and largely filmed at Les Collettes, where his brother Claude lived with his family.

Again it was a failed attempt to recapture past glories, with overtones of *Partie de campagne* and an affectionate invocation of the natural world recalling his father's own love affair with nature. It's a modern fairy tale in which another Pan-like figure, a goatherd playing a pennywhistle, casts a magical spell on the characters, including the central figure, a repressed man of science whose obsessional cause in life is artificial insemination; he succumbs (presto) to an earthy young farmwoman as others head off in pairs. But there's not enough stylization to pull off this fanciful conceit.

Ostensibly a comedy, it is hyper in tone, with theatrical posturing by the actors, and a simplistic feeling to the film dominates, like that of a made-for-TV movie. And the issue of artificial insemination is presented, dogmatically, many times — often as sermonizing or argument, but even in a chat with picnicking campers. Until the goatherd saves the day.

Back in the United States, Renoir led seminars and gave lectures at the University of Southern California and UCLA. One of his U.S.C. students was James Ivory, who admired *The River* and became another director inspired by him.

Renoir's next film, in 1962, was *Le Caporal épinglé* (*The Elusive Corporal*), set in a World War II prison camp and yet one more failure that summons up memories of a past triumph. At first Charles Spaak worked with him on the script, but the collaboration fell apart and Spaak left for another film.

In these seven years of his life, from 1956 to 1962, Renoir had consciously (or unconsciously) referred back to three of his greatest movies but had been able to come up with little of their invention or brilliance. His career was coming to an end.

Renoir made his last film in 1969. *Le Petit Théâtre de Jean Renoir* (*The Little Theater of Jean Renoir*) is a four-part film with each episode introduced by Renoir, next to a toy theater stage. The closest thing to a recurring theme is the pleasure taken by people in the misfortune of others. An odd way to unify the episodes. The first story recalls *La Petite Marchande d'allumettes* and, like his earlier movie, ends with death in the falling snow (this time a destitute couple). At times the film is embarrassingly amateurish and without life, despite the iconic presence of Jeanne Moreau singing a sad love song.

He signed it "Auteur et Réalisateur" in the credits, an acknowledgement of the stature he had attained toward the end of his filmmaking years. The film, at least, was his well-earned swan song to a life in movies, with references throughout to some of his films.

Last Years

Renoir's final years seemed difficult. He was often tired and his war wound still bothered him. Dido limited visitors, only allowing close friends like Truffaut and Leslie Caron to see him. But his works continued to be shown. In 1973 his play, *Carola*, was adapted for television, starring Caron and Mel Ferrer.

There also came a time when, although there was apparently nothing physically wrong with him, Renoir felt he was no longer able to walk and confined himself to a wheelchair. Bergan, in his biography, notes that some friends felt his illness was a psychosomatic one and that he was identifying with his father's last years. Maybe he also remembered the period, back in 1915, when son and father were "cripples" together.

Caron encouraged him to walk, but he appeared to enjoy his dependent condition. It may not seem too big a leap into psychological waters to imagine that this helplessness, with others rallying around to care for him in his old age, might have been a comfort that the little boy with long curls felt was, at last, deserved.

In 1974, Renoir published *My Life and My Films*. For a man aging rapidly, it is an assured, witty and touching memoir; it must have taken a measure of discipline to undertake the project. His passion for life and the need to express his ideas and feelings endured. When, at one point, his secretary, Eva Lothar, suggested doing a documentary film on various themes, he was interested. But Dido felt it would be too tiring for him.

Gabrielle Renard (1905) (*UCLA Charles E. Young Research Library, Department of Special Collections, Jean Renoir Collection*).

Renoir took his last trip to Europe in 1975, attending a retrospective of his films in London. That year he was also given a special Honorary Award at the Oscars, accepted for him by Ingrid Bergman; his exclusion by Zanuck from being one of "them" still remained a more significant homage. Then in 1976 he received the *croix de chevalier* of the Legion of Honor, presented by Françoise Giroud, the script girl on *La Grande Illusion* nearly 40 years earlier.

In the final two years of his life, ever expansive, he dictated three novellas. But his health continued to fail and he developed Parkinson's disease.

Jean Renoir died at 84 on February 12, 1979, at his Beverly Hills home in California.

In early March, Renoir was buried in the family plot at Essoyes in northern France. Though he had loved the United States, he was undoubtedly back where he belonged. It had been a full life. Faded, now, to black....

And one can perhaps be excused for daydreaming that he was granted his wish and that some illusory spirit of the girl who had thought him beautiful at birth was in the air above his grave, as if in the fantastical last reel of a movie called something like *La Fille de Montmartre*, to welcome Renoir home, having waited patiently for him, as requested.

20

Peaks, Valleys and Slippery Slopes (1936–1939)

"Parce que tu comprend sur cette terre il y a une chose effroyable — c'est que tout le monde a ses raisons" ("Because you know on this earth there is a frightful thing — it is that everyone has his reasons").

—Octave (Jean Renoir) in *La Règle du jeu* (1939)

"We forget one thing, that relativity exists not only in time and space. Everything, everything, absolutely everything, is relative. We are surrounded by relative truths, and indeed there are only relative truths; everything depends on the circumstances, on the moment."
—Jean Renoir in "My Next Films, Interview by Michel Delahaye and Jean-André Fieschi" (*Cahiers du Cinema in English*; March 1967; p. 47); originally in *Cahiers du Cinéma* (July 1966)

In his role as Octave in *La Règle du jeu*, Jean Renoir delivered the line often associated with him and commonly translated as "everyone has his reasons." Along with the cynical bite, it perhaps indicates a generous and sensitive nature — not judging others, in appreciating the relativity of human experience.

Whatever Renoir's own reasons, his career was an uneven one. I feel it is highlighted by the two masterpieces and a beautiful shorter film, *Partie de campagne*, as well as some other well-made and (at times) innovative movies in the 1930s like *Boudu sauvé des eaux*, *Le Crime de Monsieur Lange* and *La Bête humaine*. Many of his other films, despite flashes of vintage Renoir, verge perilously close to being overblown melodramas, especially after 1939 and *La Règle du jeu*.

This is a minority opinion. And some critics even rate his post-war films at least on a par with the earlier classics and that Renoir was always Renoir, end of argument. But an auteurist blessing of a director glosses over the fact that film is a collaborative medium, in several ways.

Although the personal stamp of a great director is certainly unmistakable in his or her films, this doesn't guarantee that the stamp will not be smeared or only partially affixed. In some criticism, the Procrustean bed of the auteur theory (or what remains of it) stretches and contorts its premises in order to dodge the issue of cinematic effectiveness and, instead, discuss the consistency of an auteur's distinctive style in shaping a film. To compartmentalize so broadly ignores the truism that everything, as Renoir put it, connects to everything else. Consistency without quality or, at the least, effectiveness is something of a hollow victory.

There was possibly in the theory's original framing an inferiority complex at work as critics felt the compulsion to raise film, as they saw it, to the level of other arts. But artistic expression in film needs also to be discussed in terms of its unique qualities and not only as the question of a director's style. It is not simply the case of an artist expressing that style in facing the work, one on one. With this perspective in mind, Renoir's unevenness can be seen even in his period of greatest productivity from 1936 through 1939. The peaks and valleys, with a few slippery slopes, are pronounced.

The three movies that Renoir released in 1936 were all, to some degree, influenced by his sympathies for the Popular Front; another film he shot that year took ten years to see the light of day.

Le Crime de Monsieur Lange, which was filmed at the end of 1935 but released in early 1936, follows the lives of workers in a publishing house run by a corrupt boss. The story also features one of the few strong women in Renoir's movies, Valentine, who runs a nearby laundry; as an ex-lover of Batala (the boss), she sees through him and resists his advances, stays loyal to the other women, helps Lange escape after he murders Batala and then convincingly defends him to win his freedom.

For the first time, Renoir exhibited his mature style at its most fluid: the long, adeptly choreographed tracking and panning shots; depth of field; interlocking relationships; and the casual, but assured, narrative.

The film suffers, however, from the unnuanced and Manichean depiction of good workers versus evil owner. Batala is a sweet-talking monster, driven by his hunger for both women and money. The grand, bordering on grandiose, performance of Jules Berry is impressive and enjoyable as a piece of highly theatrical acting, but he seems to have wandered in from another set; his performance itself becomes a focus of the movie — a caricature of a suave and very sophisticated Boudu, who is equally unimpeded by morals or legalities.

An expertly planned structure opens and closes the film at a seaside inn; the bulk of the movie recounts, in flashback, the story leading up to the murder. The first half contrasts Lange (René Lefèvre), a dreamer and sexual innocent, with the corruption of Batala as a businessman (an embezzler and con artist) and person (serial lecher and, at one point, amateur pimp). Once this is established, the last part, after Batala's faked death, covers the happy cooperative started in his absence and Lange's personal salvation with Valentine (Florelle) — only to have everything disrupted by the return of Batala.

The film is famous for a 360° pan of the courtyard confrontation and murder that André Bazin analyzed at length and that has become known as its signature moment. The scene consists of two consecutive 180° shots.

In the first shot, the camera tracks upward from Batala pawing Valentine in the courtyard to a window above and then follows Lange to the left as he rushes past other windows to a spiral staircase and then down some steps; at the doorway leading onto the courtyard, he pauses, having in essence reached 180 degrees from the shot's opening.

Then Renoir cuts to a closer shot of Lange and he heads off-camera, slightly to the right, and the camera tracks again to the left, making another 180° turn and catching up to him at the other side of the courtyard confronting Batala and then shooting him; stunned, Lange leaves the frame with Valentine.

Later, at the end of the scene, there is another 180° track, again to the left, around the cobblestones to the body of Batala at the courtyard's fountain.

This staging of the murder is grandly operatic and effective, and the tracking movements encircle the courtyard, which has been a focal point both of the cooperative and Valentine's laundry. But there is a twist to the idea of the collective as a cohesive unit — Lange and Valentine do not confide in the others at this point, only to Meunier, the cooperative's benefactor. And Meunier doesn't care that Lange has killed someone; he simply insists they must flee, and that he will drive them.

Renoir conceives a mixture of understated realism and exaggerated characterization (paralleling Lange's obsession with his pulp serial, "Arizona Jim"). But the schematic plotting of the film makes for some stilted moments. At one point, as the workers discuss plans for their cooperative and creditors express skepticism, Meunier, the son of the chief creditor, conveniently arrives on the scene and gleefully backs the workers, giving them a free hand without understanding what his backing means. He's a *deus ex machina* for the plot and pops up again at the right moment to whisk Lange and Valentine to safety.

This escape, maneuvered by Meunier, also feels a bit forced. Batala was perhaps capable of raping Valentine, and Lange might have made that case. But it works better, politically, to have him exonerated in killing the evil capitalist for the simple fact that Batala is indeed an evil capitalist. The point-blank execution puts Lange in the untenable position of deciding who lives and who dies. But not so untenable to Lange, nor to Renoir. The means justify the ends here, perhaps influenced by Renoir's dalliance with the communist movement at that time, as opposed to a more anarchistic and humanist approach. And it makes sense that *Le Crime de Monsieur Lange* is often cited for its Popular Front aspects.

There is much plot and clever dialogue in the film to advance the basic thesis, and many telling details, but Renoir does little to develop the characters. And though the film moves smoothly, and has a relaxed grace to it, there are also problematic touches. For example, after Lange admits that he selfishly lied about sleeping with Estelle, Renoir injects a sudden burst of music on the cut to a dazed Estelle, sitting in Batala's office, and the camera tracks to her for a close-up. Then two shots as the leering Batala draws close. Then Renoir cuts before he lurches onto her. All just thrown in for its melodramatic flair. And back to the more naturalistic story.

The narrative also has the amusing device of Batala returning disguised as a priest. But the subsequent argument with Lange about cooperatives, with Batala saying that a strong hand is needed, too obviously presents the thesis in dispute. And then there is the irony of Batala dying as a fake priest and asking for a real one. Check the church off as part of the capitalist cabal. Renoir and Jacques Prévert are almost too clever for their own good and Berry's flamboyance draws added attention to this cleverness.

Le Crime de Monsieur Lange ends with three shots at the border. First the camera pans from footprints in wet sand up to Lange and Valentine walking away on a windswept beach; they turn and wave. Then a shot of two men waving back to them. And, in the final shot, the fugitives turn and continue walking away into the distance, hand in hand. A poignant ending that is unresolved, as in the similar ending of *La Grande Illusion*.

But the film also has, to me, one of the most distasteful moments in a Renoir film. News of the death, in childbirth, of an illegitimate baby born to Batala and Estelle, the surviving mother, is revealed to a solemn group of Estelle's friends. Batala's cousin, Juliani, turns and says, "Hélas, c'était, tout de même, un parent" ("Alas, it was, all the same, a relative") — and everyone laughs, amused at the idea that the baby being a relative could make a difference. And the grave mood at its death punctured. Not another word about the baby or what one might assume is a newly grieving mother, the young woman Batala seduced and, also, their friend. As if claiming any human feeling or empathy is absurd in this case, considering the father in question.

Renoir then cuts to clouds and the Arc de Triomphe, backed by jaunty music, in an upbeat sequence showing the success of "Arizona Jim." Estelle's trauma quickly forgotten.

20. *Peaks, Valleys and Slippery Slopes (1936–1939)* 175

Le Crime de Monsieur Lange (1936), production still. Batala (Jules Berry) mocks Lange (René Lefèvre) with the gun that will become Lange's means of execution (*Photofest*).

Not for long, however. Lange indirectly endorses relief at the baby's death soon after when he dictates the caption for a photograph that a group in costume, including Estelle, has just taken for a new installment. He refers to "Estelle," a character in a similarly compromised position, and closes with the comment that "tout de même" (recalling Juliani's words) she had luck: "l'enfant vécu pas" ("the child lived not"). If this reflects the Popular Front ethic, giving more weight to the political negatives of a baby born to a lecherous, capitalist exploiter than to the human dimension, it is a cold-hearted formulation.

And it indicates the didactic nature of a film with points to make, instead of people to explore in their contradictions. A socially conscious film more than a humanist one. It works very well under the terms Renoir set for it, but they are modest terms.

Later in 1936, Renoir's supervision of the cooperative that made *La Vie est à nous*, a Communist Party production, can be seen as an indication of his naiveté. He was ordinarily more interested in people and their entanglements than in ideology, and he never became a member of the Party, though allying himself with it.

La Vie est à nous is unapologetically a propaganda film and embarrassing on many levels. Much of it is made up of stock documentary footage: shots of demonstrations in the first part and, near the end, a lengthy sequence of Communist Party officials ranting away at a rally, one after the other, with no more subtlety than the similar talking heads at the Nuremberg rally in Leni Riefenstahl's overrated *Triumph des Willens* (completed the previous year). There are some attempts to comment on the stock footage in *La Vie est à nous*, as in a shot of Hitler where his voice is replaced by the sound of barking dogs. But such nose-thumbing is perhaps the highest form of political analysis the film manages to reach.

Stuck into the middle of the film are three fictional stories making the stirring point that workers are noble, the Party pure, and the solidarity of the people triumphs over oppression, again and again and again. At least for these three stories.

Renoir directed the third story. An unemployed and hungry young man in a dazed state is rescued from the streets and brought to a Communist Party meeting where a group of young activists in a chorus sing an inspirational song. The visitor looks much revived and impressed by his saviors. And, eating some hearty food, he directs a spotlight on the performers. This episode could stand as a primer on how to "do" Socialist Realism — Renoir, a master of poetic realism, having unfortunately substituted socialism for poetry in the equation.

Lest we miss the point, there are then posters of Stalin and Lenin at a mass rally. Speeches by Party bigwigs end with Maurice Thorez, the Secretary General, shouting out the names of Marx — Engels — Lenin — Stalin. His incantation is dutifully illustrated with pictures of them.

La Vie est à nous returns to the fictional characters as they march along, framed against the sky (a typical Renoir composition). After a montage of marchers and more documentary images, the film ends with a close shot of workers carrying a little boy, again shot from below to boost the heroism and mythic stature of these comrades-in-arms. This final shot indicates the project's basic superficiality; its characters are presented primarily as models of moral instruction.

There are conflicting views as to how much input Renoir had in making the film. Some left-wing critics prefer to see his involvement as reflecting his political stance — and leave it at that. To be fair, it is not representative of his work (as true also of *Salute to France*).

Still, *La Vie est à nous* remains more than just an awkwardly made film. Considering that Renoir had recently visited Stalin's Russia but had missed its horrors, it is chilling to see these people reduced to determined masses marching to "The Internationale" at the end.

And yet, in the same year, Renoir shot a film that is the antithesis of *La Vie est à nous*, both in spirit and execution — his gem of a movie, *Partie de campagne*, based on a short story by Guy de Maupassant.

Renoir never completed the film as planned. Poor weather stalled production, it ran over budget, and he moved on to other films. Time passed and the original edited version was destroyed during the war but, luckily, the negatives had been saved. A collaborative effort to get it before the public was largely due to the impetus and determination of Pierre Braunberger, its producer. Marguerite Renoir edited the rushes again, Joseph Kosma added music, and it was released ten years later in 1946 in a shortened form (40 minutes).

Partie de campagne was filmed in the Loing river region where Auguste Renoir had painted and where Renoir himself filmed *La Fille de l'eau*. It is a joyous tone poem, a mood piece that brings the era of Impressionist painting to life, in black-and-white, and feels like an especially personal film for Renoir in other ways as well: he appears as an innkeeper; his companion (and the editor), Marguerite, plays the inn's servant; his son, Alain, is in the opening sequence as a boy fishing from a bridge; and Claude Renoir, his nephew, was the director of photography.

Unlike in *La Grande Illusion*, Renoir bathes the film in traditional movie music and

Partie de campagne, production still. Henriette (Sylvia Bataille) and the inn's servant (Marguerite Renoir). Photograph: Eli Lotar (*CNAC/MNAM/dist. RMN-Grand Palais/Art Resource, New York*).

relies on some close-ups and explicit dialogue. But his goals were considerably less grand. *Partie de campagne* is lushly lyrical, a meditation on the passing of time and lost love, imbued like *Boudu sauvé des eaux* with sexual tension rather than a rich narrative of fully realized characters. Taking place almost exclusively outdoors, Renoir again shares his vivid sense of nature.

A small party of Parisians is on a country outing and, at a local inn, two young men, Rodolphe (Jacques Brunius) and Henri (Georges Darnoux), plot to set their attentions on the mother and daughter in the group.

There's a memorable moment early in the film as Rodolphe opens the shutters of a window to reveal Henriette (Sylvia Bataille), the attractive young woman from Paris, and her mother, Mme. Dufour, lolling idly on nearby swings amongst the trees. As in *La Grande Illusion*, the outside world is engaged from the vantage point of a simple country place, except this time the camera acts as voyeur, at times taking the viewpoint of the playfully lecherous Rodolphe.

Renoir follows this shot with an engaging sequence of Henriette swinging more vigorously, standing and then sitting, intercut with a series of shots (seminarians passing by, boys ogling, Rodolphe and Henri commenting on the scene).

Some shots of Henriette are set on solid ground from different angles as she swings back and forth. But a few shots are fixed on the swing with Henriette, at a closer and unchanging distance from her, to create a disorienting effect, erotically charged in its apparent release from the laws of gravity. It is difficult to gauge the movement of the swing in these shots, to read what goes up and what down, and it feels similar to, though not as dizzying as, the effect in Riefenstahl's magnificent diving sequence in *Olympia* (also shot in 1936) — a more felicitous parallel to one of her films.

And Renoir closes the sequence as he began it, from the opening setup looking out the window; Henriette and her mother leave the frame.

Later, after the lazy unrolling of a summer afternoon, following the Parisian vacationers as they take in the rustic setting, the two men approach the mother and daughter, who are momentarily alone, apart from M. Dufour and his bumbling clerk, Anatole.

Renoir then cuts to a shot of Rodolphe, Mme. Dufour and Henriette, with only a bit of Henri's shoulder on the left side of the frame. Henri is a reluctant seducer and seems to be a thoughtful young man, having earlier warned his friend about the consequences of falling in love. Now he's out of the picture as Rodolphe flirts outrageously.

A cut follows to a brief medium shot of Henri rolling his eyes and turning his head in disgust. Renoir returns to the wider shot, again excluding Henri from the seduction under way. But when Henriette asks him about some boats at the river, the camera pans to include him as he responds. After a two-shot of the women, Renoir cuts to a shot of Henri and follows with one of Henriette, thus linking them apart from the others and changing the dynamic through his sequencing of shots (somewhat as in the paired close-ups of Maréchal and Elsa on Christmas morning, but on a lesser scale).

Henri soon turns from diffidence to amiable determination. He rows Henriette down the river to an isolated spot, their empathy becoming evident, these two introverted and

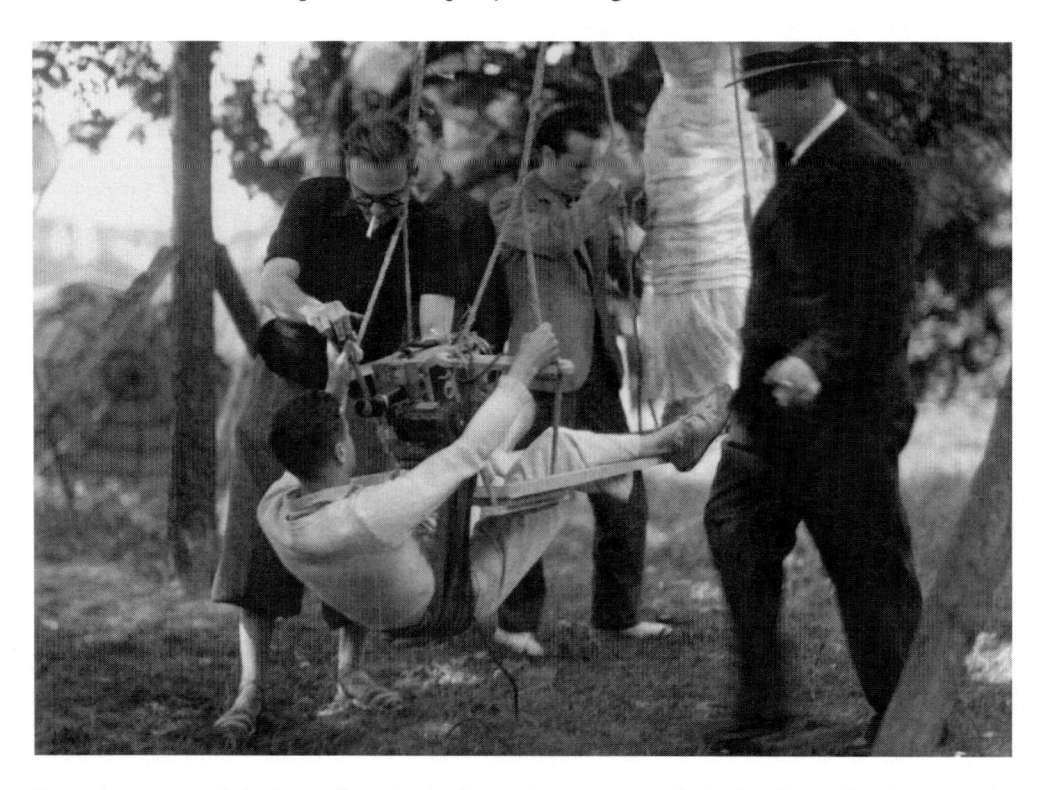

Preparing to upend the laws of gravity in *Partie de campagne*: clockwise, from Claude Renoir (at the camera) Jean-Serge Bourgoin, unidentified man, Jacques Becker, Sylvia Bataille (obscured), Jean Renoir. Photograph: Eli Lotar. (*CNAC/MNAM/dist. RMN-Grand Palais/Art Resource, New York*).

basically gentle natures, though she is an innocent and he seems already world-weary. Meanwhile Rodolphe continues his pursuit of the giggling Mme. Dufour.

A crosscut sequence then closes this opening part of the film. There is a tracking shot of Henri and Henriette walking along the riverbank. Their mutual attraction seems clear and Henri's hand on her waist guides Henriette along the path. They stop and music starts up. He reaches out his hands to embrace her and she pushes them away, but when she turns to continue their walk he puts an arm around her waist and she accepts it. Soon after, they sit down on a grassy spot and she disengages his arm, but looks at him with a serious and pensive look.

Renoir cuts to Rodolphe and Mme. Dufour engaged in their game of courtship. Then back to Henri, his arm around Henriette as she is entranced by a bird in the tree above them, wiping a tear from her face and putting her arm around Henri; he places his other arm around her.

Again back to Rodolphe and he prances lasciviously, another one of Renoir's satyrs, with sticks flourished like pipes, while he chases Mme. Dufour, who squeals in delight.

And then the final piece in the sequence. Henri kisses Henriette; she resists, falls back, and struggles against him. Renoir ups the stakes with a closer two-shot as she still resists, then goes limp and reaches up and kisses him, accompanied by swelling music — the puerile male fantasy of a man's irresistible charm and brutish aggression bringing out a young woman's sexuality.

Renoir cuts to an extreme close-up of their kiss and then Henriette turns her face to the side, nestled in Henri's hand, with tears in her eye and on her cheek, filling the screen, still with the swelling music. It is a stunning shot of the desolation beneath this unsettling disruption of innocence. Without break, the music continues through a dissolve to a full-length shot of them and she looks up at him, and then turns away; Henri also turns his head, dejected. Then shots of the river nearby.

In many ways an uncomfortable scene to watch, with Henri forcing himself on Henriette, the denouement at least defuses the passion and Henri appears to realize he must pull back from the trap about which he had warned Rodolphe. With the music continuing through the dissolve and their positions remaining largely unchanged, the implication is that Henri has stopped short in his seduction.

A storm comes up and there are strangely ominous traveling shots from a boat, moving faster than the earlier boating shots; a rain that pelts the darkened river brings solemnity to the scene. The opening part, and the bulk of the movie, comes to an end.

Renoir shifts to a lovely coda, set years later on the same river, covered again by music. The sky is overcast and a pall has settled over the landscape.

Henri rows to the same spot and Renoir reprises the earlier track as he walks along the riverbank again, but now alone. He stops, walks some more, and stops again, expressively breaking the continuity of this reprised shot. The camera moves ahead to the left, without him this time, to the spot where the earlier sequence had ended on the young couple years before, and it comes to rest on Henriette; she becomes aware of Henri's presence as Anatole, now her husband, dozes nearby, and the camera tracks back with her to the right as she runs eagerly for a few steps, then walks up to Henri — and they are, after years apart, together again in the frame, in this elaborate and complicated shot.

But immediately they are separated by Renoir's camera placement in a series of seven countershot close-ups and medium shots (with one of Anatole waking up as well) that visually captures their changed relationship. Henriette confesses that she still thinks of him and

Henri talks about his fond memories. After tears well up in Henriette's eyes, Anatole calls for her, from off-screen, and she leaves.

The fragmented variation on the original tracking shot is soon extended, and reprised, in the opposite direction. Henri ducks out of sight and the camera voyeuristically peers over his shoulder, witness to his angst in watching Henriette, in a long shot, as she walks ahead of Anatole along that same riverbank path, to the right now, then waits for her husband to catch up and put his arm around her waist before they exit the scene together. The stationary nature of the shot (there is only a slight panning adjustment at the end) further disconnects Henri (and us) from the earlier tracking shot with Henriette that took place minutes (but years) ago, in which he (not Anatole) put his arm around her waist.

This is Renoir at his greatest, repeating a particular tracking shot's setting (twice, once in each direction, this time) as he expresses both a change in feeling and the passing of time by dramatically breaking the pattern—a technique used so well in *La Grande Illusion*.

And, later, the last shot of *Partie de campagne* is a classic Renoir topper as Henriette (now more active, though subservient) rows Anatole away, and the camera pans back to Henri's empty boat at the river's edge, the boat the thwarted lovers had once shared; Renoir then pans again to take in the water, serenely and without comment, verbal or metaphoric, to disturb the implacability of the image, ending his film quietly.

Partie de campagne exemplifies a gracefully integrated piece of filmmaking. The setting and cinematic expression communicate the story as much as its plot and dialogue. Like a lyric poem, it taps into experience and memory in a sensuous way, folding the abandon of the natural world into the passions, and foibles, of its characters.

It may not quite be a masterpiece, and Renoir was not the driving force in its eventual completion, but *Partie de campagne* at least rests somewhere high on the slopes of greatness. It is open and evocative, and far different from Renoir's next film.

Les Bas-Fonds, the third film released in 1936, returns (less explicitly) to the Popular Front ethos of *Le Crime de Monsieur Lange* and *La Vie est à nous*. An adaptation of a Maxim Gorky play set at a flophouse, it is a minor and, at heart, sentimental film. That Renoir made it just before *La Grande Illusion* illustrates again the vicissitudes of moviemaking.

Gorky's characters keep their Russian names in *Les Bas-Fonds* but speak French fluently and are placed in an unspecified setting, though outdoors it looks suspiciously like France. And, to top it off, rubles are used as currency.

The long takes, tracking camera and familiar plot developments make it recognizably Renoir. But it's hard to empathize with these one-dimensional figures. They explain their inner selves directly to each other (and to us). A resident wise man with a beard even makes stock pronouncements to one and all.

Major crises take place without the necessary buildup to support them or even justify their inclusion in the plot. When Renoir introduces a secondary character named Anna, she is dying and talks anxiously about life and death; her kindly grandfather (the wise man) dispenses much philosophy. Soon afterward, her death is announced. Back to her bedside for tears and more philosophizing. Renoir plugs it for all it's worth, but she is only one among a group of unconvincing characters.

Even the suicide of an alcoholic actor near the end of the film elicits little pathos. Renoir makes him a cartoon version of the tortured artist, bug-eyed and patently theatric as played by Robert Le Vigan. Bathos is more the order of the day. And other outright mugging also mars *Les Bas-Fonds*, especially by Vladimir Sokoloff as a greedy landlord.

But the performances of Jean Gabin (Pépel) and Louis Jouvet (the Baron) are fun to watch. The early scenes featuring the Baron are delightful, marked by witty dialogue and a sense of irony. A comedy of manners. But when the flophouse is the center of attention, the flatness and sentimentality of the venture takes over. Pépel, for example, nearly strangles the landlord in a fit of rage, early on before much has been established, followed by close-ups that are over-the-top, hammering away to attempt significance for the scene.

The women in the film again conform to the extremes of the vindictive mistress and defenseless innocent. A *femme fatale* turns on her lover after trying to get him to kill her husband; another woman, Natacha, passively waits for her Galahad to rescue her (Pépel does) from an attempted seduction by a boorish police inspector, after being essentially pimped out by her sister and brother-in-law.

And, again, the real love story is the friendship of two men, this time Pépel and the Baron. In their first encounter, after Pépel tries to burglarize the Baron's apartment one night, they end up sharing a meal and getting to know each other better. The Baron even tells his new friend he can call him "tu" and puts his hand affectionately on Pépel's knee. Then, in a typical Lubitsch touch, after dollying to a lamp, Renoir dissolves to the same lamp in the morning, drawing back to show them still together, playing cards now — the stock ellipsis more frequently used in movies to indicate lovers spending the night together.

Later, there is a scene of Pépel and the Baron sitting on a grassy bank as they talk about their lives and their dreams. Two guys shooting the breeze, of a sort. The only thing to relieve the leaden exposition is a nice bit of business as the Baron toys with a snail sitting on the back of his hand. And near the end of the movie, before Pépel leaves with Natacha, he looks at the Baron with more intensity than at any woman in the film, calls him a "copain" ("pal") and grabs him for an extended kiss on the cheek. That's where the sparks fly. Natacha is more of an afterthought.

The closing shot of Pépel and Natacha, hitting the open road to start their new life together and walking toward the backtracking camera, brings no feeling of release, despite the smiles they suddenly sport after the gloom and cynicism to that point. A happy ending that, as generally distinguishes happy endings, feels tacked-on. A lot has happened; little has changed.

Les Bas-Fonds did well, unlike most of Renoir's films, and was awarded the first Prix Louis-Delluc as the best French film of the year.

La Grande Illusion followed. Though it seems a surprising leap forward in his career, ambitious and comprehensive in scope, it is also clearly the fruition of a style Renoir had been developing in his earlier sound films.

Renoir's next film, *La Marseillaise* (1938), was commissioned by the C.G.T. (Confédération Générale du Travail), a trade union influenced by the communist movement. It seems mainly an illustrated history lesson, in costume, with familiar spectacle and a series of period pieces set during the French Revolution. There are some nice mass scenes, but characters spend much of their time either discussing the historical context of the era or engaging in intellectual argument and making political speeches. A talky and informative film.

In trying to whip up human interest, Renoir presents ordinary citizens in all their Norman Rockwell goodness and simplicity, expressing their populist views. And they are broadly portrayed by the actors for maximum cuteness.

Only rarely does a welcome hiatus let something develop, as in a scene when aristocrats in exile work out the steps of a gavotte, remembering their beloved homeland. A summoning up of privilege and class that is more articulate than the surrounding verbiage.

Despite recognizable touches, including several effective pans and tracking shots, it is not Renoir's command of technique that communicates the story but the treatises serving up the revolution in manageable portions. In *La Grande Illusion* the extended tête-à-tête of Boeldieu and Rauffenstein is an aberration, an interlude that offers a change of pace. But in *La Marseillaise* such scenes make up its underlying foundation.

A few sequences like the gavotte scene are thrown in for a less didactic approach, particularly some involving the ineffectual Louis XVI, played persuasively by Pierre Renoir, who is calmer and more nuanced in his performance than most of the actors playing his subjects. But the verbalization, rather than realization, of history and of mass and individual psychology drives the film.

There is also no gradual, or even sudden, development of characters. Instead, vignettes are strung together to picture the French Revolution from the bottom up. All well and good, but the film, like *Les Bas-Fonds*, is shallow and sentimental.

Early in the story, for instance, a fort at Marseille is captured and its prisoners freed by "the people," who are less believable as real people than as symbols of the downtrodden masses. A character named Bomier happily reunites with a friend who is nearly blind from his long imprisonment. But Renoir provides no reason for the viewing audience to necessarily feel something as well; Bomier has barely been introduced and his friend appears on the screen for the first time. Heroic music, however, drenches the scene and indicates we ought to find it somewhere in our hearts to care.

Renoir even dilutes one scene near the end that attempts a more sustained, and personal, note. Bomier lies dying in a side alley, after the storming of the palace, and his girlfriend comes to his side. Behind them, a young mother gazes sadly at him, holding her baby. This symbol of life and renewal is on the level of Rauffenstein's geranium but Bomier, only sketchily developed as a person, does not warrant the weighted attention that Boeldieu commands.

In a closer two-shot, Bomier regrets that he won't see Marseille or his mother again. Renoir dissolves to a battle in the streets, then cuts to the palace, some fighting and a firing squad, to more history in the making, and finally to the last sequence in the countryside. Bomier's friends talk about the struggle ahead of them, and we only learn of his death when someone remarks that Bomier will have died in vain if they are defeated. There is not much marking the loss to his friends since he doesn't matter in the historical sweep covered by the movie, being merely a cog in the machinery of the plot. This approach keeps the characters in *La Marseillaise* at a remove.

In a medium close-up, one of the friends, Arnaud, makes an impassioned speech connecting Bomier to the cause of the people, who have now embraced "Liberté" (with a capital "L" clearly in his voice), as "La Marseillaise" fills the soundtrack; he continues the clumsy metaphor by declaiming that Liberty has not yet become the mistress of the people but that she will eventually be won.

One of the few moments where Renoir allows the image and sound to be expressive, without the redundant support of dialogue or background music, is the last shot of *La Marseillaise*, before a final scroll that provides an epilogue.

It's a medium long shot, as horses gallop past and then citizen soldiers in a long line march by the camera at a slight angle, led by drummers, and the sound of their drums, alone, beats on the soundtrack. The effect is similar to the one achieved by the window pan in *La Grande Illusion*. These fighters in the cause of "Liberté, Égalité, Fraternité" are also an organized army, and one can read into their regimented march the possible subversion of their idealism. It is at least open to interpretation.

The camera moves continuously, if only slightly, during this final shot — left to the drummers, right to a closer position, left to a wider view, then right again to a closer shot of Bomier's friends passing by ("FIN" comes up on the screen), and, finally, a very slight adjustment to the left before a fade-out, with "FIN" remaining. That floating movement imparts an unsettled feeling to the shot as the oncoming surge of soldiers flows past, in counterpoint to the meandering camera. And it is an inspiration to end this film without "La Marseillaise" sounding in the air, a leitmotif that has been used effectively throughout. Renoir confounds expectations and creates an opportunity to meditate on the image by subtracting the obvious.

This powerful shot is a reminder of how little room Renoir has carved out in his film to feel anything, or even grapple with an original idea that has not been predigested. As the drumbeats continue, the shot is followed by one of a cloudy sky, with scrolling words giving more history and, then, a quote from Goethe citing "une nouvelle époque pour l'histoire du Monde" ("a new epoch for the history of the World"). Again, too much. The obvious added back in again.

La Marseillaise premiered in February 1938, eight months after *La Grande Illusion*. Homer may nod, but this is more than a catnap. Granted, it has the feel of a Renoir, but it is an eviscerated and bland Renoir.

La Bête humaine (1938), a drama of sexual passion and murder based on a novel by Zola, again displays aspects of Renoir's style — the long takes and tracking movements; the painterly sense of landscape; some low angle shots against the skyline; a music hall performance serving as commentary; the hard-edged realism of its documentary sequences. In addition, some of his colleagues on *La Grande Illusion* worked with him on the film: Gabin (who again shines), Julien Carette, Joseph Kosma, Eugène Lourié, Claude Renoir, and of course his partner, Marguerite.

There's also a small turn by Renoir, playing Cabuche, who is falsely accused of murder in one sequence. Compared to the exquisite scene near the end of *La Règle du jeu* when Renoir, as Octave, reminisces about the past, on the terrace, this sequence comes across as padded. Octave is a central figure, already developed as a character, and his melancholy during that monologue contributes a critical element in the impressively crafted chaos that builds during the final night at the country estate. But in *La Bête humaine* Cabuche has only recently appeared in the plot and the extended scene, as he rambles on, hamming it up, seems self-indulgent; one shot of him lasts well over a minute, with Renoir clearly having fun spinning his monologue for the camera.

The larger problem is that, in not trusting the viewer to be his collaborator, Renoir sometimes uses the shortcuts of Cinema 101. Close-ups and portentous angles plead with us to pay attention now, class. And Kosma's score, although much like the music in *La Grande Illusion*, is slathered on thickly at times.

As a kind of film noir, some of these excesses can be understood as conventions of the genre. But we come to *La Grande Illusion*, while *La Bête humaine* comes all too eagerly to us. This is not reassuring. Renoir at his best doesn't insist, or even care what anyone might think. And his greatest movies are more like forces of nature than anything constructed by mere mortals.

La Bête humaine differs as well from *La Grande Illusion* in its explicit dialogue, telling us all we don't really need to know about the inner lives of the characters. Relief comes when they stop analyzing themselves and the musical support drops out as well.

It's also not a good omen that a quote from Zola's novel scrolls down the screen, after

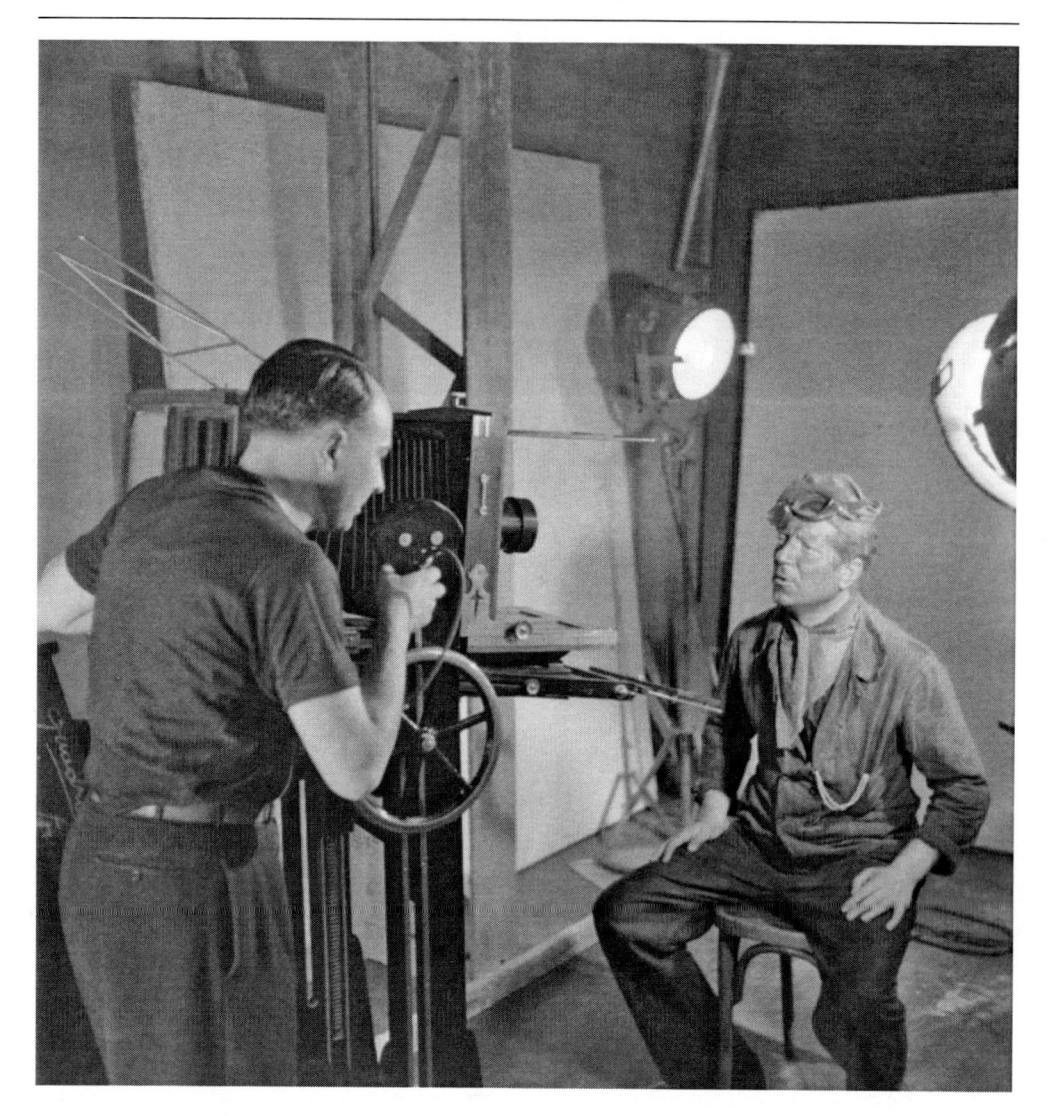

Sam Lévin photographing Gabin on the set of *La Bête humaine* (1938). Photograph: Sam Lévin (©*Ministère de la Culture/Médiathèque du Patrimoine/Sam Levin/dist. RMN-Grand Palais/Art Resource, New York*).

the opening credits, and details the alcoholism in Jacques Lantier's forebears and how this hereditary pollution has infected him so that he acts against his will. There was no more need to call on Zola than there was to end with Goethe in *La Marseillaise*. And certainly one should be suspicious of any movie that needs to explain a theme so overtly before the movie proper has even begun.

Despite this unpromising prologue, the first image of *La Bête humaine* opens a documentary-like set piece filled with more foreboding and tension than anything that follows. It is powerful filmmaking, with Renoir in top form.

In the opening shot, the camera pulls back from a close-up of a train engine's raging furnace to a medium long shot of Lantier (Gabin) steering the train and Pecqueux (Carette) stoking the fire. A screaming whistle sets the tone and the jiggling camera movement establishes a realistic edge. This apt beginning, symbolic of the fire in Lantier, does not proclaim its symbolism.

The sequence quickly generates a force that captures the train's speed and power, with the two men pantomiming instructions to each other above the screeching noise, going about their jobs. With the camera often fixed to the side of the train, thrillingly close to the overpasses shooting by, tracks whiz underneath in a rush, the train plunges into the darkness of a tunnel, gritty industrial backwaters are glimpsed along the way and signs periodically pass by, as in the documentary sequences in *La Grande Illusion*. A wonderful mishmash of shots.

And the harsh sound of the train hurtling along becomes oppressive, stirring up a feeling of unease. Consonant with Giroud's story of Renoir showing Stroheim a blank screen with the tramp of marching boots filling the theater, the sheer sound communicates more than the most grandiloquent speech.

This sequence runs a bit over four minutes, with no dialogue. An audacious way to open a film. And music only starts up toward the end and builds to an operatic pitch as the train, slowly, and majestically, pulls into Le Havre, like an ocean liner reaching its berth.

Throughout the movie, the sights and sounds of the railyard and on the train are charged with this sort of understated poetic realism. And the story never strays far from those milieus, which skillfully anchor the film. Renoir the documentary poet. But too often he relies instead on the script and music to make his points.

Some of the film's key moments show how Renoir stacks the deck. In the first major scene, before we know much about anyone, Jacques makes a pass at Flore and is rejected. He follows her up an embankment and throws her down just below some railroad tracks, as music pumps up the melodramatic fervor. In a medium shot, angled upward, she relents and they kiss (that male fantasy again). After a closer shot of Flore, Renoir cuts back to the medium shot and Jacques starts to choke her, victim of that pesky hereditary trait we had been warned about in the preamble. On a close-up of Jacques, the sound of a train makes him pause and he calms down.

Renoir returns to the two-shot, and Jacques's psychotic fit subsides as the train passes by behind him. There is almost a mystical peacefulness that comes over him — his true love being his own train's locomotive, often anthropomorphized in the dialogue. The music stops, which is refreshing, if only for the silence on the soundtrack.

Renoir soon alternates close-ups of Jacques and Flore against the sky, with background music coming up again, and they discuss his illness, already outlined in the opening quote from Zola. And the lesson ends.

By placing this scene so early in the film, Renoir makes an unwarranted and mawkish appeal, which is further weakened by the music, the close-ups and angles, and the dissertation on what ails Jacques. It is weighty without being substantial and simply provides information. Yet Renoir also seems to want us to feel something (as in *Les Bas-Fonds* or *La Marseillaise*). And this scene pales in comparison to the sensations evoked more naturally by the opening sequence, achieved obliquely through the rhythm of the editing and the blunt heaviness of sound.

The first love scene of Jacques and Séverine (Simone Simon) is even more fulsome. Once again music carries the burden. In the central shot Jacques, on a rainy night, arrives at a shack where Séverine waits for him in the doorway. She says she loves him; they kiss and, inside the shelter, drop to the floor, kissing some more. Renoir then tracks to a drainpipe with rain shooting out and (yes) overflowing a bucket filled with water (fireworks or crashing waves would be relatively tame by comparison).

But this symbolism is improbably topped by a dissolve to the same setting, after their lovemaking, with the drainpipe not spouting and the bucket no longer overflowing. Less a Lubitsch touch than a resounding thud. And excess follows excess in this closing shot of the scene as Renoir then tracks to the doorway and the feet of the lovers appear; the camera pans upward and we find them cuddling together and gazing dreamily at the heavens above, looking for all the world like Nelson Eddy and Jeanette MacDonald teetering on the brink of song, movie stars all dewy-eyed and glamourous, with Kosma's music, as if we need another tip-off, rising to a crashing climax. To paraphrase Oscar Wilde, one would have to have a heart of stone not to laugh at this pair of lovers.

At least Renoir keeps some of the biggest moments off-camera in *La Bête humaine* (the murders, sex). Séverine's murder, for example, is a memorable scene. It ends in a dimly lit bedroom, seen through a doorway, with a knife flashing as she screams and fends off Jacques; she breaks free, followed by him, both going out of sight, and the camera tracks around, as if curious, to focus on the bed, and remains outside the doorway looking dispassionately into the room, which now appears empty. Most thankfully, there is no music. Noirish in feeling, it also has the calm and tact of a classic Ozu shot, drained of people or any movement, and yet creating a sense of anticipation and impending doom. An off-screen struggle and more screams. And then they reappear as Jacques throws her onto the bed, with Séverine now hidden by the end board; he raises his knife and plunges it downward. Silence.

Renoir cuts to the café where the lovers had gone earlier. A singer croons about a woman who will not give her heart away, as is true of Séverine, and brings grief to the one who loves her.

But Renoir undercuts the impact of the murder by cutting back to a shot of Séverine's hand (with the song continuing) and, lest anyone hasn't been paying close enough attention, the camera moves up the lifeless body to her face and then to Jacques standing over her as we hear more about unhappy love on the soundtrack. In *La Grande Illusion* the incidental songs are neutral and gain greater authority by being infused with the agony of solitary confinement or the rage of separation and abandonment. But in *La Bête humaine* incidental music weighs down the plot by editorializing on it.

Near the end of the film, Renoir returns to the locomotive's engine room. As Jacques confesses in a daze to Pecqueux, an ominous double-beat of the engine's mechanism drums underneath his words. Its irregular beat, like a heart struggling, is a fitting metaphor, unspoken and indirect.

Another documentary sequence follows, recalling the opening scene, again without words or music, though not as long. The understatement is welcome. And the oppressive roar of the train once more creates a disturbing tension as Jacques breaks down and jumps off the train to his death.

La Bête humaine ends with an unflattering parallel to *La Grande Illusion*. After a long shot of Pecqueux and others by the side of the tracks, angled up against the sky, Renoir cuts to a medium close-up of Jacques, his eyes still open; Pecqueux's hand closes them. But Renoir's use of close-ups in the film has by now become devalued and his grasping for empathy falls short.

A medium shot follows as Pecqueux, choking back tears, delivers a brief eulogy about how Jacques must have suffered and how peaceful he looks now. There is no need for this explication; we have just seen the close-up — and the movie that preceded it. Renoir gives it to us anyway. True, it's also too obvious when Rauffenstein cuts the geranium, but his gesture "speaks" more eloquently than this impromptu memorial speech.

20. *Peaks, Valleys and Slippery Slopes (1936–1939)* 187

The final shot of *La Bête humaine* resembles ones that Renoir sometimes used at the end of his movies. The camera pans to Pecqueux and the others, walking away along the tracks, etched against the skyline, somewhat like the shadows that memorably end *La Règle du jeu*. So, as in *La Grande Illusion* also, the movie closes with figures walking into the distance. This subdued ending allows us to put ourselves into the scene.

Despite its weak moments, *La Bête humaine* lies at least on a slope between Renoir's two towering achievements. As an early prototype of a film noir, intended or not, its aim was clearly modest. And it turned out to be a big hit, another rarity in his career.

Renoir, eager to have greater control over his work, soon formed La Nouvelle Édition Française, a cooperative film production company, with his brother Claude and some friends. The company produced only one movie but, it can be safely said, that one movie would be quite enough as Renoir returned to the heights with *La Règle du jeu*. Has the difficult nature of filmmaking ever been better illustrated than by the astounding works, produced in 1937 and 1939, which are surrounded by such flawed ones?

Renoir's last film before the war deserves as much space and critical attention as *La Grande Illusion*. But a few random points might be of interest in comparing the two movies.

La Règle du jeu is essentially baroque, in technique and in the settings and décor, with its ubiquitous mirrors reflecting false selves and providing a reminder of the deceit and lies

La Règle du jeu, production still. Robert de la Cheyniest (Marcel Dalio), Octave (Renoir) and Christine (Nora Grégor), before the chaos. Photograph: Sam Lévin (©*Ministère de la Culture/Médiathèque du Patrimoine/Sam Levin/dist. RMN-Grand Palais/Art Resource, New York*).

that drive the film. It flows effortlessly, graced with lengthy tracking shots and the bold (even risky) strategy to film so much in long shot, as the spectacular choreography interconnects characters, rooms, doorways with dance-like precision. Dry and sophisticated, the film begins and ends at night; cynicism is the coin of the realm.

By contrast, *La Grande Illusion* is classic in structure and stripped bare, and more rooted in realism. It also moves easily, though less gorgeously than the later movie. But key scenes are often swathed in light. And it ranks lower in sophistication, while brimming with great emotion.

La Règle du jeu seems like the product of right-brain intuition and free association. It feels improvised, despite its clever organization of themes and characters, and one can imagine the film being a good deal longer — the further twirling out of a scene or another variation on a subplot. In fact, the current 106-minute version is longer than the film that opened in 1939 and the original shooting script was longer still.

Truffaut once wrote that, in watching it, "we feel we are there as the film is made." And: "For an instant, we think to ourselves, 'I'll come back tomorrow and see if it all turns out the same way.'"[1] This surreal reaction ably captures the fluid and elusive quality that makes *La Règle du jeu* so especially revered by critics and film people.

La Grande Illusion is more a left-brain film, logical and clearly structured. It seems hard to imagine much of anything added to it, or removed. And there is no chance it will turn out another way. But this is also a gross simplification. Adjust the angle of approach and the films can be discussed in similar terms. They are both strictly organized and poetically intuitive. To varying degrees.

One need only look at the first and last shots of these movies to see the mistake of categorizing them too definitively. There are some amusing synchronicities (on a technical level): the opening shots are long-held tracking shots and the closing ones are shorter still shots; the first distinguishable voice heard in both films is that of a woman, with the reporter in *La Règle du jeu* using a microphone, as the unseen singer in *La Grande Illusion* must also be doing; and the opening images feature mechanical devices (radio broadcasting equipment/the gramophone) held onto by a young man in a related setting (airport/air base), while the closing images, covered by music and without commentary, are of figures walking away (shadows of the guests/Maréchal and Rosenthal).

A major difference is that the later film, with the predominance of an ensemble and balanced pairs (even more than in *La Grande Illusion*), has no one like Maréchal; perhaps André Jurieux (Roland Toutain) comes closest. And the film starts and ends without any central characters in the frame.

Further, *La Règle du jeu* opens, with all the looseness and spontaneity of a newsreel, on the crush of an airport crowd eager to greet Jurieux, France's answer to Lindbergh; it nears the end with the squared-up proscenium of an exterior porch and steps, as well as a theatrical and controlled performance by the remaining principals in the story, establishing the tone for the last shot to finally close on dreamlike wraiths passing into the chateau. The film moves, one might say, from ultra-realism to ultra-theatricality.

La Grande Illusion also opens with a rich and complicated shot in a casually normal setting, although the dance of its characters follows a logical thread; it closes with an open-ended and minimalist image that is charged with lyricism. A similar movement, though less extreme, from realism to poetry.

More importantly, *La Règle du jeu* starts full force with a dramatic scene and André, in a sense, dooms himself with his honestly expressed disappointment at his loved one's absence, breaking the rules of polite society and drawing him into the game that ends in his death. A direct and public declaration of love, broadcast to the world. And Renoir cuts from this darkened, realistic scene to the bright, artificial interior of Christine's bedroom (linked in the foreground by the radio, which had carried André's words); it is a startling cut, connective and disconnective at the same time.

In *La Grande Illusion*, of course, no such drama takes place at the beginning. It moves along more slowly and Maréchal's downfall (and eventual recovery) is an indirect result of Boeldieu's annoyance with the smudged reconnaissance photograph. But Renoir makes an equally brilliant cut to the next setting, as well, though less extravagantly.

It is notable that, along with the ambience of refined decadence, and Renoir's inventive depth of field and tracking shots, the characters in *La Règle du jeu* talk openly about themselves. Renoir explores their psychology more directly than in *La Grande Illusion*, though the wit and artifice keeps it light, even in close-ups. And the rabbit hunt, though a shocking (and marvelous) sequence, has symbolic overtones that are too explicitly underlined later when Marceau compares Jurieux, after being shot, to an animal killed in a hunt. *La Grande Illusion*, in spite of its classicism, is far less direct and pointed, especially in its dialogue.

In the end, both works are complex and cannot be reduced to categories of romantic or classic, open or controlled. There are too many overlaps, as they each display an astonishing ability to change pace, and to surprise. And they build inexorably to riveting climaxes. In *La Règle du jeu*, the final evening's farce, both upstairs and downstairs, and its closing shots are breathtaking moments.

I can also think of few films as thoroughly beautiful, on a tactile and sensuous level, as *La Règle du jeu*. *Citizen Kane*, certainly. But not even *La Grande Illusion*. Maybe a film like Jean Cocteau's *La Belle et la Bête* (1946), but the beauty of that film is interwoven with the enchanting fairy-tale atmosphere, the costumes and sets, its movie tricks and lush chiaroscuro, making it more circumscribed in that sense. *La Règle du jeu* is abundantly and inclusively beautiful, in images and sounds — and its rhythms, in the editing and the choreography within shots. Its sheer physical presence transfixes the eye.

And there is a delicious contradiction between the formality of the theatrical framing of shots (and the stylish acting) and the naturally realistic drift of the action, almost off-the-cuff in feeling.

In brief, I admire and enjoy the brilliance of *La Règle du jeu*, and feel in awe. On the other hand, I am moved, and changed, by *La Grande Illusion*, and swept into it. They are different experiences. But both movies, in any case, achieve a level of transcendence rarely reached by other directors in the history of film.

La Règle du jeu was considered too pessimistic at a time of patriotic zeal on the eve of World War II. It did poorly and Renoir became discouraged. He agreed to make cuts, particularly in scenes involving his own role as Octave. Nevertheless, even with these changes, the film was soon withdrawn from circulation.

He would live to see it become the movie upon which his greatness and stature in the film world most securely rests.

21

Revenge of the Treatment
Le Caporal épinglé (1962)

> *"But, you know, everyone really only makes one film in his life, and then he breaks it up into fragments and makes it again, with just a few little variations each time. There's one so-called quality that's more overrated than almost any other: imagination. I've just been writing a book about my father, and I'm delighted to find that he felt this too. He really detested imagination: he thought it was the greatest possible hazard for the artist.*
>
> *He didn't believe in the idea of man as God, able to create out of nothing. He really subscribed to that text by Lavoisier which you must know: 'In nature nothing is created, nothing is lost, everything is transformed...' Well, there you are."*
> — Jean Renoir in "Conversation with Jean Renoir"; Louis Marcorelles (*Sight & Sound*; Spring 1962; p. 81), used by permission of the British Film Institute

The spirit and approach of the treatment of *La Grande Illusion* seems ascendant in Renoir's 1962 film, *Le Caporal épinglé*. Set in prison camps during World War II, there is a lifeless pallor to it, with vestigial remnants of that early outline and of *La Grande Illusion* itself. The treatment usually wins out. Unfortunately.

It appears as if Renoir tried to call once more on resonances from his glory days but, in the process, exposed the fault lines in his film. The only congruences between the two movies, other than those of plot, are purely technical ones: the formats are black-and-white, and characters talk in French and German. But it is worth looking at *Le Caporal épinglé* to further appreciate the inimitable achievement of his earlier film. The object lesson becomes clear that, even in the hands of a Jean Renoir, a movie can slip out of control.

As in his weaker films, Renoir seems impatient, telegraphing that certain scenes are to be considered important ones, as if expecting a reaction simply because they are injected into the plot. This pretense to something greater than the innate melodrama of the film, to larger themes or emotions, falls flat since the technique itself is melodramatic in nature and Renoir fails to moderate its effect.

The hero, given neither a first nor last name, is known, bloodlessly, as "the Corporal" (Jean-Pierre Cassel); imagine Maréchal being called "the Lieutenant" throughout *La Grande Illusion*. Predictably, the attempt to devise an Everyman results in No Man in Particular.

Le Caporal épinglé focuses on a series of escape attempts, as in *La Grande Illusion*'s treatment. It's an adventure film with themes slapped on and practically labeled for our convenience. The mechanics of escape (five attempts in all) take up such space that scenes resembling the tunnel-digging at Hallbach and Boeldieu's escapade at Wintersborn become the core of the movie, rather than its trimming. Characterization gets marginalized and plot assumes paramount importance.

Though not a remake, there are many moments similar in content to ones in *La Grande Illusion*: a prison commandant sternly addresses prisoners, with intercuts of them; some prisoners talk about their reasons to escape and about class divisions; a disturbance covers the escape of two men; the Corporal, haggard after being punished, is comforted by a guard; later, the Corporal corrects the grammar of a German woman speaking French; a character talks about being cuckolded; and a well-educated Frenchman undertakes a suicidal excursion. As it closes, a faint echo of *La Grande Illusion*'s finale provides a condensed and mutated ending.

There are even similar bits of business, as if to call on some talismanic power. A shot from a train, for instance, tracks to a sign for "Winterfeld." At another point, a French prisoner gives chocolate to a German guard. And, as in the analogous moment when Rosenthal and the actor cover a window before digging the tunnel in *La Grande Illusion*, the Corporal and a prisoner named Papa (Claude Brasseur) also bow to each other with grandly theatric gestures, in front of an outhouse. It is soon clear that similarities like these have little depth to them.

After some newsreel shots, *Le Caporal épinglé*'s narrative begins with a French prisoner approaching two German guards and telling them he's going home, since France has capitulated to Germany and the armistice has been signed. The guards push him back into the camp. It's a silly scene, thrown at us prematurely and starting the movie with little context, unlike the shot in *La Grande Illusion* when the actor playfully pretends to duck through the barbed wire. No irony here, like the cold gaze of the camera on marching Germans. The prisoner, instead, mutters pathetically about his cows and his wife.

Renoir pursues this strategy throughout. He rarely bothers to flesh out the characters or lay the groundwork for his story. The film, in that sense, is sentimental. After the opening sequence, another French prisoner, Ballochet (Claude Rich), searches for the Corporal; in overbearing close-ups, they reunite and embrace warmly. But this marks their first appearance. A hollow scene, reminiscent of the similar reunion in *La Marseillaise*. Nothing yet, on the emotional level at least, has been earned.

Themes are also made explicit by Renoir, instead of leaving them largely unspoken as in *La Grande Illusion*. Here he self-consciously elucidates them. People speechify about issues like escape and freedom, collaboration with the enemy, cowardice, class divisions.

In this vein, World War II is explicitly shown on the screen. The film opens with a documentary clip of a German plane; the sequence continues with the bombing of France, buildings in flames, refugees, Hitler, and the signing of the armistice. Renoir cuts to documentary sequences three more times during the film. This repeated device draws attention to the artificiality and thinness of the fictional story, since these newsreel sequences are jarringly real by contrast.

But the final documentary footage is more than merely jarring. In a close-up of the Corporal in a dentist's chair, his scream in reaction to drilling is overlapped with the sound of bombs; Renoir cuts to burning buildings during the bombing of London, pumping up the scene with a newsreel commentator's voice ("Ici, Londres") and then with soaring music (by Kosma). What sort of analogy is he suggesting? At best it is strained—at worst, tasteless and callous.

In further keeping with the strictures of an adventure film, Renoir introduces violence into the plot. Gunfire ends two of the Corporal's escape attempts and several times angry German guards drive the French around in circles, at one point kicking a prisoner.

And when the Corporal and Papa finally manage to escape, the train on which they are traveling is caught in an air raid. The exploding bombs and general confusion reaches an overblown conclusion when a drunken German passenger rants vehemently from a train window, observing the scene. Boom — and he vanishes in an explosion. Renoir follows this pomp and circumstance with churning music, grinding out the melodrama mechanically as the Corporal and Papa head off into the night.

Even with the violence, *Le Caporal épinglé* does not present a more realistic view of the world than *La Grande Illusion*. It is relatively easy to escape from these camps. At the start of his last attempt, the Corporal, with Papa and another prisoner, simply pretends to be making measurements with a long tape measure, under a watching German. They ease themselves out the gate, around the corner of a building, and run away, apparently unnoticed, accompanied by jolly background music.

Though these are not concentration camps, this is hardly the "real" World War II, and Renoir can be faulted here — the type of criticism he unjustly received in the 1940s for *La Grande Illusion*. Curiously, Rauffenstein, the Old World gentleman, almost matches these guards in toughness. But certainly Germany under the Nazis bore only a slight resemblance even to the German military culture of World War I.

In scenes where Renoir closely imitates *La Grande Illusion*, whether on purpose or not, the limitations of *Le Caporal épinglé* are most revealed. In one scene, the Corporal sits on some barrack steps, tired and drawn. After a German guard indicates sympathy for him, the Corporal explains to a fellow prisoner that he has been through two months of disciplinary punishment. We are told, rather than shown. And the scene ends with Ballochet feeding the Corporal, just as Rosenthal gets food for Maréchal after his confinement. But Ballochet also delivers a speech rationalizing his role as a collaborationist, with his psychological make-up served on a platter.

There is also a scene in which Ballochet, no longer acting as the Rosenthal of the story, becomes its Boeldieu. He freshens up to present a grand, theatrical stand; his announcement that a gratuitous gesture can be a practical action could be an approximation of Boeldieu's sacrifice, but his gesture is of a very different order. Ballochet decides to walk out and try to escape without any plan at all. Suicide without collateral benefits, with this madness probably motivated by guilt for his collaboration.

Ballochet thumps a broom handle on the floor three times to gain attention, as was traditional in the theater (a nice touch). By bathing him in garish light, Renoir further hypes his crazed manner. The Corporal tries to stop him but he is adamant and proposes meeting at a nightspot in Paris (another vestige of *La Grande Illusion*'s treatment).

After walking slowly down the hall, Ballochet, at the door, caught in a spotlight, exits. The hysterical tone continues as prisoners file by the Corporal, causing a flickering effect on him as they pass in front of the light source. Then, while imagining how far Ballochet has gotten on the prison grounds, they count out the seconds. The attempted payoff for the scene comes on a medium close-up of the Corporal over three bursts of machine-gun fire. At each burst, he flinches, teeth clenched in horror — and the close-up framing magnifies Cassel's overacting. Although Ballochet dies off-screen (as does Boeldieu), Renoir cheapens the scene by focusing on the histrionic Corporal, up close, as contrasted with Rauffenstein's simple downing of a drink. Juice up the lighting, cut a lot, add close shots.

But the clincher, showing how far from the sensibility of *La Grande Illusion* Renoir has drifted, is the scene that immediately follows. Two prisoners casually joke about working in the Metro, one with a stutter (for some misguided comic effect), and the Corporal smiles along with them. He makes no acknowledgement of his friend's death, as if nothing worthy of note has happened. The scene typifies a bloodless feeling that consistently drains *Le Caporal épinglé*.

The romance of the Corporal and Erika (Cornelia Froboess), a German dental technician working for her dentist mother, is sketched in three short scenes with direct parallels to the courtship of Maréchal and Elsa.

In the first scene at the dentist's office, the Corporal brusquely corrects Erika's grammatical mistakes as she botches the French language (a distorted echo).

During the next scene, the Corporal is now flirtatious and romantic music oozes in before he settles into the dentist's chair; he clutches her hand and kisses it. Soon, in the next room, he chooses a book and they read poetry aloud together. This time he corrects her accent lovingly and they embrace. But Erika has only just become a part of the story so the scene feels false. There's not much to go on.

Erika says she has heard that he had once escaped and dreamily adds, "J'aime un homme qui n'est pas un esclave" ("I love a man who is not a slave"). The Corporal pulls back, startled, and then swivels to face directly into the camera, looking like a cartoon character with a light bulb suddenly going on in the bubble above its head. A ridiculous moment that borders on unintentional parody.

Renoir then dissolves to the Corporal going to confront the traitorous Ballochet. After reaching him, he grabs his lapels and pushes him down on a table. The cause and effect is laughable. Words, not experience, transform the Corporal and lead him to act, as if under a spell. And Renoir regrettably tops this scene with another instant conversion from the dark side when Ballochet abruptly ends his collaboration by defiantly razzing a German guard.

In the final scene of the Corporal and Erika together, she finds civilian clothes for him and his friends, then walks out of the room, turns and stands still. This calculated come-hither move allows the Corporal to go through the doorway and approach her for an embrace, as Maréchal goes to Elsa at the farm.

But the effect is totally different here. Renoir cuts to a medium two-shot as the lovers embrace and then prepare to part. Erika says that there must be a woman who has her whole life to look at him, and adds: "Moi, je n'ai que cet instant" ("Me, I only have this moment"). It's difficult to feel anything in response to such a sentiment expressed by someone we still barely know. Renoir then undercuts their parting as they hear a patient cry out in the distance; they smile nervously and, when her mother calls for her, Erika simply walks away from the Corporal.

That is it. End of Erika. No more to be seen in the movie.

As with his handling of Ballochet's death, Renoir seems not to care about the characters in *Le Caporal épinglé*. They are disposable props, and once the needs of the plot have been met they are discarded. Erika, like the sex kitten in *La Grande Illusion*'s treatment, falls quickly into the arms of a virtual stranger. And what we learn about her relationship to the Corporal is mostly told us. A much diminished Elsa.

Renoir's compressed and reconfigured version of *La Grande Illusion*'s final part, bringing *Le Caporal épinglé* to a close, is also distressing.

Sappy music starts up with the opening shot of a murkily diffuse sunrise. Then a long shot of the Corporal and Papa, now free in the countryside. The Corporal wears a black coat, as had Maréchal during the mountain scenes (perhaps an inside reference). Check off the initial sequence of escape in *La Grande Illusion*— two men fleeing the Germans, done.

Le Caporal épinglé (1962). Renoir directing Papa (Claude Brasseur), back to camera, and the Corporal (Jean-Pierre Cassel) in his muddied black coat—a talismanic reminder of Maréchal on the run? (***Photofest***).

Next, a farm sequence, with the background music continuing throughout the scene. From their perspective on a hill, they see a man and woman farming below and run down to them. The German woman wears a shawl, like Elsa, and is a war widow; her companion is French.

The men engage in a discussion, completely out of the blue, about the fact that the farmer never owned land in France but has a spread here. The Corporal mentions having a wife in Paris, and Papa remarks that he will go wherever his friend goes. *Le Caporal épinglé*, beyond chronicling the obvious urge to escape imprisonment, is another Renoir film about male bonding (earlier Papa cries when the Corporal attempts an escape without him).

The woman never says a word and laughs good-naturedly when her companion talks about marrying her. She is an anonymous German woman, perhaps "made to bring beautiful children into the world," as the treatment of *La Grande Illusion* crudely put it about her counterpart. And the scene ends with the woman giving food to the fugitives (again like Elsa), and then she walks over to a haystack after they leave for the nearby border. At least it is not inhabited—unlike the hay in which the treatment's love triangle found itself immersed.

So much for the farm. Mercifully the music also ends.

21. Revenge of the Treatment

For the equivalent of the border sequence, the last scene is set on a bridge in Paris as the Corporal and Papa prepare to separate. Papa points out that the Corporal is going in the opposite direction, to his wife. They say goodbye and shake hands; Papa leaves but, in the same shot, returns. Another attempted reprise?

Renoir then alternates a series of eight medium close-ups as Papa asks the Corporal if, after getting reacquainted with his wife, he would do it all again. The Corporal smiles at one point and says that he despises swastikas. This excites Papa since it means they will see each other again. They smile.

If meant to be an upbeat moment, it is a strange one, implying that the class division that separates them will be temporarily overcome by their reunion as soldiers, fighting the Nazis together. This may be true, but it's a far cry from the resignation of Maréchal and Rosenthal as they anticipate having to fight again. War has its advantages in *Le Caporal épinglé*.

The friends part company in the final shot, and the Corporal walks off alone into the distance. For, ultimately, this movie belongs to the Corporal. By comparison, *La Grande Illusion* cannot be reduced to being Maréchal's movie; so much else is going on.

Le Caporal épinglé differs from *La Grande Illusion* in yet another way. It confirms, rather than questions, national divisions. The closest rapprochement between guards and prisoners comes when a German officer and a French quisling joke about the penalties commanding officers can inflict because of their authority. The scene is played for laughs, as in a sitcom. And, except for the hastily presented romance and the cardboard couple on the farm, little breaking down of national allegiances occurs beyond that of collaboration. The world of this film is divided vertically as well as horizontally.

But this is not the crux of the problem, since it could be argued that the film presents a cynical view of the world, befitting the horrors of that time. The most serious flaw, instead, remains its banality. Renoir indiscriminately presses for our empathy in *Le Caporal épinglé* and puts its themes on display. His penultimate film is a sobering reminder that the medium demands a delicate balance, which can be undermined by revealing too much and leaving less to the imagination.

That process has proven to be, many times and for many different directors, not an easy task.

Part IV
CODA

22

Film as Film — and the Music Within

"'I believe in the film as a poetic medium.... The danger in the cinema is that you see everything, because it's a camera. So what you have to do is manage to evoke, to incant, to raise up things which are not really there.'"
—Orson Welles in *World Film Directors: Volume I, 1890–1945*; edited by John Wakeman (The H.W. Wilson Company; 1987; p. 1183)

"'Something many people ignore is that there is no such thing as interesting work without the contact of the public — the collaboration, perhaps. When you are listening to great music, what you are really doing is enjoying a good conversation with a great man, and this is bound to be fascinating.... Now I am going to be very trite and say that it is easier to make a silent film than a talkie, because there is something missing. In the talkies, therefore, we have to reproduce this missing something in another way. We have to ask the actors not to be like an open book. To keep some inner feeling, some secret.'"
— Jean Renoir in *Jean Renoir: Essays, Conversations, Reviews* (p. 25)

Why indeed was *La Grande Illusion*, for Orson Welles, the "one film in the world to save" if he had to choose?[1] This question will certainly never be resolved, with some Rosebud-like answer lurking on a scrap of evidence in an old warehouse. But his admiration for the film perhaps came from an understanding that Renoir had managed "to raise up things which are not really there."

In a *Los Angeles Times* article, published six days after Renoir's death in 1979, Welles quoted at length from Renoir in a Penelope Gilliatt conversation (including portions cited in this chapter's heading) and noted that his colleague was "proclaiming the virtue of a certain degree of deliberate ambiguity." Welles seemed to sense that this approach was similar to his own methods and added that the search for "perfect clarity" ends up with something "perfectly banal."[2]

Yet their marked differences are intriguing. *Citizen Kane*, for instance, is comprehensive in its range of cinematic invention and could serve as an encyclopedia of film technique. There's no shortage of material begging for analysis. A critic's joy and salvation. *La Grande Illusion* appears to be nearer the other end of the spectrum, until closer examination.

Welles flaunts his technique in *Citizen Kane* and leaves fingerprints on every sequence, eager to be discovered; Renoir's touch is harder to detect in *La Grande Illusion*. The one extravagantly insistent, the other modest and almost disengaged. In music, the Romantic fullness perhaps of Brahms contrasted to the Baroque precision of Bach. With Brahms one can at least try to figure out the intense emotion. Bach, the craftsman, does not appear particularly interested in this area; the passion seems to emerge organically from

Orson Welles (white shirt) on the set of *Citizen Kane* (in 1940), under the floor with famed cinematographer (and significant collaborator) Gregg Toland at his side (*Photofest*).

the sequencing of notes, without more immediate prompts, like crescendos and elastic tempi.

In addition, *Citizen Kane*, discontinuous in construction, is made whole through collage and could be seen as the paragon of a closed film that funnels one's attention. *La Grande Illusion* has a more linear narrative, developing gradually into its completed form, and is essentially open (leaving one free to go over the image).

But they can not so easily be categorized. To some degree, both are "closed" and "open." Just as "Romantic" and "Baroque" are too limiting, and exclusive, in categorizing Brahms and Bach. And it would be utter fantasy to attempt some unified theory to explore the common ground of the two films, a string theory of film aesthetics winnowing out the qualities that distinguish them, at the core, beyond the glitter and allure of their surfaces. Nothing is even remotely so cut-and-dried. There are, of course, many ways to make a movie that have little relation to the approaches taken by either Renoir or Welles. Look at Yasujiro Ozu or Manoel de Oliveira, for a start.

Putting aside the elusive idea of purely cinematic attributes, these two films achieve different effects. *Citizen Kane* is filmically assured and varied, but constrained emotionally, driven by the playful energy of its 25-year-old director. *La Grande Illusion*, though also masterful cinematically, is not as prodigious and encompassing. But it has an emotional and philosophical maturity to it; Renoir, though hardly wizened at 42, seemed wise beyond his years.

Beyond their differences, the two movies generate, as in many great films, a seamless alchemy that converts watered-down elements lifted from other arts into cinematic gold. And this transmutation occurs despite the dangers of the literal, and seductively realistic, side of a movie.

Virginia Woolf, in an incisive and prescient essay, "The Cinema," which was written in 1926 just as Renoir was embarking on his film career, grasped the problem facing movies:

> For a strange thing has happened — while all the other arts were born naked, this, the youngest, has been born fully-clothed. It can say everything before it has anything to say.[3]

Her essay appeared the year before another layer of clothing, sound, would be definitively added to feature films, making it possible to say even more than "everything."

A great moviemaker struggles against this temptation to show too much, or communicate too fully. Instead, the audience is primed to be active and induced into experiencing something original. Even when using a close-up, or a pointed line of dialogue, a skillful director can suffuse, and neutralize, the abundance of the moment with a sense of mystery.

Woolf cites a film version of *Anna Karenina* in which the physical aspects are emphasized (her pearls, her teeth) instead of what goes on inside her head. A kiss or a grin represents love, happiness. But, she continues, this has nothing to do with Tolstoy and it takes an "accidental scene — like the gardener mowing the lawn —"[4] to show off the cinema.

An ingenious filmmaker can subvert the power inherent in words and images by injecting ambiguity, allusion or understatement. In short, by making room for the viewer. Then a "gardener mowing the lawn" can evoke something beyond the cutting of grass.

The materials culled from other arts and disciplines, stripped of their natural environment, can become reduced to banalities. *Citizen Kane* is filled with explications of love (and the lack thereof) and other psychological details that are simplistically reductive ("Rosebud" itself). And the script, though witty and urbane, hardly qualifies as literature. Further, the cinematography is expressive but not up to the profundities of a great painting, or perhaps even a great photograph. Yet there are not many movies that have such breadth of cinematic expression and hold together so coherently, without skipping a beat or suffering missteps.

The same can be said of *La Grande Illusion*, and its greatness rests on a similar transformation to the one in *Citizen Kane*. This change often takes place unnoticed and is a beguiling charm of film, a mongrel art form capable of spawning magnificent new creatures. Filmic invention can transform the superficial literalness of a film into something sublime, expressed implicitly by the nuts and bolts of technique.

Renoir understood the danger when that invention is missing:

> In the cinema, you can do all too much. For example, when the hero of a modern film has a phobia, you are obliged to explain it by flashbacks: I mean, to go back to the time when he was beaten by his father, or whatever thing is supposed to have had such a result. This freedom can be quite enfeebling. It makes one very literal, very anxious to make everything clear, get everything taped.[5]

At his best, Renoir did it the hard way, keeping "some inner feeling, some secret," as he had put it. He burrowed underneath and left enough open so that no particular response was necessarily more true or accurate than another one. That was essential to the style.

But, again, there is also no single way, no basic principle to be applied here, broad brush, to all films and all directors.

A film becomes a film, in more than name only, through cinematic technique. At the risk of being overly schematic, I find it useful to look at three ways that technique can have an effect. But, in isolating these differing aspects for the purpose of analysis, it's important to emphasize that of course they overlap inextricably. And also to stress that my discussion applies to traditional narrative film, not to the many experimental ways of making films, which, in their very conception, break any possible conventions in the use of cinematic language. Filmmakers working in that area must deal with a different set of problems and pitfalls.

First, at the simplest level, technique (the basis for a film's stylistic form) can merely convey the plot, characters and themes (the content) without the director's sensibility adding much of consequence. The form, in this case, is inert and the film draws its strength mainly from a combination of elements derived from other arts, and from the humanities: literature and psychology (script), painting and photography (cinematography), theater (acting), music, philosophy (themes), sociology (the social setting), and, in a movie like *La Grande Illusion*, history.

If a director uses the technique of a film simply in order to be mechanically illustrative and act as a conveyor belt to deliver other disciplines, that director is merely passing off a secondhand imitation of those disciplines. The Merchant-Ivory films adapted from great books often exemplify this brand of filmmaking. The books themselves provide a source of instant depth and seriousness. Add to that the beautifully rendered period settings, the costumes and spot-on acting. But little translates this precious beauty and high quality into something cinematic, something unexpected or original. Though it may generally be well done, and sometimes even touching, it's mainly literature, photography, theater.

Many narrative films are effective and entertaining but seem limited by that sort of clever plot, snappy dialogue, acting and stunningly photographed (and lavish) settings. The surface. Telling, not showing or implying—a throng of adverbs and adjectives, a dearth of nouns and verbs. Often genre films with a lower budget, though not so perfectly outfitted and though restricted by genre formulas, prove more satisfying. In fact, B-films with pretensions can become bloated when provided with bigger production values and stars.

Renoir once addressed a specific manifestation of being too direct:

> The danger with the cinema, now that it has become so technically perfect, is that you can detach yourself, forget the problems of translating something through image or a sound. It's all too easy. The modern director is surrounded by splendid technicians, men of skill and taste who do everything for him. The result is that the director is a bit like the station-master who makes the train run on time but hasn't actually anything to do with the train. This is dangerous and one must guard against it.[6]

To be able to reproduce the real world so closely is a Midas curse that produces dead weight—shiny and beautiful perhaps, but static, fixed, locked solidly in the grip of other arts and of the humanities. Not transformed. Or not translated "through an image or a sound." A moviemaker taking this approach insults one's intelligence. The film might be nice to look at and enjoyable, but there is no need for a second look.

A great movie, to the contrary, not only stands up after many viewings but reveals more of its greatness. And it requires an investment of attention, even energy, to watch it.

When a movie can be discussed in the language of other disciplines, without losing much in the process, it is visiting the medium rather than making itself at home. Woolf, in her essay, imagines the cinema as a beast that had hunted down its next meal (literature) as a source for raw material and then lives off it. That kind of body-snatched movie assumes the form of an actual one; light patterns simulate scenes with recognizable people acting as the characters in a story. But the essence is bled from it — that is, the expressive potential of film technique has been left untapped.

This can be comparable to a drawing transferred directly from paper to an etcher's plate, with nothing added along the way, so that the qualities peculiar to an etching remain unexplored. Such a drawing, reproduced without change in the new medium, fails to come alive. It makes little sense, as well, to describe both a body-snatched movie and a cinematically inventive one in the same language; different species need different terms.

The sort of limited movie that is substantially derivative may be seen as a "photographed story," or a story that just happens to be on film. It's certainly possible to write about *La Grande Illusion* as a photographed story, without discussing it in cinematic terms, as some critics have done. But that does not address the film's true power. By contrast, any movie that to a large extent is derivative can be well-served by the language of literature, painting, theater, philosophy and psychology.

At this most superficial level of a photographed story, analysis and critical judgment may be fairly easy. Arguments, at least, are possible, for or against, with perhaps some consensus even reached. But effects that are achieved largely by relying on the trappings of other disciplines are not lasting ones.

At the next and more complex level, technique can express the content cinematically and create a hybrid not reducible to the terms of other fields. This kind of expressive movie could be called a "story film" as opposed to a "photographed story." The essential word here is not "story," but "film."

At this level, a film can rival works in the other arts. The technique itself is able to elicit feelings beyond the characters, the actors who portray them, the words spoken, the plot, or the sets and landscapes. A great movie consistently works this way, steeped in the possibilities of the medium. But those possibilities involve much more subtlety than the obvious tricks of the trade that are also possible in film, technical gimmicks like special effects, double exposures and surreal dream sequences. Truly effective technique works through implication and suggestion, not through some finger-pointing plastered on by the latest technology of movie magic, ground out in a laboratory.

At this deeper level it is not so easy to analyze, and critical evaluations are less clear. An electric feeling grabs hold, however, when a film comes to life as a film, instead of going through the motions of a filmed play or novel, an illustrated textbook, a radio drama with pictures.

Film technique is at work, of course, throughout any movie. In every frame. At key moments, certain films take off and are especially original. But, in *La Grande Illusion*, Renoir's powers of invention are also at work in smaller moments. He cruises in mid-flight, at the least, for much of the time.

And a film like *La Grande Illusion* is more open to interpretation than a photographed story. It demands not the language of the other arts to describe it but the vocabulary of the cinema. Or, more accurately, a mix-and-match version, with the most pertinent language being the cinematic language belonging exclusively to film.

In another way of looking at this distinction, the director primarily drives a story film while a photographed story is driven by other forces, perhaps the script or the actors. And a better definition of an auteur, rather than the one that grants each movie of a sanctioned director success by fiat, might be that an auteur is a director of whom one looks forward to seeing his or her next movie, irrespective of its quality; the chance exists that at least it will be a story film, whether it works or not.

During peak periods, there are many directors for whom the next film is a must-see — as in the 1960s with Bergman, Fellini, Antonioni, Buñuel, Kurosawa, Godard (and just about every other French director at the time). In fallow times, one goes instead to see a particular movie, for itself, not because it represents the director's latest work.

In brief, the technique of a story film expresses the plot rather than just conveys it. One could say that such a film happens, at the same time, to tell a story. And the effects are substantial.

Lastly, cinematic technique has an abstract side that it shares in common with the technique in all art forms. This side derives from formal aspects intrinsic to a film and not from the narrative content. And it is where the individuality of a director can be expressed.

Beyond any meaning, a movie of course has a purely sensuous quality, shaped by the composition and placement of shots. These bare bones of technique seem especially buried in a film because its surface, so evident on the screen, is encrusted with quickly accessible elements such as plot and dialogue. Furthermore, since movies appear to be "literal" and "real," it can be hard to think of them in abstract terms. But, as in any art, a film has a visceral effect. Individual taste can perhaps be explained in part by this abstract side of technique, resonating (or failing to resonate) with personal associations and experiences. This is right-brained territory, depending more on intuition than logic.

And this is where film shares something, besides taking place in time, with music. Marcel Proust, in *À la recherche du temps perdu* (*In Search of Lost Time*), appreciated the special qualities of music, as imagined in his poetic description:

> And, just as certain creatures are the last surviving testimony to a form of life which nature has discarded, I wondered whether music might not be the unique example of what might have been — if the invention of language, the formation of words, the analysis of ideas had not intervened — the means of communication between souls.[7]

Looking at a film apart from those aspects that involve the intervention of language and ideas, a similar "communication between souls" is at play.

Like individual notes in music, the brush strokes of a painting, or sound of words in a poem, the sensuous effect of film technique is hard to certify but communicates nonetheless. It can only be analyzed by using grandly sweeping, and amorphous, language. And every movie shares equally this side of technique — the schlockiest horror movie as well as the most inscrutable art-house film.

These different aspects of film technique might be clarified by looking at an example like the climax of the Christmas morning scene in *La Grande Illusion* (the final three shots of the sequence).

As a "photographed story," these shots can be discussed in terms of the script (Rosenthal discovering the lovers and Elsa's phrase), psychology (the changed relationships), themes (national divisions breached, and the use of German and French), acting, and photography (the classic framing). That is one way of looking at it.

On the more cinematic level of a "story film," the sequence could be analyzed (as I have done) to show how those same photographed-story elements are expressed by Renoir's creative use of camera angles and positions (the distancing effect of the protagonists framed by the doorway in the tracking shot, and, in counterpoint, the two full-faced close-ups that follow), the editing placement (adjacent close-ups pairing the lovers), and the effective use of sound (reprised words and the interplay of on-screen and off-screen voices). A richer way of looking at the sequence.

La Grande Illusion, film frame. Christmas morning on the farm: Rosenthal (right) tries to ease the embarrassment of the new lovers Elsa and Maréchal (*Photofest*).

Finally, at the abstract level, which paradoxically can at least mainly be quantified by hard numbers of measurement, those three shots can be described by noting the number of seconds each lasts (20, 6, 9), the camera positions (medium long shot, head-on close-up, head-on close-up), the type of shots (tracking shot, still shot, still shot), the sound (dialogue over background music), and the placement of those shots relative to other shots — both in the scene and within the film. What effect these physical characteristics have, as physical sensation, beyond feeling right (or not right), is not as clear. But they obviously have an effect.

And one can think of this dynamic in another way (for demonstration purposes only): the content (story) rests on the surface and is immediately clear; the director generates the form (technique) throughout but it's often less consciously appreciated. This interaction of form and content at times merely keeps a film moving along; at other times, the interaction forges something original and startling. But the abstract side of technique, whether the technique itself is inert or active, plays on the senses at every point, continuously, during a movie.

To better illustrate this process, consider three basic components of cinematic technique in a shot: the visual (composition); the temporal (length and placement); and the aural (the soundtrack).

By looking at the last shot of Elsa in that climactic morning scene, one can see how a slight shift here or there might have sabotaged the sequence. Or possibly improved it.

Visually, the distance of the shot (close-up) gives the scene added impact since Renoir had rarely used close-ups until that point in the film; a medium or long shot would have greatly defused the moment. If he had angled the camera or tracked around Elsa, to lend dramatic significance to the composition, the directness and innocence that comes across uninflected in the still, head-on framing would have been lost. And filming her face against a relatively nondescript background makes the focus unflinching.

In temporal terms, if Renoir had lingered on the shot a trifle longer after her laugh, it might have lost its punch by drawing too much attention to the effect. Also, its placement before the shot of Maréchal and Rosenthal discussing their plans to leave the farm captures the transitory nature of the moment; had there been an explanatory scene inserted to make a gradual transition, the ephemeralness of the morning scene would have been diluted.

On the larger scale of the editing scheme as a whole, it would have been sentimental if Renoir had positioned the scene (and this shot) earlier in the farm sequence, thrust upon us without adequately developing the relationship of the lovers. Instead, its critical importance is warranted because of the earlier scenes on the farm.

In terms of sound, Elsa's innocuous phrase is more subtle than had some acknowledgement of a new relationship been made. In addition, if he had not covered the shot with background music, to highlight the scene, it might have been stronger since no boost is needed for this already glowing image. But at least Renoir craftily makes use of this music by dropping it when he cuts to the next shot, emphasizing the intensity that had been invested in the close-ups of Maréchal and Elsa.

Renoir could almost have had the Christmas morning scene in mind when, in his memoir, he discussed the difference between theater and film. He posited a love scene and how, in theater, language is needed to communicate the situation. Showing again his concern for the physical reality rather than an intellectual approach, he wrote about the way a close-up reduced the need to be verbally explicit:

> The texture of the skin, the glow in the eyes, the moisture of the mouth — all these can say more than any number of words. Most film dialogue seems to have been interpolated for the sake of clarification. It is a false approach. Dialogue is a part of the theme and reveals character. For the real theme is the person, whom dialogue, picture, situation, setting, temperature and lighting all combine together to depict. The world is one whole.[8]

The close-ups of Maréchal and Elsa, and her announcement to Rosenthal that the coffee is ready, are indeed the "real theme" and they reveal "character" in that world which is *La Grande Illusion*.

One way of appreciating film technique is to look at a shot in a movie and ask oneself if there is any need for it. Or, in other words, is the technique expressive?

When there seems to be, repeatedly, no reason for shot after shot, or for cutting short

La Grande Illusion, film frame. A close-up needing no words: Maréchal mesmerized by Elsa (*Photofest*).

or extending shots, or when a monotonous rhythm fits them into a comfortable pattern with no apparent rationale, a movie feels padded, as if carrying excess baggage. It becomes an academic exercise. Show all, get everything in, underline and make it crystal clear. This can be exhausting for the viewer, bombarded by such sensory overload, with shots piling up, one after another, bits of visual information accumulating to an ever-expanding degree. A Collyer-brothers equivalent of film clutter hitting the retina.

In this respect, *La Grande Illusion* has two salient characteristics: its concision (the inclusion only of "necessary shots") and its richly varied editing (the natural, non-mechanical rhythm).

Renoir's penchant for long tracking shots, and his reluctance to cut up the action into smaller bits, helps avoid clutter. He once said, after mentioning Andy Warhol, "I don't believe very much in the improvement given a picture in the cutting room." He later added, grandiosely: "ideally, the picture in the cinema should be one long take. I'm trying not to cut."[9] Some directors have even reached Renoir's ideal, like Alexander Sokurov in his 2002 *tour-de-force* film, *Russkiy kovcheg* (*Russian Ark*).

Yet it's not just a matter of economy. Renoir's precision of expression also subconsciously reassures the viewer that what he shows at a specific moment is needed. Absurd as it may seem, I think one might be able to analyze each and every shot in *La Grande Illusion* and find a possible reason for most of them. If a sequence needs to be done in one long take, so be it. But Renoir doesn't limit himself to an unrelenting dose of long, uncut tracking shots (though other filmmakers like Miklós Jancsó and Béla Tarr have brilliantly pulled off this technique). He seems to leave a shot when another one contributes something new or expressive.

A naturally flowing rhythm is set off by these changes of pace. As with a basketball player stopping and starting, hesitating, pump-faking, reversing direction to get in the flow and shoot "in rhythm" (a basketball term) instead of forcing a shot. Whatever it takes.

But film, again, cannot be reduced to one approach or another. I also believe, however, that there is an element of uncertainty in a good film, whether experimental or traditional, rule-breaking or controlled. Something that keeps it fresh.

The fact remains that the director of a film, in orchestrating an art form requiring collaboration on many levels, struggles with that volatile mix coming together in three stages: drawing on elements of the other arts and humanities for material to be molded; blending together the talents of a technical crew and the actors in the filming; and exploiting the various ways that cinematic technique can be effective in the film itself. It takes a concurrence of things coming together, a perfect storm, to produce a rare film like *La Grande Illusion*. The script before — the actors and technicians during — and, critically, the director throughout, but often most importantly afterward.

This form demands humility. A great movie may be only a few frames here, some shots there, and certain angles or sound cuts, from being merely a good, or even mediocre, movie. On this most basic level of technique — the placement and angle of the camera, the number of seconds of each shot, the order of shots, the sounds and the silences — it's a game of inches. And everything interconnects.

La Grande Illusion is a film that, as Robert Frost once said about the nature of poetry, would be lost in translation (to another medium). Successful movies absorb other arts and something original comes out of it; weaker movies opportunistically feed off those arts and are beholden to them. A film may be largely made up of appropriated materials but, at its core, a good film is original because it draws on the medium's unique resources.

There is in every art form that which resists analysis. Music, in this sense, seems the most "abstract" of all arts; film is somewhere at the other extreme. But they are alike in a basic way. It's no easier to ascribe a definitive quality to an A-flat or assign specific value for a musical phrase (except poetically) than to evaluate and pass judgment on a shot that lasts 136 frames instead of 149 frames, or on a camera angle set at a certain degree rather than a slightly greater or lesser one. There appears to be little worth to one measurable attribute over another.

Along these lines, the philosophy of music goes back to the Greeks. And, in the century marking the birth of film, Arthur Schopenhauer made the case for music's instrinsic qualities in *Die Welt als Wille und Vorstellung* (*The World as Will and Representation*) in 1819:

> Therefore music does not express this or that particular and definite pleasure, this or that affliction, pain, sorrow, horror, gaiety, merriment, or peace of mind, but joy, pain, sorrow, horror, gaiety, merriment, peace of mind *themselves*, to a certain extent in the abstract, their essential nature, without any accessories, and so also without the motives for them.

And yet, as Schopenhauer put it, without having "motives" for these feelings, "we understand them perfectly in this extracted quintessence."[10]

Adding to such philosophical writings, Walter Pater, the English writer and theorist of aesthetics, wrote in an 1877 essay, "The School of Giorgione":

> But although each art has thus its own specific order of impressions, and an untranslatable charm ... yet it is noticeable that, in its special mode of handling its given material, each art may be observed to pass into the condition of some other art, by what German critics term an *Anders-streben*—a partial alienation from its own limitations, through which the arts are able, not indeed to supply the place of each other, but reciprocally to lend each other new forces.[11]

Clearly movies draw heavily upon, and pass into, "the condition of some other art." This "*Anders-streben*" (literally, "different striving") indicates a common sharing of certain modes of aesthetic expression. But movies also have that "untranslatable charm."

Virginia Woolf, nearly half a century later, understood the same process when she wrote that filmmakers "want to be improving, altering, making an art of their own — naturally, for so much seems to be within their scope. So many arts seemed to stand by ready to offer their help."[12] And then she noted the problems of transposing literature too explicitly to the screen.

Pater, for his part, extended his analysis further and saw music as "the typical, or ideally consummate art":

> *All art constantly aspires towards the condition of music.* For while in all other kinds of art it is possible to distinguish the matter from the form, and the understanding can always make this distinction, yet it is the constant effort of art to obliterate it.[13]

It's in aspiring to "the condition of music"—that is, in counterbalancing the concrete and literal elements of a film by exploring more mysterious, and not readily identifiable, wellsprings—that a film becomes truly a film. The technique, in collision with the material, has the potential to generate heat, emotions, feelings. Beyond merely the content alone. Or, better yet, with form and content indistinguishable.

In summing up this elevated state of expression, Pater wrote that music "most completely realises this artistic ideal, this perfect identification of matter and form."[14] And so, too, does the return of Maréchal to Rosenthal after their confrontation.

In music, a layperson can have little to say about key progressions or intervals or flatted notes — they are the domain of experts. Something profound seems to come out of nothing much (notes, intervals, keys). At least to amateurs. But, in movies, novices are ready to weigh in and make decisive evaluations about the acting and the script, even a catchall category under the rubric of "direction."

Yet there are also cinematic equivalents to abstruse musical features, though they often remain unrecognized, largely because there is no end of available material in film to occupy the critical mind, trained or untrained.

As well, the musical attributes of a film are not unalloyed and distinct since, emanating from the technique, they also deliver, of course, the film's concrete side. But just as one can respond to music instinctively, without a musical background, movies too, at some unconscious level, resound beyond the story and with little knowledge of film. The shape of a movie, its feel and its rhythm — its own particular key changes and flatted intervals — have an effect, even as we also enjoy Humphrey Bogart reassuring Ingrid Bergman in *Casablanca*, "We'll always have Paris."

The effect elicited by the abstract side of film may have been understood by Woolf when she imagined characteristics in the composition of future films:

> Something abstract, something which moves with controlled and conscious art, something which calls for the very slightest help from words or music to make itself intelligible, yet justly uses them subserviently.[15]

I don't read this as applying literally, or only, to abstract and experimental movies but also to films in which the intrinsic qualities of the medium are engaged, using "words or music" in support rather than as the driving force.

Schopenhauer had earlier summed up his feeling that in music like opera, or the song, words should be subordinate: "Therefore, if music tries to stick too closely to the words, and to mould itself according to the events, it is endeavouring to speak a language not its own."[16] Filmmakers can also fail to speak film's own language, in relying too much on the foreign language of literature or philosophy, for instance, and missing the power the medium has other than through its "words" and its "events."

It's as if there is a parallel (and unseen) force created by the visible impact of the images themselves and the conjunction of those images. In an original movie something happens, beyond the screen, something universal to all great art. An extreme form of this phenomenon is montage, as theorized by Sergei Eisenstein, in which the clash of shots has an immediate effect, a separate force emerging as the result of two shots running up against each other.

Renoir makes use of that effect in a more subdued way than through montage. Instead, what he primarily does with (and within) the shot, its composition and choreography, evokes a response beyond what appears to define the frame. Welles, possibly, might be seen more as a synthesizer of the two approaches.

Here, at the creation of this unseen force, music becomes the condition to which this other art (film) "aspires," in Pater's terms, and it is where film speaks "its own" language, as Schopenhauer put it. Or where Welles referred to raising up "things which are not really there" and Renoir wrote about keeping "some inner feeling, some secret." Something not so easily explained by analysis.

And it's also where Woolf poses the question: "Is there, we ask, some secret language which we feel and see, but never speak, and, if so, could this be made visible to the eye?"[17] Certainly Renoir makes "visible" Maréchal's return to Rosenthal in the larger terms of being a friend and comrade, as opposed merely to his physical return, by his sudden, nonrealistic and magical reappearance. Without words. And the "secret language," in this case, is that of film editing.

At one point in her essay, Woolf elaborates her understanding of a poet's images: "They are compact of a thousand suggestions of which the visual is only the most obvious or the uppermost."[18] These suggestions, for a poet, include the musical side of language, at a deeper and less obvious level beyond meaning.

Film, with its uppermost means of suggestion being verbal explication as well as "the visual," in Woolf's terms, achieves a musical quality similar to poetry at the untranslatable level of technique, which works its cinematic magic much further down on the scale of suggestions.

The window pan at Hallbach is powerful not only because of Jean Gabin's acting or the themes of *La Grande Illusion*. Or even the visual beauty of the image. The intense closeness of the shot, its head-on framing, the menacing soundtrack, the languorous pace, its length, and the relationship to the shots around it also affect one viscerally. Those aspects contribute some of the shot's less obvious suggestions.

But even without being able to understand how such suggestions take hold at this deeper level, the process needs to be acknowledged. Unmodulated by thought, the resulting dynamic can be as strongly associative and gripping as music, and equally elusive. The simple mathematical dimension of a composition, the placing and length of a shot, has an effect, though it is impossible to show why certain objective, scientific values strike one viewer and not another.

Schopenhauer saw a similar dynamic in music when he wrote that "its form can be reduced to quite definite rules expressible in numbers, from which it cannot possibly depart without entirely ceasing to be music."[19] A clear contradiction also exists in film, as in the other arts, including even music (at least in opera and song), with the literal side experienced simultaneously in a tactile, non-literal way. Again, beyond meaning, as in Woolf's "suggestions" in poetry.

Further, though artists in all media are inconsistent in their output, there is often a more pronounced curve in the work of filmmakers because, I think, as Pater had put it in more general terms, and transposing his ideas to film, "it is possible to distinguish the matter from the form" in film and one's "understanding can always make this distinction." The question is how, in Pater's words again, to "obliterate" that division between content and form. And filmmakers, even great ones, don't always succeed in achieving that kind of obliteration. So many competing forces need to be harnessed for the effort.

In literature, as a case in point, a writer's style is the "abstract" element that can be personal and creative — while it expresses the literal side. At its best, the distinction between style and content, between how something is being said and the "what" being said, becomes at least hazy.

A piece of literature that works well is usually distinguished from other pieces, after all, by its style — the choice, order and sound of words. In writing, as in music or film, there is a rhythm established by specific words (notes on a stave, or shots) and the variety of accumulated sentences (musical phrases, film sequences). Perhaps an elegant, and digressive, sentence meanders around and pulls the reader deeper into the matter at hand. Followed by a short one. Or any combination, or permutation, of the same, with or without verbs.

Film, also like music, works in time while being shaped by rhythm. And in music the overtones of a particular pitch give body to, and enrich, a note by vibrating at different frequencies; movies, on the other hand, resonate with the ghosts of images, or sounds, past.

In a subliminal way, an overtone in a film can be the result of something as peripheral as the set design. In *La Grande Illusion*, there are two flat, arched forms with open-spaced patterns, which are purely decorative, on the wall of Boeldieu's office. During the next sequence, they can be seen again, behind Boeldieu and Rauffenstein at the German canteen. These insignificant background details stem perhaps from the fact that the same set was used for both scenes. But these arched forms help strengthen the parallels between the two settings (and of the French and Germans).

There are also more substantial resonances in *La Grande Illusion*. Because of Renoir's strategy of repetition and reprise, overtones vibrate throughout and enrich the film. As in the recurring camera movements. Or when "café" is lovingly gasped out by Elsa, in disjunction with the sourness of Rauffenstein earlier and then later with Rosenthal's lack of enthusiasm.

Other overtones resonate because of associations outside the film; depending on a viewer's experience, these can also have an effect. Renoir's technique in other films, for example, is similar to his technique in *La Grande Illusion*. This can lead to feelings of recognition and enhance one's reaction.

And there are the performances by members of the cast in other roles. The memory of Marcel Dalio as "Robert de la Cheyniest" in *La Règle du jeu* can come to mind during *La Grande Illusion* for anyone who has seen the later film; further, it is even pointed out during a kitchen scene in *La Règle du jeu* that Robert's grandfather was named Rosenthal though, given the chronology, it couldn't be Dalio's Rosenthal. Whether such overtones add or detract is sometimes hard to tell. Laurence Olivier, with all the technique in the world, might have achieved some semblance of a cowboy had he appeared in a western, but it would have been hard, even disturbing, to accept him in that sort of role. Too many ghosts. Ditto John Wayne as Richard III or Henry V.

The effect in *La Grande Illusion* of the ebb and flow of images with varying lengths and compositions, the physical appearance and disappearance of characters, the leitmotifs, the reprised settings, scenes and shots — all these carry musical and architectural significance. Beyond the script, beyond dialogue or themes. As sensation.

If one looks at another transcendent work like Bach's *Brandenburg Concerto No. 6*, for example, there is also that sort of breadth. Though the most thinly scored *Brandenburg*, reduced to strings alone, with no shimmering trumpets or mournful oboes, no flutes or even violins, the last movement has a rich and thrilling contrast between strings singing in unison and then breaking apart into tag-team conversations. And there are contrasts between the driving beat (difficult not to tap one's foot) and the insistent counterbalance of the off-beat, the two modes delicately shifting in importance throughout and creating a range of emotions. An unbalanced heartbeat, in and out of rhythm — the regular and irregular, the solid and ornamental — locked in seemingly perpetual motion. This single movement, in a larger piece of music, appears exhaustive in nature.

That last movement is perhaps also compelling because of Bach's judicious use of those irregular, off-beat passages; Renoir, in a similar way, does not overload his film with close-ups and angled shots. There's a sense of simplicity in the music — but also of completeness. It comes at you quietly, without undue fanfare. And Renoir, too, sneaks up on you.

La Grande Illusion encompasses a varied richness of rhythm and tone that is matched by Renoir's concise and effortless expression. Opposites in one. Also, of course, a literal side for the conscious mind and an abstract side for the unconscious. As in any work of art.

On the abstract level, all bets are off and all arguments out the window. Film, here,

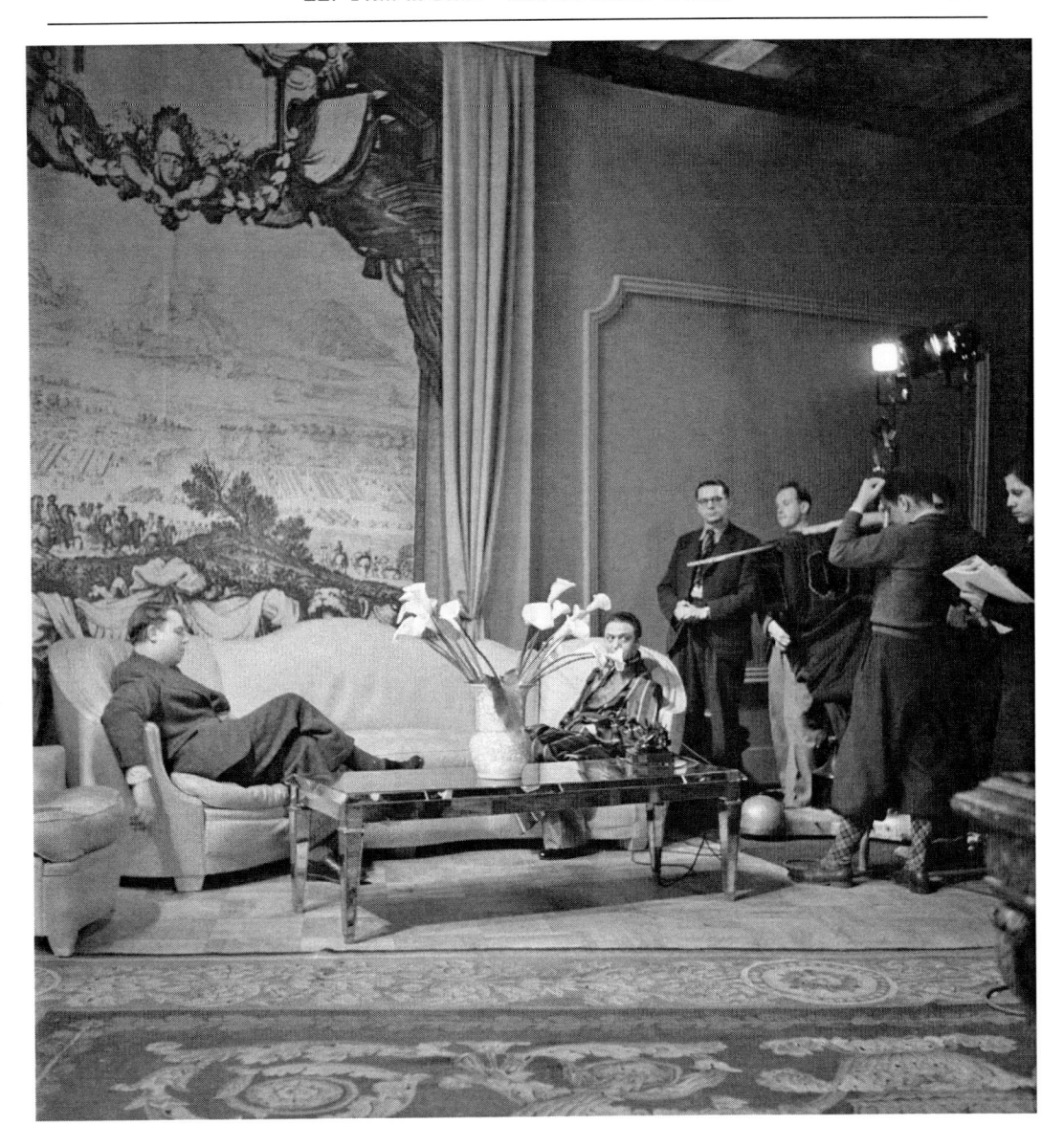

On the set of *La Règle du jeu*: Octave (Renoir, left) and Robert (Dalio), after Octave's embarrassment ("Everyone has his reasons"). And in the shadows, from the left, André Zwoboda, Henri Cartier-Bresson, unidentified man, Dido Freire (script girl). Photograph: Sam Lévin (©*Ministère de la Culture/Médiathèque du Patrimoine/Sam Levin/dist. RMN-Grand Palais/Art Resource, New York*).

can be as inexplicable as music. Woolf understood this dynamic. And Felix Mendelssohn, in an 1842 letter, wrote: "What the music I love expresses to me, is not thought too *indefinite* to be put into words, but, on the contrary, too *definite*."[20] Words also can fail in film. Why does it feel right, at a given moment, for a particular tracking shot to follow a particular still shot? Or that another shot lasts for a certain length of time? And how do these variables work together to affect one in the gut? Or not?

There are no answers to such questions. At least no incontestable answers. In trying to make some sense of this uncertainty, a discussion of content and form is simply an attempt to understand, as best one can, a film. It might help to a degree, but something else also pulls on the viewer — from somewhere.

La Grande Illusion stands alone. There exists a different version for everyone who sees it and the film needs no defense or proof, despite these pages, nearing their end, which reflect, of course, only my own take. In searching for *La Grande Illusion*, I have found a version of the film, but not a definitive version, which exists nowhere.

Renoir's film gives pleasure, when and where and how it may.

That is more than enough.

23

The Director Among Directors

"'We watch a film to know the filmmaker.'"
—Jean Renoir in *Jean Renoir: Essays,*
Conversations, Reviews (p. 25)

As one measure of Jean Renoir, the director, the credits of his movies are revealing. I found the names of 22 film directors who worked with him and had a distinguished resumé, including some working behind the scenes who went uncredited. Many of these directors had not yet started directing before their time with Renoir. And some of them were significant figures in film history.

Beyond those discoveries, there were as many more in the credits who made only a few movies, including actors like Fernandel, Mel Ferrer and Jeanne Moreau.

The presence of **Erich von Stroheim** in *La Grande Illusion* marked Renoir's most noteworthy collaboration with another director. The interaction between an actor whose illustrious directing career was over and the younger director, who was hitting his stride while also in thrall to the older man's influence, is a lovely, and intriguing, backstory.

Among others who worked on the film, **Jacques Becker** most successfully followed Renoir into directing. Becker had joined his friend on many productions before making a few classic and much-appreciated films of his own.

Eight other members of Renoir's *La Grande Illusion* family made at least one movie during their careers: Charles Spaak, Christian Matras, Eugène Lourié, Carl Koch, Pierre Blondy (general manager) and the actors, Pierre Fresnay, Gaston Modot and Georges Péclet.

From the perspective of his direct association with past and future directors, Renoir, while making history himself in the 1930s, can be seen as a link between the classics of the silent movie era and films as they evolved from the 1940s onward—from Stroheim, at one time an assistant to D.W. Griffith and then himself a master of silent films, to Luchino Visconti and Satyajit Ray.

The directors, besides Stroheim, who had already made their names before joining forces with Renoir, were:

Alberto Cavalcanti (uncredited scenarist of *Tire au flanc*),[1] the Brazilian-born director who made some early experimental films in France, *Rien que les heures* (1926) and *En rade* (1927), and contributed to *Dead of Night* (1945) before returning to Brazil and making *O Canto do mar* (1953); **Walther Ruttmann** (assistant editor on *La Nuit du carrefour*), the German director who made two important films in the 1920s, *Berlin, die Sinfonie der Großstadt* (*Berlin: Symphony of a Great City*) in 1927 and *Melodie der Welt* (*Melody of the World*) in 1929; **Paul Fejos** (assistant editor on *La Chienne*), who had made films in Hungary and the United States, continuing his career around the world until 1941; **Marcel Pagnol**

(distributor of *Toni*), who had previously made a few films and went on to direct *Regain* (1937) and *La Femme du boulanger* (1938), among others; the prolific silhouette animator, **Lotte Reiniger** (shadow puppet sequence in *La Marseillaise*), who was the wife of Carl Koch and known especially for her 1926 film, *Die Abenteuer des Prinzen Achmed* (*The Adventures of Prince Achmed*); **Pierre Kast** (assistant director on *French Cancan*), a conspicuous figure of the French New Wave; and **Guy Lefranc** (co-scenarist of *Le Caporal épinglé*), whose first movie was *Knock* (1951), starring Louis Jouvet and Pierre Renoir.

The most significant directors, in addition to Becker, who pursued their careers after working with Renoir, were:

Claude Autant-Lara (sets and a minor role in *Nana*), whose long career included the memorable film, *Le Diable au corps* (1947), followed by films like *Occupe-toi d'Amélie* (1949) and *L'Auberge rouge* (1951); **Luchino Visconti** (assistant on *Toni*), who perhaps applied the lessons of *Toni* to *Ossessione* in 1942 (adapted from *The Postman Always Rings Twice*, the novel recommended by Renoir), as he became one of the key figures in the Italian neorealist movement, following with *La terra trema: Episodio del mare* (1948) and branching out with many other films, including the sumptuous *Senso* (1954); **Yves Allégret** (assistant director on *Partie de campagne*), who had a thriving career in the 1940s and 50s; **Satyajit Ray** (unofficial advisor during the filming of *The River*), who was inspired by Renoir to go into movies, becoming one of the most respected directors of his generation after he exploded onto the scene with *Pather Panchali* (1955), the first film of his Apu trilogy, and continued with *Charulata* (1964), *Aranyer Din Ratri* (*Days and Nights in the Forest*) [1970] and a number of other good films; and there was a relationship that even links Renoir to the 21st century—**Jacques Rivette** (an assistant director trainee on *French Cancan*), whose *Paris nous appartient* (1961) is an important work of the Nouvelle Vague and who continued his idiosyncratic career with films like *L'amour fou* (1969), *Céline et Julie vont en bateau* (1974) and *Va savoir* (2001).

There were also others who would soon become established as directors: **Pierre Prévert** (co-scenarist of *On purge bébé*), whose most well-regarded films were *L'Affaire est dans le sac* (1932) and *Voyage surprise* (1947); **Jean-Paul Le Chanois** (co-director of *La Vie est à nous*), Renoir's comrade-in-arms, who later developed a film career; and **Claude Berri** (an actor cut from *French Cancan*'s final version), who became known with *Le Vieil Homme et l'enfant* in 1967 and went on to make *Jean de Florette* and *Manon des sources* in 1986.

There was also the American connection, made during Renoir's Hollywood years, particularly in conjunction with two interesting figures: **Charles Laughton** (actor in *This Land Is Mine*), Renoir's close friend, who made only a single film in his lifetime but a unique and thoroughly original one—*The Night of the Hunter* (1955); and **Robert Aldrich** (assistant director on *The Southerner*), who also assisted William Wellman, Max Ophuls and Charles Chaplin before his own long career, making films such as *Kiss Me Deadly* (1955) and *The Dirty Dozen* (1967).

Directors like **Irving Pichel** (producer of *Swamp Water*) and **Garson Kanin** (co-director and actor in *Salute to France*) already had established their careers by the 1940s.

Nunnally Johnson (uncredited collaborator on *The Southerner*'s screenplay), a seasoned screenwriter and producer, directed *The Man in the Gray Flannel Suit* (1956) and *The Three Faces of Eve* (1957) after having worked with Renoir.

And, finally, more as a footnote, there is Henri Cartier-Bresson. The great photographer had an interesting connection with Renoir, with whom he shared political views. Cartier-Bresson was an assistant director on *La Vie est à nous*, and later an assistant and actor both

Renoir and his newborn son, Alain (1922) (*UCLA Charles E. Young Research Library, Department of Special Collections, Jean Renoir Collection*).

in *Partie de campagne* (appearing as one of the seminarians) and in *La Règle du jeu* (as William, the English servant). Though he directed only a few documentaries, *Le Retour* (1945) is a touching short film on returning prisoners of war and displaced persons.

Twenty-two directors. From France, from Germany to Italy, and from India to the United States, movies sprouted under their direction, perhaps influenced in varying degrees by the Johnny Appleseed of cinema, M. Jean Renoir, Frenchman of the world.

24

24 Frames Per Second, Forever

La Grande Illusion (1937): B&W; 113 minutes

La Grande Illusion lives, today, spinning on disks, or perhaps running through a few antiquated projectors around the world at 24 frames per second, as it did in 1937. Timely and forever — or at least forever for now.

The men and women, on or off the screen, who made *La Grande Illusion*, both in large and small ways, still live in its frames as well. This extended family includes, but is not limited to, a varied cast of 31 accomplices (in Renoir's term of endearment), with a few others noted in passing:

Jacques Becker (Paris, 9/15/1906–Paris, 2/21/1960)
Assistant Director; Actor: English officer (Hallbach)

Becker, born 12 years after Renoir, shared the same birthday. He was a close friend and an assistant on nine Renoir films, and also appeared in some of them. Becker became a well-known director in his own right, including: *Goupi mains rouges* (1943); *Rendez-vous de juillet* (1949); most famously, *Casque d'or* (1952); *Touchez pas au grisbi* (1954); and *Le Trou* (1960). He died at 53, having directed only 13 feature films.

Habib Benglia (Oran, Algeria, 8/25/1895–Paris, 12/2/1960)
Actor: Senegalese officer (Wintersborn)

After serving in World War I, Benglia played the starring role (at 28) in Eugene O'Neill's *The Emperor Jones* at the Théâtre National de l'Odéon. He was the first black actor in France to play white characters in the classical repertoire, also at the Odéon. His film career covered 35 years and his most significant role was as one of the stars of *Daïnah la métisse* (1932), directed by Jean Grémillon. Some other films: Marcel Carné's *Les Enfants du paradis* (1945) and John Huston's *The Roots of Heaven* (1958).

Raymond Blondy (Paris, 5/21/08–?)
Director of Production

Blondy offered Erich von Stroheim the role of Rauffenstein in *La Grande Illusion*. His younger brother, Pierre, was the general manager on the film and appeared as an extra. Raymond Blondy also worked as production manager on a few films into the 1960s.

Julien Carette (Paris, 12/23/1897–Saint-Germain-en-Laye, 7/20/1966)
Actor: Cartier, the music hall actor (Hallbach)

Born Julien Victor. Coming from a background in theater, Carette was a character actor for more than 30 years and appeared in over 100 movies. He worked with Renoir on five films, including *La Bête humaine* and, most memorably, as Marceau, the poacher, in

La Règle du jeu. Other films include: Pierre Prévert's *L'affaire est dans le sac* (1932); Carné's *Les Portes de la nuit* (1946); Yves Allégret's *Une si jolie petite plage* (1949); and Claude Autant-Lara's *Occupe-toi d'Amélie* (1949) and *L'Auberge rouge* (1951).

Marcel Dalio (Paris, 7/17/1900–Paris, 11/20/1983)
Actor: Lt. Rosenthal

Born Israel Moshe Blauschild. Dalio appeared mainly as a character actor in over 100 movies, from 1931 until 1981. His only other role in a Renoir film was possibly his greatest achievement, as the marquis, Robert de la Cheyniest, in *La Règle du jeu*. At the start of World War II, Dalio, who was Jewish, went into exile; his parents were killed in the Holocaust. From 1941, he acted in many American movies, before dividing his career between France and the United States.

Some of his more widely known films: Julien Duvivier's *Pépé le Moko* (1937), starring Jean Gabin; Josef von Sternberg's *The Shanghai Gesture* (1941); Michael Curtiz's *Casablanca* (1942); Howard Hawks's *To Have and Have Not* (1944) and *Gentlemen Prefer Blondes* (1953); Billy Wilder's *Sabrina* (1954); and Mike Nichols's *Catch-22* (1970).

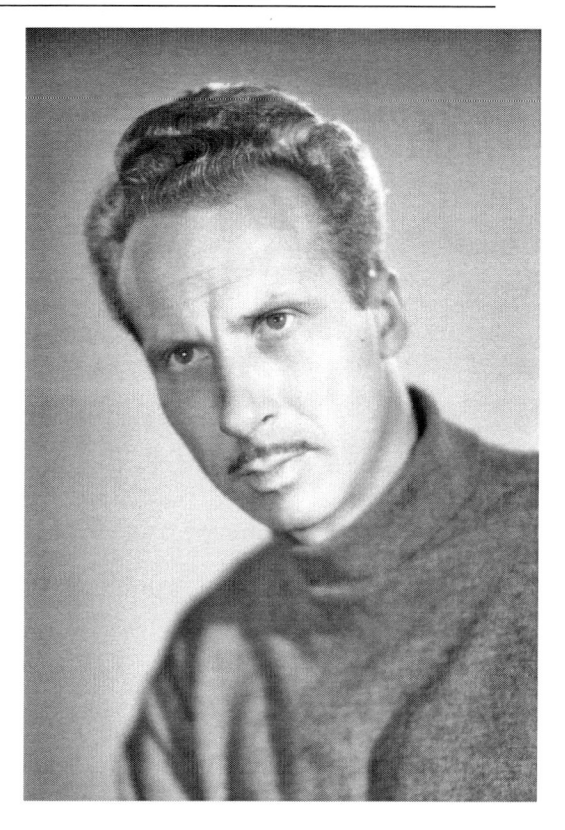

Jacques Becker, Renoir's close friend. Photograph: Sam Lévin (©*Ministère de la Culture/ Médiathèque du Patrimoine/Sam Levin/dist. RMN-Grand Palais/Art Resource, New York*).

Jean Dasté (Paris, 9/18/1904–Saint-Étienne, 10/15/1994)
Actor: the teacher (Hallbach)

Primarily an actor in the theater, Dasté appeared in four Renoir movies. His first major film role was as the school supervisor in Jean Vigo's brilliant *Zéro de conduite* (1933) and he co-starred (coincidentally) with Dita Parlo in Vigo's other masterpiece, *L'Atalante* (1934). After *La Grande Illusion*, he returned to theater work and formed a successful stage company. Dasté had roles in a few Alain Resnais films, including *La Guerre est finie* (1966), and was also in François Truffaut's *L'Enfant sauvage* (1970).

Joseph de Bretagne (Vaudricourt, 11/21/1901–Cagnes-sur-Mer, 12/4/1986)
Director of Sound

A frequent colleague of Renoir, de Bretagne worked on nine films with him, including *La Règle du jeu*. Some of his other films: Duvivier's *Panique* (1946); and, in the United States, William Wyler's *Roman Holiday* (1953), Nicholas Ray's *Bitter Victory* (1957), the omnibus *The Longest Day* (1962), and John Frankenheimer's *The Train* (1964).

Werner Florian ( )
Actor: Sgt. Arthur Krantz (Hallbach)

The only other movie Florian appeared in was *La Marseillaise* (though uncredited).

Fréhel (Paris, 7/14/1891–Paris, 2/3/1951)
Singer of "Frou-Frou" (soundtrack)

Born Marguerite Boulc'h. While only in her teens, Boulc'h was a noted singer. Despite struggling with alcoholism, she was able to establish her career, took the stage name "Fréhel," and became a star. She appeared as a singer and actress in some films of the 1930s and 40s — including Duvivier's *Pépé le Moko* (1937) with Gabin. Fréhel's voice opens *La Grande Illusion*, singing "Frou-Frou," an 1898 song with lyrics by Hector Monréal and Henri Blondeau, and music of Henri Chatau.

Pierre Fresnay (Paris, 4/4/1897–Neuilly-sur-Seine, 1/9/1975)
Actor: Capt. de Boeldieu

Born Pierre Jules Louis Laudenbach. Fresnay was a soldier in World War I. As an 18-year-old, he started at the Comédie-Française and became a noted stage actor. He made his movie debut in silent films but got his big break by playing the title role, which he had performed on stage, in Alexander Korda's *Marius* (1931), the film version of a Marcel Pagnol play; he also played Marius in two sequels. Alec Guinness once called him his favorite actor.

Fresnay never worked with Renoir again after *La Grande Illusion*. Other memorable films: Alfred Hitchcock's *The Man Who Knew Too Much* (1934); G.W. Pabst's *Mademoiselle Docteur* (1937) with Dita Parlo; Henri-Georges Clouzot's *L'Assassin habite au 21* (1942) and *Le Corbeau* (1943); and Maurice Cloche's *Monsieur Vincent* (1947). Fresnay directed his own film, *Le Duel*, in 1939. He returned to the theater in the 1960s and later did television work.

Jean Gabin (Paris, 5/17/1904–Neuilly-sur-Seine, 11/15/1976)
Actor: Lt. Maréchal

Born Jean Alexis Moncorgé. The son of cabaret performers, Gabin worked in music halls early in his career, including the Folies Bergère and the Moulin Rouge. He appeared in his first movie in 1930 and made nearly 100 films. Gabin was one of France's great stars of the 1930s and also acted in a few American productions during World War II. He joined the Forces Françaises Libres and was awarded the *Croix de guerre* and the *Médaille militaire* for his service in North Africa.

In addition to *La Grande Illusion* and three other Renoir movies, Gabin is known for his starring roles in some notable films: Duvivier's *La Bandera* (1935), *La Belle Équipe* (1936) and *Pépé le Moko* (1937), which was released just before filming began on *La Grande Illusion*, with some fellow actors from Renoir's film in the cast — Dalio, Gaston Modot and Georges Péclet (as well as the singer Fréhel); Grémillon's *Gueule d'amour* (1937) and *Remorques* (1941); Carné's classic films, *Le Quai des brumes* (1938) and *Le Jour se lève* (1939); Max Ophuls's lovely *Le Plaisir* (1952); and Becker's *Touchez pas au grisbi* (1954).

Ever a romantic leading man, Gabin played opposite Josephine Baker in Marc Allégret's *Zouzou* (1934) in an early role and, later, opposite Brigitte Bardot in Autant-Lara's *En cas de malheur* (1958).

Françoise Giroud (Lausanne, Switzerland, 9/21/1916–Neuilly-sur-Seine, 1/19/2003)
Script girl

Born France Gourdji; her credit in *La Grande Illusion* is as "Gourdji." Giroud started in movies as the script girl for Marc Allégret's *Fanny* (1932). She was an assistant director on films in the 1930s and then a scriptwriter through the 1950s. A journalist, essayist and author, she co-founded the magazine, *L'Express*, in 1953. Giroud was politically active and

Jean Gabin on the set of *La Grande Illusion*. Photograph: Sam Lévin (©*Ministère de la Culture/ Médiathèque du Patrimoine/Sam Levin/dist. RMN-Grand Palais/Art Resource, New York*).

served as France's Minister for Women's Affairs (1974–76) and as Minister of Culture (1976–77).

Marguerite Houllé-Renoir (born 1907–died in Paris, July 1987)
Editor

Also known as Marguerite Renoir or Marguerite Houllé. A woman of many names (and spellings) in her 40 years as an editor. And a mysterious figure, rarely mentioned in film histories despite her productive career. In the credits of *La Grande Illusion*, she is listed simply as "Margueritte" *(sic)* and was assisted by Marthe Huguet.

Houllé-Renoir was the editor on all 13 of Renoir's movies from *La Chienne* through *La Règle du jeu*. They lived together for nearly ten years and she became known as an editor under the name of Marguerite Renoir. A Communist Party member, she influenced the politics of Renoir in the 1930s. She edited all but one of Jacques Becker's feature films and also worked with Luis Buñuel.

Sylvain Itkine (Paris, 12/8/1908–Lyon, 8/1/1944)
Actor: Lt. Demolder (Wintersborn)

Itkine appeared in four Renoir movies. His other films, in his short life, include Grémillon's *Gueule d'amour* (1937), Abel Garce's *J'accuse* (1938) and Ophuls's *De Mayerling à Sarajevo* (1940). In World War II, Itkine was heroically active in the Resistance during the occupation of France and was murdered by the Gestapo in August 1944.

Carl Koch (Nümbrecht, Germany, 7/30/1892–Barnet, England, 12/1/1963)
Technical advisor; Actor: German soldier at the farmhouse window

In Germany, Koch co-directed *Mann ist Mann* (1931), a short he made with Bertolt Brecht that starred Peter Lorre. A good friend of Renoir, he collaborated with him on the screenplays of *La Marseillaise* (a film on which his more well-known wife, Lotte Reiniger, also worked) and *La Règle du jeu*. In 1940 Koch completed the Italian production of the film, *La Tosca* (1941), replacing Renoir, who had returned to France.

Joseph Kosma (Budapest, Hungary, 10/22/1905–La Roche-Guyon, France, 8/7/1969)
Music

Kosma joined Brecht's touring company in 1929 and immigrated to France in 1933. He often partnered with Jacques Prévert, setting his poems to music, including the popular standard, "Autumn Leaves," ("Les Feuilles mortes"). Having studied with Béla Bartók, he wrote symphonic and vocal works. His two principal themes in *La Grande Illusion* are derived from motifs in Igor Stravinsky's *Symphony No. 1 in E-flat*. Kosma composed the music for ten other Renoir films, including *La Règle du jeu*. Other major films include: Carné's *Les Visiteurs du soir* (1942), as well as the director's greatest film, *Les Enfants du paradis* (1945), and *Les Portes de la nuit* (1946); and Georges Franju's *Le Sang des bêtes* (1949).

Sam Lévin (Kharkov, Russia, 7/19/1904–Paris, 11/5/1992)
Still photographer

Lévin's parents fled Russia for France in 1906 because of growing anti–Semitism. He was a set photographer from 1937–1955 and worked on some other Renoir films, including *La Règle du jeu*—and on Ophuls's *La Ronde* (1950). Lévin also worked for MGM and Cinecittà. As an acclaimed celebrity portrait photographer, he became best known for his photographs of Brigitte Bardot in the mid–1950s, bringing out her sexual appeal and mystery for the first time.

Renée Lichtig (born Shanghai, China, 1921–Paris, 10/16/2007)
Editor of the restored 1958 version of La Grande Illusion

In 1958, Lichtig worked as an editor (assisted by Ginette Courtois-Doynel), under the supervision of Renoir and Charles Spaak, to restore *La Grande Illusion* to its original form. She then further developed her own editing career with other directors — and with Renoir, on three more films. Lichtig was also a close collaborator of Henri Langlois at the Cinémathèque Française.

Eugène Lourié (Kharkov, Russia, 4/8/1903–Woodland Hills, California, 5/26/1991)
Set Decorator

Lourié designed ballet sets before moving on to film. He was assisted on *La Grande Illusion* by Georges Wakhévitch (uncredited), who briefly replaced Lourié when he had to leave before the end of filming; in addition, René Decrais was in charge of costume design. Lourié worked with Renoir on eight films, including *La Règle du jeu* and *The River*. Other notable movies include Charles Chaplin's *Limelight* (1952) and Samuel Fuller's *Shock Corridor* (1963) and *The Naked Kiss* (1964). He directed several science fiction films in Hollywood as well, including *The Beast from 20,000 Fathoms* (1953) and *The Colossus of New York* (1958).

Christian Matras (Valence, 12/29/1903–Paris, 5/4/1977)
Director of Photography

Matras began making short documentaries in 1926. Trained as a newsreel photographer, he worked as a cinematographer on over 100 movies, starting with Grémillon's first feature, *Maldone* (1928). *La Grande Illusion* was his only film with Renoir.

Most memorably, Matras was the director of photography for many of Max Ophuls's greatest films: *La Ronde* (1950); *Le Plaisir* (1952); *Madame de...* (1953); and *Lola Montès* (1955). He also worked with other prominent French directors like Christian-Jaque, Jean Cocteau, Julien Duvivier and Jean Epstein—and with Vittorio De Sica and Luis Buñuel (*La Voie lactée* in 1969).

Gaston Modot (Paris, 12/31/1887–Paris, 2/24/1970)
Actor: the engineer (Hallbach)

After studying design and architecture, Modot pursued painting and knew Picasso and Modigliani, among others. He made seven films with Renoir and is best known for his key roles as Schumacher in *La Règle du jeu* and as the hero of Buñuel's powerful *film maudit*, *L'Âge d'or* (1930). Modot acted in more than 100 movies. Some other appearances of note: René Clair's *Sous les toits de Paris* (1930); Pabst's *Die Dreigroschenoper [The Threepenny Opera]* (1931) and *Mademoiselle Docteur* (1937); Duvivier's *Pépé le Moko* (1937); Carné's *Les Enfants du paradis* (1945); and Becker's *Casque d'or* (1952). He also directed a film in 1930, *Conte cruel*.

Dita Parlo (Stettin, Germany, 9/4/1906–Paris, 12/13/1971)
Actor: Elsa

Born Grethe Gerda Kornstädt. Parlo studied classical dance and then moved on to theater. She became a star of the German cinema after her first film in 1928. Signed to a four-year Hollywood contract in 1930, she made a few undistinguished movies and returned to Europe, settling in France to escape Hitler's Germany.

Parlo is memorable in her starring role as the young wife (opposite Jean Dasté) in Vigo's *L'Atalante* (1934). *La Grande Illusion* was her only film with Renoir. Also in 1937 she appeared both in Pabst's *Mademoiselle Docteur* with Fresnay and in Edmond T. Gréville's English version of the same film, released as *Under Secret Orders*, with Erich von Stroheim in the cast. The French authorities arrested Parlo, as a German citizen, and deported her in 1940 to Germany. After the war she made some more movies in France; her career ended in 1965.

Georges Péclet (La Brillanne, 7/27/1897–Marseille, 1/11/1974)
Actor: French prisoner (Wintersborn)

Born Prosper Désiré Péclet. He fought in World War I as a pilot (like Renoir) and received the *Croix de guerre*. In the 1920s he acted in many silent movies. Péclet made only two more films with Renoir. Other films: Duvivier's *Pépé le Moko* (1937) and Pabst's *Mademoiselle Docteur* (1937). After the war, he gave up acting to make his own movies and founded "l'Aéro-club du cinéma."

La petite Peters (born ca. 1930–died May 1937)
Actor: Lotte

Though she has a significant role in the film, the girl who played Lotte is not listed in the credits of *La Grande Illusion*. "La petite Peters" ("The little [girl] Peters"), as she is identified by Olivier Curchod, did not live to see the film. A few weeks before the premiere, she tragically died of influenza. It is hard to watch the four minutes she appears on the screen, knowing of her death, without feeling the weight of that tragedy and reflecting on the unique way film immortalizes, in its modest way, an actor.

Albert Pinkevitch (   )
Co-producer (at Réalisations d'Art Cinématographique)

A friend of Jean Renoir, Pinkevitch was, with Frank Rollmer, an uncredited co-producer of *La Grande Illusion*. In addition to helping secure financial backing, his input was critical in expanding the role of Rosenthal into a specifically Jewish character; he also provided some dialogue for Cartier, the music hall actor.

Captain Armand Pinsard (Nercillac, 5/28/1887–Paris, 5/10/1953)

A leading French ace, Pinsard saved Renoir from an attacking German plane during World War I; Renoir ran into him again, in 1934, while shooting *Toni*. Although he has no title credit, his war stories gave Renoir the initial idea for *La Grande Illusion*. Pinsard also served in World War II and lost a leg during a bombing raid in 1940.

Claude Renoir (Paris, 12/4/1913–Troyes, 9/5/1993)
Second camera operator

Son of Pierre Renoir, the actor, and nephew of Jean Renoir. He joined his uncle on seven films, including (as cinematographer) *Partie de campagne*. Under Christian Matras on *La Grande Illusion*, he was backed up by Jean-Serge Bourgoin and Ernest Bourreaud, who were assistant operators; Bourgoin replaced Renoir for three weeks of shooting in Alsace when he had to withdraw due to ill health. After the war, he worked on many films around the world, including Cloche's *Monsieur Vincent* (1947), Clouzot's documentary, *Le Mystère Picasso* (1956), Joseph L. Mankiewicz's *Cleopatra* (1963) and Roger Vadim's *Barbarella* (1968).

Jean Renoir (Paris, 9/15/1894–Beverly Hills, California, 2/12/1979)
Director; Co-scriptwriter

The second son of the Impressionist painter, Pierre Auguste Renoir, Jean was a model for some of his father's paintings. His older brother, Pierre, became an accomplished actor; his younger brother, Claude, also worked in film. Jean's only child, Alain, was born in 1921.

Renoir directed his first film, *La Fille de l'eau*, in 1924. His career began to blossom during the early 1930s and reached its peak later in the decade. With World War II, he came to the United States, where he completed six movies. After making *The River* in India and *The Golden Coach* in Italy, he returned to France in 1955 to finish his film career (though also living in California).

An engaging writer, he published, among other writings, *Renoir, My Father* (1962) and *My Life and My Films* (1974), a memoir.

Jean Renoir is considered among the greatest directors in film history. His influence on other filmmakers, and the spell he cast on critics as well, is nearly unmatched. He remains best known as the director of *La Règle du jeu* (especially) and *La Grande Illusion*.

In his long life in film, the following titles could be cited to characterize Renoir's status as one of the towering figures of cinema, though they only cover the 1930s: *Boudu sauvé des eaux*; *Le Crime de Monsieur Lange*; *Partie de campagne*; *La Grande Illusion*; *La Bête humaine*; and *La Règle du jeu*. And I would add, as particularly good examples of his originality, *Nana*, *La Chienne* and *The Woman on the Beach*. (This list would surely be deemed inadequate by many critics.)

Frank Rollmer ( )
Co-producer (at Réalisations d'Art Cinématographique)

Rollmer bankrolled *La Grande Illusion* with 3 million francs and was, with Albert Pinkevitch, an uncredited co-producer of *La Grande Illusion*. A banker, he also put money into Carné's *Jenny* (1936) after having some success in the stock market.

Jean Renoir (ca. 1937). Photograph: Sam Lévin (©*Ministère de la Culture/Médiathèque du Patrimoine/Sam Levin/dist. RMN-Grand Palais/Art Resource, New York*).

Charles Spaak (Brussels, Belgium, 5/25/1903–Nice, 3/4/1975)
Co-scriptwriter

A journalist early in his life, Spaak also wrote plays and came to Paris in 1928 where he worked as a secretary to Jacques Feyder, the filmmaker, for whom he wrote his first script. He was the brother of Paul-Henri Spaak, the Belgian foreign minister who (ironically) banned *La Grande Illusion* in Belgium, soon after its release, and who later was the first president of the United Nations's General Assembly.

Over a period of 45 years, Charles Spaak became a highly respected scenarist, writing screenplays for over 100 movies. He worked as well with Renoir on *Les Bas-Fonds* and briefly on *Le Caporal épinglé*. Spaak wrote scripts for some interesting films: Feyder's *Le Grand Jeu* (1934) and *La Kermesse héroïque* (1935); Duvivier's *La Bandera* (1935) and *La Belle Équipe* (1936); Grémillon's *Gueule d'amour* (1937); and André Cayatte's *Nous sommes tous des assassins* (1952). He also directed a film, *Le Mystère Barton* (1949).

Erich von Stroheim (Vienna, Austria, 9/22/1885–Maurepas, 5/12/1957)
Actor: Capt. von Rauffenstein

Born Erich Oswald Stroheim. One of the most famous filmmakers of the silent era. Earlier in his career, Stroheim worked as an assistant to D.W. Griffith and was an extra in *Intolerance*. A perfectionist as a director, he refused to give in to the Hollywood system; his career ended within ten years. Continuing as a screenwriter and actor (known as "The Man You Love to Hate"), he had roles in over 40 movies. *La Grande Illusion* was his high point as an actor. Stroheim also appeared in two Billy Wilder films, *Five Graves to Cairo* (1943) and *Sunset Boulevard* (1950), and in Sacha Guitry's *Napoléon* (1955) as Ludwig van Beethoven (!), with an all-star cast including Gabin and Orson Welles among many others.

An early version of Stroheim's best-known work, *Greed*, was eight hours long. It is a key "lost film" in movie history, having eventually been shortened to a little over two hours; the rest of the footage was, outrageously, destroyed. His major films: *Blind Husbands* (1919); *Foolish Wives* (1922); *Greed* (1924); *The Merry Widow* (1925); and *The Wedding March* (1928).

And then there was *Queen Kelly* (1929) — a movie on which he was fired by the producers, Joseph P. Kennedy (!!) and Gloria Swanson, midway through shooting, making Stroheim's final directorial effort only nominally a Stroheim film and, though finally released in a mutilated version, establishing it, in essence, as also "lost" or, at the least, unfinished.

Appendix A: Title Credits

(blank screen)

• RÉALISATIONS D'ART
RAC
CINÉMATOGRAPHIQUE •
présent

(fade-out)
(fade-in)

JEAN GABIN

(flip)

DITA PARLO

(dissolve)

PIERRE FRESNAY
et

(flip)

ERIC von STROHEIM
dans

(dissolve)

LA GRANDE ILLUSION

(flip)

Réalisation de
JEAN RENOIR

(dissolve)

avec
CARETTE

(flip)

225

PECLET
WERNER FLORIAN
DASTE
ITKINE
MODOT

(dissolve)

et
DALIO

_____ (flip)

Scénario et Dialogues:
CHARLES SPAAK et JEAN RENOIR
Conseiller technique: CARL KOCH
Montage:
MARGUERITTE   MARTHE HUGUET
Assistant metteur en scène:
JACQUES BECKER

(dissolve)

Chef opérateur:
CHRISTIAN MATRAS
Second opérateur: CLAUDE RENOIR
Assistants opérateurs:
BOURGOIN
BOURREAUD
Décorateur: LOURIÉ

_____ (flip)

Ingénieur du son: De BRETAGNE
Script girl: GOURDJI
Photographie: SAM LEVIN

(dissolve)

Directeur de Production
RAYMOND BLONDY

_____ (flip)

Régie générale: PIERRE BLONDY
Chef de plateau: ROBERT RIPS
Régie extérieure: BARNATHAN
Accessoiristes:
ALEXANDRE   LAURIÉ
PILLON
Maquilleur: RAFFELS

Costumier: DECRAIS

(dissolve)

Musique de JOSEPH KOSMA
Orchestre VUILLERMOZ
Éditions SMYTH
Tirage G.M. FILM
groupes électrogènes LUXTONE
PARIS – STUDIOS – CINÉMA
Western Electric
SYSTÈME SONORE

(fade-out)

C'est une production
des
RÉALISATIONS
D'ART
CINÉMATOGRAPHIQUE

(fade-out)

Uncredited actors

Jacques Becker (English officer with the watch, at Hallbach)
Habib Benglia (Senegalese officer)
Pierre Blondy (soldier)
Albert Brouett (Russian prisoner)
Roger Forster (Maisonneuve)
Georges Fronval
Karl Heil (German officer)
Carl Koch (German soldier at the farmhouse window)
"La petite Peters" (Lotte)
Claude Sainval (Captain Ringis)
Michel Salina
Claude Vernier (German officer)

Appendix B: The Story

Time: World War I, during the years 1915–1917. Each significant time shift in the story is indicated by a corresponding shift to a new paragraph.

French air base (French territory)

Lt. Maréchal, a young French mechanic by trade, sings "Frou-Frou" along with a gramophone record, looking forward to an evening on the town with a woman named Josephine. He is interrupted and told to report to Capt. de Boeldieu, an upper-class career officer. Boeldieu informs Maréchal that they will conduct a reconnaissance mission to clear up details of an aerial photograph.

German canteen (German territory)

Capt. von Rauffenstein, a German fighter pilot, enters the canteen and celebrates his shooting down of Boeldieu and Maréchal.

They soon enter as his guests at a lavish meal and the two captains develop an immediate rapport based on class affinities. A German soldier carrying a memorial wreath for a fallen French pilot interrupts the meal. And the prisoners are notified that they are to be moved to a prison camp.

Interlude — landscape along railroad tracks (Germany)

A documentary shot, from a moving train, shows the passing countryside, followed by a shot of the sign for a prison camp: "Hallbach."

Hallbach prison camp (Germany)

Newly arrived prisoners of war have been assembled in a courtyard as the German commandant oversees the reading of camp regulations by Arthur, a guard. Maréchal and Boeldieu are soon searched. Meanwhile, some of their future roommates inspect a food package in the mailroom. And, in a somber setting, three German guards eat together. Lt. Rosenthal, from a well-off banking family, then provides a feast for his compatriots, including the new arrivals. The meal is marked by high spirits and light repartee, especially by Cartier, a music hall actor, who teases the aloof Boeldieu.

But more serious business is at hand. In the next scene, another prisoner, an engineer, washes Maréchal's feet and tells him about an escape tunnel the French prisoners are digging.

At night Cartier climbs down into the tunnel. After digging a bit, he starts to suffocate and pulls the string tied to a can, which serves as an alarm. It takes a while for the warning signal to be noticed; he is barely rescued in time.

During the day, the French head off to the prison garden where they dump earth from the previous night's digging. With the arrival of costumes for their planned musical revue, some prisoners gather to go through the clothes. When one of the men dresses up as a woman, the room falls silent at the strange, but evocative, sight.

Young German soldiers drill in formation. And the French prepare costumes for the show, sharing their reasons for wanting to escape. They are briefly mesmerized by the sight and sound of the soldiers drilling below their window.

One evening a poster (dated February 26, 1916) announces that the Germans have captured the fort at Douaumont. The Germans celebrate; the prisoners decide to go ahead with their show.

The lively revue features Cartier as its central figure, supported by a line of English "chorus girls." Maréchal interrupts the show to announce that Douaumont has been recaptured by the French, inspiring the prisoners to sing "La Marseillaise" in defiance.

As punishment for his action, Maréchal is placed in solitary confinement and futilely attempts to escape. Bells ring as news is posted that the Germans have recaptured Douaumont.

Some time afterward, an old German guard tries to console Maréchal in his cell and leaves a harmonica for him. Maréchal rouses himself enough to peck absent-mindedly at "Frou-Frou"; the guard sings along, outside the cell.

The French discuss their escape plans, and Maréchal is returned to the room.

As the prisoners wait for nightfall to escape, Arthur enters and announces that all officers are to change camp immediately. Later, assembled with the others for the transfer, Maréchal is unable to communicate with an English officer about the tunnel.

Interlude — landscape along railroad tracks (Germany)

A series of documentary shots, from a moving train, shows the countryside and train stations passing by, interspersed with signs for two prison camps (indicating a substantial passage of time), leading finally to a long shot of a castle in the distance, followed by the sign for another camp: "Wintersborn."

Wintersborn prison camp (Germany)

Rauffenstein, badly wounded, has been reduced to the role of commandant at Wintersborn. He greets three new prisoners (Boeldieu, Maréchal and Lt. Demolder) and discusses prison regulations before leading them on a tour of the castle to discourage any idea of escape; he reconnects with Boeldieu in the process.

Maréchal and Boeldieu are reunited with Rosenthal, as they also share their room with other prisoners. Studying a map together, the two junior officers discuss a plan to escape.

As the Germans are about to make a spot inspection, Boeldieu saves the day by hiding an escape rope, suspending it from an exterior drainpipe. Rauffenstein gets Boeldieu's word of honor that there is nothing in the room against regulations.

The two captains enjoy a quiet tête-à-tête at the German's quarters in a converted chapel. Rauffenstein regrets that they are part of a dying class. But Boeldieu expresses ambivalence and is, at least, resigned to the new order.

In a parallel scene, Maréchal and Rosenthal draw closer to each other as they talk about Boeldieu and their projected escape from Wintersborn.

Russian prisoners invite the French to share the contents of a wooden crate, a gift from the Czarina. They anticipate vodka and caviar, but the box is filled with books and some angry Russians set it on fire. Boeldieu suggests to Maréchal and Rosenthal that the resulting commotion, with guards occupied, has provided a dress rehearsal for a possible escape plan. He insists on taking charge and, against their objections, says that the plan will only work for two people (them).

In their quarters, Boeldieu discusses his plan with Maréchal, who is embarrassed to be escaping without his commanding officer. But Boeldieu cuts him off.

Maréchal again tries to communicate his uneasiness as Boeldieu washes his gloves, but he is foiled once more.

Evening. The prisoners at the camp start a ruckus, making loud noises and playing pennywhistles. The Germans confiscate the flutes and momentarily restore order. But, on cue, the prisoners start up again, singing and banging pots and pans. A general roll call is announced and Maréchal awkwardly says goodbye to Boeldieu. Soon after, in the courtyard, with Rauffenstein presiding, Boeldieu's name is called; after a moment of silence, a solitary flute tootling a children's song can be heard high in the ramparts. Searchlights find Boeldieu and the chase is on. Maréchal and Rosenthal slip away and escape out a window. Back in the courtyard, Rauffenstein stops a guard's gunfire and pleads with Boeldieu, in English, to come down. Boeldieu defies him and Rauffenstein is forced to shoot, attempting to wound him in the leg. The French captain falls. Rauffenstein learns that Maréchal and Rosenthal have escaped.

Later that evening, the mortally wounded Boeldieu lies on the bed in Rauffenstein's quarters. The German commandant regrets his poor aim. Boeldieu, however, realizes that death is a good solution for men like themselves in such a rapidly changing world. He dies and Rauffenstein, in mourning, cuts the potted geranium that his friend had admired earlier.

Country roads and mountains (Germany)

Maréchal and Rosenthal, in civilian clothes, hide from a passing stranger and then continue on their way in enemy territory.

Rosenthal has twisted his ankle and Maréchal becomes frustrated at their slow progress in the cold and wintry countryside. They argue angrily on a mountain road and Maréchal storms off after letting loose an anti–Semitic slur. Defiantly, they exchange verses of the same children's song that had been played by Boeldieu. But Maréchal returns and, reconciled, they head on together. Seeing a shack in the distance, they decide to risk hiding there for the evening.

Elsa's farm (Germany)

It is later that night as Maréchal and Rosenthal hide in a barn. The door opens and a cow enters, followed by Elsa, a German war widow. Unafraid of the two men, she invites them into her farmhouse. She offers them food and milk as they settle down in the kitchen area. Troops are heard passing by; Elsa responds to a knock on the shutters and says nothing to a German soldier about her guests. She returns to them and attends to Rosenthal's ankle.

One day Elsa shows Rosenthal photographs of her husband and brothers, killed in the war, as her little daughter, Lotte, eats at a nearby table. Outside, in the barn, Maréchal feeds the cow and then enters the house. Elsa, scrubbing the floor, asks him to get water; their growing attraction for each other has become evident.

Christmas Eve. Maréchal and Rosenthal have fashioned a homemade crèche. At midnight, Elsa wakes Lotte, who is enchanted by the scene. After Maréchal learns a few words in German, and addresses them to Lotte, she is put to bed. The two men say goodnight to Elsa. But Maréchal returns and Elsa embraces him.

It's Christmas morning. Rosenthal finds the lovers standing close together by a window. They have already made coffee and Elsa has learned a simple phrase in French.

Soon the men realize they must leave their refuge. Rosenthal tells Elsa of their plans. Maréchal tries to reassure her, as she cries, and says he will return after the war if he makes it out alive.

Later that day, the final evening on the farm. The Frenchmen bid goodbye to Elsa and Lotte; Maréchal repeats his few German words once more, before leaving. Elsa is again alone with her daughter.

The border (Germany & Switzerland)

Maréchal and Rosenthal, near the Swiss border, vow to join their units and fight again. Maréchal hopes that this will be the last war and Rosenthal gently chides him for his illusions. They hug goodbye in case they are surprised by German soldiers and must separate. Meanwhile, a patrol follows their tracks in the snow. The soldiers raise their rifles and fire a few shots. But one of them orders another to stop firing since the fugitives have crossed the border into Switzerland. Maréchal and Rosenthal, far in the distance, scramble onward, breaking unevenly through the crusted snow.

FIN

Appendix C: Breakdown of Shots

KEY

Moving shot (track or pan)
Still shot

X = group shot (4 or more characters)
3 = 3 characters
2 = 2 characters
1 = 1 character
0 = no characters

(#) = Length of shot (to the nearest second)

Centered (dissolve)/(fade-out) = new day
Flush left (dissolve)/(fade-out) = gap in time within the same day

---

Shot **Length (seconds)**
no. 0 5 10 15 20 25 30 35 40 45 50 55 60 65 70 75 80 85 90 95 100

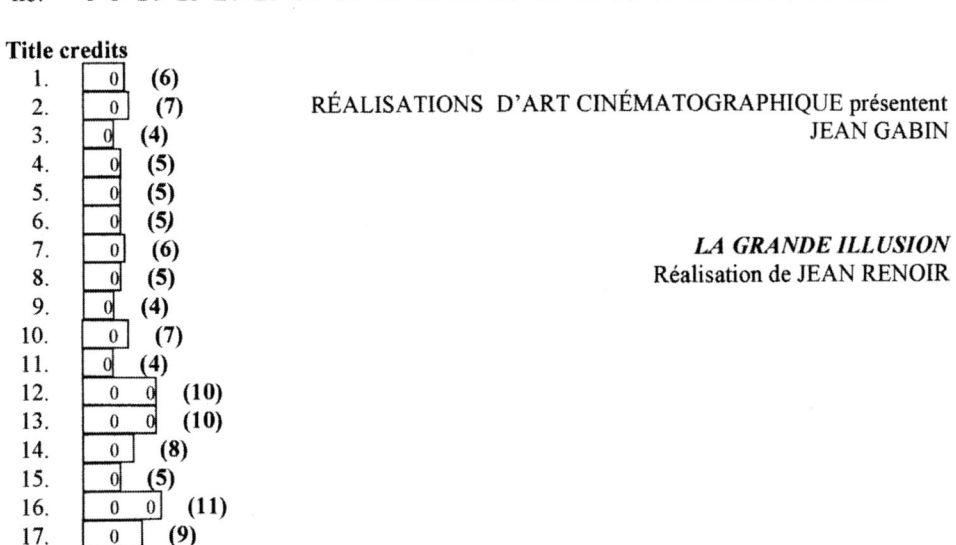

Title credits

Shot	Length	Text
1.	0 (6)	
2.	0 (7)	RÉALISATIONS D'ART CINÉMATOGRAPHIQUE présentent
3.	0 (4)	JEAN GABIN
4.	0 (5)	
5.	0 (5)	
6.	0 (5)	
7.	0 (6)	*LA GRANDE ILLUSION*
8.	0 (5)	Réalisation de JEAN RENOIR
9.	0 (4)	
10.	0 (7)	
11.	0 (4)	
12.	0 0 (10)	
13.	0 0 (10)	
14.	0 (8)	
15.	0 (5)	
16.	0 0 (11)	
17.	0 (9)	

Appendix C

```
Shot   Length (seconds)
no.    0  5  10  15  20  25  30  35  40  45  50  55  60  65  70  75  80  85  90  95  100

18.    [ 0 ]  (7)
                                      (fade-out/fade-in)
```

French air base

```
19.    [x x x x x x x x x x]  (56)              Maréchal at the gramophone
20.    [x x]  (14)
21.    [1]  (5)                                 Boeldieu in his office
22.    [3 3 3 3 3 3 3 3 3 3]  (51)
```
(dissolve)

German canteen

```
23.    [x x x x x x x x x x x]  (64)            Rauffenstein at the canteen
```
(fade-out/fade-in)
```
24.    [x x x x x x x x x x]  (58)              Boeldieu & Maréchal arrive
25.    [2 2 2 2]  (20)                          The shared meal of the French and Germans
26.    [x x x x]  (23)
27.    [1]  (5)
28.    [0]  (8)
29.    [3]  (6)
30.    [x x x]  (17)
31.    [1]  (8)
```
(dissolve)

German landscape (with a dissolve)
```
32.    [0]  (9)
33.    [0]  (6)                                 "Hallbach"
```
(dissolve)

Hallbach prison camp
```
34.    [x x]  (11)                              Courtyard: the first day
35.    [x x x x]  (27)
36.    [x x x]  (19)
37.    [x x x]  (19)
38.    [x]  (3)
39.    [x x x]  (19)
40.    [x x]  (12)
41.    [x x x x]  (20)
42.    [x]  (5)
43.    [x x x x x x x x x]  (50)                Boeldieu and Maréchal searched
44.    [x x x x x x x x x x x x x x]  (75)      The mailroom
45.    [3 3 3]  (17)                            German guards at their meal
46.    [x x x x x x x x x]  (56)                Rosenthal's feast
47.    [1]  (8)
48.    [x x x]  (19)
49.    [x x x x x x]  (34)
50.    [2 2]  (10)
51.    [3]  (8)
52.    [x x x x]  (22)
                                      (fade-out)
53.    [x x x x x x x x]  (44)                  The engineer washes Maréchal's feet
54.    [1]  (2)
```

Breakdown of Shots

Shot no.	Length (seconds) 0 5 10 15 20 25 30 35 40 45 50 55 60 65 70 75 80 85 90 95 100	
55.	1 (6)	
56.	1 (5)	
57.	2 (6)	
58.	2 2 2 2 2 (27)	
59.	2 2 2 2 (24)	
(fade-out)		
60.	3 3 3 3 (24)	*Preparing to dig the tunnel*
61.	X X X X (24)	
62.	X X X X X X X X X X X X X X X X X X X X X (117)	*Cartier goes down into the tunnel*
63.	2 2 (10)	
64.	1 1 1 (15)	
65.	X X X X X X (34)	
66.	1 (9)	
67.	3 (8)	
68.	2 2 2 2 2 2 2 (39)	*Rescuing Cartier*
69.	3 3 3 (16)	
70.	1 (5)	
71.	X X X X X X X (37)	
72.	X X X X X X X X X (49)	
(fade-out)		
73.	2 (7)	*Courtyard*
74.	X (3)	
75.	X X X X X X X X (41)	
76.	X X X X X X X X X X (59)	*Cartier at the barbed wire*
77.	X X X X X X X X X X X X (66)	*Gardening scene*
78.	X X X X X X X X X X X (57)	*Inspecting the costumes*
79.	X X X X X X X X X (46)	
80.	X X X X X X X (35)	
81.	X X (13)	
82.	X X X X (21)	*Maisonneuve in a dress*
(fade-out)		
83.	X X (11)	*Prison yard*
84.	3 (4)	
85.	X (6)	*German soldiers drill*
86.	X X X (19)	
87.	3 3 (11)	*The French work on their costumes*
88.	X X (12)	
89.	X X X X (22)	
90.	X X X X X (29)	
91.	2 (3)	
92.	X X X X X X (31)	
93.	3 (7)	
94.	2 (2)	
95.	2 2 2 (17)	
96.	2 (4)	
97.	1 (3)	

Appendix C

Shot no.	Length (seconds)	
98.	x x x (16)	
99.	x x x (16)	CU pan at the window
100.	x x x x x (29)	
	(fade-out)	
101.	x x x x x x x x x x x x (60)	Courtyard: Douaumont falls
102.	x x x (17)	
	(fade-out)	
103.	x x x x x x x x (43)	Musical revue
104.	x x x x x (29)	
105.	x (7)	
106.	x x x x (20)	
107.	x (7)	
108.	x x x x x (26)	
109.	x (9)	
110.	x x (14)	
111.	x x x (19)	
112.	x x (11)	
113.	1 1 (11)	
114.	x x (11)	
115.	x (2)	
116.	x (5)	
117.	x x (10)	Maréchal rushes onto the stage
118.	x (5)	
119.	x x x x x x x x x x x (60)	"La Marseillaise"
120.	x (8)	
	(fade-out)	
121.	x x x x x x x x x x x x x (65)	Maréchal in solitary confinement
122.	x x x x (20)	
	(fade-out)	
123.	2 2 2 2 2 2 2 2 2 2 2 2 2 2 2 2 2 2 2 2 2 (104)	Maréchal picks up the harmonica
124.	2 2 2 2 2 2 2 2 (40)	"Frou-Frou"
	(fade-out)	
125.	x x x x x x (38)	French quarters: Maréchal returns
126.	x x x x (23)	
127.	1 (5)	
	(fade-out/fade-in)	
128.	x x x x x x (34)	The last day
129.	1 (3)	
130.	x x x (18)	
(dissolve)		
131.	x x x x x x (30)	The French assemble to leave Hallbach
132.	x x (14)	
133.	x (6)	
134.	x (5)	
135.	x (4)	
136.	x (6)	

Breakdown of Shots

Shot **Length (seconds)**
no.   **0 5 10 15 20 25 30 35 40 45 50 55 60 65 70 75 80 85 90 95 100**

137.   xxxx (24)   Maréchal and an English officer
                     (dissolve)

German landscape (with dissolves)
138.   0 (5)
139.   0 (7)
140.   x x x (16)
141.   0 (4)
142.   0 (7)   "Alsheim"
143.   2 (7)
144.   0 (3)
145.   3 (9)
146.   0 (5)
147.   0 (8)   "Sente"
148.   x x (10)
149.   0 (6)
150.   0 (8)
151.   0 (5)   "Wintersborn"
                     (dissolve)

Wintersborn prison camp
152.   2 2 2 2 2 2 2 2 2 2 2 2 2 2 (73) Rauffenstein's quarters
153.   1 1 1 (15)
154.   2 2 (12)   Rauffenstein's office
155.   3 (8)
156.   x x x x x x x x x x (51)   Greeting the new prisoners
157.   1 1 (14)
158.   1 (3)
159.   1 (9)
160.   1 (3)
161.   1 (7)
162.   1 (6)
163.   1 1 (14)
164.   x x x (19)
165.   1 1 (10)
166.   x x x x x (26)
(dissolve)
167.   x x x (16)   Tour of Wintersborn
168.   x x x (19)
169.   x x x x x x x x x (54)
170.   x x x x x x x (41)
171.   x (6)
172.   x x x (21)
173.   x x x x x x (32)
174.   x x x x x x x x (40)
                     (fade-out)
175.   x x (10)   Snowball fight in the yard
176.   2 (7)   French quarters

Appendix C

Shot no.	Length (seconds) 0 5 10 15 20 25 30 35 40 45 50 55 60 65 70 75 80 85 90 95 100	
177.	1 (4)	
178.	1 1 1 (15)	
179.	x x x x x x x x x (49)	
180.	3 3 3 3 3 3 3 3 3 (47)	*Planning an escape*
	(dissolve)	
181.	x x x x x x (31)	*The room search*
182.	1 (7)	
183.	2 (2)	
184.	1 (3)	
185.	3 (6)	
186.	x x x x x x x x x x x x (62)	*Rauffenstein enters*
187.	3 (2)	
188.	1 (3)	
189.	x x x (19)	*Boeldieu & Rauffenstein: tête-à-tête*
190.	1 (7)	
191.	2 (4)	
192.	1 (4)	*Rauffenstein: "Peut-être"*
193.	2 (7)	
194.	x x x x x x x x x x x x x (65)	
	(fade-out)	
195.	2 2 2 (19)	*Rauffenstein's quarters: another tête-à-tête*
196.	2 2 2 (19)	
197.	1 (9)	
198.	1 (2)	
199.	1 1 1 1 1 1 (33)	
200.	1 (2)	
201.	1 (5)	
202.	1 1 (11)	
203.	1 1 (10)	
204.	1 (3)	
205.	1 (4)	
206.	1 (2)	
207.	1 (3)	
208.	1 (6)	
209.	1 (5)	
210.	1 (3)	
211.	1 (4)	
212.	1 (2)	
213.	1 (3)	
214.	1 (9)	*Boeldieu: "Peut-être"*
215.	2 2 (14)	
	(fade-out)	
216.	2 2 2 2 2 2 2 2 2 2 2 2 (65)	*Maréchal & Rosenthal together*
	(fade-out)	
217.	x x x x (22)	
218.	x x x x x x x x x (52)	*Russian quarters*

Shot no.	Length (seconds) 0–100	Scene
219.	x x x x (21)	
220.	x x x (15)	Book burning by the Russians
221.	x x (13)	
222.	x (4)	
223.	x (7)	
224.	x x x x x x x x x x x x (65)	Boeldieu's plan
	(dissolve)	
225.	2 2 2 2 2 2 2 2 2 2 (58)	French quarters: Boeldieu & Maréchal
	(dissolve)	
226.	2 2 2 2 2 2 2 (37)	Later, Boeldieu & Maréchal in their quarters
227.	3 3 3 3 3 3 3 3 3 3 (50)	
	(fade-out/fade-in)	
228.	0 (4)	The prison disturbance
229.	2 2 2 2 2 2 2 2 2 2 (50)	
230.	x x x x x (28)	
231.	x (8)	
232.	x (8)	
233.	x x x x x (27)	The French surrender their pennywhistles
234.	x x x x x x (31)	
235.	x (9)	
236.	2 (2)	
237.	2 (2)	
238.	2 (2)	
239.	2 (2)	
240.	x x (11)	
241.	x x (13)	
242.	x (9)	
243.	x x x x x x x x x x x x x (67)	Maréchal & Boeldieu part
(dissolve)		
244.	x x (14)	Courtyard: the roll call
245.	x (7)	
246.	x x (11)	
247.	2 2 (14)	
248.	x (8)	
249.	1 (5)	
250.	1 (7)	Boeldieu plays his pennywhistle
251.	1 (2)	
252.	1 (5)	
253.	1 (6)	
254.	x (5)	
255.	x (8)	
256.	x x (14)	
257.	1 1 1 (19)	Pursuit of Boeldieu
258.	x (8)	
259.	x (5)	
260.	1 1 1 (17)	

Appendix C

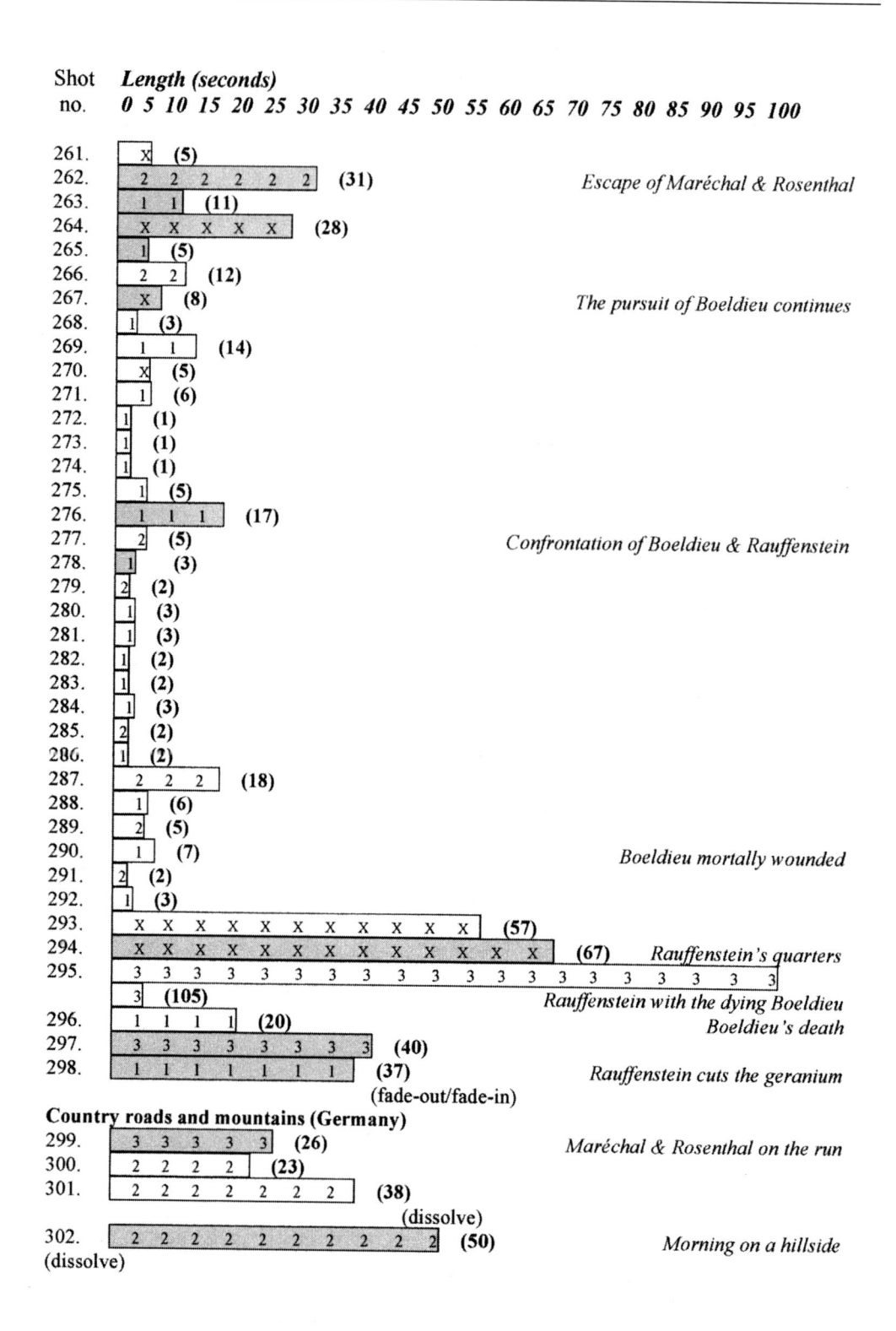

Shot no.	Length (seconds)	
261.	x (5)	
262.	2 2 2 2 2 2 (31)	Escape of Maréchal & Rosenthal
263.	1 1 (11)	
264.	x x x x x (28)	
265.	1 (5)	
266.	2 2 (12)	
267.	x (8)	The pursuit of Boeldieu continues
268.	1 (3)	
269.	1 1 (14)	
270.	x (5)	
271.	1 (6)	
272.	1 (1)	
273.	1 (1)	
274.	1 (1)	
275.	1 (5)	
276.	1 1 1 (17)	
277.	2 (5)	Confrontation of Boeldieu & Rauffenstein
278.	1 (3)	
279.	2 (2)	
280.	1 (3)	
281.	1 (3)	
282.	1 (2)	
283.	1 (2)	
284.	1 (3)	
285.	2 (2)	
286.	1 (2)	
287.	2 2 2 (18)	
288.	1 (6)	
289.	2 (5)	
290.	1 (7)	Boeldieu mortally wounded
291.	2 (2)	
292.	1 (3)	
293.	x x x x x x x x x x x (57)	
294.	x x x x x x x x x x x x x (67)	Rauffenstein's quarters
295.	3 3 3 3 3 3 3 3 3 3 3 3 3 3 3 3 3 3 3 3 3 (105)	Rauffenstein with the dying Boeldieu
296.	1 1 1 1 (20)	Boeldieu's death
297.	3 3 3 3 3 3 3 3 (40)	
298.	1 1 1 1 1 1 1 (37)	Rauffenstein cuts the geranium
	(fade-out/fade-in)	

Country roads and mountains (Germany)

299.	3 3 3 3 3 (26)	Maréchal & Rosenthal on the run
300.	2 2 2 2 (23)	
301.	2 2 2 2 2 2 2 (38)	
	(dissolve)	
302.	2 2 2 2 2 2 2 2 2 (50)	Morning on a hillside

(dissolve)

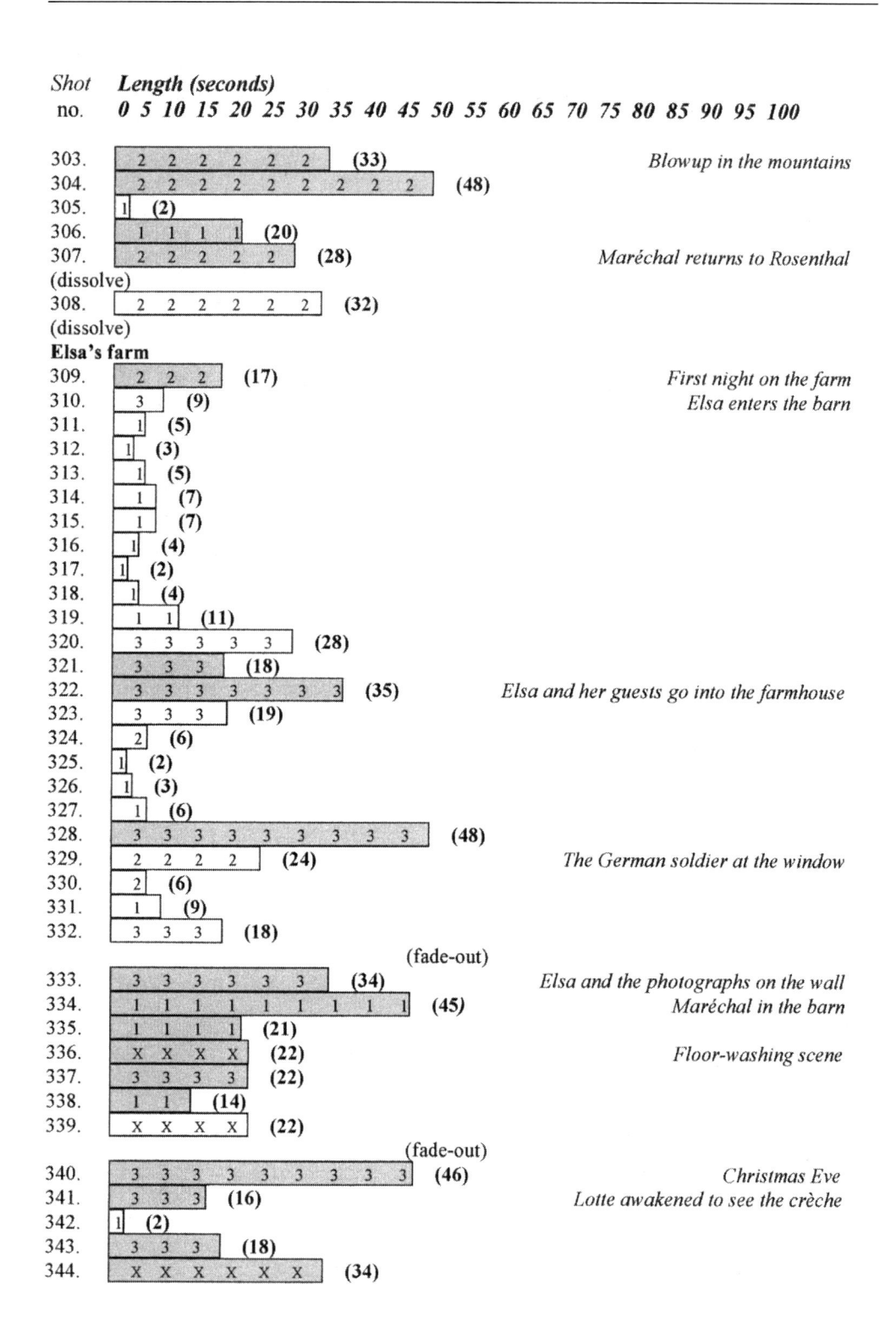

Shot **Length (seconds)**
no.   0 5 10 15 20 25 30 35 40 45 50 55 60 65 70 75 80 85 90 95 100

Shot	Bar data	Scene
303.	2 2 2 2 2 2 (33)	Blowup in the mountains
304.	2 2 2 2 2 2 2 2 2 (48)	
305.	1 (2)	
306.	1 1 1 1 (20)	
307.	2 2 2 2 2 (28)	Maréchal returns to Rosenthal
(dissolve)		
308.	2 2 2 2 2 2 (32)	
(dissolve)		

Elsa's farm

Shot	Bar data	Scene
309.	2 2 2 (17)	First night on the farm
310.	3 (9)	Elsa enters the barn
311.	1 (5)	
312.	1 (3)	
313.	1 (5)	
314.	1 (7)	
315.	1 (7)	
316.	1 (4)	
317.	1 (2)	
318.	1 (4)	
319.	1 1 (11)	
320.	3 3 3 3 3 (28)	
321.	3 3 3 (18)	
322.	3 3 3 3 3 3 (35)	Elsa and her guests go into the farmhouse
323.	3 3 3 (19)	
324.	2 (6)	
325.	1 (2)	
326.	1 (3)	
327.	1 (6)	
328.	3 3 3 3 3 3 3 3 (48)	
329.	2 2 2 2 (24)	The German soldier at the window
330.	2 (6)	
331.	1 (9)	
332.	3 3 3 (18)	
	(fade-out)	
333.	3 3 3 3 3 3 (34)	Elsa and the photographs on the wall
334.	1 1 1 1 1 1 1 1 1 (45)	Maréchal in the barn
335.	1 1 1 1 (21)	
336.	X X X X (22)	Floor-washing scene
337.	3 3 3 3 (22)	
338.	1 1 (14)	
339.	X X X X (22)	
	(fade-out)	
340.	3 3 3 3 3 3 3 3 3 (46)	Christmas Eve
341.	3 3 3 (16)	Lotte awakened to see the crèche
342.	1 (2)	
343.	3 3 3 (18)	
344.	X X X X X X (34)	

Appendix C

Shot no.	Length (seconds)		
	0 5 10 15 20 25 30 35 40 45 50 55 60 65 70 75 80 85 90 95 100		

345. x x x x x x x (38) — Maréchal: "Lotte hat blaue Augen"
346. 3 3 3 3 3 3 3 3 3 3 3 (55)
347. 3 3 3 3 3 3 3 3 (43) — Maréchal & Elsa embrace
(fade-out)
348. 0 (4) — Christmas morning
349. 1 1 (12)
350. 3 3 3 3 (20)
351. 1 (6)
352. 1 (9) — Elsa: "Le café est prêt"
(fade-out/fade-in)
353. 2 2 2 (18) — Maréchal & Rosenthal prepare to leave
354. 3 3 3 3 3 3 3 3 (41)
355. x x x x x x (32)
356. 2 (4)
357. 2 (6)
358. 2 2 2 2 2 2 2 2 2 2 2 (56) — Maréchal comforts Elsa
(dissolve)
359. x x x x (20) — The last night on the farm
360. 2 (5) — Maréchal: "Lotte hat blaue Augen"
361. 1 (4)
362. x x x x (20) — The two men leave
363. 2 (6)
364. 2 (6)
365. 2 2 2 (19) — Elsa & Lotte alone on the farm
(fade-out/fade-in)

The border (Germany & Switzerland)
366. 0 0 0 (15) — Near the border
367. 2 2 2 2 2 2 2 2 2 2 2 (58) — Maréchal & Rosenthal goodbyes
368. 2 2 (12)
369. x x x x x (25) — The German patrol
370. 2 (6)
371. x x (14) — Maréchal & Rosenthal in Switzerland
372. 2 2 2 (18)
(fade-out)

End credit
373. 0 (6) — FIN
(fade-out)

*   *   *   *   *

Filmography of Jean Renoir
(Dates are the release years)

Catherine. 1924; released as *Une Vie sans joie* in 1927.
   Co-director: Albert Dieudonné (Jean Renoir uncredited). Scenarist (Sc): Renoir & Pierre Lestringuez. Director of Photography (DP): Jean Bachelet & Alphonse Gibory. Cast: Catherine Hessling (Catherine), Albert Dieudonné (Maurice), Jean Renoir (the sub-prefect).

La Fille de l'eau. 1924.
   Sc: Pierre Lestringuez. DP: Jean Bachelet & Alphonse Gibory. Cast: Catherine Hessling (Viriginia), Pierre Lestringuez (Uncle Jef), Harold Lewingston (Georges Reynal).

Nana. 1926.
   Sc: Pierre Lestringuez. DP: Edmund Corwin & Jean Bachelet. Cast: Catherine Hessling (Nana), Werner Krauss (Count Muffat), Jean Angleo (Count de Vandeuvres), Pierre Lestringuez (Bordenave).

Sur un air de Charleston (short). 1927.
   Sc: Pierre Lestringuez. DP: Jean Bachelet. Cast: Catherine Hessling (The Dancer), Johnny Huggins (The Explorer).

Marquitta. 1927.
   Sc: Pierre Lestringuez. DP: Jean Bachelet & Raymond Agnel. Cast: Marie-Louise Iribe (Marquitta), Jean Angelo (Prince Vlasco).

La Petite Marchande d'allumettes (short). 1928.
   Co-director: Jean Tedesco. Sc: Jean Renoir. DP: Jean Bachelet. Cast: Catherine Hessling (Karen), Jean Storm (Young Man/Wooden Soldier), Manuel Raaby (Policeman/Death), Amy Wells (Mechanical Doll).

Tire au flanc. 1928.
   Sc: Renoir, Claude Heymann & André Cerf. DP: Jean Bachelet. Cast: Georges Pomiès (Jean Dubois d'Ombelles), Michel Simon (Joseph), Fridette Fatton (Georgette), Félix Oudart (Colonel Brochard).

Le Tournoi dans la cité. 1928.
   Sc: Henry Dupuy-Mazuel & André Jaeger-Schmidt. DP: Marcel Lucien & Maurice Desfassiaux. Cast: Aldo Nadi (François de Baynes), Jackie Monnier (Isabelle Ginori), Enrique Rivero (Henri de Rogier).

Le Bled. 1929.
   Sc: Henry Dupuy-Mazuel & André Jaeger-Schmidt. DP: Marcel Lucien & Léon Morizet. Cast: Jackie Monnier (Claudie Duvernet), Enrique Rivero (Pierre Hoffer), Manuel Raaby (Manuel Duvernet).

On purge bébé. 1931.

Sc: Renoir & Pierre Prévert. DP: Théodore Sparkuhl & Roger Hubert. Cast: Jacques Louvigny (Follavoine), Marguerite Pierry (Julie Follavoine), Sacha Tarride (Toto), Michel Simon (Chouilloux).

La Chienne. 1931.

Sc: Renoir & André Girard. DP: Théodore Sparkuhl. Cast: Michel Simon (Maurice Legrand), Janie Marèse (Lulu), Georges Flamant (Dédé), Magdeleine Bérubet (Adèle Legrand).

La Nuit du carrefour. 1932.

Sc: Jean Renoir. DP: Marcel Lucien & Georges Asselin. Cast: Pierre Renoir (Inspector Maigret), Georges Térof (Lucas), Winna Winfried (Else Andersen), Georges Koudria (Carl Andersen).

Boudu sauvé des eaux. 1932.

Sc: Jean Renoir. DP: Marcel Lucien. Cast: Michel Simon (Boudu), Charles Granval (M. Lestingois), Marcelle Hainia (Mme. Lestingois), Séverine Lerczinska (Anne-Marie).

Chotard et cie. 1933.

Sc: Jean Renoir. DP: Joseph-Louis Mundwiller. Cast: Fernand Charpin (François Chotard), Georges Pomiès (Julien Collinet), Jeanne Boitel (Reine Chotard).

Madame Bovary. 1934.

Sc: Jean Renoir. DP: Jean Bachelet. Cast: Valentine Tessier (Emma Bovary), Pierre Renoir (Charles Bovary), Max Dearly (M. Homais), Fernand Fabre (Rodolphe).

Toni. 1935.

Sc: Renoir & Carl Einstein. DP: Claude Renoir. Cast: Charles Blavette (Toni), Jenny Hélia (Marie), Celia Montalvan (Josefa), Max Dalban (Albert).

Le Crime de Monsieur Lange. 1936.

Sc: Renoir & Jacques Prévert. DP: Jean Bachelet. Cast: René Lefèvre (Amédée Lange), Jules Berry (Batala), Florelle (Valentine), Nadia Sibirskaïa (Estelle), Sylvia Bataille (Edith).

La Vie est à nous. 1936.

Principal co-directors (collective): Jean-Paul Le Chanois, Jacques Becker, Pierre Unik & Jacques Brunius. Sc: Renoir, Le Chanois, Becker, & Zwoboda. DP: Louis Page, Jean-Serge Bourgoin, Jean Isnard, Alain Douarinou & Claude Renoir. Cast: Jean Dasté (Teacher), Charles Blavette (Tonin), Gaston Modot (Philippe), Julien Bertheau (René).

Partie de campagne. 1936; released in 1946.

Sc: Jean Renoir. DP: Claude Renoir. Cast: Sylvia Bataille (Henriette Dufour), Georges Darnoux (Henri), Jane Marken (Madame Dufour), Jacques Brunius (Rodolphe), Jean Renoir (Poulain), Marguerite Renoir (servant), Alain Renoir (boy on bridge).

Les Bas-Fonds. 1936.

Sc: Renoir, Charles Spaak, Yevgeni Zamyatin & Jacques Companeez. DP: Fedote Bourgasoff & Jean Bachelet. Cast: Jean Gabin (Pépel), Louis Jouvet (The Baron), Junie Astor (Natacha), Suzy Prim (Vassilissa), Valdimir Sokoloff (Kostilev).

La Grande Illusion. 1937.

Sc: Renoir & Charles Spaak. DP: Christian Matras. Cast: Jean Gabin (Maréchal), Marcel

Dalio (Rosenthal), Pierre Fresnay (Boeldieu), Erich von Stroheim (Rauffenstein), Dita Parlo (Elsa), Julien Carette (Cartier).

La Marseillaise. 1938.
   Sc: Renoir, Carl Koch & Nina Martel-Dreyfus. DP: Jean-Serge Bourgoin, Alain Douarinou, Jean-Marie Maillols, Jean-Paul Alphen & Jean Louis. Cast: Pierre Renoir (Louis XVI), Edmond Ardisson (Bomier), Andrex (Arnaud), Nadia Sibirskaïa (Louison), Louis Jouvet (Roederer).

La Bête humaine. 1938.
   Sc: Jean Renoir. DP: Curt Courant. Cast: Jean Gabin (Jacques Lantier), Simone Simon (Séverine), Fernand Ledoux (Roubaud), Julien Carette (Pecqueux), Jean Renoir (Cabuche).

La Règle du jeu. 1939.
   Sc: Renoir & Carl Koch. DP: Jean Bachelet. Cast: Marcel Dalio (Robert de la Cheyniest), Nora Grégor (Christine), Roland Toutain (André Jurieux), Jean Renoir (Octave), Mila Parély (Geneviève), Gaston Modot (Schumacher), Paulette Dubost (Lisette), Julien Carette (Marceau).

Swamp Water. 1941.
   Sc: Dudley Nichols. DP: J. Peverell Marley & Lucien Ballard. Cast: Dana Andrews (Ben Ragan), Walter Brennan (Tom Keefer), Walter Huston (Thursday Ragan), Anne Baxter (Julie Keefer).

This Land Is Mine. 1943.
   Sc: Renoir & Dudley Nichols. DP: Frank Redman. Cast: Charles Laughton (Albert Lory), Maureen O'Hara (Louise Martin), George Sanders (George Lambert), Walter Slezak (Major von Keller).

Salute to France (short). 1944.
   Co-director: Garson Kanin. Sc: Renoir, Philip Dunne & Burgess Meredith. DP: George Webber. Cast: Garson Kanin (Joe), Burgess Meredith (Tommy), Claude Dauphin (Narrator and various Frenchmen).

The Southerner. 1945.
   Sc: Jean Renoir. DP: Lucien Andriot. Cast: Zachary Scott (Sam Tucker), Betty Field (Nona Tucker), Beulah Bondi (Grandma), J. Carrol Naish (Devers).

The Diary of a Chambermaid. 1946.
   Sc: Renoir & Burgess Meredith. DP: Lucien Andriot. Cast: Paulette Goddard (Célestine), Burgess Meredith (Captain Mauger), Hurd Hatfield (Georges Lanlaire), Francis Lederer (Joseph), Judith Anderson (Mme. Lanlaire).

The Woman on the Beach. 1947.
   Sc: Renoir & Frank Davis. DP: Harry J. Wild & Leo Tover. Cast: Robert Ryan (Scott Burnett), Joan Bennett (Peggy Butler), Charles Bickford (Tod Butler), Nan Leslie (Eve Geddes).

The River. 1951.
   Sc: Renoir & Rumer Godden. DP: Claude Renoir. Cast: Patricia Walters (Harriet), Thomas E. Breen (Captain John), Radha Sri Ram (Melanie), Adrienne Corri (Valerie), Arthur Shields (Mr. John).

The Golden Coach. 1953.
Sc: Renoir, Jack Kirkland, Renzo Avanzo, Giulio Macchi & Ginette Doynel. DP: Claude Renoir & Ronald Hill. Cast: Anna Magnani (Camilla), Duncan Lamont (The Viceroy), Riccardo Rioli (Ramon), Paul Campbell (Felipe).

French Cancan. 1955.
Sc: Jean Renoir. DP: Michel Kelber. Cast: Jean Gabin (Danglard), Maria Félix (Lola), Françoise Arnoul (Nini), Jean-Roger Caussimon (Baron Walter), Giani Esposito (Prince Alexandre).

Elena et les hommes. 1956.
Sc: Jean Renoir. DP: Claude Renoir. Cast: Ingrid Bergman (Princess Elena), Jean Marais (Général Rollan), Mel Ferrer (Henri de Chevincourt), Pierre Bertin (Martin-Michaud).

Le Testament du Docteur Cordelier. 1959.
Sc: Jean Renoir. DP: Georges Leclerc. Cast: Jean-Louis Barrault (Dr. Cordelier/Opale), Teddy Bilis (Maître Joly), Michel Vitold (Dr. Séverin).

Le Déjeuner sur l'herbe. 1959.
Sc: Jean Renoir. DP: Georges Leclerc. Cast: Paul Meurisse (Prof. Alexis), Catherine Rouvel (Nénette), Fernand Sardou (Nino), Charles Blavette (Gaspard).

Le Caporal épinglé. 1962.
Sc: Renoir & Guy Lefranc. DP: Georges Leclerc. Cast: Jean-Pierre Cassel (The Corporal), Claude Brasseur (Papa), Claude Rich (Ballochet), Cornelia Froboess (Erika).

Le Petit Théâtre de Jean Renoir. 1969.
Sc: Jean Renoir. DP: Georges Leclerc. Cast: Jean Renoir (The Presenter); Nino Formicola & Milly Monti (tramps); Marguerite Cassan (Émilie) & Pierre Olaf (Gustave); Jeanne Moreau (The Singer); Fernand Sardou (M. Duvallier) & Françoise Arnoul (Mme. Duvallier).

Chapter Notes

Acknowledgments

1. Jean Renoir, "Introduction" in "Jean Renoir's *Grand Illusion*," DVD (USA: The Criterion Collection, 1999).

Preface

1. Orson Welles, on "Jean Renoir's *Grand Illusion*." Publicity postcard for Canal+ Image International, Janus Films and Rialto Pictures (USA: 1-800-Postcards, 1999).

2. Jean Renoir, *My Life and My Films*, trans. Norman Denny (London: William Collins Sons & Co., Ltd., 1974), 141.

Chapter 1

1. When dialogue or written words from the film are quoted in the text, they are transcribed directly and the English translation (in parentheses) is by the author; in addition, all shot descriptions and timings (rounded to the nearest second) are based on the 1999 DVD of the film (The Criterion Collection).

Chapter 2

1. Wallace Stevens, "Thirteen Ways of Looking at a Blackbird," in *Harmonium* (New York: Alfred A. Knopf, 1923), 135–7.

2. Leonard Bernstein, *Findings* (New York: Simon and Schuster, 1982), 218. Tribute to John F. Kennedy at United Jewish Appeal benefit, Madison Square Garden, New York City, on November 25, 1963.

Chapter 3

1. For the title credits, and a list of uncredited actors, see Appendix A.

Chapter 4

1. See Appendix C for a graph of those 373 shots; this visual representation gives a sense of the pace and diversity of shots.

Chapter 5

1. Renoir, *My Life and My Films*, 57.
2. Ibid., 157.
3. André Bazin, *Jean Renoir*, trans. W.W. Halsey II and William H. Simon (New York: Simon and Schuster, 1973), 90.
4. Alexander Sesonske, *Jean Renoir: The French Films, 1924–1939* (Cambridge, Massachusetts: Harvard University Press, 1980), 312.
5. Penelope Gilliatt, *Jean Renoir: Essays, Conversations, Reviews* (New York, St. Louis and San Francisco: McGraw-Hill Paperbacks, 1975), 9.

Chapter 6

1. This image reminds me of the horrifying long shot in Leni Riefenstahl's 1935 *Triumph des Willens* (*Triumph of the Will*) as Hitler and two prominent aides, also unmatched in their uniforms and hats, stride out of step, surrounded by massed troops. In *La Grande Illusion*, the effect is of course much lighter, but similar implications darken the scene.

Chapter 8

1. Renoir, *My Life and My Films*, 145.
2. William Wordsworth, "Preface" to *Lyrical Ballads*, in *Wordsworth and Coleridge: Lyrical Ballads*, ed. R.L. Brett and A.R. Jones (London and New York: Routledge Classics, 2008), 307.

Chapter 11

1 There is even Blue Mimi, the thoroughbred filly ridden by Rauffenstein to victory in the Prince of Wales Cup, as remembered by Boeldieu; her hollowed-out hoof appears to serve them as an ashtray.

2. Verdun, during its lengthy siege in World War I, was surrounded by a group of forts, including Fort Douaumont. Thus Elsa's loss is subliminally linked to her countrymen's earlier celebration (at least for those aware of the connection). And Hindenburg, honored by Rauffenstein's improvised altar, was a hero of Tannenberg.

3. Jean Renoir, *Renoir, My Father*, trans. Randolph and Dorothy Weaver (Boston: Little, Brown and Company, 1962), 294.

Chapter 12

1. This story is related in the preface of Sesonske's *Jean Renoir: The French Films*.
2. Ibid., 322.

Chapter 13

1. Gilliatt, *Jean Renoir*, 6.
2. This bit of information and some other details in this chapter are contained in Olivier Curchod's important study, *La Grande Illusion: Jean Renoir* (Ligugé, Poitiers: Éditions Nathan, 1994), which was updated slightly in 1998.
3. One photograph of Pinsard shows similarities to Boeldieu, as portrayed by Fresnay — a whiff of superiority in his bored gaze, a mustache (though a much fuller one) and a similar insignia on his collar.
4. Françoise Giroud vividly told this story in "Souvenirs," as translated in Sesonske's *Jean Renoir: The French Films*, 319.
5. Renoir, *My Life and My Films*, 142.
6. Ibid., 233.
7. Ibid., 94.

Chapter 14

1. The quotes from the treatment that follow in this chapter are from "An Early Treatment of *Grand Illusion*" in Bazin's *Jean Renoir*, 172–82.
2. There's a similar line in *La Grande Illusion* as they hide in the barn and hear Elsa approaching; Rosenthal urges Maréchal to escape and leave him to deal with the threat. It is, however, barely audible and Renoir makes nothing of it.
3. Bazin, *Jean Renoir*, 172.
4. Jean Renoir, "Introduction" in "Jean Renoir's *Grand Illusion*," DVD.
5. Digby Diehl, "Directors Go to Their Movies: Jean Renoir,"*Action*, vol. 7, no. 3 (May–June 1972): 8.

Chapter 15

1. Curchod's study includes an interesting and informative section, "Les trois scénarios de *La Grande Illusion*," which outlines changes from the treatment to the continuity scenario with dialogue (September–October 1936) to the final technical scenario that details shots (November–December 1936).
2. Jean Renoir, "La Grande Illusion: Jean Renoir," *l'Avant-Scène du Cinéma*, No. 44 (January 1, 1965): 8–42.
3. Diehl, "Directors Go to Their Movies," 5.

Chapter 16

1. Renoir, *My Life and My Films*, 152.
2. Jean Renoir, "M. RENOIR SPEAKS OF WAR," *New York Times*, October 23, 1938, section 9.

Chapter 17

1. John Wakeman, ed., *World Film Directors: Volume I, 1890–1945* (New York: The H.W. Wilson Company, 1987), 930.
2. Diehl, "Directors Go to Their Movies," 8.
3. Satyajit Ray, "Renoir in Calcutta," in *Great Film Directors*, ed. Leo Braudy and Morris Dickstein (New York: Oxford University Press, 1978), 643.
4. Erich von Stroheim, "My First Meeting with Jean Renoir," in *Grand Illusion: a film by Jean Renoir*, trans. Marianne Alexandre and Andrew Sinclair (New York: Simon and Schuster, 1968), 10.
5. Eugene Lourie, *My Work in Films* (San Diego and New York: Harcourt Brace Jovanovich, 1985), 30.
6. This translated quote from Giroud's "Souvenirs" is in Sesonske's *Jean Renoir: The French Films*, 322.
7. Renoir, *My Life and My Films*, 265.

Chapter 18

1. Jean Renoir, *Letters*, ed. David Thompson and Lorraine LoBianco (London: Faber and Faber, 1994), 39.
2. Georges Altman, "Franc-Tireur, 29 août 1946," *l'Avant-Scène du Cinéma*, No. 44 (January 1, 1965): 43.
3. Marc Ferro, *Cinema and History*, trans. Naomi Greene (Detroit: Wayne State University Press, 1988), 135–6.
4. Roy Armes, *French Cinema* (New York: Oxford University Press, 1985), 106.
5. Martin O'Shaughnessy, *La Grande Illusion (Jean Renoir, 1937)* (London and New York: I.B. Tauris & Co Ltd, 2009), 3.
6. James Kerans, "Classics Revisited: 'La Grande Illusion,'" *Film Quarterly*, Vol. 14, No. 2 (Winter 1960): 13, 15.
7. Peter Harcourt, *Six European Directors* (Harmondsworth, UK and Baltimore: Penguin Books Ltd., 1974), 93.
8. François Truffaut, "*La Grande Illusion* de Jean Renoir est d'une brûlante actualité," *Arts*, No. 691 (October 8–14, 1958): 7.
9. Bazin, *Jean Renoir*, 7–9.
10. The quotes about *La Grande Illusion* that follow are from Truffaut's entry in the filmography of Bazin's *Jean Renoir*, 248–9.
11. Ibid., 257.
12. Robert Hughes, ed., *Film: Book 2— Films of*

Peace and War (New York: Grove Press, Inc., 1962), 189.
   13. François Truffaut, *The Films in My Life*, trans. Leonard Mayhew (New York: Simon & Schuster, 1978), 39.
   14. The quotes that follow are from the "Préface" by François Truffaut in Jean Renoir's *La Grande Illusion: Jean Renoir*, ed. Gérard Vaugeois (Nantes: Balland, 1974), 7–13.

Chapter 19

1. Renoir, *My Life and My Films*, 282.
2. Renoir, *Renoir, My Father*, 275.
3. Renoir, Ibid., 276.
4. Renoir, *My Life and My Films*, 37.
5. Renoir, *Renoir, My Father*, 327.
6. Ibid., 357.
7. Ibid., 394.
8. Renoir, *My Life and My Films*, 24.
9. Ibid., 25–6.
10. Ibid., 33.
11. Renoir, *Renoir, My Father*, 337.
12. Renoir, *My Life and My Films*, 30.
13. Renoir, *Renoir, My Father*, 3.
14. Ibid., 451.
15. Renoir, *My Life and My Films*, 47.
16. Ronald Bergan, *Jean Renoir: Projections of Paradise* (Woodstock, NY: The Overlook Press, 1995), 46.
17. Renoir, *Renoir, My Father*, 5.
18. Ibid., 6.
19. Ibid., 21.
20. Renoir, *My Life and My Films*, 47.
21. Renoir, *Renoir, My Father*, 457.
22. Ibid., 220.
23. Ibid., 443.
24. Renoir, *My Life and My Films*, 90.
25. Ibid., 199.
26. Bazin, *Jean Renoir*, 263.
27. Renoir, *My Life and My Films*, 191.
28. Ibid., 199.
29. Bergan, *Jean Renoir*, 327.
30. Ibid., 247.
31. Bazin, *Jean Renoir*, 273.
32. Renoir, *My Life and My Films*, 247.

Chapter 20

1. Truffaut, *The Films in My Life*, 42.

Chapter 22

1. Although his comment about *La Grande Illusion* was apparently not a direct quote taken from Welles, it probably comes from an appearance on The Dick Cavett Show on July 27, 1970. Cavett asked Welles to name two films he would save for posterity on an hypothetical ark. He hesitated, before blurting out: "Two films, *Grande Illusion*, of Renoir...and uh...uh...something else." Even though he soon reverted to being mischievous by pretending that "*Something Else*" was a film by James Cruze, his initial, unfiltered response is a sincere homage to Renoir's film. ["The Dick Cavett Show: Hollywood Greats," DVD (USA: Daphne Productions, Inc., 2006) http://www.youtube.com/watch?v=YjfaIGFwmUA (accessed October 10, 2010).]
   2. Orson Welles, "Jean Renoir: 'the Greatest of All Directors,'" *Los Angeles Times*, February 18, 1979, Part V.
   3. Virginia Woolf, "The Cinema," in *The Captain's Death Bed and Other Essays* (San Diego and New York: Harcourt Brace Jovanovich, Inc., 1950/1978), 186. Originally published in *Arts* (June 1926).
   4. Ibid., 183.
   5. Gilliatt, *Jean Renoir*, 30.
   6. Rui Nogueira and François Truchaud, "Interview with Jean Renoir," *Sight & Sound*, Vol. 37, No. 2 (Spring 1968): 59.
   7. Marcel Proust, *In Search of Lost Time* (Volume V: *The Captive* and *The Fugitive*), trans. C.K. Scott Moncrieff and Terence Kilmartin, rev. D.J. Enright (New York: The Modern Library, 1993), 344.
   8. Renoir, *My Life and My Films*, 123.
   9. Diehl, "Directors Go to Their Movies," 5.
   10. Arthur Schopenhauer, *The World as Will and Representation* (Volume 1), trans. E.F.J. Payne (New York: Dover Publications, Inc., 1966), 261.
   11. Walter Pater, "The School of Giorgione," in *The Renaissance* (New York: Random House/The Modern Library, 1924), 110.
   12. Woolf, "The Cinema," 182.
   13. Pater, "The School of Giorgione," 111.
   14. Ibid., 114.
   15. Woolf, "The Cinema," 184–5.
   16. Schopenhauer, *The World as Will and Representation*, 262.
   17. Woolf, "The Cinema," 184.
   18. Ibid.
   19. Schopenhauer, *The World as Will and Representation*, 256.
   20. Felix Mendelssohn, "To Marc-André Souchay, Lübeck [Berlin, October 15th, 1842]" in *Letters of Felix Mendelssohn Bartholdy, from 1833 to 1847*, ed. Paul Mendelssohn Bartholdy and Dr. Carl Mendelssohn Bartholdy, trans. Lady Wallace (Freeport, NY: Books for Libraries Press, 1970), 269–70.

Chapter 23

1. Though some of these directors worked on more than one film with Renoir, only the earliest collaboration is noted in parentheses.

Bibliography

Altman, Georges. "Franc-Tireur, 29 août 1946." *l'Avant-Scène du Cinéma*, No. 44 (January 1, 1965): 43.

Armes, Roy. *French Cinema*. New York: Oxford University Press, 1985.

Bazin, André. *Jean Renoir*. Translated by W. W. Halsey II and William H. Simon. New York: Simon and Schuster, 1973.

Bergan, Ronald. *Jean Renoir: Projections of Paradise*. Woodstock, NY: Overlook Press, 1995.

Bernstein, Leonard. *Findings*. New York: Simon and Schuster, 1982.

Cowie, Peter. Insert. In "Jean Renoir's *Grand Illusion*" (DVD). USA: The Criterion Collection, 1999.

Curchod, Olivier. *La Grande Illusion: Jean Renoir*. Ligugé, Poitiers: Éditions Nathan, 1994.

Davis, Colin. *Scenes of Love and Murder: Renoir, Film and Philosophy*. London and New York: Wallflower Press, 2009.

Delahaye, Michel, and Jean-André Fieschi. "My Next Films: Interview with Jean Renoir." *Cahiers du Cinema in English*, No. 9 (March 1967): 40–52.

Diehl, Digby. "Directors Go to Their Movies: Jean Renoir." *Action*, vol. 7, no. 3 (May–June 1972): 2–8.

Faulkner, Christopher. *Jean Renoir: A Conversation with His Films 1894–1979*. Edited by Paul Duncan. Köln: Taschen, 2007.

_____. *Jean Renoir, a guide to references and resources*. Boston: G.K. Hall & Co., 1979.

_____. *The Social Cinema of Jean Renoir*. Princeton: Princeton University Press, 1986.

Ferro, Marc. *Cinema and History*. Translated by Naomi Greene. Detroit: Wayne State University Press, 1988.

Gilliatt, Penelope. *Jean Renoir: Essays, Conversations, Reviews*. New York, St. Louis and San Francisco: McGraw-Hill Paperbacks, 1975.

"Grand Illusion: Story." In *Janus Films Catalogue*, n.p. New York: Janus Films, Inc., 1973.

Harcourt, Peter. *Six European Directors*. Harmondsworth, UK, and Baltimore: Penguin Books, 1974.

Hughes, Robert, ed. *Film: Book 1—The Audience and the Filmmaker*. New York: Grove Press, 1959.

_____. *Film: Book 2—Films of Peace and War*. New York: Grove Press, 1962.

Jackson, Julian. *La Grande Illusion*. London: Palgrave Macmillan, 2009.

Kaplan, Alice Yaeger. *Relevé des Sources et Citations dans* Bagatelles pour un massacre. Tusson: Éditions du lérot, 1987.

Kauffmann, Stanley. *Living Images*. New York: Harper & Row, 1975.

Kerans, James. "Classics Revisited: 'La Grande Illusion.'" *Film Quarterly*, Vol. 14, no. 2 (Winter 1960): 10–17.

Leprohon, Pierre. *Jean Renoir*. Translated by Brigid Elson. New York: Crown Publishers, 1971.

Lourie, Eugene. *My Work in Films*. San Diego and New York: Harcourt Brace Jovanovich, 1985.

Marcorelles, Louis. "Conversation with Jean Renoir." *Sight & Sound*, Vol. 31, No. 2 (Spring 1962): 78–83, 103.

Mendelssohn, Felix. "To Marc-André Souchay, Lübeck [Berlin, October 15th, 1842]." In *Letters of Felix Mendelssohn Bartholdy, from 1833 to 1847*, edited by Paul Mendelssohn Bartholdy and Dr. Carl Mendelssohn Bartholdy, translated by Lady Wallace, 269–70. Freeport, NY: Books for Libraries Press, 1970.

Montgomery, Paul. "Jean Renoir, Director of 'Grand Illusion' Film, Dies." *New York Times*, February 14, 1979, D19.

Nogueira, Rui, and François Truchaud. "Interview with Jean Renoir." *Sight & Sound*, Vol. 37, No. 2 (Spring 1968): 56–62.

O'Shaughnessy, Martin. *La Grande Illusion (Jean Renoir, 1937)*. London and New York: I.B. Tauris, 2009.

_____. *Jean Renoir*. Manchester and New York: Manchester University Press, 2000.

Pater, Walter. "The School of Giorgione." In *The Renaissance*, 107–27. New York: Random House/Modern Library, 1924.

Proust, Marcel. *In Search of Lost Time*. Translated by C.K. Scott Moncrieff and Terence Kilmartin, revised by D.J. Enright. New York: Modern Library, 1993.

Ray, Satyajit. "Renoir in Calcutta." In *Great Film Directors*, edited by Leo Braudy and Morris Dickstein, 638–43. New York: Oxford University Press, 1978.

Renoir, Jean. *Grand Illusion: A Film by Jean Renoir*. Translated by Marianne Alexandre and Andrew Sinclair. New York: Simon and Schuster, 1968.

———. "La Grande Illusion: Jean Renoir." *l'Avant-Scène du Cinéma*, No. 44 (January 1, 1965): 8–42.

———. *La Grande Illusion: Jean Renoir*. Edited by Gérard Vaugeois. Nantes: Balland, 1974.

———. *An Interview: Jean Renoir*. Copenhagen: Green Integer Books, 1998.

———. "Introduction." In "Jean Renoir's *Grand Illusion*" (DVD). USA: The Criterion Collection, 1999. http://www.youtube.com/watch?v=l63xhUUZOH8 (accessed October 22, 2010).

———. "Jean Renoir's *Grand Illusion*" (DVD). USA: Criterion Collection, 1999.

———. *Letters*. Edited by David Thompson and Lorraine LoBianco. London: Faber and Faber, 1994.

———. "M. Renoir Speaks of War." *New York Times*, October 23, 1938, section 9.

———. *My Life and My Films*. Translated by Norman Denny. London: William Collins Sons, 1974.

———. *Renoir, My Father*. Translated by Randolph and Dorothy Weaver. Boston: Little, Brown, 1962.

———. *Renoir on Renoir: Interviews, Essays, and Remarks*. Translated by Carol Volk. New York: Cambridge University Press, 1989.

Schopenhauer, Arthur. *The World as Will and Representation*. Translated by E.F.J. Payne. New York: Dover Publications, 1966.

Serceau, Daniel. *Jean Renoir, l'insurgé*. Paris: Le Sycomore, 1981.

Sesonske, Alexander. *Jean Renoir: The French Films, 1924–1939*. Cambridge, MA: Harvard University Press, 1980.

———. "Renoir: A Progress Report." *Cinema*, Vol. 6, No. 1 (1969): 16–20.

Stevens, Wallace. "Thirteen Ways of Looking at a Blackbird." In *Harmonium*, 135–7. New York: Alfred A. Knopf, 1923.

Stroheim, Erich von. "My First Meeting with Jean Renoir." In *Grand Illusion: a film by Jean Renoir*, translated by Marianne Alexandre and Andrew Sinclair, 8–10. New York: Simon and Schuster, 1968.

Truffaut, François. *The Films in My Life*. Translated by Leonard Mayhew. New York: Simon & Schuster, 1978.

———. "*La Grande Illusion* de Jean Renoir est d'une brûlante actualité." *Arts*, No. 691 (October 8–14, 1958): 7.

———. "Préface" to *La Grande Illusion: Jean Renoir*, edited by Gérard Vaugeois, 7–13. Nantes: Balland, 1974.

Vinneuil, François [Lucien Rebatet]. "*L'Action française*, 11 juin 1937." In *La Grande Illusion: Jean Renoir*, by Olivier Curchod, 113–4. Ligugé, Poitiers: Éditions Nathan, 1994.

Viry-Babel, Roger. *Jean Renoir: films/textes/références*. Nancy: Presses Universitaires de Nancy, 1989.

———. *Jean Renoir: Le jeu et la règle*. Évreux: Éditions Ramsay, 1994.

Wakeman, John, ed. *World Film Directors: Volume I, 1890–1945*. New York: H.W. Wilson Company, 1987.

Weightman, John. Introduction. *Masterworks of the French Cinema*. London: Harper & Row, 1974.

Welles, Orson. "Jean Renoir's *Grand Illusion*." Quote on publicity postcard for Canal+Image International, Janus Films and Rialto Pictures. USA: 1-800-Postcards, 1999.

———. "Jean Renoir: 'The Greatest of All Directors.'" *Los Angeles Times*, February 18, 1979, Part V.

———. "Orson Welles: July 27, 1970." In "The Dick Cavett Show: Hollywood Greats" (DVD). USA: Daphne Productions, Inc. 2006. http://www.youtube.com/watch?v=Yjfa1GFwmUA (accessed October 10, 2010).

Woolf, Virginia. "The Cinema." In *The Captain's Death Bed and Other Essays*, 180–6. San Diego and New York: Harcourt Brace Jovanovich, 1950/1978.

Wordsworth, William. "Preface" to *Lyrical Ballads*. In *Wordsworth and Coleridge: Lyrical Ballads*, edited by R.L. Brett and A.R. Jones, 287–314. London and New York: Routledge Classics, 2008.

Index

Page numbers in **_bold italics_** indicate pages with illustrations.

À la recherche du temps perdu 203
Die Abenteuer des Prinzen Achmed 214
The Adventures of Prince Achmed see *Die Abenteuer des Prinzen Achmed*
l'Aéro-club du cinéma 222
L'Affaire est dans le sac 214, 217
Africa 161, 218
L'Âge d'or 221
Aldrich, Robert 214
Alexandra, Czarina 55, 83
Algeria 216
Allégret, Marc 218
Allégret, Yves 214, 217
Alsace 116, 132, 222
Altman, Georges 136–7
L'Amour fou 214
Amsterdam 3, 84
anarchism 3, 174
Andersen, Hans Christian 157
Angell, Norman 116
Anna Karenina 200
Annabella 110
anti-Semitism 9, 54, 57, 58, 60, 103, 118, 124, 220
Antonioni, Michelangelo 161, 203
Apu trilogy 214
Aranyer Din Ratri 214
Arc de Triomphe 174
Arles 168
Armes, Roy 137
Armstrong, Louis 29
Around the World in 80 Days 3
L'Assassin habite au 21 218
L'Atalante 217, 221
L'Auberge rouge 214, 217
Augusta Viktoria (Kaiserin) 67, 85
Austria 223
Autant-Lara, Claude 214, 217, 218
auteur theory 142, 172–3, 202–3
Automaboul 151
"Autumn Leaves" 220

B-films 3, 201
Bach, Johann Sebastian 16, 17, 30–1, 167, 198–9, 210
"Bagatelles pour un massacre" 118
Baker, Josephine 218
La Bandera 218, 223
Barbarella 222
Bardot, Brigitte 218, 220
Barnet (England) 220

Baronet Theater 3
Barrault, Jean-Louis 169
Bartók, Béla 220
Les Bas-Fonds 110, 126, 142, 158–9, 160, 165, 180–1, 182, 185, 223
Bataille, Sylvia **_177_**, **_178_**
Battleship Potemkin see *Bronenosets Potyomkin*
Bazin, André 142, 143, 168, 169, 173
The Beast from 20,000 Fathoms 221
Becker, Jacques 77, 116, 131, 156, **_157_**, 158, 169, **_178_**, 213, 214, 216, **_217_**, 218, 220, 221
Beethoven, Ludwig van 16, 224
Belgium 118, 223
La Belle Époque 168
La Belle Équipe 218, 223
La Belle et la bête 189
Benglia, Habib 50, 216
Bennett, Joan **_166_**
Bergan, Ronald 152, 155, 171
Bergman, Ingmar 203
Bergman, Ingrid 165, 169, 171, 208
Berlin 84, 119, 213
Berlin, die Sinfonie der Großstadt 213
Berlin: Symphony of a Great City see *Berlin: Die Sinfonie der Großstadt*
Bernard, Raymond 112
Bernstein, Leonard 16–7
Berri, Claude 214
Berry, Jules 173, 174, **_175_**
Besançon 115, 151
La Bête humaine 143, 158, 160, 172, 183–7, 216, 223
Beverly Hills 142, 171, 222
Bible 90, 150
Bicycle Thieves see *Ladri di biciclette*
Billancourt studios 117
The Birth of Venus (Botticelli) 64
The Bitch see *La Chienne*
Bitter Victory 217
Blauschild, Israel Moshe see Dalio, Marcel
Blind Husbands 224
Blondeau, Henri 218
Blondy, Pierre 213, 216
Blondy, Raymond 112, 216
blowup in the mountains 3, 4, 8–12, 14, 32, 53, 80–1, 82, 92, 138;

Maréchal's return to Rosenthal 10–2, 73, 82, 207, 208–9
Bogart, Humphrey 208
Bondi, Beulah 165
Bordeaux 84
Botticelli, Sandro 64
Boudu sauvé des eaux 159, 171, 177, 223; "Boudu" (character) 169, 173
Boudu Saved from Drowning see *Boudu sauvé des eaux*
Boulc'h, Marguerite see Fréhel
Bourgoin, Jean-Serge **_115_**, **_178_**, 222
Bourreaud, Ernest 222
Boyer, Charles 162
Brahms, Johannes 198, 199
Brandenburg Concerto No. 6 210
Le Brasier ardent 146, 154
Brasseur, Claude 191, **_194_**
Braunberger, Pierre 176
Brecht, Bertolt 220
Bresson, Robert 167
Brialy, Jean-Claude 168
Bronenosets Potyomkin 119
Brunius, Jacques 177
Brussels 119, 169, 223
Budapest 220
Buñuel, Luis 203, 220, 221
Butler, Hugo 165

"Cadet Rousselle" 32
Cagnes-sur-Mer 152, 217
Cahiers du Cinéma 142, 168, 169
Cain, James M. 160
California 163, 168, 171, 221, 222
Camus, Albert 168
O Canto do mar 213
Le Caporal épinglé 170, 190–5, 214, 223
Capra, Frank 118, 134
Caravaggio 84
Carette, Julien 18, 28, **_35_**, **_38_**, **_39_**, **_41_**, 42, **_61_**, 131, **_132_**, 183, 184, 216–7
Carné, Marcel 110, 216, 217, 218, 220, 221, 223
Un Carnet de bal 118
Carola (play) 170
Caron, Leslie 168, 170, 171
Le Carrosse d'or see *The Golden Coach*
Cartier-Bresson, Henri **_161_**, **_164_**, **_211_**, 214–5

253

Casablanca 139, 208, 217
Casanova (book) 50
Casque d'or 216, 221
Cassel, Jean-Pierre 190, 192, *194*
Catch-22 217
Catherine see *Une Vie sans joie*
Cavalcanti, Alberto 155, 213
Cayatte, André 223
Ce Soir 117, 160
Céline, Louis-Ferdinand 118
Céline et Julie vont en bateau 214
Cézanne, Aline *111*
Cézanne, Jean-Pierre *111*
Cézanne, Paul, Jr. *111*, 161
C.G.T. (Confédération Générale du Travail) trade union 181
Chabrol, Claude 268
Chamonix 116
Chaplin, Charles 119, 141–2, 153, 165, 169, 214, 221
Charleroi (World War I battle) 84
Charulata 214
Chatau, Henri 218
Château des Brouillards 147
La Chienne 117, 158, 159, 213, 220, 223
Child with Toys — Gabrielle and the Artist's Son, Jean (Renoir, 1895–1896) *149*
China 220
Christian-Jaque 221
Cinecittà 220
"The Cinema" (Woolf) 200
Cinema and History 137
Cinémathèque de Toulouse 119
Cinémathèque Française 220
Citizen Kane 1–2, 3, 17, 120, 142, 163, 189, 198–200
Clair, René 221
"Classics Revisited: 'La Grande Illusion'" 138
Cleopatra (film) 222
Cloche, Maurice 218, 222
Clouzot, Henri-Georges 218, 222
Cocteau, Jean 189, 221
Les Collettes 153, 161, 170
Colmar 112, 116
The Colossus of New York 221
Comédie-Française 218
commedia dell'arte 168
communism 117, 160, 174, 175–6, 181, 220
Communist Party see communism
Conrad, Joseph 163
Conte cruel 221
Le Corbeau 218
Cotten, Joseph 3
Courtois-Doynel, Ginette 119, 220
Le Crime de Monsieur Lange 158–9, 160, 163, 172, 173–5, 180, 223
The Crime of Mr. Lange see *Le Crime de Monsieur Lange*
Curchod, Olivier 13, 118, 137, 138, 141, 222
Curtiz, Michael 217

Daily News (New York) 141
Daïnah la métisse 216
Dalio, Marcel 8, *9*, *12*, 28, *31*, 32, *35*, *39*, *41*, *61*, *83*, *94*, *95*, *100*, *106*, 114, 116, 118, 124, *187*, *204*, *211*, 217, 218
Darnoux, Georges 177
Dasté, Jean 28, *35*, 37, *39*, *41*, *61*, *132*, 160, 217, 221
Davis, Colin 138
A Day in the Country see *Partie de campagne*
Days and Nights in the Forest see *Aranyer Din Ratri*
Dead of Night 213
de Bretagne, Joseph 131, 217
Decrais, René 221
De Mayerling à Sarajevo 220
Le Déjeuner sur l'herbe 170
De Sica, Vittorio 119, 221
des Vallières, Jean 112
Le Diable au corps 214
The Diary of a Chambermaid 158, 165–6, 168
Dieudonné, Albert 154
The Dirty Dozen 214
Douaumont (fort) 42, 43, 45, 46, 61, 84, 85, 86, 90, 91, 114, 118
Die Dreigroschenoper (film) 221
Dreyer, Carl Theodor 120, 165, 167, 169
Dubost, Paulette *164*
Le Duel 218
Dufayel department store 150
Dumas, Alexandre 150
Duvivier, Julien 118, 217, 218, 221, 222, 223

Éclair studios 116
Egyptian art 17
Eisenstein, Sergei 119, 208
Elena and Her Men see *Elena et les hommes*
Elena et les hommes 169
Elsa's farm 14–5, 26, 32–3, 65, 77–8, 80–101, 103, 115, 116, 138; Christmas eve 65, 84, 86–7, 88, 92, 94–6; Christmas morning 5, 87, 91–2, 96–9, 105, 203–5; embrace of Maréchal and Elsa 88–90, 92, 96; final evening 82, 88, 92, 99–101; first evening 80, 81, 82–3, 84, 87–8, 92, 93
The Elusive Corporal see *Le Caporal épinglé*
The Emperor Jones (play) 216
En cas de malheur 218
En rade 213
L'Enfant sauvage 217
Les Enfants du paradis 3, 216, 220, 221
Engels, Friedrich 176
England 220
Épernay 77
Épinay-sur-Seine 116
Epstein, Jean 221
"The Escapes of Colonel Pinsard" see "Les Évasions du Colonel Pinsard"
Esquire 3
Essoyes 171
L'Étranger (book) 168

Europe 119, 164, 171, 221
"Les Évasions du Colonel Pinsard" 111
L'Express 218

Fanny 218
Faulkner, Christopher 138
Faulkner, William 165
Fejos, Paul 213
Fellini, Federico 203
La Femme du boulanger 214
Fernandel 213
Ferrer, Mel 170, 213
Ferro, Marc 137
"Les Feuilles mortes" see "Autumn Leaves"
Feyder, Jacques 223
Field, Betty 165
La Fille de l'eau 154, 176, 222
film noir 84, 162, 163, 166, 183, 187
Filmarte (theater) 118
Five Graves to Cairo 224
Flaherty, Robert 161, 163
Flaubert, Gustave 159
Florelle 173
Florian, Werner 38, *132*, 217
Folies Bergère 218
Foolish Wives 112–3, 146, 154–5, 224
Forces Françaises Libres 218
Forster, Roger 38, *39*
The 400 Blows see *Les Quatre Cents coups*
France 23, 54, 59, 99, 102, 111, 112, 118, 119, 136, 146, 153, 160, 161, 165, 166, 168, 170, 171, 176, 180, 188, 191, 194, 213, 214, 215, 216, 217, 218, 219, 220, 221, 222
Franju, Georges 220
Frankenheimer, John 217
Fréhel 218
Freire, Dido see Renoir, Dido
French Cancan 168–9, 214
French Cinema 137
French Resistance 220
French Revolution 71, 181–2
"Frère Jacques" 32, 35
Fresnay, Pierre 18, 20, *23*, 28, *35*, *41*, *61*, *64*, *68*, *72*, *76*, 114, 124, *132*, 133, 213, 218, 221
Froboess, Cornelia 193
Frost, Robert 206
"Frou-Frou" 19, 22, 31, 32, 46–7, 48, 80, 101, 104, 218
Fuller, Samuel 221

Gabin, Jean 8, *9*, *12*, 18, *19*, *23*, 28, *29*, 32, *35*, *39*, *41*, *42*, *47*, *61*, *64*, *68*, *83*, *89*, *94*, *95*, *97*, *98*, *100*, *106*, 110, *115*, 116, 118, 122, 124, 131, *132*, 133, *134*, *140*, 141, 156, 168–9, 181, 183, *184*, *204*, *205*, 217, 218, *219*, 224; biographical summary 218; performance in *La Grande Illusion* 28, 46, 63, 126, 133, 209
Gance, Abel 154, 220
Gentlemen Prefer Blondes 217

Georgia (U.S.) 162
Germany 26, 81, 84, 103, 105, 118, 128, 138, 161, 165, 191, 192, 215, 220, 221
Gestapo 220
Gilliatt, Penelope 198
Giroud, Françoise *56*, 112, ***115***, 134, 171, 185, 218–9
Godard, Jean-Luc 163, 168, 203
Goddard, Paulette 165–6
Godden, Rumer 167
Goebbels, Joseph 118
Goethe, Johann Wolfgang von 183, 184
The Gold Rush 119
Goldberg Variations 30–1
The Golden Coach 168, 222
Gorky, Maxim 180
Gosfilmofond 119
Goupi mains rouges 216
Gourdji, France *see* Françoise Giroud
Grand Illusion see La Grande Illusion
Le Grand Jeu 223
La Grande Illusion 1–108, 198–200, 202, 206, 210–2; analysis 1–108; anti-war film 2, 13, 21, 24, 32, 102, 128–30; background music (Kosma) 24, 32, 71, 74, 78, 80, 82, 96, 99, 102, 103–4, 105, 183, 204, 205, 220; as *Bildungsroman* 14; class divisions 2, 9, 13, 14, 21, 32, 54, 57, 59–60, 64, 66, 70, 73, 144; collaborators 131–5; comparison to *Le Caporal épinglé* 190–5; credits 18, 32; critical reception 13, 118–20, 136–44; gender issues 20, 39–40, 43, 54, 55, 57–8, 79, 80, 83, 86, 101; humor 20, 35, 37, 42, 45, 59, 67, 69, 82, 85–6, 94–5; illusions 36, 100, 101, 102–3, 105, 108; incidental music 19–20, 21, 32, 43–5, 73–4, 96, 186; interruptions 19, 23–4, 32–3, 42, 43, 45, 48, 55, 58, 62, 75, 77, 87, 95, 99–100, 103–5; irony 10, 15, 32, 38, 45, 48, 63, 67, 68, 74, 77, 82, 84, 86, 93, 105; languages 54, 62, 66, 67–8, 71, 75, 92–6, 98–9, 104–5; meals 20, 22–4, 31, 32, 34–5, 46, 51, 58, 59, 84–5, 87, 101; national divisions 2, 9, 23, 32, 43–5, 46–8, 54, 57, 60–1, 67, 74, 80–1, 85, 91, 93, 105, 143; poetic style 11, 19, 24, 30, 84, 108, 114, 143, 188; pre-production 110–6; production 116–7; relationships 55–8; repetitions 10, 12, 19–20, 24, 25, 30–1, 37–8, 47, 54–5, 63, 67, 72–3, 76–7, 91, 95–6, 97–9, 100–1, 102–3; restoration of film 119; scenarios 125–7, 137, 138; separations 9–10, 19, 24, 32–3, 46, 48, 49, 55, 58, 65, 71–2, 75, 77, 81, 87, 99–100, 103, 107; structure 25–6; style 27–33; symbolism 49, 63, 78, 90, 108; themes 53–5; treatment of film 121–4, 190, 192, 193–4; windows 90–2; *see also* blowup in the mountains; Elsa's farm; Hallbach prison camp; opening part; Swiss border; Wintersborn prison camp
La Grande Illusion (Jackson) 138
La Grande Illusion: Jean Renoir (Curchod) 137
La Grande Illusion (Jean Renoir, 1937) 138
The Great Dictator 141
The Great Escape 139
The Great Illusion 116
Greed 224
Grégor, Nora ***187***
Grémillon, Jean 216, 218, 220, 221, 223
Gréville, Edmond T. 221
Griffith, D.W. 213, 223
Groupe Octobre 160
La Guerre est finie 217
Gueule d'amour 218, 220, 223
Guignol 151
Guinness, Alec 218
Guitry, Sacha 224

Hallbach prison camp 25, 26, 32, 34–48, 59–62, 85–7, 88, 91, 92, 114–5; CU window pan 40–2, 70, 91, 98, 138, 209; Maisonneuve in a dress 38–9, 83, 98; "La Marseillaise" shot 43–5, 139, 143, 144; musical revue 42–5; solitary confinement sequence 45–8; tunnel-digging scene 36–7, 60, 90
Handel, George Frideric 103–4
Harcourt, Peter 139
Haut-Koenigsbourg (castle) 116, 133
Hawks, Howard 143, 217
Heart of Darkness (book) 163
Hensel, Frank 119
Hessling, Catherine *see* Heuschling, Andrée (Dédée)
Heuschling, Andrée (Dédée) 146, 153–5, ***155***, 157, 158
Hindenburg, Paul von 22, 50, 87
Hinduism 167, 168
Hines, Earl 29
Hitchcock, Alfred 27, 218
Hitler, Adolf 3, 119, 128, 142, 176, 191, 221
Hollywood 110, 112, 118, 160, 162, 165, 166–7, 214, 221, 224
Holocaust 136–7, 217
homosexuality 43, 67, 101, 156
Houllé, Marguerite *see* Houllé-Renoir, Marguerite
Houllé-Renoir, Marguerite *56*, ***115***, 131, ***140***, 155, 158, 160, 176, ***177***, 185, 219–20
House Un-American Activities Committee 167
Huguet, Marthe 220
The Human Beast see La Bête humaine
Hungary 213, 220
Huston, John 216

"Il était un petit navire" 9–10, 32, 73–4, 125
Impressionism 146, 176, 222
In Search of Lost Time see *À la recherche du temps perdu*
India 132, 167, 215, 222
"L'Internationale" 176
Intolerance 223
Italy 118, 160–1, 168, 215, 222
Itkine, Sylvain 28, 49, ***68***, 160, 220
"It's a Long Way to Tipperary" 32, 38, 43
It's a Wonderful Life 134
Ivory, James 170, 201

J'accuse (1938) 220
Jackson, Julian 138, 141
Jancsó, Miklós 206
Janus Films 139
Jean de Florette 214
Jean Renoir (Bazin) 142
Jean Renoir (O'Shaughnessy) 138
Jean Renoir: A Conversation with His Films 1894–1979 138
Jean Renoir, a guide to references and resources 138
Jean Renoir: films/textes/références 137
Jean Renoir: Le jeu et la règle 137
Jean Renoir: Projections of Paradise 155, 171
Jean Renoir: The French Films, 1924–1939 137
Jehovah 73
Jenny 110, 223
Jerusalem 60, 84
Jesus (Christ) 65, 88, 94, 103
Joan of Arc 165
Johnson, Nunnally 165, 214
Le Jour se lève 218
Jouvet, Louis 114, 160, 181, 214
Jules et Jim 143
Julius Caesar (play) 168

Kamenka, Alexandre 110
Kanin, Garson 165, 214
Kast, Pierre 214
Kauffmann, Stanley 138
Kavalier Scharnhorst 112, 136
Kennedy, John F. 16
Kennedy, Joseph P. 224
Kerans, James 138
La Kermesse héroïque 223
Kharkov 220, 221
Kiss Me Deadly 214
Knock 214
Koch, Carl *56*, 91, 112, 114, ***115***, 119, 161, 213, 214, 220
Korda, Alexander 218
Kornstädt, Grethe Gerda *see* Parlo, Dita
Kosma, Joseph 32, 71, 96, 105, 131, 160, 176, 183, 186, 191, 220
Krauss, Werner ***155***
Kurosawa, Akira 4, 203

La Brillanne 221
La Roche-Guyon 220
Ladri di biciclette 119–20
The Lady from Shanghai 142
The Ladykillers 3
Lanchester, Elsa 165
Lang, Fritz 161, 163
Langlois, Henri 119, 220
Last Year at Marienbad 3
Laudenbach, Pierre Jules Louis *see* Fresnay, Pierre
Laughton, Charles 163–4, 165, 214
Lausanne 218
Le Havre 185
Le Chanois, Jean-Paul 214
Lefèvre, René 173, *175*
Lefranc, Guy 214
Legion of Honor 171
Lenin, Vladimir 176
Lestringuez, Pierre *155*, 156
Le Vigan, Robert 114, 180
Lévin, Sam *184*, 220
Lichtig, Renée 119, 220
A Life Without Joy see *Une Vie sans joie*
Limelight 221
Lindbergh, Charles 188
Lindström, Pia 169
The Little Match Girl see *La Petite Marchande d'allumettes*
The Little Theater of Jean Renoir see *Le Petit Théâtre de Jean Renoir*
Liverpool 71, 84
Living Images 138
Loing river 176
Lola Montès 221
London 171, 191
The Longest Day 217
Lorre, Peter 220
Los Angeles Times 198
Lothar, Eva 171
Louis XVI 182
Lourié, Eugène 116, *122*, 131, 133, 165, 183, 213, 221
The Lower Depths see *Les Bas-Fonds*
Lubitsch touch 181, 186
Lumière brothers 150
Lüttich (World War I battle) 84
Lyon 84, 220

Macdonald, Dwight 3–4
MacGuffin 27
Madame Bovary (book) 159
Madame Bovary (Renoir film) 159
Madame de... 221
Mademoiselle Docteur 218, 221
Magnani, Anna 168
Maldone 221
The Man in the Gray Flannel Suit 214
The Man Who Knew Too Much (1934) 218
Mankiewicz, Joseph L. 222
Mann ist Mann 220
Manon des sources 214
Many Wars Ago see *Uomini contro*
Marcorelles, Louis 127

Marèse, Janie 158
Marius (film) 218
Marivaux cinema 117
La Marseillaise 126, 160, 181–3, 184, 185, 191, 214, 217, 220
"La Marseillaise" 43–5, 46, 48, 93, 121, 139, 143, 144, 182, 183
Marseille 182, 221
Marthe Richard au service de la France 112, 116
Marx, Groucho 167
Marx, Karl 176
Mast, Gerald 3
Matras, Christian 31–2, 97, 133, 213, 221, 222
Maupassant, Guy de 176
Maurepas 223
Maxim gun 67
Maxim's 59, 67, 83, 123
Melodie der Welt 213
Melody of the World see *Melodie der Welt*
Men Against see *Uomini contro*
Mendelssohn, Felix 211
Merchant-Ivory films 201
Meredith, Burgess 165–6
The Merry Widow 224
Messiah 103–4
MGM 220
The Milkmaid (Vermeer) 87
Minister for Women's Affairs (France) 219
Minister of Culture (France) 219
Mr. Arkadin 142
Modigliani, Amedeo 221
Modot, Gaston 28, *35*, 36, *41*, *42*, *61*, 124, 131, *132*, 160, *161*, 213, 218, 221
Moncorgé, Jean Alexis *see* Gabin, Jean
Monréal, Hector 218
Monsieur Vincent 218, 222
Montmartre 147
Moreau, Jeanne 170, 213
Morgan, Michèle 168
Moscow 119
Mosjoukine, Ivan 146
Moulin Rouge 218
music, in relation to film 25–6, 29, 30–1, 103–4, 107, 198–9, 203, 207–12
Mussolini, Benito 118, 136, 160
Muste, A.J. 130
"My First Meeting with Jean Renoir" (Stroheim) 132
My Life and My Films 4, 147, 171, 222
Le Mystère Barton 223
Le Mystère Picasso 222

The Naked Kiss 221
Nana 154–5, 156, 214, 223
Napoléon (Gance) 154
Napoléon (Guitry) 224
Nazis 118–9, 119, 128, 136–7, 138, 141–2, 161, 164–5, 192, 195
neorealism 130, 159–60, 214
Nercillac 222
Neuilly-sur-Seine 218

New Wave (French) *see* Nouvelle Vague
New York 3, 118, 141, 221
New York Film Critics Circle 118
New York Times 130, 141
The New Yorker 3
New Yorker Theater 4
Nice 223
Nicholas II, Czar 133
Nichols, Dudley 164
Nichols, Mike 217
Night at the Crossroads see *La Nuit du carrefour*
The Night of the Hunter 214
9/11 attacks 16–7
Ninth Symphony (Beethoven) 16
Nobel Peace Prize 116
Normandy 156
Nous sommes tous des assassins 223
La Nouvelle Édition Française 187
Nouvelle Vague 141, 169, 214
La Nuit du carrefour 159, 213
Nümbrecht 220
Nuremberg rally 175

Occupe-toi d'Amélie 214, 217
Office of War Information (U.S.) 165
Oliveira, Manoel de 199
Olivier, Laurence 210
Olympia 178
On purge bébé 158, 214
O'Neill, Eugene 216
opening part 18–24, 25–6, 133, 210; first shot 18–20, 45, 47, 77, 96, 101, 105, 107, 188–9; French air base 18–21, 32, 55–6, 85, 114; German canteen 21–4, 32, 66, 85, 91, 92, 114
Ophuls, Max 214, 218, 220, 221
Oran 216
Orvet 168
Oscars (Hollywood) 118, 171
O'Shaughnessy, Martin 138, 141
Ossessione 160, 214
Ozu, Yasujiro 3, 186, 199

Pabst, G.W. 218, 221
pacifism 21, 55, 105, 114, 121, 128–30, 136, 143
Pagnol, Marcel 213–4, 218
Pan 74, 159, 167, 170
Panique 217
Paris 35, 59, 84, 86, 112, 116, 117, 119, 147, 151, 159, 161, 177, 192, 194, 195, 214, 216, 217, 218, 219, 220, 221, 222, 223
Paris nous appartient 214
Parkinson's disease 171
Parlo, Dita 18, 28, 82, *83*, *85*, *89*, *94*, *95*, *98*, *100*, *115*, *117*, 118, 124, 163, *204*, 217, 218, 221
Partie de campagne 160, 170, 172, 176–80, 214, 215, 222, 223
La Passion de Jeanne d'Arc 120, 165
The Passion of Joan of Arc see *La Passion de Jeanne d'Arc*
Passions (Bach) 167
Pater, Walter 207, 208, 209

Index

Pather Panchali 167, 214
"Le Pâtre des montagnes" 32, 37
Péclet, Georges 50, 213, 218, 221–2
Péclet, Prosper Désiré *see* Péclet, Georges
Pépé le Moko 217, 218, 221, 222
Père Noël 87
Peters *see* "La petite Peters"
Le Petit Théâtre de Jean Renoir 170
La Petite Marchande d'allumettes 157, 170
"La Petite Peters" 29, 84, *94*, *95*, *100*, 222
Piaf, Edith 168
Picasso, Pablo 221, 222
Pichel, Irving 214
Picnic on the Grass see *Le Déjeuner sur l'herbe*
Pindar 54, 62, 101; "Pindar" (character) 49
Pinkevitch, Albert 110, 114, 222, 223
Pinsard, Armand 111, 115, 124, 128, 222
Le Plaisir 218, 221
poetic realism 158, 176, 185
Popular Front 136, 138, 160, 173, 174, 175, 180
Les Portes de la nuit 217, 220
Portugal 161
The Postman Always Rings Twice (book) 160, 214
Prévert, Jacques 160, 174, 220
Prévert, Pierre 214, 217
Prix Louis-Delluc 181
Proust, Marcel 17, 90, 203
La P'tite Lili 155

Le Quai des brumes 218
Les Quatre Cents coups 141
Queen Kelly 224

Ray, Nicholas 217
Ray, Satyajit 132, 167, 213, 214
Réalisations d'Art Cinématographique (RAC) 108, 110
Rebatet, Lucien 136
Regain 214
La Règle du jeu 1, 2, 15, 30, 117, 156, 158, 160, 162, 165, 169, 172, 183, 210, 215, 217, 220, 221, 223; comparison to *La Grande Illusion* 187–9; failure 160, 189; final shot 79, 187, 188; first shot 188–9; production 117, 187; reputation 120, 141, 143, 163, 169, 189
Reichsfilmarchiv 119
Reiniger, Lotte 214, 220
Remorques 218
Renard, Gabrielle *see* Renard-Slade, Gabrielle
Renard-Slade, Gabrielle 90, *147*, 148, *149*, 150–1, 156, 163, 165, 169, *171*
Rendez-vous de juillet 216
Renoir, Alain 154, 155, *157*, 163, 176, *215*, 222
Renoir, Aline 146, 147–8, 149, 151–2, 153

Renoir, Claude ("Coco") 148, 153, 170, 187, 222
Renoir, Claude (Jr.) 131, 176, *178*, 183, 222
Renoir, Dédée *see* Andrée Heuschling
Renoir, Dido 155, 160, 161, 162, *164*, 170, 171, *211*
Renoir, Jean *15*, *56*, *107*, *111*, *115*, *117*, *129*, *132*, *140*, *142*, *149*, *153*, *155*, *161*, *164*, *166*, *178*, *187*, *194*, *211*, *215*, *223*; American films 160–7, 214; biographical sketch 146–71, 222–3; birth 147; childhood 147–51; classic films (1930s) 158–60, 172–89; death 141, 170, 198; documentarian's eye 90, 96, 159, 162, 167, 183, 184–5, 186, 188; early films 154–7; film influences 146, 150–1, 153, 154, 213; *La Grande Illusion* (as director) 1–108, 198–200, 202, 203–6, 209, 210–2; leftist politics 160, 165, 167, 173, 174, 175–6, 180, 220; post–Hollywood films 167–70, 172, 190–5; theater 151, 168, 170; World War I service 151–2; *see also La Grande Illusion*; Heuschling, Andrée; Houllé-Renoir, Marguerite; *La Règle du jeu*; Renard-Slade, Gabrielle; Renoir, Alain; Renoir, Aline; Renoir, Dido; Renoir, Pierre Auguste (Auguste)
Renoir, Marguerite *see* Houllé-Renoir, Marguerite
Renoir, Pierre 112, 114, 148, 153, 159, 182, 214, 222
Renoir, Pierre Auguste (Auguste) 132, 146–50, 151–2, *153*, 154, 155, 156, 169, 170, 171, 176, 222
Renoir, My Father 90, 147, 152, 156, 163, 169, 222
Resnais, Alain 217
Le Retour 215
Rich, Claude 191
Richard-Willm, Pierre 114
Richthofen, Baron von 112
Riefenstahl, Leni 175, 178
Rien que les heures 213
The River (book) 167
The River (film) 132, 167–8, 170, 214, 221, 222
Rivette, Jacques 166–7, 168, 214
Rivière, Georges *111*
Rohmer, Eric 168
Rollmer, Frank 110, 222, 223
Roman Holiday 217
La Ronde 220, 221
Roosevelt, Eleanor 118
Roosevelt, Franklin D. 118, 136
The Roots of Heaven 216
Rosi, Francesco 130
Rossellini, Roberto 169
Rubens, Pierre Paul 153
The Rules of the Game see *La Règle du jeu*
Russia 160, 176, 220, 221
Russian Ark see *Russkiy kovcheg*

Russkiy kovcheg 206
Russo-Japanese War (1904–5) 133
Ruttmann, Walther 213
Ryan, Robert 166

Sabrina 217
Saint-Étienne 217
Saint-Exupéry, Antoine de 162
Saint-Germain-en-Laye 216
Sainval, Claude 19
Salute to France 165, 176, 214
Le Sang des bêtes 220
Scenes of Love and Murder: Renoir, Film and Philosophy 138
"The School of Giorgione" 207
Schopenhauer, Arthur 207, 208, 209
Scott, Zachary 165
Seine river 159
Selznick, David O. 165
Senso 214
Serceau, Daniel 137
Sergeant York 143
Sergine, Véra 115
Sesonske, Alexander 13, 30, 108, 137–8
The Seven Samurai 4
Shanghai 142, 217, 220
The Shanghai Gesture 217
Shock Corridor 221
A Short History of the Movies 3
Une si jolie petite plage 217
"Si tu veux ... Marguerite" 43, 83
Sight & Sound 120
Simon, Michel 156, 158, 159, 160, 161
Simon, Simone 185
Siodmak, Robert 163
Six European Directors 139
Slade, Conrad 163
Slezak, Walter 164
The Social Cinema of Jean Renoir 138
Socialist Realism 176
Sokoloff, Vladimir 180
Sokurov, Alexander 206
Sous les toits de Paris 221
The Southerner 142, 143, 165, 214
Spaak, Charles 32, 110, 111–2, 115, 118, 119, 121, 124, 125, 133, 170, 213, 220, 223
Spaak, Paul-Henri 118, 223
Stalag 17 139
Stalin, Joseph 3, 176
The Steel Trap 3
Sternberg, Josef von 217
Stettin (Germany) 221
Stevens, Wallace 14
Stevenson, Robert Louis 169
Strange Case of Dr. Jekyll and Mr. Hyde 169
The Stranger (book) see *L'Étranger* (book)
The Stranger (film) see *Lo straniero*
Lo straniero 168
Strauss, Johann, Jr. 22
Stravinsky, Igor 220
Stroheim, Erich Oswald *see* Stroheim, Erich von

Stroheim, Erich von 3, 18, 22, **23**, **51**, **68**, **70**, **76**, 101, 110, 112, **113**, 114, 116, 118, 119, 124, 125, 133, 164, 185, 216, 221; biographical summary 223–4; performance in *La Grande Illusion* 28, 58, 70, 77, 141; relationship with Jean Renoir 112–4, 132–3, 146, 154–5, 169, 213
Studio Publicis 119
Sunset Boulevard 224
Swamp Water 162–3, 165, 214
Swanson, Gloria 224
Swiss border 14, 26, 56, 65, 81, 101, 102–8, 116; final shot 26, 33, 58, 86, 105–8, 187, 188
Switzerland 26, 58, 73, 81, 84, 102, 103, 105, 107, 123, 125, 139, 218
Symphony No. 1 in E-flat (Stravinsky) 220

Tannenberg (World War I battle) 84, 85
Tarr, Béla 206
Tedesco, Jean 154, 157
La terra trema: Episodio del mare 214
Terre des hommes 162
Le Testament du Docteur Cordelier 169–70
Théâtre Montmartre 151
Théâtre National de l'Odéon 216
This Land Is Mine 163–5, 214
Thorez, Maurice 176
The Three Faces of Eve 214
The Threepenny Opera see *Die Dreigroschenoper*
Tibremont 116
Tire au flanc 213
Titian 153
To Have and Have Not 217
Tobis studios 116
Toland, Gregg **199**
Tolstoy, Leo 200
Toni 111, 117, 142, 159, 214, 222
La Tosca (film) 160–1, 220
La Tosca (play) 160
Touchez pas au grisbi 216, 218
Toulouse 119
Tourneur, Jacques 163
Toutain, Roland **161**, 188

The Train 217
The Trial 142
Triumph des Willens 175
Le Trou 216
Troyes 222
Truffaut, François 123–4, 141, **142**, 143–4, 167, 168, 170, 188, 217
20th Century–Fox 162

Under Secret Orders 221
United Nations's General Assembly 223
United States 118, 136, 162, 163, 170, 171, 213, 215, 217, 222
University of California, Los Angeles (UCLA) 103, 170
University of Southern California (U.S.C.) 170
Uomini contro 130

Va savoir 214
Vadim, Roger 222
Valence 221
Vaudricourt 217
Velazquez, Diego 153
Venice Film Exposition (Festival) 118, 169
Verdun (World War I battle) 84
Vermeer, Jan 17, 48, 87
Vichy government 118, 137
Victor, Julien see Carette, Julien
La Vie est à nous 160, 175–6, 180, 214
Une Vie sans joie 154
Le Vieil Homme et l'enfant 214
Vienna 84, 118, 223
Vigo, Jean 217, 221
Vinneuil, François see Rebatet, Lucien
Viry-Babel, Roger 117, 137
Visconti, Luchino 159–60, 161, 168, 214
Les Visiteurs du soir 220
Vivaldi, Antonio 168
La Voie lactée 221
Voyage surprise 214

"Die Wacht am Rhein" 43
Wakhévitch, Georges 221
Warhol, Andy 206
Wayne, John 210
The Wedding March 224

Welles, Orson 1–2, 17, 156, **163**, 169, 198, **199**, 208, 224
Wellman, William 214
The Well-Tempered Clavier 167
Die Welt als Wille und Vorstellung 207
White House 118
Wild, Harry J. **166**
Wilde, Oscar 16, 156, 186
Wilder, Billy 217, 224
Wilhelm II (Kaiser) 34, 67, 85, 87, 116
Wind, Sand and Stars see *Terre des hommes*
Wintersborn prison camp 25, 26, 32, 49–52, 62–5, 66–79, 86–7, 91–2, 116, 133; Boeldieu and Rauffenstein tête-à-têtes 50, 69–73, 76, 78, 85, 98, 137; death of Boeldieu 49, 75–9, 81; final confrontation 74–5, 104; final shot 78–9; first shot 50–1; opening scenes (reception and tour) 66–9; parting of Boeldieu and Maréchal 64–5, 73; prison diversion 50, 73–4, 77, 78–9, 90, 92; room search 62, 69–70
The Woman on the Beach 166–7, 223
Woodland Hills 221
Woolf, Virginia 200, 201, 207, 208–9, 211
Wordsworth, William 55
The World as Will and Representation see *Die Welt als Wille und Vorstellung*
World War I 2, 8, 13, 55, 102, 110, 111–2, 116, 119, 124, 128, 137, 139, 146, 151, 192, 216, 218, 221, 222
World War II 118, 161, 170, 189, 190, 191, 192, 217, 218, 220, 222
World's Fair (Brussels) 119, 169
Wyler, William 217

You Can't Take It with You 118

Zanuck, Darryl F. 162, 167, 171
Zéro de conduite 217
Zola, Émile 154, 183–4, 185
Zouzou 218
Zwoboda, André **164**, **211**